Critical Essays on
Joseph Heller

Critical Essays on Joseph Heller

James Nagel

G. K. Hall & Co. • Boston, Massachusetts

Library of Congress Cataloging in Publication Data
Main entry under title:

Critical essays on Joseph Heller.

  (Critical essays on American literature)
  Includes index.
  1. Heller, Joseph — Criticism and interpretation —
Collected works.   I. Nagel, James.   II. Series
PS3558.E476Z62 1984   813'.54   84-4656
ISBN 0-8161-8685-5

CRITICAL ESSAYS ON AMERICAN LITERATURE

This series seeks to anthologize the most important criticism on a wide variety of topics and writers in American literature. Our readers will find in various volumes not only a generous selection of reprinted articles and reviews but original essays, bibliographies, manuscript sections, and other materials brought to public attention for the first time. This volume on Joseph Heller, edited by James Nagel, is a welcome addition to our list. There are reprinted reviews and articles by many leading critics and writers, including Kurt Vonnegut, Jr., John W. Aldridge, Clive Barnes, Walter Kerr, Robert Brustein, Thomas LeClair, Susan Strehle, and Benjamin DeMott, among others. In addition to an extensive introduction, which surveys the history of criticism on this important writer, there are original essays by Melvin J. Friedman, James M. Mellard, Joan DelFattore, and Linda McJ. Micheli. We are confident that this volume will make a permanent and significant contribution to American literary study.

For Joseph Satin

CONTENTS

Films and Plays

INTRODUCTION

The historical record of the serious study of the life and works of Joseph Heller has been shaped by the development of his career. Although he has published three novels, three plays, and a dozen short stories, and despite the fact that he has been a professional writer for almost thirty years, he is still most widely known as the author of *Catch-22* (1961), a comic masterpiece of tragic seriousness that set the tone for a generation of Americans in the 1960s. His other works, especially *Something Happened* (1974) and *Good as Gold* (1979), have occasioned a good deal of comment in reviews and scholarly articles, but the fact remains that well over half the important criticism on Heller is addressed to his sensational first novel.

The professional study of Heller has been influenced by other factors as well. Perhaps the most serious is that despite the enormous impact that Heller's works have had on American letters over the past two decades, there is still no extended and reliable biographical account. Scholars are still writing about Heller based on fragmentary and often erroneous information, some of which grossly distorts even the most basic facts of his life, and yet critics persist in making easy equations of Heller with various of his characters, their views with his, as though there were a solid body of biographical data on which to draw. Unfortunately, such is not the case. Until an authorized biography is added to the critical canon, scholars will be forced to use the best of the existing documents, cautioned by an awareness that even the most reliable of these are not without problems.

Among the biographical essays that should be consulted is an early piece in the *New York Herald Tribune* published in 1962 that outlines Heller's life and describes the initial reception of *Catch-22*.[1] Also of some value are the accounts in *Who's Who in America*, *Who's Who in the East*, *Contemporary Authors*, and other standard reference works, although these brief statements tend to repeat information from one volume to another.[2] Of somewhat greater utility are the comments in *200 Contemporary Authors* and *Current Biography Yearbook* and, especially, the entry in the *Dictionary of Literary Biography*, although all three contain minor errors. Also of value is Barbara Gelb, "Catching Joseph Heller," a lengthy essay in the *New York Times Magazine* that provides information not available else-

1

where, especially with regard to Heller's childhood and family background.[3] By far the most influential biographical essay is one filled with misinformation, Richard Lehan and Jerry Patch, "*Catch-22*: The Making of a Novel" in the *Minnesota Review* in 1967. As Heller has recorded in a letter, in just one paragraph of their account, Lehan and Patch err in Heller's age when his father died, the sex of his siblings, the influence of the Coney Island Renaissance, and other such matters. Suffice it to say, scholars beginning a study of the life and works of Joseph Heller should not rely on this essay for biographical data, despite the fact that it has been reprinted in two major collections.[4]

One fortuitous circumstance that somewhat relieves this situation is the fact that Heller has over the years granted more than fifty interviews, many of them containing valuable biographical information. Although the list is far too long to cover in detail, a few of these deserve special mention. Two of the best on *Catch-22* are Paul Krassner's "An Impolite Interview with Joseph Heller," published in *The Realist* in 1962, which deals largely with technique, and W. J. Weatherby's "The Joy Catcher," which covers the personal background and literary influences, matters also addressed in "So They Say" in *Mademoiselle* in 1963.[5] Elenore Lester's "Playwright in Anguish" in 1967 provided the same function for *We Bombed in New Haven*. Of more general interest is Susan Braudy, "Laughing All the Way to the Truth," which is largely biographical and contains the fascinating suggestion that Heller has used humor over the years as a protective shield. Dale Gold, "Portrait of a Man Reading," is another interview that explores literary influences and the assessment of other writers, whereas Ken Barnard, "Interview with Joseph Heller," is more specifically focused on *Catch-22*, particularly Heller's experiences in World War II. Perhaps the most extensive of the important interviews is Richard B. Sale's piece in *Studies in the Novel* in 1973, in which Heller talks about the art of his fiction, Yossarian's moral responsibility in *Catch-22*, the seriousness of *Something Happened*, and his beginnings as a writer.[6] A number of other interviews have also dealt with *Something Happened*, all of them containing intriguing and enigmatic comments, perhaps the best of which is George Plimpton's for the *New York Times Book Review* in 1974. Another interview of considerable value is Sam Merrill's long piece in *Playboy* in 1975, in which Heller discusses his books, places of writing, his views of current political and social issues, as well as his personal background.[7] Although there are a great many others of merit, the general point is that in the current state of Heller scholarship these interviews provide a valuable source of background information.

Students of Heller are in somewhat better shape with regard to primary and secondary bibliographies, for although there are no definitive lists in either category, there are several good ones. An early bibliography of considerable merit was published in *A "Catch-22" Casebook*, edited by Frederick Kiley and Walter McDonald, in 1973. Their secondary listing is broken into useful categories of concern, but it is not annotated. Robert M. Scotto provided another brief listing in his *Joseph Heller's "Catch-22": A Critical Edition*, also published in 1973. The following year James Nagel included a brief annotated bibliography in his *Critical Essays on "Catch-22."*[8] But all of these were superseded in 1975 by Joseph Weixlmann, "A Bibliography of Joseph Heller's *Catch-22*," in the *Bulletin of Bibliography*. Weixlmann limits himself to *Catch-22* criticism, but he lists all known reviews and essays on the novel through 1973 along with a partial list of the primary works. Robert M. Scotto improved on Weixlmann in 1977 with *Three Contemporary Novelists: An Annotated Bibliography of Works by and about John Hawkes, Joseph Heller, and Thomas Pynchon*. Scotto includes a primary and secondary bibliography including Heller's stories, novels, plays, interviews as well as articles, books, dissertations, and bibliographies regarding Heller. Scotto's volume is a major contribution, one which remains useful because of its organization and coverage. Another major contribution to Heller bibliography is Brenda M. Keegan, *Joseph Heller: A Reference Guide*, an annotated listing of Heller scholarship from 1961 to 1977.[9] Although there are occasional errors, this is a valuable book: the introduction is a bibliographical essay that is thorough and objective; the annotations are descriptive; the index comprehensive and easy to use. In short, in addition to the standard listings in periodical bibliographies of American literature, Heller scholars have been well served by the work of Weixlmann, Scotto, and Keegan.

The existence of three extensive bibliographies dealing largely with *Catch-22* obviates the need for an exhaustive survey of reviews and criticism, but a discussion of selected items can suggest the historical development of response to Heller's first novel. *Catch-22* was published in October of 1961 to what are known in the trade as mixed reviews, none of which recognized the full complexity of the book. Robert Brustein was among the most enthusiastic reviewers, calling the novel an "explosive, bitter, subversive, brilliant book" in his review in *The New Republic*. Brustein read *Catch-22* as essentially a social satire of the "malevolent, mechanical, and incompetent world" that confronts the "humbug, hypocrisy, cruelty, and sheer stupidity of our mass society." Subsequent comment has done little to improve on the clarity of Brustein's initial formulation. Nelson Algren followed Brustein's tack in calling *Catch-22* "the strongest repudiation of our civilization, in fiction, to come out of World War II." He went on to conclude, in a much quoted sentence, that the "novel is not merely the best American novel to come out of World War II; it is the best American novel that has come out of anywhere in years." Julian Mitchell joined the chorus in the *Spectator* with the observation that "*Catch-22* is a book of enormous richness and art, of deep thought and brilliant writing, [a] surrealist *Iliad*, with a lunatic High Command instead of gods, and a coward for hero." Other reviews in *Newsweek, Time, Mademoiselle, Saturday Review*, the London *Observer*, and elsewhere responded positively to the serious comedy of the novel. Norman Mailer remarked that "*Catch-22* is the debut of a writer with merry gifts," perhaps his most prophetic observation.[10]

But there were dissenters as well, legions of them, who found Heller's social satire unpatriotic, its sexual references offensive, its style repetitious, its structure incoherent, its characters unbelievable. Writing in the *New York Times Book Review*, Richard G. Stern complained that "*Catch-22* has much passion, comic and fervent, but it gasps for want of craft and sensibility. A portrait gallery, a collection of anecdotes, some of them wonderful, a parade of scenes, some of them finely assembled, a series of descriptions, yes, but the book is no novel." Douglas Day regarded the book as a "perverted Boy Scout's Oath of a novel" that represented a "mass of tastelessness and vulgarity." Many reviewers regarded the comedy in the novel as too insistent: Granville Hicks felt that Heller "shoots way over the mark" with his humor; Whitney Balliet, in the *New Yorker*, concluded that "Heller wallows in his own laughter, and finally drowns in it." Spencer Klaw complained of the strained humor of the novel and expressed his disappointment with it in the *New York Herald Tribune*. In his review for the *New York Times*, Orville Prescott expressed ambivalence: it was not a good novel, a bit strange, and yet an unforgettable "dazzling performance." But there was nothing equivocal about the extended review by Roger H. Smith in *Daedalus*: in the most negative of all the reviews, Smith judged the novel to be a "worthless" effort by an author who cannot write; there was no story and no characters; the book was "immoral."[11]

The scholarship on *Catch-22* since these early reviews has been largely confined to the concerns of the initial readers: matters of social satire, black humor, war protest, absurdity, and structural organization, with only the occasional foray into comparative analysis, origins and influences, style, and the aesthetics of the novel. However, in what has become a body of several hundred essays, *Catch-22* criticism has steadily developed in depth and sophistication despite its relatively narrow range. One of the early scholarly landmarks is Frederick R. Karl, "Joseph Heller's *Catch-22*: Only Fools Walk in Darkness," published in 1964, in which he took the provocative posture that the absurdity of life in the novel was not so much literary invention as a devastating portrayal of modern life. Yossarian is thus not so much comic figure as a character in isolation, the only one who sees life as it is, who must therefore accept total responsibility for his actions. Karl is thus led to the conclusion that Yossarian is justified in his defiance of the military bureaucracy and in his desertion for in both actions he defies "death in the name of reason and life." Norman Podhoretz developed essentially the same argument in "The Best Catch There Is" in *Doings and Undoings* the same year. He describes the modern world as a "gigantic insane asylum" and *Catch-22* as one of the "the bravest and most nearly successful attempts we have yet had to describe and make credible the incredible reality of American life in the middle of the 20th century." Joseph J. Waldmeir's contemplation of these issues, however, lead him to a rather different assessment. His conclusion, in "Joseph Heller: A Novelist of the Absurd," is that the book is a "magnificent failure" in that its "complexity is superficial, that its variety is only apparent, that its apparent repetitiveness is unfortunately all too real." He also finds Yossarian's assertion at the end of the novel that he has been fighting all along for his country "totally unconvincing," a charge echoed by a great many other readers. In one of the very best scholarly essays on Heller, Ihab Hassan regards black humor as an affirmation of life through comedy: "The buffoonery of Heller's *Catch-22* settles for nothing less than sanity and freedom."[12]

If Hassan's essay is valuable as representing the definitive statement of the role of Black Humor in the novel, Sanford Pinsker's "Heller's *Catch-22*: The Protest of a *Puer Eternis*" in 1965 was instrumental in provoking a new approach to Yossarian. Pinsker's contention was that Heller's protagonist refuses to mature, unlike other American figures, and he remains a "perennial innocent." Constance Denniston, in "The American Romance-Parody: A Study of Heller's *Catch-22*," is similarly provocative, although she advances the issue of generic classification. She finds that the use of flat characters, repeated events, and a chaotic structure, matters often criticized, are all consistent with the standards of the romance-parody. G. B. McK. Henry, the following year, argued that *Catch-22* should be studied as a "tragic-farce." However, a more valuable portion of his essay, "Significant Corn: *Catch-22*," deals with a comparison of Heller's novel to those by Charles Dickens in the mixture of popular entertainment and serious themes. Also of interest is Vance Ramsey's "From Here to Absurdity: Heller's *Catch-22*," which presents Yossarian as an anti-hero in a world in which the sane and the insane have switched places. Ramsey echoes Waldmeir in feeling that the book loses its dramatic quality in the last four chapters.[13]

In *Quests Surd and Absurd*, James E. Miller groups Heller with Ken Kesey as writers who "hold the greatest promise of major work that will have a permanent impact on American fiction." He says that *Catch-22* "creates a paradigm of the modern world in the madness and violence of the U.S. Air Force in World War II."[14] In "An Experiment in Therapy: A Study of *Catch-22*," Donald Monk argues the somewhat eccentric but nonetheless interesting thesis that given the insanity of modern warfare, Heller's novel functions as an inversion of therapy. Standard therapy, says Monk, consists of stripping away illusion to deal with the facts; by introducing fantastic elements into the conclusion of the novel (Orr's escape; Yossarian's flight to Sweden; the persistence of Nately's whore), "Heller seems explicitly to deny the moral claims of the world of facts." Of related interest is Nelvin Vos's position in *For God's Sake Laugh!* He contends that the humor is directed at a "world so highly organized and institutionalized that it manifests itself only in anarchy and chaos." Jan Solomon presented in "The Structure of Joseph Heller's *Catch-22*" an often challenged thesis that the chronology of the novel employs an impossible series of events to underscore the theme of absurdity. Caroline Gordon and Jeanne Richardson published an article in the *Southern Review* in 1967 in which they argue that Heller uses a fictional technique borrowed from Lewis Carroll's *Alice in Wonderland* in his play with language and control of absurdity through logic.[15] Minna Doskow's "The Night Journey in *Catch-22*" is an excellent discussion of the importance of Chapter 39, "The Eternal City," in Yossarian's moral development and final desertion. Of special value is Heller's own article in *Holiday*, "*Catch-22* Revisited," in which he recounts his return to the scene of his war adventures in Rome, Corsica, and Avignon. His reflections are informative, touching, and of considerable biographical significance in understanding how his personal experiences inform specific scenes in the novel, especially those involving the missions to Poggibonsi and Avignon.[16]

To this growing body of scholarship, several important articles were added in 1968. Brian Way maintained that *Catch-22* is a brilliant novel in the tradition of radical protest with a strong antimilitarist and anticapitalist theme and an endorsement of freedom and justice. His view is that because the object of the satire is nonrational, Heller uses the techniques of the literature of the absurd. James L. McDonald's "I See Everything Twice! The Structure of Joseph Heller's *Catch-22*" is an excellent early study of the formal values of the novel, especially its structure and handling of time. McDonald's point is that the chronology is related to Yossarian's consciousness, which accounts for the interplay between the present narrative and the repetitions of scenes from the past. In "*Catch-22*: *Deja vu* and the Labyrinth of Memory," James M. Mellard regards *deja vu* as not only a device of organization but also a concept central to the sense of reality (disjunctive). He goes on to demonstrate how Yossarian is involved in, and to some extent responsible for, nearly all of the major events.[17] "War and the Comic Muse: *The Good Soldier Schweik* and *Catch-22*," by J. P. Stern, offers an excellent comparison of Heller's novel to Jaroslav Hasek's in their portrayals of war and bureaucracy, twisted logic, sex, death, and a fight for survival. Stern maintains that they both show war as meaningless and death as irrational rather than heroic; however, Stern sees no social protest against war in *Catch-22*. John W. Hunt gave precise formulation to what was becoming a common insight in his "Comic Escape and Anti-Vision: Joseph Heller's *Catch-22*." Hunt's point is that the novel has a classic structure for a comedy based on the absurd, one that compels the realization that it is the modern world that is absurd, not that of the novel. In other essays of lesser moment, Josh Greenfeld outlined the background of the composition and publication of the novel, Eugene McNamara explored absurdity in the style of *Catch-22*, Hamlin Hill further refined the role of Black Humor, and Max F. Schulz argued that Colonel Cathcart and Yossarian share "the anxiety that afflicts man faced with his own helplessness and insignificance before the diffusion of twentieth-century mass society."[18]

Scholarship in 1969 produced only two notable contributions, Eric Solomon's "From Christ in Flanders to *Catch-22*: An Approach to War Fiction," in which he discusses Heller's book in the context of novels about war, and the section on *Catch-22* in Joseph J. Waldmeir's *American Novels of the Second World War*, essentially a repeat of his article from 1964.[19] The following year publication on Heller took on renewed vigor, in part because of the release of the movie of *Catch-22*. Judith Crist gave the film an essentially negative review as "another antiwar black comedy that ranges from the very very good to the pretentious mediocre" despite her praise of the performance by Alan Arkin as Yossarian. Hollis Alpert concurred, saying that the film lacks the style and depth of characterization that made the novel a success. But other reviewers were more enthusiastic: Susan Larder wrote a largely positive review for the *New Yorker* in which she praised the "ingeniously laid-out, unobtrusive line of the plot." Writing in *Esquire*, Jacob Brackman praised Arkin as Yossarian. Vincent Canby called it "the most moving, the most intelligent, the most humane — oh, to hell with it! — it's the best American film I've seen this year" in his piece for the *New York Times*. But, however entertaining this critical disputation might be, the most substantial essay on the film was Ken Barnard's interview with Heller for the *Detroit News Sunday Magazine*, in which Heller talks about the novel and the movie, his war experiences (including a mission to Avignon on which a gunner in his plane was wounded), and other background events. Anyone exploring the relationship of novel to film should read this interview carefully.[20]

There were also several important essays on the novel in 1970, among them Wayne Charles Miller's chapter in *An Armed American: Its Face in Fiction*, in which he discusses *Catch-22* in the tradition of the war novel. His contention is that Pianosa is a mirror of America, a device that allows Heller to satirize justice, romantic love, heroism, the military, and capitalism. Miller feels that the ending rings false and yet Yossarian emerges as a "symbol of humanistic faith." Victor J. Milne took a somewhat different twist in "Heller's 'Bolstered': A Theological Perspective on *Catch-22*," exploring the novel as a conflict between the "Christian ethic of universal benevolence" and the competitive ethic of capitalism. Jim Castelli developed a similar thesis in an article in which he argues that Yossarian is fundamentally Christian and represents the "new hero" who questions the logic of society, affirms humanity, and restores sanity to the world.[21] Doug Gaukroger took issue with Jan Solomon's reading of the structure of the novel by countering that the time scheme *does* make sense and by producing a chart to make his point. Alvin Greenberg wrote that Orr's desertion is essentially a withdrawal within himself that inspires Yossarian to a sense "that human possibility is to be found and the possibility of a meaningful life to be explored." W. K. Thomas did a study of the misuses of logic in the novel, a device that forces the reader to look at the irrationality of modern life. He is especially good on Clevinger's trial and the role of the old man at the Roman brothel. Another valuable discussion is by Jerry H. Bryant in *The Open Decision*, particularly with regard to the vagaries of catch-22 and Yossarian's desertion. Bryant contends that the theme of the novel is "survival through defiance."[22]

Perhaps the best known study published the following year is Tony Tanner's *City of Words*, in which he gives *Catch-22* a reading marred by limited research and occasional errors of fact. Tanner is very good on Yossarian's struggle for survival and on the roles of individual characters, but his attempt to interpret distortions of language as the center of the novel is not sustained. Another notable essay is Robert Protherough's "The Sanity of *Catch-22*," in which he makes a case for the sanity and coherent structure and theme of the novel. Protherough outlines a variety of satiric devices in the novel very persuasively and is similarly perceptive on the developing thematic patterns as the novel progresses. An often reprinted essay is Jean Kennard's "Joseph Heller: At War with Absurdity," a study of *Catch-22* as an "illustration of the absurdity of the human condition itself." To reinforce the sense of absurdity, Kennard argues, Heller interrupts chronological flow, presents contradictory statements, and gives contradictory accounts of events; finally, the only value is the perpetuation of human existence.[23] Thomas Blues contends that Yossarian deserts not because he must be human but because he hears about Orr; nor does Blues find Yossarian's assertion that he has been fighting for his country all along very compelling because the historical war seems as of little consequence save as metaphor. Thomas Allen Nelson contributed to the debate about the structure of the novel in an essay in *Renascence* in which he maintains that the novel contains a "cyclical pattern of action" related to the central issue of responsibility: "Events and characters which may be outrageously funny when first introduced acquire a philosophical significance in the last part of the novel as the degeneration of values increases to alarming proportions." In "Violence in the Eternal City: *Catch-22* as a Critique of American Culture," Lucy Frost advanced what was by then a familiar thesis that "*Catch-22* is a serious critique of the total culture, not just of war." Heller eliminates Germany from the conflict, she says, to focus on a criticism of American society. Her best observation is that "the Army's goals are no longer shaped by a governing civilian society; they are predominately internal and autonomous."[24]

There were two essays of special interest in 1972. Richard B. Sale did a long interview with Heller that touches on Heller's concern for the integrity of his art and his career as a writer from his early short stories to *We Bombed in New Haven* and *Something Happened*, which was at that point in progress. In *Beyond the Waste Land*, Raymond M. Olderman gave *Catch-22* a reading in the tradition of T. S. Eliot, seeing Yossarian as both Fisher King and Grail Knight. The real enemy in the novel is the military-industrial complex, not the Germans. The terror is that social institutions have seized control over individual human life; the quest of the novel is thus for a way to "affirm life against the forces of negation without violating what is human." Olderman's contribution would have been more valuable had he read the previous scholarship on the subject.[25]

In the following year, 1973, several remarkable critical publications appeared, chief among them two collections of criticism. In his *Catch-22: A Critical Edition*, Robert M. Scotto published not only the novel itself but "Love, Dad," a deleted chapter from the manuscript, and eight previously published articles on the novel. Of much greater utility is A *"Catch-22" Casebook*, edited by Frederick Kiley and Walter McDonald.[26] This book contains an excellent collection of reviews, critical articles, interviews, comments on the movie, and an extensive bibliography. And, in addition to reprinted criticism, the volume contains several original pieces, including a transcription of remarks by Heller at the Young Men's Hebrew Association in New York in December of 1970 about the background of the novel and the script for the film (pp. 346–62). Of special interest is Clayton L. Balch's "Yossarian to Catchcart and Return: A Personal Cross-Country," a reminiscence by an officer in a bomber group (not Heller's) stationed on Corsica that portrays events and people parallel to those in the novel (pp. 301–06). Balch's general reflection is that the men did not realize the seriousness of the situation, or the meaning of what they were doing, until much later, a sentiment shared by Heller. Also of value is Howard J. Stark's "The Anatomy of *Catch-22*," an excellent discussion of the concepts of *deja vu*, *jamais vu*, and *presque vu* as the basis for the structure of the novel (pp. 145–58). Jesse Ritter's study of *Catch-22* as a "Social Surrealist Novel" is also of interest; he defines this genre as a form that features "outcast heroes of mythical stature, the parody and fusion of conventional literary forms, the structural juxtaposition of unrelated elements, and the bitter mixture of black humor and tragicomedy" (pp. 73–86). In his essay on the film, Wayne Charles Miller argues that Mike Nichols misread the novel and missed important themes; the novel is not only anti-war, as the movie suggests, but a book about American culture and its direction since 1945 (pp. 383–90).

Beyond the items in *Casebook*, there were only a few valuable studies in 1973. One of the best was Clinton S. Burhans, Jr., "Spindrift and the Sea: Structural Patterns and Unifying Elements in *Catch-22*," a useful discussion of the chronology and structure of the novel, complete with a time chart. Burhans also identifies the major lines of thematic development and demonstrates that although the surface of the novel is chaotic, there are unifying patterns of development beneath the surface. Walter R. McDonald's "He Took Off: Yossarian and the Different Drummer" is a good brief essay on Yossarian's desertion that places him in the tradition of other American protagonists who light out for the territory. In "The Radical Vision," Paul Loukides argues that the novel posits a nontraditional, radical vision that offers an "alternative vision of reality," one that affirms a belief in the self.[27]

One of the contributions in 1974 was *Critical Essays on "Catch-22,"* edited by James Nagel.[28] This volume contains a selection of reviews and reprinted articles on the novel along with five original essays, an annotated bibliography, and a list of suggested readings. Among the original essays is Jess Ritter's "What Manner of Men are These," a reading of the novel in terms of Northrop Frye's definition of Menippean satire and an insightful analysis of the roles of individual characters (pp. 45–56). Daniel Walden's " 'Therefore Choose Life': A Jewish Interpretation of Heller's *Catch-22*" develops the idea that the values of the book, especially those expressed by Yossarian, grow out of Jewish tradition, particularly the commitment to preserve existence and to lead a moral life (pp. 57–63). In "*Catch-22*: The Ultimate Irony," Howard J. Stark argues that because the world is absurd, all meaning generates from the individual through a revolt against inhumanity. From this perspective, Yossarian is wrong in deserting; he should have stayed with his unit and tried to persevere, as did the chaplain (pp. 130–41). James J. Martine, in "The Courage to Defy," presents a good survey of Heller's short stories as a prelude to discussing the weaknesses of *Catch-22*, especially its verbosity, discursive elements, and Heller's failure to realize that greed and inhumanity are not restricted to capitalistic countries (pp. 142–49). And in "Yossarian, the Old Man, and the Ending of *Catch-22*," James Nagel develops the thesis that the old man of the brothel serves as a guide to the ethic of survival that Yossarian gradually endorses in the novel, especially after his night journey through Rome and his epiphany about the meaning of Snowden's death. Contra Stark, Nagel thus maintains that Yossarian's desertion is emblematic of his growth, his affirmation of moral principle, and his rejection of compromise (pp. 164–74).

In other scholarship in 1974, Alfred Kazin discussed *Catch-22* in *Bright Book of Life* as representing the "hypothesis of a totally rejectable world," a situation expressive of what many Americans felt in the post-war period. Of greater substance is Bruce Janoff's "Black Humor, Existentialism, and Absurdity: A Generic Confusion," in which Janoff argues that the first thirty-eight chapters are a brilliant example of Black Humor but that the novel changes tone during the final four chapters to one of existential optimism, a shift that "severely impede[s] its thematic momentum." David H. Richter's section on *Catch-22* in *Fable's End* is an extensive essay (29 pp.) that relies heavily on paraphrase of the key scenes of the novel. His thesis is that the form of the narrative "represents an achievement towards which contemporary rhetorical fiction had been groping." Richter sees Yossarian's desertion in positive terms as "the only meaningful and sane form of heroism Heller's world allows." James Nagel had two essays in 1974, a note in *Modern Fiction Studies* that contains two manuscript fragments, one of which shows Yossarian to have been Jewish at the earliest stage of composition, and another hospital scene in which Yossarian and Dunbar seem to be writing a novel. In "*Catch-22* and Angry Humor: A Study in the Normative Values of Satire," Nagel attempts to define the shared assumptions of the novel from which all deviation appears ludicrous. His conclusion is that the novel is essentially a Juvenalian satire with a radical, or idealistic, frame of reference, and this perspective serves as a base for a critique of American society.[29]

In the next two years *Catch-22* scholarship abated somewhat, probably because of the interest in *Something Happened*, published in 1974. In Mike Frank's "Eros and Thanatos in *Catch-22*" his best point is that the enemy is the Protestant ethic, not the Germans, and the conflict is between capitalistic greed allied with war (thanatos) and the forces of sex and life (eros). H. R. Swardson used his article in *College English* to express his contempt for *Catch-22* as a sentimental novel not worth teaching: "I find it phony on every page." In a more appreciative article, Carol Pearson suggested that "the novel is an examination of the destruction power of language when language is used for manipulation rather than communication." Fred M. Fetrow explored "Joseph Heller's Use of Names in *Catch-22*" and concluded that the characters have symbolic functions suggested by their names. In *War and the Novelist*, Peter G. Jones discusses *Catch-22* at some length in what is essentially a summary of major critical issues. Jones interprets Yossarian's desertion as a commitment to "his responsibilities as a rational human being." James Nagel once again based his research on the Heller manuscripts for "The *Catch-22* Note Cards," an essay that discusses the notes Heller made in the planning stages of composition and their relationship to the published novel.[30]

In 1977 Morris Dickstein presented some valuable comments on the temper of the 1960s, Yossarian's embodiment of this spirit, and the theme of insanity. Dickstein calls *Catch-22* "the best novel of the sixties," a judgment that has steadily gained in support. The following year Peyton Glass, III, published a note in *Explicator* to the effect that in the final chapter two lines of action come together, one humanistic (involving Snowden and his secret) and another mechanistic (involving Milo and capitalism). In two persuasive studies, Robert Merrill addressed the use of repetition for thematic emphasis in the scene with the Soldier in White and concludes that "*we* contribute to death and dehumanization through our amused tolerance for life's injustices," and Gary W. Davis discussed how the world of the novel reveals "how society's institutions reflect fundamental discontinuities in language, thought, and behavior." He says that Yossarian's search is for a more meaningful discourse, in which language and reality are brought together.[31]

In 1979 Leon F. Seltzer published "Milo's 'Culpable Innocence': Absurdity as Moral Insanity in *Catch-22*," the most extensive and most persuasive article thus far on Milo and the capitalistic ethic. Seltzer's thesis is that the absurd world of Pianosa is used as a vehicle to explore the inhumanity of modern society. In his article Adam J. Sorkin finds that in Heller's novel "man seems imprisoned in language as a conceptual matrix, and the connections among words, perception, and reality, either external actuality or moral and metaphysical realms, are transient, oblique, and elusive." Michael J. Larsen explored the allusions to Shakespeare throughout the novel

and suggested that they link the human situation in the modern world to that of the ages. Also of interest is Thomas L. Hartshorne's discussion of *Catch-22* and Kurt Vonnegut's *Slaughterhouse-Five* as expressions of the "left-tending protest movements" of the 1960s, fables, in effect, consisting of antiwar sentiments, Black Humor, and absurdity.[32]

In the 1980s of much greater substance is James M. Mellard's discussion in *The Exploded Form* of Heller's use of "modern lyrical fiction" in the concept of *deja vu*, "a term that suggests something of the delusive experience, hallucinatory quality, and disjunctive expression of reality in *Catch-22*." The impact of this structural device is an emphasis on Yossarian's moral growth, his recognition of his mortality and responsibility for his participation in the war, and his development of a new set of values. In *The American 1960s* Jerome Klinkowitz regards Yossarian and Randall Patrick McMurphy of *One Flew Over the Cuckoo's Nest* as "culture heroes for the bold new decade of the American 1960s." He says they are the "first underground literary heroes of the new activist generation, proclaiming revolutionary new values. . . ." James S. Mullican presented again Jess Ritter's argument that *Catch-22* can be read as Menippean satire with flat, stylized characters that embody thematic traits. P. Merivale's attempt to demonstrate that *Catch-22* was modelled on Joseph Conrad's *The Secret Agent* shows some affinities of theme and character but no direct influence. Gary Lindberg takes a more promising tack in *The Confidence Man in American Literature* in discussing Yossarian and Milo as con men. And Jeffrey Walsh, in *American War Literature 1914 to Vietnam*, presents an excellent discussion of the concept of the "catch" and the satiric method of the novel.[33]

The scholarship on *Catch-22* thus represents a rich reservoir of insight on many of the major issues of the novel, especially the method of its satire, its relationship to literature of the absurd, its blend of humor and serious themes, and the complexity of its chronology and structure, matters still unresolved. If there is a persistent weakness in this critical record it is that far too many scholars do not do their homework. This lapse has led to a good deal of repetition in the scholarly record and some perpetuation of error of biographical facts. However, the developing critical approaches, especially those involving basic background research and the use of manuscripts, along with a close reading of the text, promise to contribute to the study of the best American novel of the 1960s.

Something Happened received a good deal of attention, largely in the form of interviews with Heller about his work in progress, even before it was published on October 16, 1974. In one of these, Heller spoke with James Shapiro in 1971 about his protagonist, "Joe" Slocum and the basic plot of the novel, and commented that he was almost through with the writing. In another, with Barbara Bannon, Heller again made general remarks about his forthcoming novel and added the comment, "I do not think novels are like life. Novels are better than life." The best of these prepublication interviews is the one with George Plimpton in the *New York Times Book Review*

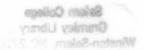

in which Heller explains how he started the novel with a sentence that expanded into a chapter, comments on his working habits, and reflects on *Catch-22* and its relationship to his new novel.[34]

Despite the advance interest in the novel, the reviews were once again mixed, many of them harshly negative. Even Nelson Algren, who had given *Catch-22* its most positive review, had a negative reaction to *Something Happened*, saying that the jokes are not funny, the protagonist is phony, and that there "simply isn't enough of a dramatic conflict to sustain a long novel." Pearl K. Bell saw the novel as "a willful, disastrous exercise in futility. Throughout its almost 600 pages we are forced to listen to the turgid, self-pitying, unintelligent, scandalously repetitive, childishly narcissistic, suffocatingly tedious monologue of a faceless organization man named Bob Slocum." In a review in the *Boston Globe*, Margaret Manning voiced a common complaint: "The principal trouble with Heller's novel is that Bob Slocum is a zombie, impossible to identify with." John Thompson wrote in the *New York Review of Books* that "the ruminations of Slocum . . . become as insidious as muck." And L. E. Sissman followed in the *New Yorker* with the observation that the novel is a "painful mistake," the characters "do not command respect or empathy," and "the flatness, the blankness, the nonhumanity of these characters makes the book tractarian," views echoed by Joseph Epstein in the *Washington Post*, John B. Breslin in *America*, Melvin Maddocks in *Time*, Edward Grossman in *Commentary*, and Wilfrid Sheed in the *New York Times Book Review*. Some of the reviews contained at least qualified praise: D. Keith Mano thought that there was "fine writing" but that the novel was told in "first person compulsive," and Caroline Blackwood thought it too long, too uneven, but finally a more ambitious effort than *Catch-22*.[36]

Among the positive reviewers, and there were many, none was more enthusiastic than John W. Aldridge, who described *Something Happened* as not only a "major work of fiction" but as an "abrasively brilliant commentary on American life that must surely be recognized as the most important novel to appear in this country in at least a decade." Susan Fromberg Schaeffer saw it as a "triumph" that would be impossible to forget, and William Kennedy remarked that it was "exhaustive and exhausting, a major contemporary novel" that maintains Heller in the "first rank of American writers." In the *Los Angeles Times*, Robert Kirsch reflected that "Heller's deliberate choice of narrator appears a mistake, but in a virtuoso performance he sustains our attention." Walter Clemons and Paul Desruisseaux both reviewed the novel as an important book that was thoughtful and impressive, and Kurt Vonnegut, Jr., wrote in the *New York Times Book Review* that "it is splendidly put together and hypnotic to read. It is as clear and hard-edged as a cut diamond." In an especially positive and intelligent review in the *Yale Review*, Patricia Meyer Spacks observed that "the novelist, expertly evoking our masochism, implies that his punishing vision of upper-middle-class anguish reflects the truth of our condition."

Subsequent comment in scholarly journals and other forums has continued this diversity of opinion, although in general the reputation of the
novel has gradually improved over the years, as has Heller's. In "Joe Heller,
Author on Top of the World," Charles T. Powers covered Heller's appearance at the University of Southern California to discuss *Something Happened*. Powers remarks that Heller is one of the most important writers in
America. Heller's comments, widely quoted, are directed to influences on
his novel, the stature of Slocum (a monster who turns out to be much like
everyone else), and his views on modern novels. He also speculates that he
might like to write a novel about Henry Kissinger, an idea that may have
sparked the beginning of *Good As Gold*. George J. Searles in 1977 was
among the first serious scholars to give the novel extended treatment. His
view was that *Something Happened* is a more subtle and sophisticated
novel than *Catch-22* in that it works through implication and understate-
ment. A more mature work that captures the American situation, it has not
been fully appreciated, Searles maintained, because of its use of an unheroic protagonist, its narrative method, and its pessimistic theme. In "Joseph Heller: Something Happened to the American Dream," Nicholas
Canaday portrayed Slocum as the Willy Loman of the 1970s. He sees
Slocum's reflections as "efforts to screw down his life so tight that discovery
and change and the unknown cannot possibly threaten him." In another
essay in 1977, Susan Strehle wrote briefly that the device of the "parenthetical tic is particularly appropriate in *Something Happened* because it serves
as a metaphor for Slocum's thematically central problem of uncertainty."[38]

Of greater value in 1978 are the comments on *Something Happened* by
Christopher Lasch in *The Culture of Narcissism* that explore Slocum's narcissism, his relationships with his children, and his daughter's need for punishment.[39] Susan Strehle Klemtner presents some views that are certain to
spark controversy in an article in which she concludes that Slocum "deliberately murders his son," the unacknowledged hero of the novel. By so doing
"Slocum succeeds in ridding himself of the poignant reminder of his freedom and responsibility" (p. 556). The only article worthy of note in the
following year is Wayne D. McGinnis, "The Anarchic Impulse in Two Recent Novels." McGinnis sees *Something Happened* as a "brilliant satire" that
will endure; Slocum is a "crazy paranoid" but his voice is enchanting and
transcends the limitations of the novel. Perhaps McGinnis's best observation is that the liberating vision of the novel is Slocum's humanity.[40]

The best scholarship on Heller's second novel has appeared in the
1980s, and perhaps the finest essay thus far is Thomas LeClair's "Joseph
Heller, *Something Happened*, and the Art of Excess" (1981). LeClair reads
the book as a novel of "unsettling massiveness or multiplicity of implication
that exceeds the norms of conventional fiction," a form he terms the novel of
excess. He regards *Something Happened* as a better work than *Catch-22*,
one that shows Heller's growth as an artist in that "a work of excess has the
rhetorical advantage of soliciting conventional responses which are then

overturned because excess forces the reader to reconsider such notions as proportions, propriety, quantity, and value." In another notable article, George Sebouhian's "From Abraham and Isaac to Bob Slocum and My Boy: Why Fathers Kill Their Sons," the novel is discussed in the context of American works that examine the "disintegration of the personality" in terms of fathers destroying sons as a rejection of the son's potential for renewal; in this instance, Slocum is regarded as a helpless instrument in his son's death. Another article from 1981 that deserves attention is "Notes from a Dark Heller: Bob Slocum and the Underground Man" by Richard Hauer Costa. His view is that *Something Happened* is "really concerned principally with the forces in man which cause him to be terrified of himself," and he goes on to explore this theme in a comparison of Heller's novel to Dostoevsky's underground man, especially with regard to tonal and rhetorical devices. One item of interest in 1983 is John W. Aldridge, *The American Novel and the Way We Live Now*, a volume in which he comments (pp. 35–41) on Slocum as a reliable narrator, with an emphasis on how Slocum's fantasies distort his sense of reality. Aldridge feels that Slocum is, in at least one sense, realistic: he sees life in entropic terms.[41] Also worthy of note are the two original essays on *Something Happened* published in this volume. In "*Something Happened*: The Imaginary, the Symbolic, and the Discourse of the Family," James M. Mellard gives the novel a Lacanian reading with an emphasis on Bob Slocum and his relationship to his family. Joan DelFattore, in "The Dark Stranger in Heller's *Something Happened*," directs her attention to the meaning of Slocum's dreams, especially those involving a dark stranger with a concealed knife. DelFattore shows how these dreams are related to Slocum's fear of powerlessness, his concern for sexual performance, and his obsession with public speaking. These issues help explain and put into context the conclusion of the novel.

The publication of *Good As Gold* in 1979 prompted even more negative reviews than did *Something Happened*, although the basis of the objections changed somewhat. The review in the *New Yorker*, for example, complained that "Mr. Heller is trying for very black and very broad comedy, but he achieves only tastelessness." Morris Dickstein agreed, faulting the tone and unity of the narrative, and concluding that "the result is a very funny book but a weak and unconvincing novel." One of the most hostile reactions was that of Pearl K. Bell. In her review for *Commentary* she suggested that *Gold* had been praised only because of *Catch-22*. Further, she says, Bruce Gold is "Heller's version of Jewish infantilism, an opportunist who will suck at any alien teat to get ahead." In Bell's view, in doing a "Jewish" novel, Heller "has appropriated every moldy cliché of the school of Philip Roth." The reference to Roth was not uncommon in negative reviews: Gene Lyons suggested that Heller should "give Woody Allen a cut of the take, who should pass most of it on to Philip Roth." Lyons went on to say that the satire "seems like simple malice" and is too dependent on stereotypes and finally reads like a "transcript of a twelve-hour Henny Youngman routine." Larry Simonberg considered the novel to be "funny" but too much like "warmed-over Philip Roth." His basic judgment was that it is a "wonderfully ambitious book, spilling over with crazy events and lunatic lines. Yet too much of it is out of control." Peter S. Prescott agreed with this line of reasoning in *Newsweek*, observing that satire must be "fixed firmly to some standard of decency or restraint." Rather, he suggests, the novel "resembles nothing so much as a self-indulgent ventilation of private spleen."[42]

In a similar vein, R. Z. Sheppard described the novel as a "polemic finger-painted in bile." He found *Gold* to be a "savage, intemperately funny satire on the assimilation of the Jewish tradition of liberalism into the American main chance." A host of other reviews echoed these views and added their individual objections, Benjamin DeMott that *Gold* is "a rather listless and dispirited piece of work," Jeffrey A. Tannenbaum that the novel "doesn't have a likeable character in it," Aram Bakshian, Jr., that it is peopled with "wall-to-wall rats and zombies," and Clara Claiborne Park that it lacks a "locus of value."[43] Margaret Manning protested that "insufficient madness will not sustain anger nor such a long book," and Doris Grumbach that "nothing in it succeeds as it seems it was planned to do." Several reviewers objected to the portrayal of Henry Kissinger, Roderick Nordell on the grounds that Heller's satire "is an example of the overkill that eventually becomes suicidal for the book." Raymond A. Schroth went on to suggest that the problem with Kissinger is also the problem with Gold, he is "corrupted by the mere smell of power." Schroth speculates that Gold is also like Heller, who "dreams of being a celebrity when he has nothing more substantial to celebrate than his own half-baked fame."[44]

Those reviewers who responded positively to the novel, some of them exuberantly so, praised precisely those elements the negative reviewers lamented. In the *New York Review of Books* Thomas R. Edwards called *Gold* "continuously alive, very funny, and finally coherent." Edwards particularly praised three major strands in the novel, the Jewish family ("more perceptive about human nature than anything else Heller has done"), the satire on Washington, and the satire on Kissinger. Edwards concludes that "Heller is among the novelists of the last two decades who matter." In the *New Republic*, Jack Beatty expressed approval of these same three elements, especially the Kissinger satire: "Not since Tolstoy eviscerated Napoleon . . . has a central historical figure been so intimately castigated by the Word. Score one for literature." John W. Aldridge exalted the Black Humor in *Gold*, as well as *Catch-22* and *Something Happened*, and says that it portrays "the collapse of those values that once made humanity and rationality necessary." Aldridge regards the Washington scenes as a "masterful burlesque of government bureaucracy." Leonard Michaels gave *Gold* a largely positive reading, calling it a novel that "seems to have combined Einstein's theory of relativity with Kafka's agonies." Although he suggested that the novel might have been tighter, Lee Eisenberg praised the novel in *Esquire* as "recklessly wise, thunderously funny, and, sad to say, long-winded." In addition to the reviews, which constitute a considerable body of opinion about the novel, there are a few other pieces worthy of consultation for the student of American literature. Two interviews are of some substance. In the first, "Talking with Joseph Heller," Heller responded to a question by Charlie Reilly by saying that the idea for *Gold* came from a reading in Wilmington, Delaware, during which a woman asked him why he had never written about the Jewish experience. Heller said he then invented Bruce Gold to write such a book. In his interview with Chet Flippo in *Rolling Stone*, Heller talked at length about *Gold* and, to a lesser extent, *Catch-22*, and reflected that capitalism is dead but that socialism will not work either.[46]

Formal scholarship on *Gold* thus far has been extremely limited, but what has been written has been informative and engrossing. In 1979, in "Ethnic Identity as Moral Focus: A Reading of Joseph Heller's *Good as Gold*," Wayne C. Miller argues that ethnicity is at the heart of the moral vision of the novel and that Bruce Gold finds himself in the values of the American Jewish experience. He contends that Heller portrays several generations of that experience interacting and shows the ethical deterioration as each succeeding generation moves further away from its racial identity. Charles Berryman mounts an energetic attempt in the *Chicago Review* in 1981 to demonstrate that *Gold* is Heller's best novel, that it has the virtues of the first two efforts but not the faults. Where they were rambling and repetitive, he says, *Gold* is structurally unified. It has a more sophisticated humor closely interwoven with the plot and people in the book. "Heller's skill at the craft of fiction has made clear advances in characterization, narrative control, and most of all in dramatic timing." In "Joseph Heller and the University," James Nagel discusses all of Heller's fiction, including *Gold*, in terms of its portrayal of education as a means of socio-economic advancement, a matter also explored in Frances K. Barasch, "Faculty Images in Recent American Fiction."[47] The best single discussion of *Gold* thus far is Melvin J. Friedman, "Something Jewish Happened: Some Thoughts about Joseph Heller's *Good as Gold*," an original essay written for publication in this volume. Friedman draws on his considerable background as a scholar of Jewish writing in America to place *Gold* in that tradition and to explore the ways in which its satire, portrayal of the family, regard for education, and especially its language relate to the traditions of Jewish literature.

Despite the considerable scholarly record that has been compiled on Heller as the writer of fiction, very little has been written on him as dramatist. Of *We Bombed in New Haven*, *Catch-22: A Dramatization*, and the one-act play *Clevinger's Trial*, only the first has received any sustained attention, even with regard to reviews. *We Bombed*, which ran for eighty-six performances on Broadway in 1968, starring Jason Robards and Diana Sands, received the same broad mix of reviews that characterized the reception of Heller's earlier books. On the negative side, critics did not spare Heller's play their wit. The review in *Time* observed that "it takes a certain concentrated foolishness to let a show bomb twice. *We Bombed in New Haven* did just that. It is now rebombing in New York," a reference to the fact that the play first opened at Yale. Even Heller's enthusiastic supporters were sometimes negative on the play: Tom Driver responded by saying that "Heller is great and *Catch-22* the greatest and *We Bombed in New Haven* a dud of the first magnitude." Stanley Reynolds suggested that the play was simply the "tailfire" from *Catch-22* and complained that it was "incredibly boring to read." B. H. Fussell called the play a "bag of burlesque skits" and speculated that the next use of *Catch-22* material would probably be a television series starring Woody Allen as Yossarian. In his review in the *New York Times*, Walter Kerr concluded that the play simply does not work, that the audience feels itself inaccurately presented in its views and is not told anything it does not already know. Robert Hatch said the play was filled with "wit, schmaltz, buffoonery, scenic legerdemain" but that ultimately it does not work: "A theatre is not a pulpit; it is a place where you must show, not tell, what you believe." The review in *Variety*, responding to the opening at the Yale University Theatre on December 4, 1967, complained that the play was "terribly overwritten" but allowed that it was "an overwhelming tragedy of irresistible personal compulsion." The reviewer for *Time*, responding to the same staging of the play, had a somewhat different reaction: "By the time the captain has to order his own son on a mission, it would take a rug rather than a handkerchief to sop up the teary sentimentality."[48]

But the play had its supporters as well. Jack Kroll gave the Yale production a positive assessment, calling it "very likely the most powerful play about contemporary irrationality an American has written." He went on to say that "this is one of those rare productions that advance the whole notion of the theater." Writing in the *Christian Science Monitor*, Roderick Nordell also responded favorably: "Among the obscenities of war, Joseph Heller's first play finds a blend of satire, comedy, and tragedy that cuts to the quick." Writing about the Broadway production, Clive Barnes called it "a bad play any good playwright should be proud to have written, and any good audience fascinated to see." His general assessment was that "any way you look at it, this is a pretty remarkable theatrical debut for Mr. Heller." And other reviewers too found things to praise, Jane Foster that the "dominant tone here is tragic disbelief and an almost pitiful plea for escape from war. Very strong medicine, very timely reading." William Hogan called the play "grade-A Heller that should delight champions of *Catch-22*."[49]

Beyond the reviews, there is very little on the scholarly record to examine. Elenore Lester did an interview with Heller at Yale before the opening of the play for the *New York Times* that is worthy of attention. In it Heller says that in general he does not like the theater, that he does not consider himself to be a writer of Black Comedy, that, in any event, *New Haven* is not comic, and that he is somewhat concerned about the quality of his script. On the other end of the public performances of the play, Israel

Shenker did another interview for the *New York Times* on December 29, 1968, the day the play closed its New York run. In this piece, "Did Heller Bomb on Broadway?" Heller comments that the play is modeled on Greek tragedies and comedies and that most of all he wanted to move the conscience of the audience.[50] The most substantial discussion of Heller as dramatist, however, is Linda McJ. Micheli's "In No-Man's Land: The Plays of Joseph Heller," an original essay written especially for this volume. In her essay Micheli discusses all three of Heller's plays in terms of the art of theatre. She concludes that Heller is a dramatist who must be taken seriously, especially for his skill with dialogue and for the drafting of memorable individual scenes. Micheli's essay will always be valuable as the first comprehensive treatment of Heller's controversial but nonetheless remarkable plays.

There are a few scholarly publications that might be classified as "general studies" of Heller that deserve additional mention. Josephine Hendin's *Vulnerable People: A View of American Fiction Since 1945* is a book that needs to be approached with both caution and scepticism. She gives *Catch-22* what must be regarded as a distorted reading, seeing it as a book that "mocks both power and vulnerability," thus she misses the point of Yossarian's obsession with Snowden's death and his protest against his superiors. With regard to *Something Happened*, she says that Slocum (whom she mistakenly calls "Bill" throughout her essay) is a man whose enemy "is what remains of his capacity for caring" (pp. 110–13). Another study of limited value is Stephen W. Potts, *From Here to Absurdity: The Moral Battlefields of Joseph Heller*, which is basically an unresearched study guide consisting of plot summaries of the Heller canon. The opinions expressed in this slim volume (64 pp.) are best ignored. *The Modern American Novel*, by Malcolm Bradbury, published in 1983, is typical of recent scholarship that does not take into account previous criticism: it presents commonplace ideas as original insights. Bradbury regards *Catch-22* as a "founding text for the Sixties" but offers only the most standard comments about it and the rest of the Heller canon, along with a number of factual errors.[51]

As a review of the scholarship reveals, a great deal has been written on Heller and a great deal remains to be done. Although *Catch-22* has been examined from numerous perspectives, most of the central issues of the book, and most of the basic technical aspects of it, have yet to receive definitive treatment, and only a few scholarly essays take into account the rich legacy of the manuscripts of the novel. Heller's other novels have been studied in only a preliminary way, and his short stories and plays have received only scant attention. Beyond specific works, a reliable and extended biographical account would be of use to scholars of all persuasions as would a full primary and secondary bibliography. It is perhaps too early to contemplate an edition of Heller's letters, but scholars who seek them out in libraries and private collections will find them fascinating reading and patently quotable for scholarly purposes. At some point a full scholarly study would help to draw together Heller's life with his creative work, but until such time as one is produced, this volume may have to serve as the best compilation of scholarly insight into the life and works of one of the most important contemporary American writers.

James Nagel

Notes

1. Anon., "Writers at Work: Joseph Heller," *New York Herald Tribune Books*, Oct. 7, 1962, p. 3.

2. See *Who's Who in America*, 34 (Chicago: Marquis, 1966), 936; *Who's Who in the East* (Chicago: Marquis, 1967), p. 471.

3. See Barbara Harte and Carolyn Riley, ed., *200 Contemporary Authors*, 5–8 (Detroit: Gale, 1969), pp. 533–34; "Joseph Heller," *Current Biography Yearbook* (New York: H. W. Wilson, 1973), pp. 174–77; Inge Kutt, "Joseph Heller," *Dictionary of Literary Biography*, II (Detroit: Gale, 1978), 231–36; Barbara Gelb, "Catching Joseph Heller," *New York Times Magazine*, March 4, 1979, pp. 14–16, 42–55.

4. Richard Lehan and Jerry Patch, "*Catch-22*: The Making of a Novel," *Minnesota Review*, 7 (1967), 238–44. Joseph Heller's letter to James Nagel outlining the numerous errors in this article is dated April 4, 1974, and a copy of the letter has been placed in the Brandeis University Library.

5. Paul Krassner, "An Impolite Interview with Joseph Heller," *The Realist*, 39 (Nov., 1962), 18–31; W. J. Weatherby, "The Joy Catcher," *The Guardian*, Nov. 20, 1962, p. 7; "So They Say," *Mademoiselle*, 57 (Aug. 1963), 234–35.

6. Elenore Lester, "Playwright-in-Anguish," *New York Times*, Dec. 3, 1967, Sec. 2, pp. 1, 9; Susan Braudy, "Laughing All the Way to the Truth," *New York*, 1 (Oct. 14, 1968), 42–45; Dale Gold, "Portrait of a Man Reading," *Washington Post Book World*, July 20, 1969, p. 2; Ken Barnard, "Interview with Joseph Heller," *Detroit News Magazine*, Sept. 13, 1970, 18–19, 24, 27–28, 30, 65; W. K. Thomas, "The Mythic Dimension of *Catch-22*," *Texas Studies in Language and Literature*, 15 (1973), 189–98.

7. George Plimpton, "How It Happened," *New York Times Book Review*, Oct. 6, 1974, 2, 3, 30; Barbara Bannon, "PW Interviews: Joseph Heller," *Publishers' Weekly*, 204 (Sept. 30, 1974), 6; Thomas Collins, "*Something Happened*: A Story of America," *Newsday*, Oct. 16, 1974, p. 13; Peter Gorner, "13 Years After *Catch-22*, Heller's Happened Again," *Chicago Tribune*, Sept. 30, 1974, p. 14; Sam Merrill, "*Playboy* Interview: Joseph Heller," *Playboy*, 22 (June 1975), 59–61, 64–66, 68, 70, 72–74, 76.

8. Frederick Kiley and Walter McDonald, ed., *A "Catch-22" Casebook* (New York: Crowell, 1973); Robert M. Scotto, ed., *"Catch-22": A Critical Edition* (New York: Delta, 1973); James Nagel, ed., *Critical Essays on "Catch-22"* (Encino: Dickenson, 1974).

9. Joseph Weixlmann, "A Bibliography of Joseph Heller's *Catch-22*," *Bulletin of Bibliography*, 31 (1974), 32–37; Robert M. Scotto, *Three Contemporary Novelists: An Annotated Bibliography of Works by and about John Hawkes, Joseph Heller, and Thomas Pynchon* (New York: Garland, 1977); Brenda M. Keegan, *Joseph Heller: A Reference Guide* (Boston: G. K. Hall, 1978). Indeed, Keegan's account is so complete that it obviates the need for a full listing here. In particular, her list should be consulted for information about dissertations on Heller, which, for reasons of length, I have eliminated from this survey.

10. Robert Brustein, "The Logic of Survival in a Lunatic World," *New Republic*, 145 (Nov. 13, 1961), 11–13; Nelson Algren, "The Catch," *Nation*, 193 (Nov. 4, 1961), 357–58; Julian Mitchell, "Under Mad Gods," *Spectator*, June 15, 1962, p. 801; "Lunacracy," *Newsweek*, 58 (Oct. 16, 1961), 116–18; "Good Soldier Yossarian," *Time*, 78 (Oct. 27, 1961), 97–98;

"Christmas Classified," *Mademoiselle*, 54 (Nov. 1961), 103–09; "Christmas Books for Varied Tastes," *Saturday Review*, 44 (Dec. 2, 1961), 32; see Kenneth Tynan in the London *Observer*; Dec. 17, 1961, p. 22; Norman Mailer, "Some Children of the Goddess: Norman Mailer vs. Nine Writers," *Esquire*, 60 (July 1963), 63–69, 105.

11. Richard G. Stern, "Bombers Away," *New York Times Book Review*, Oct. 22, 1961, p. 50; Douglas Day, "*Catch-22*: A Manifesto for Anarchists," *Carolina Quarterly*, 15 (Summer 1963), 86–92; Granville Hicks, "Medals for Madness," *Saturday Review*, 44 (Oct. 14, 1961), 32; Whitney Balliet in the *New Yorker*, 27 (Dec. 9, 1961), 247–48; Spencer Klaw, "Airman's Wacky War," *New York Herald Tribune*, Oct. 15, 1961, Sec. 6, p. 8; Orville Prescott, "Books of the Times," *New York Times*, Oct. 23, 1961, p. 27; [Roger H. Smith] in *Daedalus* (Winter 1963), pp. 155–65.

12. Frederick R. Karl, "Joseph Heller's *Catch-22*: Only Fools Walk in Darkness," in *Contemporary American Novelists*, ed. Harry T. Moore (Carbondale: Southern Illinois Univ. Press, 1964), pp. 134–42; Norman Podhoretz, *Doings and Undoings* (New York: Farrar, Straus & Giroux, 1964), pp. 228–35; Joseph J. Waldmeir, "Joseph Heller: A Novelist of the Absurd," *Wisconsin Studies in Contemporary Literature*, 5, No. 3 (1964), 192–96; Ihab Hassan, "Laughter in the Dark: The New Voice in American Fiction," *American Scholar*, 33 (Autumn 1964), 636–39.

13. Sanford Pinsker, "Heller's *Catch-22:* The Protest of a *Puer Eternis*," *Critique*, 7, No. 2 (1965), 150–62; Constance Denniston, "The American Romance-Parody: A Study of Heller's *Catch-22*," *Emporia State Research Studies*, 14, No. 2 (1965), 42–59; G. B. McK. Henry, "Significant Corn: *Catch-22*," *Melbourne Critical Review*, 9 (1966), 133–44; Vance Ramsey, "From Here to Absurdity: Heller's *Catch-22*," *Seven Contemporary Authors: Essays on Cozzens, Miller, West, Golding, Heller, Albee, and Powers*, ed. Thomas B. Whitbread (Austin: Univ. of Texas Press, 1968), 99–118.

14. James E. Miller, Jr., *Quests Surd and Absurd: Essays in American Literature* (Chicago: Univ. of Chicago Press, 1967), pp. 24–25.

15. Donald Monk, "An Experiment in Therapy: A Study of *Catch-22*," *London Review*, No. 2 (Autumn 1967), 12–19; Nelvin Vos, *For God's Sake Laugh!* (Richmond: John Knox Press, 1967), pp. 53–58; Jan Solomon, "The Structure of Joseph Heller's *Catch-22*," *Critique*, 9, No. 2 (1967), 46–57; Caroline Gordon and Jeanne Richardson, "Flies in Their Eyes? A Note on Joseph Heller's *Catch-22*," *Southern Review*, 3 (1967), 96–105.

16. Minna Doskow, "The Night Journey in *Catch-22*," *Twentieth Century Literature*, 12 (1967), 186–93; Joseph Heller, "*Catch-22* Revisited," *Holiday*, 41 (April 1967), 45–60, 130, 141–42, 145.

17. Brian Way, "Formal Experiment and Social Discontent: Joseph Heller's *Catch-22*," *Journal of American Studies*, 2 (1968), 253–70; James L. McDonald, "I See Everything Twice! The Structure of Joseph Heller's *Catch-22*," *University Review*, 34 (1968), 175–80; James M. Mellard, "*Catch-22*: Deja vu and the Labyrinth of Memory," *Bucknell Review*, 16, No. 2 (1968), 29–44.

18. J. P. Stern, "War and the Comic Muse: *The Good Soldier Schweik* and *Catch-22*," *Comparative Literature*, 20 (1968), 193-216; John W. Hunt, "Comic Escape and Anti-Vision: Joseph Heller's *Catch-22*," *Adversity and Grace: Studies in Recent American Literature*, ed. Nathan A. Scott, Jr. (Chicago: Univ. of Chicago Press, 1968), pp. 91–98; Josh Greenfeld, "22 Was Funnier Than 14," *New York Times Book Review*, March 3, 1968, pp. 1, 49-51, 53; Eugene McNamara, "The Absurd Style in Contemporary American Literature," *Humanities Association Bulletin*, 19, No. 1 (1968), 44–49; Hamlin Hill, "Black Humor: Its Cause and Cure," *Colorado Quarterly*, 17 (Summer 1968), 57–64; Max F. Schulz, "Pop, Op, and Black Humor: The Aesthetics of Anxiety," *College English*, 30 (Dec. 1, 1968), 230–41.

19. See Eric Solomon, "From *Christ in Flanders* to *Catch-22*: An Approach to War Fiction," *Texas Studies in Literature and Language*, 11 (1969), 851–66; Joseph J. Waldmeir, *American Novels of the Second World War* (The Hague: Mouton, 1969), pp. 160–65.

20. Judith Crist, "All That Glitters is Not Nichols," *New York*, 3 (June 29, 1970), 54; Hollis Alpert, "The Catch," *Saturday Review*, 53 (June 27, 1970), 24; Susan Larder, "The Current Cinema: No Comparison," *New Yorker*, 46 (June 27, 1970), 62–63; Jacob Brackman, "Review of *Catch-22*," *Esquire*, 74 (Sept. 1970), 8, 12, 14; Vincent Canby, "A Triumphant *Catch*," *New York Times*, June 28, 1970, Sec. 2, p. 1; Ken Barnard, "Joseph Heller Tells How *Catch-18* Became *Catch-22* and Why He Was Afraid of Airplanes," *Detroit News Sunday Magazine*, Sept. 13, 1970, pp. 18–19, 24, 27–28, 30, 65.

21. Wayne Charles Miller, *An Armed America: Its Face in Fiction* (New York: New York Univ. Press, 1970), pp. 205–43; Victor J. Milne, "Heller's 'Bologniad': A Theological Perspective on *Catch-22*," *Critique*, 12, No. 2 (1970), 50–69; Jim Castelli, "*Catch-22* and the New Hero," *Catholic World*, 211 (1970), 199–202.

22. Doug Gaukroger, "Time Structure in *Catch-22*," *Critique*, 12, No. 2 (1970), 70–85; Alvin Greenberg, "Choice — Ironic Alternative in the World of the Contemporary Novel," in *American Dreams, American Nightmares*, ed. David Madden (Carbondale: Southern Illinois Univ. Press, 1970), pp. 175–87; W. K. Thomas, "What Difference Does It Make," *Dalhousie Review*, 50 (1970), 488–95; Jerry H. Bryant, *The Open Decision: The Contemporary American Novel and Its Intellectual Background* (New York: Free Press, 1970).

23. Tony Tanner, *City of Words: American Fiction 1950-1970* (London: Jonathan Cape, 1971), pp. 72–84; Robert Protherough, "The Sanity of *Catch-22*," *Human World*, 3 (May 1971), 59–70; Jean Kennard, "Joseph Heller: At War With Absurdity," *Mosaic*, 4, No. 3 (1971), 75–87.

24. Thomas Blues, "The Moral Structure of *Catch-22*," *Studies in the Novel*, 3 (1971), 64–79; Thomas Allen Nelson, "Theme and Structure in *Catch-22*," *Renascence*, 23 (1971), p. 178; Lucy Frost, "Violence in the Eternal City: *Catch-22* as a Critique of American Culture," *Meanjin Quarterly*, 30 (1971), 447–53.

25. Richard B. Sale, "An Interview in New York with Joseph Heller," *Studies in the Novel*, 4 (1972), 63–74; Raymond M. Olderman, *Beyond the Waste Land: A Study of the American Novel in the Nineteen-Sixties* (New Haven: Yale Univ. Press, 1972), pp. 94-116.

26. See Scotto, *Critical Edition*, and Kiley, *Casebook*. The page numbers for individual essays are given in the text.

27. Clinton S. Burhans, Jr., "Spindrift and the Sea: Structural Patterns and Unifying Elements in *Catch-22*," *Twentieth-Century Literature*, 19 (1973), 239–49; Walter R. McDonald, "He Took Off: Yossarian and the Different Drummer," *CEA Critic*, 36 (Nov. 1973), 14–16; Paul Loukides, "The Radical Vision," *Michigan Academician*, 5 (1973), 497–503.

28. See Nagel, *Critical Essays on "Catch-22."* The page numbers for individual original essays are given in the text.

29. Alfred Kazin, *Bright Book of Life: American Novelists and Storytellers from Hemingway to Mailer* (New York: Delta, 1974), pp. 82–85; Bruce Janoff, "Black Humor, Existentialism, and Absurdity: A Generic Confusion," *Arizona Quarterly*, 30 (1974), 293-304; David H. Richter, *Fable's End: Completeness and Closure in Rhetorical Fiction* (Chicago: Univ. of Chicago Press, 1974), p. 136; James Nagel, "Two Brief Manuscript Sketches: Heller's *Catch-22*," *Modern Fiction Studies*, 20 (1974), 221–24; James Nagel, "*Catch-22* and Angry Humor: A Study in the Normative Values of Satire," *Studies in American Humor*, 1 (1974), 99–106.

30. Mike Frank, "Eros and Thanatos in *Catch-22*," *Canadian Review of Ameican Studies*, 8, No. 1 (1976), 77–87; H. R. Swardson, "Sentimentality and the Academic Tradition," *College English*, 37 (April 1976), 747–66; Carol Pearson, "*Catch-22* and the Debasement of Language," *CEA Critic*, 38, No. 4 (1976), 30–35; Fred M. Fetrow, "Joseph Heller's Use of Names in *Catch-22*," *Studies in Contemporary Satire*, 1, No. 2 (1975), 28–38; Peter G. Jones, *War and the Novelist: Appraising the American War Novel* (Columbia: Univ. of Missouri Press, 1976); James Nagel, "The *Catch-22* Note Cards," *Studies in the Novel*, 8 (1976), 394–405.

31. Morris Dickstein, *Gates of Eden: American Culture in the Sixties* (New York: Basic

Books, 1977), pp. 113–17; Peyton Glass, III, "Heller's *Catch-22*," *Explicator*, 36, No. 2 (1978), 25–26; Gary W. Davis, "*Catch-22* and the Language of Discontinuity," *Novel*, 12 (1978), 66–77; Robert Merrill, "The Rhetorical Structure of *Catch-22*," *Notes on Contemporary Literature*, 8, No. 3 (1978), 9–11.

32. Leon F. Seltzer, "Milo's 'Culpable Innocence': Absurdity as Moral Insanity in *Catch-22*," *Papers on Language and Literature*, 15 (1979), 290–310; Adam J. Sorkin, "From Papa to Yo-Yo: At War with All the Words in the World," *South Atlantic Bulletin*, 44, No. 4 (1979), 48–65; Michael J. Larsen, "Shakespearean Echoes in *Catch-22*," *American Notes and Queries*, 17 (1979), 76–78; Thomas L. Hartshorne, "From *Catch-22* to *Slaughterhouse V*: The Decline of the Political Mode," *South Atlantic Quarterly*, 78 (1979), 17-33.

33. James M. Mellard, *The Exploded Form: The Modernist Novel in America* (Urbana: Univ. of Illinois, Press, 1980); Jerome Klinkowitz, *The American 1960s: Imaginative Acts in a Decade of Change* (Ames: Iowa State Univ. Press, 1980); James S. Mullican, "A Burkean Approach to *Catch-22*," *College Literature*, 8, No. 1 (1981), 42–52; P. Merivale, "*Catch-22* and *The Secret Agent*: Mechanical Man, the Hole in the Center, and the 'Principle of Inbuilt Chaos'," *English Studies in Canada*, 7, No. 4 (1981), 426–37; Gary Lindberg, *The Confidence Man in American Literature* (New York: Oxford Univ. Press, 1982); Jeffrey Walsh, *American War Literature 1914 to Vietnam* (New York: St. Martin's Press, 1982).

34. James Shapiro, "Work in Progress: An Interview with Joseph Heller," *Intellectual Digest*, 2 (Dec. 1971), 6, 8, 10-11; Barbara Bannon, "Joseph Heller," *Publisher's Weekly*, 206 (Sept. 30, 1974), 6; George Plimpton, "How It Happened," *New York Times Book Review*, Oct. 6, 1974, pp. 2, 3, 30.

35. Nelson Algren, "*Something Happened* by Joseph Heller," *Critic*, 33, No. 1 (1974), 90-91; Pearl K. Bell, "Heller's Trial by Tedium," *New Leader*, Oct. 28, 1974, p. 17; Margaret Manning, "Heller Back with Somber Work," *Boston Globe*, Oct. 14, 1974, p. 33; John Thompson, "Caught Again," *New York Review of Books*, 21 (Oct. 17, 1974), 24–26.

36. L. E. Sissman, *New Yorker*, 50 (Nov. 25, 1974), 193; Joseph Epstein, "Joseph Heller's Milk Train: Nothing More to Express," *Washington Post Book World*, Oct. 6, 1974, pp. 1-2; John B. Breslin, "Living with Absurdity," *America*, Oct. 26, 1974, pp. 235–36; Melvin Maddocks, "Boring from Within," *Time*, Oct. 14, 1974, pp. 87-88; Edward Grossman, "Yossarian Lives," *Commentary*, 58 (Nov. 1974), 78-84; Wilfrid Sheed, "The Good Word: The Novel of Manners Lives," *New York Times Book Review*, Feb. 2, 1975, p. 2; D. Keith Mano, "Fine Writing that Irks," *National Review*, 26 (Nov. 22, 1974), 1974; Caroline Blackwood, "The Horrors of Peace," *Times Literary Supplement*, Oct. 25, 1974, p. 1183.

37. John W. Aldridge, "Vision of Man Raging in a Vacuum," *Saturday Review World*, 2 (Oct. 19, 1974), 18–22; Susan Fromberg Schaeffer, "Heller's New 'Catch': The Man in the Gray-Flannel Cubicle," *Chicago Tribune Book World*, Oct. 13, 1974, p. 1; William Kennedy, "Endlessly Honest Confession," *New Republic*. Oct. 19, 1974. pp. 17–19: Robert Kirsch. "Heller's Catch-23: The Entrapment of Everyman," *Los Angeles Times*, Oct. 13, 1974, pp. 1, 68; Walter Clemons, "Comedy of Fear," *Newsweek*, Oct. 14, 1974, pp. 116, 118; Paul Desruisseaux, "A Powerful, Tragic Novel of a Life Coming Apart," *San Francisco Examiner*, Oct. 13, 1974, p. 30; Kurt Vonnegut, Jr., "*Something Happened*," *New York Times Book Review*, Oct. 6, 1974, pp. 1–3; Patricia Meyer Spacks, "New Novels: In the Dumps," *Yale Review*, 64 (Summer 1975), 583-84.

38. Charles T. Powers, "Joe Heller, Author on Top of the World," *Los Angeles Times*, March 30, 1975, Part 7, pp. 1, 12; George J. Searles, "*Something Happened*: A New Direction for Joseph Heller," *Critique*, 18, No. 3 (1977), 74–81; Nicholas Canaday, "Joseph Heller: Something Happened to the American Dream," *CEA Critic*, 40, No. 1 (1977), 34–38; Susan Strehle, "Slocum's Parenthetical Tic: Style as Metaphor in *Something Happened*," *Notes on Contemporary Literature*, 7, No. 5 (1977), 9–10.

39. Christopher Lasch, *The Culture of Narcissism: American Life in an Age of Diminishing Expectations* (New York: Norton, 1978), pp. 85-86, 98, 180.

40. Susan Strehle Klemtner, " 'A Permanent Game of Excuses': Determinism in Heller's *Something Happened," Modern Fiction Studies*, 24 (1978–79), 556; Wayne D. McGinnis, "The Anarchic Impulse in Two Recent Novels," *Publications of the Arkansas Philological Association*, 5, Nos. 2–3 (1979), 36–40.

41. Thomas LeClair, "Joseph Heller, *Something Happened*, and the Art of Excess," *Studies in American Fiction*, 9 (1981), 245–60; George Sebouhian, "From Abraham and Isaac to Bob Slocum and My Boy: Why Fathers Kill Their Sons," *Twentieth-Century Literature*, 27 (1981), 43–52; Richard Hauer Costa, "Notes from a Dark Heller: Bob Slocum and the Underground Man," *Texas Studies in Literature and Language*, 23 (1981), 159–82; John W. Aldridge, *The American Novel and the Way We Live Now* (New York: Oxford Univ. Press, 1983).

42. [Review of *Good as Gold*] *New Yorker*, 55 (April 16, 1979), 158; Morris Dickstein, "Something Didn't Happen," *Saturday Review*, 6 (March 31, 1979), 49–52; Pearl K. Bell, "Heller & Malamud, Then and Now," *Commentary*, 67 (1979), 71–72; Gene Lyons, "Contradictory Judaism," *Nation*, 228 (June 16, 1979), 727-28; Larry Simonberg, [Review of *Good as Gold*], *Boston Phoenix*, April 10, 1979, Section 3, pp. 1, 12; Peter S. Prescott, "Private Spleen," *Newsweek*, March 12, 1979, p. 91.

43. R. Z. Sheppard, "Speaking About the Unspeakable," *Time*, March 12, 1979, p. 92; Benjamin DeMott, "Heller's Gold and a Silver Sax," *Atlantic Monthly*, 243 (March 1979), 129–32; Jeffrey A. Tannenbaum, "The Relentless Cynicism of Joseph Heller," *Wall Street Journal*, 193 (March 16, 1979), 22; Aram Bakshian, Jr., "Books in Brief," *National Review*, 31 (July 20, 1979), 932, 935; Clara Claiborne Park, "Fiction Chronicle," *Hudson Review*, 32 (1979), 584.

44. Margaret Manning, "Through Joseph Heller's Looking Glass," *Boston Sunday Globe*, March 18, 1979, p. A8; Doris Grumbach, "Unheralded Joys from a Writer's Writer and a First Novelist: But Heller's *Gold* does not Succeed as Planned," *Chronicle Review*, March 19, 1979, pp. 14–15; Roderick Nordell, "Heller's Black Comedy of Society's Errors," *Christian Science Monitor*, March 28, 1979, p. 17; Raymond A. Schroth, "I Wonder Who's Kissinger Now?" *Commonweal*, 106 (May 11, 1979), 284–85.

45. Thomas R. Edwards, "On the Gold Standard," *New York Review of Books*, 26 (April 5, 1979), 10; Jack Beatty, *"Good as Gold* by Joseph Heller," *New Republic*, 180 (March 10, 1979), 42–44; John W. Aldridge, "The Deceits of Black Humor," *Harper's*, 258 (March 1979), 115–18; Leonard Michaels, "Bruce Gold's American Experience," *New York Times Book Review*, March 11, 1979, pp. 1, 24–25; Lee Eisenberg, "Jewish Questions," *Esquire*, p. 91 (Feb. 29, 1979), 17–18.

46. Charlie Reilly, "Talking with Joseph Heller," *Inquiry Magazine*, May 1, 1979, pp. 22–26; Chet Flippo, "Checking in with Joseph Heller," *Rolling Stone*, April 16, 1981, pp. 51–52.

47. Wayne C. Miller, "Ethnic Identity as Moral Focus: A Reading of Joseph Heller's *Good as Gold*," *MELUS*, 6, No. 3 (1979), 3-17; Charles Berryman, "Heller's Gold," *Chicago Review*, 32, No. 4 (1981), 108-18; James Nagel, "Joseph Heller and the University," *College Literature*, 10 (1983), 16–27; Frances K. Barasch; "Faculty Images in Recent American Fiction," *College Literature*, 10 (1983), 28–37.

48. "Indiscriminate Bombing," *Time*, 92 (Oct. 25, 1968), 69; Tom Driver, "Curtains in Connecticut," *Saturday Review*, 51 (Aug. 31, 1968), 22–24; Stanley Reynolds, "A Damp Squib," *Guardian Weekly*, July 17, 1969, p. 20; B. H. Fussell, "On the Trail of the Lonesome Dramaturge," *Hudson Review*, 26 (1973), 753-54; Walter Kerr, "Walter Kerr vs. Joseph Heller," *New York Times*, Oct. 27, 1968, Section 2, pp. 1, 5; Robert Hatch, "Theatre," *Nation*, 207 (Nov. 4, 1968), 477–78; "We Bombed in New Haven," *Variety*, Dec. 13, 1967, p. 58; "Catchall-22," *Time*, 90 (Dec. 15, 1967), 87.

49. Jack Kroll, "War Games," *Newsweek*, 70 (Dec. 18, 1967), 96; Roderick Nordell, "Premiere of *We Bombed in New Haven*," *Christian Science Monitor*, Dec. 8, 1967, p. 14; Clive Barnes, "Theater: Heller's *We Bombed in New Haven* Opens," *New York Times*, Oct. 17, 1968,

p. 51; Jane Foster, *Library Journal*, March 15, 1969, pp. 1346–47; William Hogan, "Joseph Heller's *Catch-22* Cont'd," *San Francisco Chronicle*, Aug. 19, 1968, p. 41.

50. Elenore Lester, "Playwright-in-Anguish," *New York Times*, Dec. 3, 1967, Section 2, pp. 1, 19; Israel Shenker, "Did Heller Bomb on Broadway?" *New York Times*, Dec. 29, 1968, Section 2, pp. 1, 3.

51. Josephine Hendin, *Vulnerable People: A View of American Fiction Since 1945* (New York: Oxford Univ. Press, 1978), pp. 110-13; Stephen W. Potts, *From Here to Absurdity: The Moral Battlefields of Joseph Heller* (San Bernardino: Borgo, 1982); Malcolm Bradbury, *The Modern American Novel* (New York: Oxford Univ. Press, 1983), pp. 165–67.

Catch-22

The Logic of Survival in a Lunatic World
Robert Brustein[*]

Like all superlative works of comedy — and I am ready to argue that this is one of the most bitterly funny works in the language — *Catch-22* is based on an unconventional but utterly convincing internal logic. In the very opening pages, when we come upon a number of Air Force officers malingering in a hospital — one censoring all the modifiers out of enlisted men's letters and signing the censor's name "Washington Irving," another pursuing tedious conversations with boring Texans in order to increase his life span by making time pass slowly, still another storing horse chestnuts in his cheeks to give himself a look of innocence — it seems obvious that an inordinate number of Joseph Heller's characters are, by all conventional standards, mad. It is a triumph of Mr. Heller's skill that he is so quickly able to persuade us 1) that the most lunatic are the most logical, and 2) that it is our conventional standards which lack any logical consistency. The sanest looney of them all is the apparently harebrained central character, an American bombardier of Syrian extraction named Captain John Yossarian, who is based on a mythical Italian island (Pianosa) during World War II. For while many of his fellow officers seem indifferent to their own survival, and most of his superior officers are overtly hostile to his, Yossarian is animated solely by a desperate determination to stay alive:

> It was a vile and muddy war, and Yossarian could have lived without it — lived forever, perhaps. Only a fraction of his countrymen would give up their lives to win it, and it was not his ambition to be among them. . . . That men would die was a matter of necessity; *which* men would die, though, was a matter of circumstance, and Yossarian was willing to be the victim of anything but circumstance.

The single narrative thread in this crazy patchwork of anecdotes, episodes, and character portraits traces Yossarian's herculean efforts — through caution, cowardice, defiance, subterfuge, strategem, and subversion, through feigning illness, goofing off, and poisoning the company's food with laundry soap — to avoid being victimized by circumstance, a force represented

*Reprinted, with the permission of the author, from the *New Republic*, 145 (Nov. 13, 1961), 11–13.

27

in the book as Catch-22. For Catch-22 is the unwritten loophole in every written law which empowers the authorities to revoke your rights whenever it suits their cruel whims; it is, in short, the principle of absolute evil in a malevolent, mechanical, and incompetent world. Because of Catch-22, justice is mocked, the innocent are victimized, and Yossarian's squadron is forced to fly more than double the number of missions prescribed by Air Force code. Dogged by Catch-22, Yossarian becomes the anguished witness to the ghoulish slaughter of his crew members and the destruction of all his closest friends, until finally his fear of death becomes so intense that he refuses to wear a uniform, after his own has been besplattered with the guts of his dying gunner, and receives a medal standing naked in formation. From this point on, Yossarian's logic becomes so pure that everyone thinks him mad, for it is the logic of sheer survival, dedicated to keeping him alive in a world noisily clamoring for his annihilation.

According to this logic, Yossarian is surrounded on all sides by hostile forces: his enemies are distinguished less by their nationality than by their ability to get him killed. Thus, Yossarian feels a blind, electric rage against the Germans whenever they hurl flak at his easily penetrated plane; but he feels an equally profound hatred for those of his own countrymen who exercise an arbitrary power over his life and well-being. Heller's huge cast of characters, therefore, is dominated by a large number of comic malignities, *genus Americanus*, drawn with a grotesqueness so audacious that they somehow transcend caricature entirely and become vividly authentic. These include: Colonel Cathcart, Yossarian's commanding officer, whose consuming ambition to get his picture in the *Saturday Evening Post* motivates him to volunteer his command for every dangerous command, and to initiate prayers during briefing sessions ("I don't want any of this Kingdom of God or Valley of Death stuff. That's all too negative. . . . Couldn't we pray for a tighter bomb pattern?"), an idea he abandons only when he learns enlisted men pray to the same God; General Peckem, head of Special Services, whose strategic objective is to replace General Dreedle, the wing commander, capturing every bomber group in the US Air Force ("If dropping bombs on the enemy isn't a special service, I wonder what in the world is"); Captain Black, the squadron intelligence officer, who inaugurates the Glorious Loyalty Oath Crusade in order to discomfort a rival, forcing all officers (except the rival, who is thereupon declared a Communist) to sign a new oath whenever they get their flak suits, their pay checks, or their haircuts; Lieutenant Scheisskopf, paragon of the parade ground, whose admiration for efficient formations makes him scheme to screw nickel-alloy swivels into every cadet's back for perfect ninety degree turns; and cadres of sadistic officers, club-happy MPs, and muddleheaded agents of the CID, two of whom, popping in and out of rooms like farcical private eyes, look for Washington Irving throughout the action, finally pinning the rap on the innocent chaplain.

These are Yossarian's antagonists, all of them reduced to a single exaggerated humor, and all identified by their totally mechanical attitude towards human life. Heller has a profound hatred for this kind of military mind, further anatomized in a wacky scene before the Action Board which displays his (and their) animosity in a manner both hilarious and scarifying. But Heller, at war with much larger forces than the army, has provided his book with much wider implications than a war novel. For the author (apparently sharing the Italian belief that vengeance is a dish which tastes best cold) has been nourishing his grudges for so long that they have expanded to include the post-war American world. Through the agency of grotesque comedy, Heller has found a way to confront the humbug, hypocrisy, cruelty, and sheer stupidity of our mass society — qualities which have made the few other Americans who care almost speechless with baffled rage — and through some miracle of prestidigitation, Pianosa has become a satirical microcosm for many of the macrocosmic idiocies of our time. Thus, the author flourishes his Juvenalian scourge at government-subsidized agriculture (and farmers, one of whom "spent every penny he didn't earn on new land to increase the amount of alfalfa he did not grow"); at the exploitation of American Indians, evicted from their oil-rich land; at smug psychiatrists; at bureaucrats and patriots; at acquisitive war widows; at high-spirited American boys; and especially, and most vindictively, at war profiteers.

This last satirical flourish, aimed at the whole mystique of corporation capitalism, is embodied in the fantastic adventures of Milo Minderbinder, the company mess officer, and a paradigm of good natured Jonsonian cupidity. Anxious to put the war on a businesslike basis, Milo has formed a syndicate designed to corner the world market on all available foodstuffs, which he then sells to army mess halls at huge profits. Heady with success (his deals have made him Mayor of every town in Sicily, Vice-Shah of Oran, Caliph of Baghdad, Imam of Damascus, and the Sheik of Araby), Milo soon expands his activities, forming a private army which he hires out to the highest bidder. The climax of Milo's career comes when he fulfills a contract with the Germans to bomb and strafe his own outfit, directing his planes from the Pianosa control tower and justifying the action with the stirring war cry: "What's good for the syndicate is good for the country." Milo has almost succeeded in his ambition to pre-empt the field of war for private enterprise when he makes a fatal mistake: he has cornered the entire Egyptian cotton market and is unable to unload it anywhere. Having failed to pass it off to his own mess hall in the form of chocolate-covered cotton, Milo is finally persuaded by Yossarian to bribe the American government to take it off his hands: "If you run into trouble, just tell everybody that the security of the country requires a strong domestic Egyptian cotton speculating industry." The Minderbinder sections — in showing the basic incompatibility of idealism and economics by satirizing the patriotic cant which usually accompanies American greed — illustrate the procedure of the entire book: the ruthless ridicule of hypocrisy through a technique of farce-fantasy, beneath which the demon of satire lurks, prodding fat behinds with a red-hot pitch-fork.

It should be abundantly clear, then, that *Catch-22*, despite some of the most outrageous sequences since *A Night at the Opera*, is an intensely serious work. Heller has certain technical similarities to the Marx Brothers, Max Schulman, Kingsley Amis, Al Capp, and S. J. Perelman, but his mordant intelligence, closer to that of Nathanael West, penetrates the surface of the merely funny to expose a world of ruthless self-advancement, gruesome cruelty, and flagrant disregard for human life—a world, in short, very much like our own as seen through a magnifying glass, distorted for more perfect accuracy. Considering his indifference to surface reality, it is absurd to judge Heller by standards of psychological realism (or, for that matter, by conventional artistic standards at all, since his book is as formless as any picaresque epic). He is concerned entirely with that thin boundary of the surreal, the borderline between hilarity and horror, which, much like the apparent formlessness of the unconscious, has its own special integrity and coherence. Thus Heller will never use comedy for its own sake; each joke has a wider significance in the intricate pattern, so that laughter becomes a prologue for some grotesque revelation. This gives the reader an effect of surrealistic dislocation, intensified by a weird, rather flat, impersonal style, full of complicated reversals, swift transitions, abrupt shifts in chronological time, and manipulated identities (*e.g.* if a private named Major Major Major is promoted to Major by a faulty IBM machine, or if a malingerer, sitting out a doomed mission, is declared dead through a bureaucratic error, then this remains their permanent fate), as if all mankind was determined by a mad and merciless mechanism.

Thus, Heller often manages to heighten the macabre obscenity of total war much more effectively through its gruesome comic aspects than if he had written realistic descriptions. And thus, the most delicate pressure is enough to send us over the line from farce into phantasmagoria. In the climactic chapter, in fact, the book leaves comedy altogether and becomes an eerie nightmare of terror. Here, Yossarian, walking through the streets of Rome as though through an Inferno, observes soldiers molesting drunken women, fathers beating ragged children, policemen clubbing innocent bystanders until the whole world seems swallowed up in the maw of evil:

> The night was filled with horrors, and he thought he knew how Christ must have felt as he walked through the world, like a psychiatrist through a ward of nuts, like a victim through a prison of thieves. . . . Mobs . . . mobs of policemen. . . . Mobs with clubs were in control everywhere.

Here, as the book leaves the war behind, it is finally apparent that Heller's comedy is his artistic response to his vision of transcendent evil, as if the escape route of laughter were the only recourse from a malignant world.

It is this world, which cannot be divided into boundaries or ideologies, that Yossarian has determined to resist. And so when his fear and disgust have reached the breaking point, he simply refuses to fly another mission. Asked by a superior what would happen if everybody felt the same way, Yossarian exercises his definitive logic, and answers, "Then I'd be a damned fool to feel any other way." Having concluded a separate peace, Yossarian maintains it in the face of derision, ostracism, psychological pressure, and the threat of court martial. When he is finally permitted to go home if he will only agree to a shabby deal white-washing Colonel Cathcart, however, he finds himself impaled on two impossible alternatives. But his unique logic, helped along by the precedent of an even more logical friend, makes him conclude that desertion is the better part of valor; and so (after an inspirational sequence which is the weakest thing in the book) he takes off for neutral Sweden—the only place left in the world, outside of England, where "mobs with clubs" are not in control.

Yossarian's expedient is not very flattering to our national ideals, being defeatist, selfish, cowardly, and unheroic. On the other hand, it is one of those sublime expressions of anarchic individualism without which all national ideals are pretty hollow anyway. Since the mass State, whether totalitarian or democratic, has grown increasingly hostile to Falstaffian irresponsibility, Yossarian's anti-heroism is, in fact, a kind of inverted heroism which we would do well to ponder. For, contrary to the armchair pronouncements of patriotic ideologues, Yossarian's obsessive concern for survival makes him not only *not* morally dead, but one of the most morally vibrant figures in recent literature—and a giant of the will beside those weary, wise and wistful prodigals in contemporary novels who always accommodate sadly to American life. I believe that Joseph Heller is one of the most extraordinary talents now among us. He has Mailer's combustible radicalism without his passion for violence and self-glorification; he has Bellow's gusto without his compulsion to affirm the unaffirmable; and he has Salinger's wit without his coquettish self-consciousness. Finding his absolutes in the freedom to *be*, in a world dominated by cruelty, carnage, inhumanity, and a rage to destroy itself, Heller has come upon a new morality based on an old ideal, the morality of refusal. Perhaps—now that Catch-22 has found its most deadly nuclear form — we have reached the point where even the logic of survival is unworkable. But at least we can still contemplate the influence of its liberating honesty on a free, rebellious spirit in this explosive, bitter, subversive, brilliant book.

Under Mad Gods

Julian Mitchell*

Joseph Heller's *Catch-22* is an extraordinary book. Its basic assumption is that in war all men are equally mad; bombs fall on insane friend and crazy enemy alike. But wherever bombs fall, men die, and no matter how often the process of bombs falling and men dying is repeated, it is always terrible. Ostensibly a black farce about an American bomber squadron stationed on an island in the Mediterranean towards the end of the Second World War, it is, in fact, a surrealist *Iliad*, with a lunatic High Command instead of gods, and a coward for hero.

Yossarian, the coward, is a rational man trying not to be killed in a wholly irrational world, forced to resort to even more irrational behavior than that of his superiors in order to survive. He is an expert malingerer; he performs minor acts of sabotage on his own plane; he takes every possible form of evasive action. But he cannot succeed against the appalling Colonel Cathcart, who continually raises the number of missions the men have to fly before they can be sent home, solely to get a reputation as a tough leader of men. Whatever Yossarian does, there is always a catch — Catch-22: 'Catch-22 says they have a right to do anything we can't stop them from doing.' It is an unwritten law which is ruthlessly enforced.

Epic in form, the book is episodic in structure. Each chapter carries a single character a step nearer madness or death or both, and a step, too, into legend. The action takes place well above the level of reality. On leave or in action the characters behave with a fine disregard for the laws of probability. Yet they follow the law of Catch-22 and its logically necessary results. Within its own terms the book is wholly consistent, creating legend out of the wildest farce and the most painful realism, constructing its own system of probability. Its characters are as boldly unlikely as its events, but when they die, they die with as much pain as any 'real' men, and when they are dead, they are wept for with real tears. There is a scene in which Yossarian bandages the wounded leg of one of his crew, only to find that inside the man's flak-suit his vital organs have mortally spilled, a scene which is repeated again and again, each time with more detail and more dread. It acts as a reminder that *Catch-22*, for all its zany appearance, is an extremely serious novel. Against Catch-22 the man who does not wish to die has only his wits: war is not civilized, and to be caught up in it is to be reduced to a state of nature far worse than that visualised by Hobbes. *Catch-22* is a book of enormous richness and art, of deep thought and brilliant writing.

*Reprinted, with the permission of the author and publisher, from the *Spectator*, June 15, 1962, p. 801.

"It Was All Yossarian's Fault": Power and Responsibility in *Catch-22*

Stephen L. Sniderman*

There are so many villains and power-mongers in *Catch-22* that it is easy to minimize or overlook Yossarian's culpability in the world Heller describes. The characters in the novel who are most often cited as the "real" controllers of power are Milo Minderbinder and ex-P.F.C. Wintergreen. Jan Solomon believes that Milo "begins the novel as a hard-working young hopeful dreaming of a syndicate and ends wielding absolute power."[1] Joseph J. Waldmeir feels it is ex-P.F.C. Wintergreen "who, for all practical purposes, runs the war from his clerk's desk by manipulating orders and memoranda."[2] To Sanford Pinsker both of these characters "ultimately evolve as the real manipulators of power in *Catch-22*."[3] Yossarian, on the other hand, is generally identified with the powerless. James L. McDonald, discussing a group that obviously includes the protagonist, claims that "the victims of the officials are bewildered and virtually helpless."[4] Gerald B. Nelson says that Yossarian "sees what is wrong, the corruption that greed and envy have brought in their wake, but he can do nothing save run away."[5]

In one sense, of course, these positions are unchallengeable. Milo and Wintergreen, or their real-life counterparts, must have greatly influenced the outcome of the war, while the Yossarians undoubtedly had little effect at all. In the fictional sense, however, it is Yossarian who controls things, not Wintergreen or Milo. In one way or another, Yossarian is responsible for nearly every significant event mentioned in the novel, including most of the deaths we witness. Within the framework of the novel, Yossarian cannot be considered the helpless victim of a monolithic system. In fact, he wields more potential power than any other character in the book. Until he learns to use it, however, his efforts to save himself from destruction are not only futile, but lead to catastrophe and death for those around him. The irony of the novel is that Yossarian is unaware of his power and spends much of his time blaming others — Cathcart, Milo, "they" — for his predicament. What Yossarian learns in the course of the book is that he, and no-one else, is in control of his fate. The novel seems to be designed to hide this fact from the reader until Yossarian himself sees it. The world in which he exists is made to appear inescapable and uncontrollable, but the sequence of events we are shown and Yossarian's relationship to them indicates that he is the center of his universe and, though he does not know it at first, capable of turning it topsy-turvy or setting it straight.

In Chapter nineteen Colonel Cathcart makes a list of "Black Eyes!!!" Next to two of the items, "Ferrara" and "Naked man in formation (after

*Reprinted, with permission, from *Twentieth-Century Literature*, 19 (1973), 251–58.

Avignon)," he writes "Yossarian!" Next to the other items, "he wrote in a bold, decisive hand:

?

Those entries labeled '?' were the ones he wanted to investigate immediately to determine if Yossarian had played any part in them."[6] Of course, Yossarian did play a part in making every item on the list (with the exception of "Skeet Range") a "Black Eye" for Cathcart. He moved the bomb line on the map during the Great Big Siege of Bologna (p. 123), had Corporal Snark put laundry soap in the sweet potatoes which caused the "Food Poisoning (during Bologna)" (pp. 126–7), started the "Moaning (epidemic of during Avignon briefing)" (p. 225), and encouraged the chaplain to hang around the officers' club every night (pp. 194–5).

But Yossarian's influence is even more pervasive than Cathcart's list indicates. He is directly responsible for Dobbs' decision not to murder Cathcart (pp. 231–2 and pp. 308–9) and for Nately's broken nose (pp. 368–71). His habit of signing Washington Irving's name to the letters he censors eventuates in the appearance of two C.I.D. men on the base and the subsequent interrogations of Major Major (p. 93 and pp. 96–100). His signing of the chaplain's name to one letter (p. 8) leads to the brow-beating of the chaplain in the cellar of Group Headquarters (p. 97 and pp. 387–96). The punch that Yossarian receives from Appleby (after Orr had smashed open Appleby's forehead with his ping-pong paddle) causes Chief White Halfoat to bust Colonel Moodus in the nose, which in turn causes General Dreedle to have the chaplain thrown out of the officers' club and to order Chief White Halfoat moved into Doc Daneeka's tent (p. 57). Yossarian also provides the impetus for Milo's international cartel, as James M. Mellard points out, since it is Yossarian's letter from Doc Daneeka authorizing him to get all the fruit he wants which makes it possible for Milo to start his syndicate.[7]

More significantly, Yossarian can be linked to the deaths of many of his acquaintances. He is most clearly responsible for the deaths of Kraft, his crew, and Lieutenant Coombs, who were killed over Ferrara: "the bridge was not demolished until the tenth mission on the seventh day, when Yossarian killed Kraft and his crew by taking his flight of six planes in over the target a second time" (p. 141). Earlier we had been told about "Lieutenant Coombs, who had gone out on a mission as a guest one day just to see what combat was like and had died over Ferrara in the plane with Kraft" (p. 109). Since Yossarian is responsible for Lieutenant Coombs's death, he is "responsible" for Chief White Halfoat's presence on Pianosa (p. 109) and therefore for the living death of the "ghostly" Captain Flume (p. 104) who was driven to live by himself in the forest by Chief White Halfoat's threat to slit his throat from ear to ear (p. 58).

Yossarian's responsibility for Mudd's death can also be established. Mudd was killed over Orvieto when "Milo contracted with the American

military authorities to bomb the German-held highway bridge . . . and
with the German military authorities to defend the highway bridge . . .
with antiaircraft fire against his own attack" (p. 261). Obviously, Milo is to
blame for Mudd's death — although he denies it vehemently by saying, "I
wasn't even there that day" (p. 262) — but Yossarian could have prevented
the fiasco by stopping Milo from buying the entire harvest of Egyptian cotton when they were in Cairo together and eliminating the need for a
money-making scheme like the Orvieto contract (p. 263). Wintergreen asks
Yossarian why he let Milo buy all the cotton in the world: " 'Me?' Yossarian
answered with a shrug. 'I have no influence on him' " (p. 125). But Yossarian's rationalization is as weak as Milo's. It is Yossarian, after all, who convinces Milo to give up the idea of chocolate-covered cotton and to bribe the
government instead (pp. 268–74). And it is to Yossarian Milo comes when he
needs advice or comfort: "Milo was even more upset by the possibility that
someone had poisoned his squadron again, and he came bristling fretfully
to Yossarian for assistance" (p. 128). On the trip to the Middle East, in fact,
Milo tells Yossarian: " 'That's what I like about you,' he exclaimed. 'You're
honest! You're the only one I know that I can really trust' " (p. 239). Milo is
right, then, in turning Yossarian's accusation around: " 'Yossarian, what am
I going to do with so much cotton? It's all your fault for letting me buy it' "
(p. 263). It *is* Yossarian's "fault," in the sense that his failure to stop Milo
from buying the cotton, which results from his failure to see the potential
ramifications of Milo's purchase, leads to the death of Mudd. Unless we
wish to argue, as Milo does, that the Americans would have bombed the
bridge anyway and the Germans would have defended it anyway and, by
implication, Mudd would have been killed anyway, we are forced to acknowledge Yossarian's contribution, albeit indirect and involuntary, to the
tragedy at Orvieto.

Yossarian's relation to Doc Daneeka's death is more obvious. It is
Yossarian "who made it possible for Dan Daneeka to collect his flight pay
each month without ever climbing back into the womb [i.e., an airplane].
Yossarian would persuade McWatt to enter Doc Daneeka's name on his
flight log for training missions or trips to Rome" (p. 34). Without this arrangement, of course, Doc would not have been assumed dead when
McWatt crashed his plane: "The first person in the squadron to find out that
Doc Daneeka was dead was Sergeant Towser, who had been informed earlier by the man in the control tower that Doc Daneeka's name was down as
a passenger on the pilot's manifest McWatt had filed before taking off" (p.
350).

Yossarian's part in the deaths of Kid Sampson and McWatt is also
hinted at. Although McWatt had buzzed the wooden raft long before he
killed Kid Sampson (p. 18), the implication in the following passage is that
he began to do so more frequently after Yossarian convinced him not to buzz
his tent any more: "McWatt was incorrigible, and, while he never buzzed
Yossarian's tent again, he never missed an opportunity to buzz the beach

and roar like a fierce and low-flying thunderbolt over the raft in the water" (p. 344). In an earlier passage we are told that he "flew his plane as low as he dared over Yossarian's tent as often as he could, just to see how much it would frighten him, and loved to go buzzing with a wild, close roar over the wooden raft floating on empty oil drums" (p. 18). After he no longer flies over Yossarian's tent "as often as he could," McWatt "never missed an opportunity" to buzz the beach and the raft, thus immensely increasing the chances of an accident like the one which actually occurs when his plane dips suddenly and chops Kid Sampson in half.

Finally, and perhaps most important, Yossarian is to blame for Nately's death. Heller plants and nurtures this idea, first, by having Nately's whore attack Yossarian immediately after she learns of her lover's fate, second, by having Yossarian swear "that Nately's death had not been his fault" (p. 402) and say, " 'What do you *want* from me? . . . I didn't kill him' " (p. 403), third, by making Nately's whore ubiquitous once she starts trying to kill Yossarian, and fourth, by letting Yossarian offer several unsatisfactory explanations of her behavior: " 'She never did like me. Maybe it's because I broke his nose, or maybe it's because I was the only one in sight she could hate when she got the news' " (p. 407); "Yossarian thought he knew why Nately's whore held him responsible for Nately's death and wanted to kill him. Why the hell shouldn't she? It was a man's world, and she and everyone younger had every right to blame him and everyone older for every unnatural tragedy that befell them" (p. 414). The inadequacy of these reasons is obvious, since each explains only the whore's initial reaction, not her fanatic international pursuit of Yossarian that presumably extends beyond the final pages of the novel. But the conspicuous lack of any better explanation forces us to supply our own. The only possibility is that Nately's whore knows intuitively what Yossarian has not yet learned, that he is to blame for Nately's death, not in an impersonal way, but in a way that justifies her behavior toward him personally.

In an enigmatic passage, the narrator apparently places blame explicitly on Yossarian for Nately's death: "In a way it was all Yossarian's fault, for if he had not moved the bomb line during the Big Siege of Bologna, Major —— de Coverley might still be around to save him, and if he had not stocked the enlisted men's apartments with girls who had no other place to live, Nately might never have fallen in love with his whore" (p. 294). The first and second parts of this sentence appear to be causally related, when in fact they are not, at least not on a literal level. After Yossarian moved the bomb line, Major —— de Coverley had flown to Florence, but it was in Rome that Nately had found his whore, several months *before* the Big Siege of Bologna.[8] Literally speaking, Yossarian cannot be at fault, even indirectly, for Nately's falling in love with his whore. Therefore, Yossarian cannot be considered the catalyst for Nately's decision to fly more missions so he could continue courting his whore after he had finished his tour of duty. Yet the narrator seems to imply in this passage that Yossarian *is* to blame ("in a way") for Nately meeting the whore, the first link in the chain that leads to his death. "It was all Yossarian's fault," the structure of the passage seems to say, because he moved the bomb line, which made Major —— de Coverley fly to Florence and stock the enlisted men's apartments (in Rome) with girls, including the whore Nately meets and falls in love with, then refuses to leave behind when he finishes his 70 missions. Significantly, it is on Nately's 71st mission that he is killed; if he had not wanted to stay and court his whore, he would never have flown his fatal mission.

Yossarian can also be blamed in more tangible ways for Nately's death. First, his refusal to sanction Dobbs's plot to murder Cathcart after the missions have been raised to 60 (p. 233) means that Carthcart is around to raise the missions to 80, guaranteeing that Nately flies his 71st, on which, ironically, Dobbs is killed, too. Second, Yossarian does not have the courage to kill Cathcart himself when Dobbs refuses to go along with him (p. 315). Third, as we have seen, Yossarian can be blamed for the deaths of Kid Sampson, McWatt, and Doc Daneeka, which make Colonel Cathcart so upset that he raises the missions to 70 (pp. 349–50). And, fourth, Yossarian's decision to ask Milo for help in stopping Nately from flying more missions leads to Milo's discussion with Cathcart in which Cathcart realizes Milo's indispensability and Nately's availability (" 'Yes, Nately will fly more.' ") and decides to raise the number of missions to 80 (p. 383).

There is yet another way that Yossarian is personally responsible for Nately's death and for the deaths of all the other men in his squadron — including Clevinger and Snowden — who die during a mission. In a word, Yossarian is guilty of complicity. His essential sin is in lending his presence and his tacit sanction to the system perpetrated by the USAF and distorted by Cathcart and Korn. By not deserting and by continuing to fly missions, his feeble protests against bureaucracy are worse than useless because they not only do not stop anyone from getting killed but they engender further tragedy. The chaplain is brutally interrogated because Yossarian, out of boredom and impatience with red tape, had signed the name A. T. Tappmann to a letter he was censoring. Worse yet, Yossarian's refusal to wear his uniform after Avignon and his threat to cause trouble about the number of missions only makes Colonel Cathcart more nervous and insecure (pp. 213–8) and therefore more willing to raise the missions again, "the most tangible achievement he had going for him" (p. 219).

Perhaps the most telling case, though, is Yossarian's most daring and most futile exploit of silent rebellion — the moving of the bomb line during the great Big Seige of Bologna, which serves only to delay the inevitable and to get rid of Major —— de Coverley, the one person on Pianosa capable of cutting through the red tape and ending Cathcart's tyranny. When the narrator tell us, "In a way it was all Yossarian's fault, for if he had not moved the bomb line during the Big Siege of Bologna, Major —— de Coverley might still be around to save him," the implication is clear — he might still be around to save all of them from the spiraling missions requirement and from the grasp of Catch-22 itself.

Major —— de Coverley's ability to sweep away the horrors and absurdities of military life is firmly established in the scene describing his return to the base during the Glorious Loyalty Oath Crusade (p. 120). His power over the other officers, including Colonels Cathcart and Korn, is established several times, as in the following passage: "so many other people treated Major —— de Coverley with such profound and fearful veneration that Colonel Cathcart had a hunch they might all know something. Major —— de Coverley was an ominous, incomprehensible presence who kept him on edge and of whom even Colonel Korn tended to be wary. Everyone was afraid of him and no one knew why" (p. 217). His very name is indicative of his awe-inspiring qualities: "No one even knew Major —— de Coverley's first name, because no one had ever had the temerity to ask him" (p. 217).

In "real" life, of course, it would be true that all the men who continued to fly their missions could be considered partners in evil as much as Yossarian, but the structure of the novel places the fictional burden almost entirely on him. He can be held personally responsible for virtually everything in the book: "In a way it was all Yossarian's fault." This is true, first, because he — far more than any other single character — is intimately related to every significant event in the novel, either as a primary cause (e.g., with Kraft's death), as a secondary cause (e.g., with Mudd's death), as a catalyst (e.g., with the fight in the officers' club), or as a participant (e.g., with Snowden's death). Secondly, of all the characters in the book, Yossarian is the only one flying missions (i.e., going along with the system) who fully understands the absurdity, the danger, and the evil of doing so. His complicity, therefore, is the most obvious and the most hypocritical. Thirdly, of all the characters in the book, Yossarian has the most charisma, so his complicity is the most influential: Milo, Dobbs, the chaplain, and Doc Daneeka seek him out for advice and sympathy; Orr works for months to make the tent livable for him; Clevinger tries desperately to find holes in his argument; Chief White Halfoat won't drive until he's sure Yossarian is in his jeep (p. 130); Hungry Joe spends most of the time with Yossarian, hoping to photograph him sexually engaged with some girl; McWatt buzzes Yossarian's tent and nobody else's; the "last person in the squadron Major Major wanted to be brought down with a flying tackle by was Yossarian" (p. 104); and Colonel Cathcart turns "white as a sheet" upon hearing his name (pp. 276–7).

Finally, the enormous success of Yossarian's refusal to fly more missions further emphasizes his powerful influence over the affairs on Pianosa and his blameworthiness for not trying such a ploy earlier, before all his pals were killed. Even Havermeyer and Appleby, his least friendly acquaintances, come to ask questions and offer encouragement when Yossarian begins to walk backwards with his gun on his hip and refuses to fly more missions (pp. 408–11). In addition, "people kept popping up at him out of the darkness to ask him how he was doing. . . . People in the squadron he barely knew popped into sight out of nowhere as he passed and asked him how he was doing. Even men from other squadrons came one by one to conceal themselves in the darkness and pop out. . . . Even one of his room-mates popped out to ask him how he was doing and pleaded with him not to tell any of his other roommates he had popped out" (p. 411). Significantly, the narrator uses the same phrase to indicate his success that he had used earlier to describe his bungling: "The men with seventy missions were start-ing to grumble because they had to fly eighty and there was a danger some of them might put on guns and begin walking around backward too. Mo-rale was deteriorating and *it was all Yossarian's fault*" (p. 414, italics added). Later, Heller has Colonel Korn drive the point home: " 'The men were perfectly content to fly as many missions as we asked as long as they thought they had no alternative. Now you've given them hope, and they're unhappy. So the blame is all yours' " (p. 431).

Clearly, of all the people on Pianosa after Major —— de Coverley's disappearance, Yossarian had the best chance of destroying, or at least un-dermining, the mechanism by which men were being killed every day, for Cathcart and Korn rather than for their country. The fact that he does not use his leverage fully until the end of the novel suggests that he, rather than Milo or Wintergreen, is the real culprit of *Catch-22* and that, at its most basic level, Heller's work is the story of Yossarian's education in power and responsibility. By making everything in the novel, the good as well as the evil, Yossarian's "fault," Heller argues that the individual, not bureaucracy or the establishment, still holds the final trump.

Notes

1. "The Structure of Joseph Heller's *Catch-22*," *Critique*, 9, No. 2 (1967), 47–8.

2. "Two Novelists of the Absurd: Heller and Kesey," *Wisconsin Studies in Contemporary Literature*, V (Autumn 1964), 193.

3. "Heller's *Catch-22*: The Protest of a *Puer Eternis*," *Critique*, 7, No. 2 (Winter, 1964–65), 156.

4. "I See Everything Twice! The Structure of Joseph Heller's *Catch-22*," *The University Review*, 34, No. 3 (March 1968), 178.

5. *Ten Versions of America* (New York: Alfred A. Knopf, 1972), p. 173.

6. Joseph Heller, *Catch-22* (New York: Dell Publishing Co., 1962), p. 8. Subsequent ref-erences to this edition will appear in the text.

7. "*Catch-22*: Déja Vu and the Labyrinth of Memory," *Bucknell Review*, 16, No. 2 (1968), 37–8.

8. Nately must have already been in love with his whore before Milo was made mess officer, since Yossarian tells Milo about it just after Milo has been promoted (p. 63). On p. 139, we learn that it was Major —— de Coverley who made Milo mess officer. This must have occurred before de Coverley's trip to Florence, since he never returns after that trip, as we are told on p. 135 and in the passage quoted from p. 294.

Spindrift and the Sea: Structural Patterns and Unifying Elements in *Catch-22*

Clinton S. Burhans, Jr.*

If my experience is at all representative, a particular and unusual danger lurks in the serious study of this work. Inevitably, there comes a time when, looking around at accumulations of notes, charts, and commentaries, you suddenly bust out laughing at yourself in an unexpected illumination of your own absurdity in taking the thing so seriously. In that strange flash of disorientation, you feel like one of Heller's characters, like maybe a bookkeeper for Milo Minderbinder.

Fortunately, this fit of sudden sanity dissolves, as it rightly should; for the comic anarchy which provokes it is only the surface of *Catch-22*, not its sustaining structure. Critics have consistently been challenged by the question of the work's structure and unity and with various and conflicting results. In the main, such discussions center around two viewpoints: some critics argue that the work is episodic and formless; others find it organized according to some particular principle or method.[1] Neither position, it seems to me, need necessarily, nor in fact does, exclude the other. The narrative surface is obviously episodic and apparently chaotic; but this surface formlessness is central to the novel's thematic experience, and it rises from strong and multi-level structural patterns and a variety of unifying devices.

Seeking these patterns and devices in *Catch-22* involves a long and often frustrating analysis, beginning with an elusive sense of underlying structure and unity and ending with that sense becoming conviction amidst an overwhelming mass of supporting information. Despite the constant episodic zigzags which comprise *Catch-22's* narrative surface, the novel is built on a central conflict, two sub-plots, and a host of motifs. What Heller has done is to break up the logical and chronological development of these narrative elements by taking bits and pieces of all three and mixing them together with dashes of expository and rhetorical comment without regard to logical or temporal or spatial connection. The result is an apparent — but only apparent — jumble of comment, character, and event consistent with contemporary esthetic tendencies away from reason, time, and space as ordering categories.

Nevertheless, a basic narrative structure can be discovered holding the novel subtly together. This structure can best be visualized as a kind of narrative tree, with the trunk comprised primarily of the main plot (Yossarian's efforts to get off flying status either by achieving the required number of missions or by having himself declared insane) and two sub-plots (the struggle between Peckem and Dreedle for command of the Wing, and Milo's syndicate). Around this trunk grow in abundance two kinds of branches, arranged for visual convenience one on either side. Those on the

*Reprinted, with permission, from *Twentieth Century Literature*, 19 (1973), 239–50.

left, whether simple references or detailed episodes, are expository flash-backs made once for informational purposes or repeated for thematic ef-fect. Those on the right are a different kind of flashback, one which I have not encountered elsewhere. The best way to describe them, I think, is to call them foreshadowing flashbacks; that is, again whether simple reference or detailed episode, most of them after the first add links in a chain of informa-tion drawn out and completed at some length. Thereafter, references to these subjects become conventional flashbacks repeated for thematic effect. The result is the paradox of suspense through flashbacks; and, I think, as this paradox suggests, an ingenious fusion of time planes into the simultane-ity of existential time, a fusion entirely consistent with what seems to me the fundamental existential theme of the work.

Visualizing this narrative tree and looking down it, one discovers that Heller has done something in each chapter to link it to the preceding chap-ter — a continuing action or condition, references to time or to historical events, mention of the number of missions required or flown. Sometimes these links are slight and tenuous, as in Chapters Six, Eight and Twenty-four; they may appear at the beginning or to buried in the middle or only surface in the end; still, they are usually there, and they do function, if only subliminally, to tie the narrative together.

Amplifying this masked but functional narrative continuity, *Catch-22* develops in a five-part alternating structure. The trunk of the narrative tree bends twice, breaking its straight line into three sections and two substan-tial bulges. The first part, through Chapter Ten, establishes and develops the narrative present; that is, each chapter, however fragmented in time or place, event or character, does something to maintain and advance the nar-rative present and its problems established in the opening chapters. The second part flashes back to the Great Big Siege of Bologna in Chapters Eleven through Sixteen; and a third part returns to the narrative present as in the first part in Chapters Seventeen to Twenty-two. Another long flash-back, this time to Milo Minderbinder's operations and to the origins and growth of his M & M enterprises, forms a fragmentary but essentially sus-tained fourth part in Chapters Twenty-two through Twenty-four. A fifth part returns again to the narrative present in Chapter Twenty-five and re-mains there with increasingly less fragmentation to the end.

That these structural sections are neither arbitrary nor accidental is suggested by the clearly transitional chapters with which Heller surrounds the two major flashbacks. Chapter Ten ends by introducing the Great Big Siege of Bologna, and Chapter Seventeen opens shortly after the two Bolo-gna missions by returning Yossarian to the hospital at the time of Chapter One and ends with Yossarian out of the hospital again and coming to Doc Daneeka a second time for aid after Major Major had refused to help him in Chapter Nine. Similarly, Chapter Twenty-two introduces the earlier trip to Cairo on which Milo had tried to corner Egyptian cotton; and Chapter Twenty-five refers both to the Chaplain's seeing a naked man in a tree at

Snowden's funeral — the episode which ends Chapter Twenty-four — and to his continuing efforts in the narrative present to help Yossarian and the other men by trying to get the required number of missions reduced.

Despite *Catch-22's* many and sudden shifts in scene, episode, character, motif, and time, then, the narrative trunk makes it clear that Heller has distributed sufficient elements of continuity and transition to give the work a controlling structural design beneath its kaleidoscopic surface. However much this narrative surface may disguise it, *Catch-22* is built on a five-part alternating structure in which sections developing the central conflict and sub-plots in the narrative present (parts one, three, and five) alternate with long flashback sections providing additional background and exposition and also functioning to fuse the work's time planes (parts two and four).

Another glance down the narrative tree suggests a second structural pattern, a tonal structure. Beginning with the end of Chapter Twenty-nine and Chapter Thirty and culminating in Chapter Thirty-nine, the novel darkens measurably into almost insupportable horror. The crucial episode is the mission against the undefended mountain village, a totally unnecessary mission in which poor people unconnected with the war are to be killed without warning for publicity photos of tight bomb patterns. The tonal shift in this episode is clear and sharp. Earlier episodes focus on individual combatants as voluntary or involuntary participants in a familiar if horrifying and ridiculous game with ultimate consequences, like the descriptions of Yossarian's experiences on missions; or on perils and death remote in time, like the Ferrara mission; or on horrors contained within farcical situations, like Milo's bombing of the squadron. Such episodes reflect real horrors but to some degree, at least, cushion the reader against experiencing them, insulate their effects on him. Not so with the mission against the mountain village. It is immediate; it is probable; it is barren of justification; it is stark murder; it is unspeakable outrage; it is uncushioned horror. Even Dunbar, who has up to this point looked primarily after himself and sought only to lengthen his life span by taking no unnecessary risks whatever, rises in protest, denounces the mission, and risks court-martial by intentionally missing the village.

The tonal shift I am suggesting here is indicated in several other ways as well. Four of the novel's five basic structural sections and the beginning of the fifth precede the mission to the mountain village; no basic structural change follows it. Clearly, something different is going on in this final third of the novel from the structural alternation of the first two-thirds: something more focused, more concentrated, more intense. Similarly, most of the novel's riotous fragmentation of time, place, character, and event occurs in its first two-thirds: most of the flashbacks, for example, appear in these chapters. The ratio is around four or five to one, not only in number but also in the variety of their subjects, again suggesting a more intense focus in the novel's final third on the narrative present and its immediate problems. Finally, despite the long months of peril, neither Yossarian nor any of his friends, the central characters in the novel, die before the mission to the mountain village. But one by one they die or disappear thereafter, like lights going out in a gathering darkness.

A three-part tonal structure, then, seems evident. The first part, Chapters One through Twenty-nine, establishes the tone by which the novel is usually characterized: a predominantly and broadly humorous tone, a mixed tone in which fear and desperation are contained within and controlled by exploding jokes, gags, puns, parodies, and satiric attacks, the tone of a fireworks display in a thunderstorm. The second part, Chapters Twenty-nine through Thirty-nine, pivoting on the mission to the mountain village, shifts to a much different and more consistent tone, one of deepening despair whose growing darkness envelops the humor and turns it increasingly sick and savage. The third part, the last three chapters, shifts again to another mingled tone, one of resigned desperation broken by revelation and release.

Within these general structural patterns of organization and tone, *Catch-22's* central conflict develops in a conventional plot and sub-plot structure. The central conflict is, of course, Yossarian's struggle to survive the war either by flying the required number of missions or by getting himself removed from combat status. In each purpose, he finds himself constantly blocked: Col. Cathcart keeps raising the required number, and the military system functions by insuperable devices for keeping Yosssarian on combat status. The resulting conflict develops in a generally classical pattern: exposition, initiation, complication, rising tension, crisis, and climax moving in the main chronologically and climactically within a welter of expository and foreshadowing flashbacks and providing points of departure for a host of related puns, jokes, parodies, and satiric attacks.

Catch-22 begins *in medias res* with Yossarian in full and close pursuit of the magic number: 45 missions are required, and he has flown 44. In Chapter Two, Col. Cathcart raises the number to 50 and in Chapter Six, when Yossarian has 48, to 55. In Chapters Nine and Seventeen, Yossarian has reached 51, but in Chapter Nineteen, the magic number rises to 60. By Chapter Twenty-eight, Yossarian is once more closing in; but Cathcart raises the ante again, to 65 in Chapter 30 and to 70 in Chapter 31. In Chapter Thirty-five, Cathcart raises to 80; and Yossarian, after reaching 71, decides in Chapter Thirty-eight to end this exercise in futility and fly no more.

Flashbacks provide additional information on Yossarian's efforts to gain this elusive military brass ring. Chapter Six returns to the previous Fall when 25 missions were required and Yossarian reached 23 by flying six missions in six days. At that point, Col. Cathcart became the new group commander and raised the number to 30 in celebration. By the time of the Orvieto mission the following Spring, 35 missions were required (Chapter Ten); and after the two Bologna missions, when Yossarian had 32, the number increased to 40 (Chapter Sixteen). In Chapter Seventeen, Yossarian reached 38, and Cathcart raised again to the 45 required in Chapter One.[2]

A similar pattern emerges from the second aspect of Yossarian's struggle to survive: his efforts to get off combat status. After leaving the hospital in Chapter One, he tries unsuccessfully to persuade Doc Daneeka to help him (Chapters Four and Five) and considers refusing to fly any more missions (Chapter Six). He decides to go to Major Major; and when he refuses to help (Chapter Seven and Nine), Yossarian tries Doc Daneeka again (Chapter Seventeen). He asks the Chaplain for help, and the Chaplain responds vigorously but without result (Chapters Nineteen, Twenty, Twenty-five). After Yossarian is wounded over Leghorn, the psychiatrist at the hospital certifies him insane but confuses him with another patient, who gets sent home instead of Yossarian; and he tries Doc Daneeka again (Chapter Twenty-Seven). In Chapter Thirty-eight, he refuses to fly any more missions; and after recognizing that he cannot go through with his deal with Cathcart and Korn (Chapters Forty and Forty-one), he deserts.

Here, too, flashbacks fill in important background material. In Chapter Ten, Yossarian decides not to fly the first Bologna mission; and in Chapter Fourteen, he aborts by forcing Kid Sampson to turn back. On the Avignon mission, he is smeared with Snowden's blood and viscera and refuses to wear a uniform again (Chapter Twenty-four). And a final flashback revealing the full import of Snowden's secret reveals as well the deepest motivation of Yossarian's struggles (Chapter Forty-one).

Like the structural and tonal patterns, then, this two-pronged central conflict functions coherently at the heart of *Catch-22*, though it is not always immediately or continuously available. In less detailed and more fragmentary form, two sub-plots work similarly within the apparent welter of the novel's surface. The lesser of these is the contest between Generals Peckem and Dreedle for command of the Wing. The background and opening moves of this contest are suggested in Chapter Three, and Peckem's aims and campaign appear in Chapters Twelve and Nineteen. General Dreedle's position and ultimate defeat are indicated in Chapter Twenty-one, and Scheisskopf joins Peckem and learns of his real war in Chapter Twenty-nine. In Chapter Thirty-six, Peckem replaces Dreedle, only to discover that his command is now under the broader jurisdiction of the newly promoted Scheisskopf (Chapters Thirty-seven and Forty).

A more fully developed sub-plot describes the rise of Milo Minderbinder from new mess officer to business manager of the whole war as head of M & M Enterprises. As with Yossarian, Milo's story begins *in medias res*. Chapters Two, Seven, and Nine reveal his extravagant and luxurious mess-hall operations in full bloom; and flashbacks in Chapters Ten, Twelve, and Thirteen explain how Milo became a mess officer and describes some of the operations of M & M Enterprises.[3] Syndicate operations and Milo's spreading influence and power appear in Chapters Nineteen, Twenty-one, and Twenty-two; and Chapter Twenty-four is a flashback to the beginnings of M & M Enterprises and its major operations. Chapters Twenty-eight, Thirty-five, Thirty-nine, Forty-one, and Forty-two reflect

further glimpses of Milo's gourmet mess halls and his increasingly ubiquitous syndicate. In Chapter Forty-two, Col. Cathcart and ex-P.F.C. Wintergreen have joined Milo; and he is well on his way not only to controlling the
war but also to owning the world by giving everyone a share in it.

As the narrative tree suggests, then, the episodic and fragmented narrative surface of *Catch-22* masks and is sustained by a complex and multi-
dimensional structural design compounded of an alternating five-part basic
structure, a three-part tonal structure, and a conventional plot and sub-plot
structure. Moreover, this complex structural design is reinforced by several
unifying devices: chronology, recurring characters, and a variety of motifs.
The result is paradox: structure and unity sustaining and controlling episodic chaos.

However much the narrative surface may obscure it, the events of
Catch-22 are chronologically related. Heller refers to several specific dates
and occasions and to historical events, and these can be supplemented by
time references and cross-references in the text. We know, for example, that
it is late August when the Chaplain talks to Col. Cathcart about lowering
the missions from the new number of 60 (203, 283)[4] and that this conversation occurs at least several weeks after Yossarian leaves the hospital at the
beginning of the story. We also know, from a reference to his rest leaves in
Rome (18), that Yossarian leaves the hospital and returns to his tent at least
several weeks after the fall of Rome on June 6, 1944. We can thus infer that
the narrative present at the beginning of the story is sometime in July, 1944.
When Yossarian returns from the hospital at that time, he learns that Col.
Cathcart has raised the required missions to 50; and a short time later, probably in middle or late July, he raises the number to 55. At this point,
Yossarian recalls the death of Mudd "three months earlier" (111–12); therefore, since Mudd died on the Orvieto mission, we can date that mission as
sometime in April, 1944.

By thus using firm dates and events as constant reference points and by
cross-checking against them and against each other the main episodes of the
novel, it is possible to organize an occasionally loose but generally reliable
chronology for *Catch-22*:

1941	:	Yossarian in Army — qualifies for transfer to Air Cadet training
1941-1943	:	Yossarian an Air Cadet at Santa Ana, California, and Lowery Field, Colorado — Grand Conspiracy of Lowery Field
NOVEMBER 26, 1941	:	Yossarian in hospital at Lowery Field
NOVEMBER 26, 1942	:	Yossarian in hotel room with Mrs. Scheisskopf
1943	:	Yossarian goes overseas via Puerto Rico — Splendid Atabrine Insurrection

SEPTEMBER, 1943   :   Required missions at 25

Yossarian flies his 23rd, to Arezzo — Col. Nevers killed — time of Salerno beach-head — missions raised to 30

APRIL, 1944   :   Beginning of M & M Enterprises — Orvieto mission — death of Mudd

MAY, 1944   :   Required missions at 35

Development of M & M Enterprises — Milo tries to corner Egyptian cotton

Ferrara mission — deaths of Kraft and Coombs — first soap poisoning of mess

Milo bombs squadron

General Peckem schemes to take over combat command

Great Big Siege of Bologna — second soap poisoning of mess — Yossarian's 32nd mission — missions raised to 40

Yossarian goes into hospital

JUNE, 1944   :   Yossarian leaves hospital, flies six more missions — time of fall of Rome

Yossarian and Orr on leave trip with Milo

Avignon mission — death of Snowden

Yossarian naked in tree at Snowden's funeral

Yossarian naked at decoration for bravery in Ferrara mission

Clevinger disappears in cloud

JULY, 1944   :   Missions raised to 45 — Yossarian has 38, goes into hospital again — time of beginning of book

Yossarian leaves hospital — missions raised to 50

AUGUST, 1944   :   Yossarian flies four more missions — missions raised to 55

Yossarian flies 51st mission

Yossarian tries to punch Col. Cathcart in Officer's Club

Missions raised to 60; Paris liberated (August 25, 1944)

General Peckem gaining in struggle with General Dreedle

SEPTEMBER, 1944	:	Yossarian wounded over Leghorn — goes into hospital again — Americans pushing into Germany, 8th Army takes Rimini, Gothic Line collapsing
		Yossarian returned to combat status — flies two more missions — second Avignon mission — Orr shot down again
		Third Bologna mission — Orr shot down and disappears
		Scheisskopf joins General Peckem's command
		Raid on small Italian mountain village — Germans above Florence
		Deaths of Kid Sampson and McWatt — missions raised to 65
OCTOBER, 1944	:	Missions raised to 70
		Yossarian gets new roommates — two months after invasion of Southern France (August 15, 1944)
NOVEMBER, 1944	:	Yossarian breaks Nately's nose on Thanksgiving Day — goes into hospital to see Nately — Dunbar to be disappeared
		Yossarian has 70 missions — Chief White Halfoat dies
DECEMBER, 1944	:	Missions raised to 80 — Dobbs and Nately killed on La Spezia mission
		General Peckem becomes wing commander — under General Scheisskopf
		Yossarian has 71 missions, refuses to fly any more — Dunbar and Major Major disappear
		Yossarian knifed by Nately's whore — goes back into hospital
		Hungry Joe dies
		Col. Cathcart and Ex-P.F.C. Wintergreen partners in M & M Enterprises
		Yossarian deserts — Germans driving towards Antwerp in Battle of Bulge

Despite the general consistency of this chronology, Heller occasionally errs in computation. For one, it seems unlikely that Cathcart would increase the required number of missions only by ten in the seven or eight months between September, 1943, and May, 1944; and it seems even more unlikely that Yossarian would fly only nine missions in the same period — especially after flying six missions in six days in September. The relationship between the number required and the number Yossarian flies is consistent, but the totals are implausible. For another, Heller says at one point that Milo bombed the squadron "seven months" after the period in which Yossarian was an air cadet at Lowery Field in Colorado (109). But Milo formed his syndicate after April, 1944 (247), and Yossarian had already flown 23 missions seven months earlier in September, 1943 (54). Clearly, then, Heller is off here by a year or two. Again, Captain Black's Glorious Loyalty Oath Crusade is ended by Maj. —— de Coverly when he returns to the squadron from Rome shortly after the fall of the city in June, 1944[5] (119–20). But Captain Black began his Crusade when Major Major was made squadron commander instead of him (116), and Major Major was already squadron commander when Yossarian joined the squadron some time before September, 1943 (109).

Such errors raise some interesting problems. To begin with, they are few and relatively insignificant when measured against the number of events and their generally consistent chronological relationship. Moreover, Heller occasionally makes almost offhand expository comments which indicate that he does have a clear chronology in mind. In describing Yossarian's and Hungry Joe's missions in September, 1943, for example, he concludes with the observation that shipping orders could have saved Hungry Joe "seven days earlier and five times since" (54). At that time, 25 missions were required; and Col. Cathcart, until late in the story, raises the ante by fives. "Five times" would put the number at 50 — which is precisely the number required in the narrative present from which Heller is writing at this point.

It is tempting, therefore, to argue that Heller's errors are intentional, that he means them to disguise his general chronological consistency or to contribute to the fusing of time planes which, it seems to me, is an essential element in his thematic purposes. On the other hand and more likely, I believe, they could be the results of simple carelessness. Either way, such errors are insufficient to destroy the basic and generally consistent chronology or to prevent its functioning as a unifying element in the matrix of the story.

Another unifying element is Heller's use of recurring characters. Counting the characters in *Catch-22* poses the same problem as counting them in Chaucer's "Prologue": the sum depends on those you decide *not* to count. The full total of all the characters in *Catch-22* would number armies and hosts; but if the count is restricted to those who are named or otherwise individualized, the result is some eighty or ninety characters. And if the count is only of those whose recurrence is sufficient in number and in distribution to suggest a unifying effect, the total becomes a manageable but still significantly large twenty-six. Yossarian (40), Cathcart (30), Korn (25), Daneeka (22), Dunbar (22), Hungry Joe (21), McWatt (21), Milo (21), Nately (21), Black (19), Orr (18), Aarfy (17), Chaplain (16), Dreedle (16),

Wintergreen (16), Nately's whore (15), Snowden (15), Major Major (14), Appleby (13), Danby (13), Halfoat (13), Peckem (13), Clevinger (12), Dobbs (12), Havermeyer (11), Duckett (10) — each recurs throughout the novel in the number of chapters indicated in parentheses.

Another interesting and valuable way to assess Heller's use of recurring characters is to note how many of these twenty-six appear or are mentioned in each chapter. Two chapters (Six and Thirty) contain some mention or broader function of eighteen of these twenty-six characters, and only one chapter (Eighteen) has a few as one of them. The average is about fourteen per chapter; only three chapters contain less than five, and only fifteen chapters less than ten characters. Clearly, then, Heller uses recurring characters to further the paradox at the heart of his novel's structure: with so large a number of characters (supplemented by the other sixty or so recurring less frequently) in as many chapters, he can achieve a turbulent variety in any single chapter while evoking a subtle sense of unity between the chapters.[6]

Even more interesting and effective, it seems to me, is Heller's use of motifs as unifying elements. Two motif patterns function throughout *Catch-22*: general and climactic. By general motif I mean simply the conventional repetition of concept, theme, image, or event for thematic or stylistic or structural effect; and at least eight such general motifs recur in *Catch-22*: death (36), insanity (30), Yossarian and death (16), Yossarian and sex (14), disappearance (12), Yossarian and hospitals (11), Catch-22 (9) and Washington Irving signatures (7).

Here, again, as with the recurring characters, I have listed the motifs in the order of the number of chapters in which they are at least mentioned. Moreover, these motifs are distributed throughout the novel; and they reflect intriguing thematic suggestions. Supporting and illuminating the earlier discussion of the novel's central conflict, these motifs emphasize that death and insanity characterize the world of *Catch-22*, a closed-system world of sudden disappearance in which hospitals and bizarre behavior are Yossarian's only refuge, and sex and the life-force it represents his true rebellions.

More dramatic and much more complicated are the novel's climactic motifs, by which I mean essentially what I outlined earlier in discussing Heller's use of foreshadowing flashbacks — that is, a progressive repetition in which successive occurrences provide additional details up to a climactic point at which the motif is completed or its full significance revealed. At least six such climactic motifs recur in *Catch-22*: Nately and his whore (17), Avignon and the death of Snowden (14), Ferrara and the deaths of Kraft and Coombs (12), Orvieto and the death of Mudd (10), Orr's whore, stove, and ditching (9), and Milo's bombing of the squadron (7).

Clearly, these motifs are closely related thematically to the general motifs and with them to the central conflict: if the general motifs shade in the conditions of the world in which Yossarian struggles to survive and the means which he employs in his struggles, the climactic motifs highlight the principal events and persons through which he comes to know the real nature of his world and his dire need to contend with it. Furthermore, these climactic motifs function even more carefully and effectively than the general motifs as unifying elements. Each one begins early in the novel; with one exception, each develops through a wider range of chapters; and, again with one exception, each one ends its development in a late chapter. Like the general motifs, then, these climactic motifs recur with sufficient frequency and distribution to work as unifying elements; but they contribute even more valuably to this end both in their function as foreshadowing flashbacks and also in the overlapping pattern of their development.

No one or two of these structural and unifying elements would do much to support or control the apparent episodic chaos of *Catch-22*. But, taken together, the narrative links between chapters, the multi-dimensional structural design, the disguised but generally consistent chronology, the recurring characters, and the two kinds of motifs form a surprising and impressive foundation of structure and unity beneath the shifting shapes and colors of the novel's narrative surface.

Despite its occasional flaws, Heller's artistry in *Catch-22* is both more effective and also more impressive than is sometimes granted. Moreover, this artistry is thematically significant. Its combination of formal elements working subtly within and sustaining an obvious surface formlessness argues strongly that the novel's bombardment of jokes and its satiric barrage are equally linked and that both derive from a shaping thematic concern at its core. The sea, too, has its spindrift; but the spindrift is not the sea.

Notes

1. John Aldridge sees *Catch-22* as an anti-novel, a parody on the novel form ("Contemporary Fiction and Mass Culture," *New Orleans Review*, I:1, [Fall, 1968], 4–9); similarly, Constance Denniston sees it not as a novel but as an episodic and formless mixture of genres — a romance-parody ("The American Romance-Parody: A Study of Purdy's *Malcolm* and Heller's *Catch-22*," *Emporia State Research Studies*, Vol. 14 [1965], 42–49, 63–4); and Douglas Day considers it a grab-bag, an anatomy in Northrop Frye's sense of the term ("*Catch-22*: A Manifesto for Anarchists," *Carolina Quarterly*, XV:3 [Summer, 1963], 86–92). In contrast, G. B. McHenry thinks *Catch-22* is constructed carefully on cinematic principles ("Significant Corn: *Catch-22*," *Critical Review*, Vol. 40 [1966], 134–44); Jan Soloman argues that behind its apparent chaos is a careful system of time sequences involving two distinct and mutually contradictory chronologies ("The Structure of *Catch-22*," *Critique: Studies in Modern Fiction*, Vol. IX:2 [1967], 46–57); James Mellard and James L. McDonald each picks up Heller's use of *déja vu* in several incidents and makes it the structural principle of the whole work (Mellard, "*Catch-22*: Déja Vu and the Labyrinth of Memory," *Bucknell Review*, XVI:2 [May 1968], 29–44, and McDonald, "I See Everything Twice!: The Structure of Joseph Heller's *Catch-22*," *University Review* [Kansas City], 34:3 [March, 1968], 175–80); Gabriel Chanan points to an intricate molecular structure whose avenues of communication can reach out to any direction at any time ("The Plight of the Novelist," *Cambridge Review*, Vol. 89: 2170 [April 26, 1968], 399–401); and Minna Doskow finds in *Catch-22* a close reworking of the conflict and develop-

ment of the archetypal classical hero ("The Night Journey in *Catch-22*," *Twentieth Century Literature*, XII:4 [January, 1967], 186–93).

2. Heller seems to have miscounted here. After leaving the hospital when he has 32 missions and 40 are required, Yossarian flies six more missions and reaches 38. Col. Cathcart then raises the number to 45, and Yossarian goes back into the hospital. This is the number required when he is in the hospital at the beginning of the book; and the day he gets out of the hospital, he learns from Doc Daneeka (at the end of Chapter Two) that the number has been raised to 50. Yossarian is outraged because, as he tells Doc Daneeka, he has 44. But if he had 38 when he went into the hospital, how could he have 44 when he came out – unless, of course he flew six missions while he was in the hospital! Or perhaps Yossarian came out of the hospital, flew six more missions, and went back in during the time 45 missions were required without Heller saying anything about it. It seems more likely that Heller, in completing his long Bologna flashback, either carelessly or intentionally forgot the 44 number he had Yossarian state at the end of Chapter Two.

3. Heller's chronology is way off here. Major —— de Coverley makes Milo the squadron mess officer after the Major returns from his triumphal entry into Rome in early June, 1944 (pp. 138–9). When Yossarian gets out of the hospital in July, Milo's mess-hall operation has grown gourmet in quality and international in scope (21, 62, 66), and he is thinking about forming his syndicate (68). But in Chapter Twenty-four, M & M Enterprises is already worldwide and flourishing in April.

4. After quotations and other references, I have put in parentheses page numbers from the Dell edition (New York, 1962).

5. This reflects another error in Heller's chronology. At the beginning of Chapter Twenty-six, Heller writes that if Yossarian "had not moved the bomb line during the Big Siege of Bologna, Major —— de Coverley might still be around to save him . . ." (294). But the bomb-line moving and Major —— de Coverley's consequent trip to Florence (135) were sometime in May; and the Jovean old Major had entered Rome with the liberating forces in June and been hit in the eye with a rose, had later arranged leave apartments in the city, and then had returned, ending the Loyalty Oath Crusade. If he disappeared and was thus unable to save Yossarian from being wounded in September, it must have been after June, not after May.

6. Gabriel Chanan makes what seems to me a brilliant and provocative observation about this aspect of Heller's dense net of characters. It gives us, Chanan suggests, a way to conceive that non-chronological aspect of our lives which exists laterally in a web of interrelationships not dependent on time or consequence (see note one above for documentation).

The *Catch-22* Note Cards

James Nagel*

One of the most intriguing aspects of the composition history of Joseph Heller's *Catch-22* is the existence of a large number of detailed note cards on which the author planned the structure of the novel before writing and analyzed its contents after the first complete draft. These note cards are lined, 5 X 8″ Kardex cards of a type used by the Remington Rand office Heller worked in during the composition of the novel. The most important of these is a group of more than thirty cards, written in Heller's hand and headed "CHAPTER CARDS (outlines for chapters before they were written.)"[1] Given what Heller has said in a letter about the period of composition of the

*Reprinted, with permission, from *Studies in the Novel*, 8 (1976), 394–405.

novel,[2] the date of these cards would be sometime around 1953, at which point, of course, the novel was still entitled "Catch-18."

Perhaps the most striking feature of these cards, especially in light of the frequent charges that the novel is "unstructured," "disorganized," or even "chaotic," is the detail of the planning stage of composition.[3] Not only are the main events in each chapter suggested, but characters are named and described, relationships among events are indicated, and key sentences are drafted. These cards correspond only roughly to what are now the forty-two chapters of *Catch-22*, but they are fascinating in their revelation of the acceptance and rejection of ideas and of the total growth of the novel. For example, a typical card, one now located about twelfth from the beginning,[4] treats the characters and events for what was evidently considered to be a single chapter.[5]

1. Cathcart's background & ambition. Puzzled by —— de Coverley.
2. Hasn't a chance of becoming general. Ex-corporal Wintergreen, who evaluates his work, also wants to be a general.
3. For another, there already was a general, Dreedle.
4. ↑Tries to have Chaplain say prayer at briefing.↑
5. Description of General Dreedle. His Nurse.
6. Dreedle's quarrel with Moodis [*sic*].
7. Snowden's secret revealed in argument with Davis.
8. Dreedle brings girl to briefing.
9. Groaning. Dreedle orders Korf shot.
10. That was the mission in which Yossarian lost his balls.

The section of the published novel that relates to the items listed now comprises much of chapter 19, "Colonel Cathcart," and chapter 21, "General Dreedle," with chapter 20, "Corporal Whitcomb," almost entirely unrelated to these matters, interspersed between them. Thus the ten items on the card were developed into roughly twenty-one pages of the novel.[6]

The business of Colonel Cathcart's background and ambition now begins in chapter 19 with a description of Cathcart as a "slick, successful, slipshod, unhappy man of thirty-six who lumbered when he walked and wanted to be a general" (p. 185). The descriptive and background attention to Cathcart covers a bit over two pages and then gives way to what is listed on the card as Item 4, "Tries to have Chaplain say prayer at briefing." This sentence had directional arrows pointing up, and, indeed, it was moved into second position in the manuscript. It relates logically to Cathcart's ambition: "Colonel Cathcart wanted to be a general so desperately he was willing to try anything, even religion . . ." (p. 187). The idea is developed carefully: Cathcart is impressed by a photograph in *The Saturday Evening Post* of a colonel who has his chaplain conduct prayers before each mission. Cathcart's sudden interest in religion is related to his ambition: "Maybe if we say prayers, they'll put my picture in *The Saturday Evening Post*" (p. 188). The humor of the situation progresses as Cathcart's thinking develops:

"Now, I want you to give a lot of thought to the kind of prayers we're going to say. . . . I don't want any of this Kingdom of God or Valley of Death stuff. That's all too negative. What are you making such a sour face for?"

"I'm sorry, sir," the chaplain stammered. "I happened to be thinking of the Twenty-third Psalm just as you said that."

"How does that one go?"

"That's the one you were just referring to, sir. 'The Lord is my shepherd I——' "

"That's the one I was just referring to. It's out. What else have you got?" (p. 189).

It leads ultimately to Cathcart's admission, "I'd like to keep away from the subject of religion altogether if we can," and to the true object of his thinking: "Why can't we all pray for something good, like a tighter bomb pattern?" (p. 190). But the plan for prayer is abandoned when the chaplain reveals that the enlisted men do not have a separate God, as Cathcart had assumed, and that excluding them from prayer meetings might antagonize God and result in even looser bomb patterns. Cathcart concludes "The hell with it, then" (p. 193). Thus the first item on the card, about Cathcart, and the elevated item regarding prayer grew to comprise the entire content of chapter 19. The secondary notions of each of these items were moved: Cathcart's puzzlement at —— de Coverely was delayed to chapter 21, and the revelation that Milo is now the mess officer was placed earlier, in chapter 13, when Major —— de Coverely promotes him out of a desire for fresh eggs.

The remaining items on the card were saved to become chapter 21, "General Dreedle." This chapter pursues two main concerns: obstructions to Cathcart's promotion to general, one of which is General Dreedle, and to General Dreedle himself. In the novel, the chapter is about equally divided between these two topics. The balance is enriching: the ambitious Colonel trying to get promoted is contrasted to the entrenched General trying to preserve what he has. Cathcart's problems here are precisely those that Heller listed as items two and three:

> Actually, Colonel Cathcart did not have a chance in hell of becoming a general. For one thing, there was ex-P.F.C. Wintergreen, who also wanted to be a general and who always distorted, destroyed, rejected or misdirected any correspondence by, for or about Colonel Cathcart that might do him credit. For another, there already was a general, General Dreedle, who knew that General Peckem was after his job but did not know how to stop him (p. 212).

Wintergreen has, of course, been demoted from "ex-corporal" in the notes to "ex-P.F.C." in the novel. General Peckem, called P. P. Peckenhammer throughout the note cards, has been added as a further complication.

The business of General Dreedle, items five through nine, now occupies the last half of the chapter (pp. 212-20) with only minor alterations from the notes. "Moodis" is changed to "Moodus"; in the incident of the "groaning" at the staff meeting, Dreedle orders Major Danby shot, not Korn (p. 218). Two items are not treated: the business of Snowden's secret was saved for the conclusion of the novel (p. 430), a wise decision in that the Snowden incident is the major *déjà vu* scene and it becomes climactic of that device placed at the end. And, further, Snowden's secret, that man is matter, emphasizes the theme of mortality just when Yossarian is most concerned with death and survival.

The second matter not treated, relating to Yossarian's castration, is itself a startling revelation but one Heller later rejected in manuscript revision. The incident of Yossarian's wound was ultimately moved to chapter 26: Aarfy, known as "Aarky" throughout the notes, gets lost on the mission to Ferrara and, before McWatt can seize control of the plane, flies back into the flak and the plane is hit. Yossarian's wound is, in fact, in his thigh, but his first analysis follows the suggestion of the note card:

> He was unable to move. Then he realized he was sopping wet. He looked down at his crotch with a sinking, sick sensation. A wild crimson blot was crawling upward rapidly along his shirt front like an enormous sea monster rising to devour him. He was hit! . . . A second solid jolt struck the plane. Yossarian shuddered with revulsion at the queer sight of his wound and screamed at Aarfy for help.
> "I lost my balls! Aarfy, I lost my balls! . . . I said I lost my balls! Can't you hear me? I'm wounded in the groin!" (pp. 283-84).

Yossarian's mistake reveals, perhaps, a normal fear and an understandable confusion; it also unites the sexual theme with the dangers of war and, especially, to the destructive insensitivity of Aarfy. Yossarian's wound also serves the plot in getting him back into the hospital where the themes of absurdity, bureaucracy, and insanity are explored: Nurse Cramer insists to Yossarian that "it certainly is not your leg! . . . That leg belongs to the U.S. government" (p. 286); Dunbar moves a temperature card to become A. Fortiori (p. 285); Major Sanderson mistakes Yossarian for A. Fortiori and then pronounces him a manic-depressive because he is depressed by misery, ignorance, violence, greed, and crime (pp. 297-98).

Another note card of particular interest is one entitled "Night of Horrors" in the notes, and in the manuscript chapter derived from it, but "The Eternal City" in the published novel. The note card contains seven entries, the first four of which concern matters not eventually made part of the chapter. These have to do with the discovery of penicillin, which Yossarian apparently needs for syphilis, his attempts to get the drug through Nurse Duckett, and the acquisition of penicillin by "Aarky." The discovery by Yossarian that the old man in the whorehouse is dead, and that the girls have been driven out of the apartment by the vagaries of "Catch-18," is thus the result of his search for a cure. He has come to the apartment in Rome to see Aarky. The villain in this episode turns out to be Milo, as Item 7 explains: "Milo is exposed as the source of penicillen, [*sic*] tricking both Aarky &

Yossarian, and as the man who infected the girl to create a demand for his new wonder drug. Yossarian breaks with him." This concept, finally rejected, of course, would have been an interesting but perhaps unnecessary further development of Milo's corruption.

This idea, and all but one of the other suggestions on the card, were finally abandoned or subordinated to what appears as note 5: "Yossarian walks through the streets of Rome witnessing various horrors, among them the maid, who has been thrown from the window by Aarky." It is this concept which ultimately becomes the heart of "The Eternal City": Yossarian discovers that the apartment is in shambles, that the girls have been driven out, that the old man is dead. In the novel, of course, Milo is not pushing pencillin; instead, he initially agrees to assist Yossarian in finding Nately's whore's kid sister, but in the "grip of a blind fixation," he abandons Yossarian when he hears of a scheme to smuggle illegal tobacco (p. 402). This leads to Yossarian's "Night of Horrors," his surrealistic walk through Rome at night in which greed, violence, corruption, insanity, and death bombard his consciousness from all sides.[7] Aarfy has raped Michaela and thrown her out the window, and Yossarian is arrested for being AWOL.

The development of this note from initial conception to the finished novel is demonstrated by the manuscript draft of the chapter. "Night of Horrors" in manuscript is labelled "11 B" and covers fifty pages. It is essentially what is now known as "The Eternal City" (pp. 396–410). Of the alterations from manuscript to final publication, most are minor, single-word revisions. In the first paragraph, for example, the description of Milo "with pious lips pursed primly" became "with pious lips pursed." That he speaks to Yossarian in "wounded, ecclesiastical tones" became simply "ecclesiastical tones." Only a few other such revisions are worthy of mention. In the manuscript, Yossarian, on his walk through Rome, comes upon a "man" on the ground in convulsions. The novel was revised so that Yossarian now discovers an "Allied soldier." The implication of this revision would extend the universality of human suffering, which Yossarian is discovering in this chapter, to military men not in combat but within the civilian world. The "military" as an organization is the perpetrator of the violence in the novel; the soldiers as individuals share in being its victims. That the individual is an "Allied soldier" rather than an "American" is consistent with a pattern of revision in this chapter. In another passage, Yossarian, in the manuscript, comes upon a "crying American sergeant" in a doorway; in the novel the man is simply a "crying soldier" (p. 406). Another point revealed in these revisions, one of particular interest to biographical scholarship, is that the island on which Yossarian is based, called Pianosa throughout the novel, is clearly identified as Corsica throughout the manuscript. Heller, of course, spent most of his active duty on this island.

Beyond these simple revisions there are only a few other passages of substantial alteration. Yossarian's discovery of Nately's whore's apartment in shambles originally, as note card Item 6 suggested, contained the information of the death of the old man. The deleted passage read: "The old man had died of a stroke a few days earlier — once again he had marched with the majority — and the only one there was the old woman." In the novel, the news of the death of the old man is delayed two pages and the cause is made somewhat obscure: " 'Something broke in here,' " the old woman says, pointing to her head. " 'One minute he was living, one minute he was dead' " (p. 399). It is now possible that "Catch-22" has contributed to his death.[8] On the other hand, somewhat more emphasis is given in the manuscript to Yossarian's outrage at "Catch-18," the justification offered for the raid on the apartment, a matter reduced in the novel to only a few sentences (p. 398). The "stout woman with warts and two chins" (p. 402) Yossarian passes as he leaves the police headquarters in the novel does not appear in the manuscript. Her addition would seem to signify an intensification of the grotesquerie of the scene and an implication that she may be involved with the police commissioner who has just chased Yossarian out of his office.

In the novel, "At the Ministry of Public Affairs on the next block, a drunken lady was backed up against one of the fluted Corinthian columns by a drunken young soldier . . ." (p. 404). This passage is a considerable improvement over the manuscript version: "At the Ministry of Public Affairs, a drunken girl was backed up against one of the fluted Corinthian columns by a drunken soldier trying to insinuate his you-know-what into her and-how. . . ." Another wise alteration a few pages later was the deletion of a moralizing narrative intrusion into the action asserting that "Justice was a blind-folded brute with a club, a pimp with a knife." This interpretive remark was deleted[9] and is simply implicit in the events rather than stated by the narrator. In other matters, Aarfy's justification for killing Michaela after raping her is, in the novel, that " 'I couldn't very well let her go around saying bad things about us, could I?' " (p. 408). In the manuscript, the "us" was originally "an American officer," and another sentence followed: "That would have been bad propaganda for our country." These are changes of a certain amount of substance, but, in general, what a comparison of this note card with the manuscript and novel reveals is that the substance of the chapter does indeed follow the note suggestion and that what Heller wrote in his first draft is remarkably close to what was ultimately published.

There are numerous other note cards as intriguing and significant as these two and several individual ideas that were developed or abandoned after their first conception in the notes. One important point that must be stressed, however, is that the heart of *Catch-22*, the basic plot and character formulations, the underlying conflicts and themes, were all devised at the initial stage of note card composition. That Snowden will be killed on the mission to Avignon, that in response Yossarian will parade in the nude and sit naked in a tree during the funeral, are all established on a card entitled "Ferrara." The kind of minor detail that Heller frequently changed is the suggestion on this card that when Yossarian is awarded his medal, still standing naked in formation, "Dreedle orders a zoot suit for him." Another such revision concerns what is finally chapter 30, "Dunbar" (pp. 324–33), but is called "McAdam" in the notes.[10] The two most dramatic events of the chapter are here suggested: McAdam dives low over the beach, slicing Kid Sampson in half, and then commits suicide. The note card indicates an indefinite "man" as the victim and also suggests that "McAdam kills himself & Daneeker," which, of course, was revised, but the focus of the chapter is all there. This card, incidentally, also contains a fascinating suggestion: "Nurse Cramer's family tree traced back to include all known villains in History. She completes the line by being a registered Republican who doesn't drink, smoke, fornicate, or lust consciously & [is] guiltless of similar crimes."

Other random points of interest throughout these cards deserve comment. There are two suggestions that Yossarian and Dunbar are going to write a war novel in parody of Hemingway but they are having problems getting their "Jew" to conform and they lack a "radical" to make the plan complete.[11] An entry for chapter 40, "Catch-22," entitled "Catch-18" in the notes, reads "in the morning, Cathcart sends for Yossarian and offers him his deal. Big brother has been watching Yossarian." The concluding phrase makes explicit an underlying thematic allusion to George Orwell's 1984, one now more subtly beneath the action of the novel. The same card contains the suggestion that Nately's whore will stab Yossarian as he leaves Cathcart's office, which occurs in the novel, and that she will shout "olé" as she plunges the knife in, which does not.

The note for the final chapter, "Yossarian," contains not only plot suggestions but some interpretive remarks as well. There is a good deal of interest in Yossarian's mortality: "Yossarian is dying, true, but he has about 35 years to live." Another provocative entry, one rejected, is that "Among other things, he really does have chronic liver trouble. Condition is malignant & would have killed him if it had not been discovered." But perhaps the most important comments on the card are those relating to the thematic significance of Yossarian's refusal of Cathcart's deal. In the note card, Yossarian is to discuss the ethics of the deal, and his alternatives, with an English deserter: "Easiest would be to go home or fly more missions. Hardest would be for him to fight for identity without sacrificing moral responsibility." The following entry reads "He chooses the last, after all dangers are pointed out to him."

In the novel, the English deserter has been replaced by Major Danby, who, since he does not appear in the preliminary notes, would seem to be a late invention. The conception of the "fight for identity" has been slightly altered: Yossarian says, " 'I've been fighting all along to save my country. Now I'm going to fight a little to save myself. The country's not in danger any more, but I am' " (p. 435). The "identity" motif has been submerged into the "survival" theme, one centered on Yossarian's physical and moral survival. Thus Yossarian can now claim: " 'I'm not running away from my responsibilities. I'm running to them' " (p. 440). In thematic terms, this change is perhaps the most important discovery to emerge from a study of the preliminary note cards.

But the preliminary cards comprise less than half of all the cards there are. There are other groups of note cards detailing the activities of each of the characters in the novel, its structure and chronology, and the themes of sex and "Catch-18." There are even a group of cards which provide a page by page analysis of several chapters, listing items in much the manner of the preliminary notes but keyed to the page numbers of the manuscript. These cards are headed "Chapter Cards (Analysis of Chapter After They Were Written) [.]" A typical card is the one for the first chapter:

[MS pp.]	[Catch-22 pp.]
p. 3. – Catch-18 leads Y. to censor letters with Washington Irving's name. CID man arrives	[p. 8.]
p. 4. – The Texan, Dunbar, and the warrant officer	[p. 9.]
p. 5. – Soldier in White	[p. 10.]
p. 7. – Nurse Cramer discovers that the Soldier in White is dead	[p. 10.]
p. 7. – Chaplain visits Yossarian.	[p. 11.]
p. 10. – Chaplain mentions Nately	[p. 12.]
p. 15. – Texan drives out everybody but CID man	[p. 15.]

These cards all contain this level of detail and demonstrate Heller's close scrutiny of his manuscript. One item of interest throughout these entries is the concern for the number of missions required relative to the number Yossarian has flown. Two points are clearly stressed: that Yossarian is working against a progressive requirement which advances at about the same rate he completes missions; that the novel does not proceed chronologically and thus the number of required missions is a key to the historical sequence of events.

The entries indicate the important elements of the chapters and many of these are familiar: the T. S. Eliot business, Yossarian's willingness to be "the victim of anything but circumstance," the Loyalty Oath Crusade. Other items were revised in manuscript: Corsica was, at the last moment, changed to Pianosa; the death of Mudd (p. 107) has, in these notes, something to do with $E = MC^2$; P. P. Peckem is still called Peckenhammer; and chapter 12, published as "Bologna," is here entitled "Sgt. Knight." One card, labelled "Plans For Revision," suggests some of the changes to be made.

Heller has apparently decided, for example, to "build up" the role of

Nately and to concentrate on his love for the whore. After the entry "Whores," Heller wrote: "Nately's whore mentioned more, together with her apartment & old Folks." There are also other plans: to increase the references to the Soldier in White, presumably to deepen the *déjà vu* effect; to concentrate on "Aark," soon to be "Aarfy," and to stress his interest in Nately, his getting lost on missions, and his righteousness ("world is full of the girls he wouldn't prod"). As even these few entries suggest, Heller's revision and planning at this stage of the composition of *Catch-22* were serious and meticulous, the depth of which is easily revealed by several related groups of cards.

There is a card, for example, entitled "Combat Targets" on which the key events of each of the major missions are listed, the most significant of which is the mission to Avignon when "Dobbs goes crazy & Snowden is killed." Another important card lists, in chronological order, each of the main events in Yossarian's career, from "Feigns illness at Lowery Field" to "Accepts Englishman's terms. Runs off with penicillan [*sic*] and gun, whore behind him with knife," a suggestion contained in the preliminary notes and continued here, but eliminated in final manuscript. For the most part, however, the events here suggested are those of the novel, with a few intriguing exceptions: the notation "Treats Snowden (Loses Balls, wrong wound: no morphine)" is certainly one of them. This entry is followed two cards later with "Wounded in legs when Aarky gets lost (Doesn't lose Balls)" which suggests that at least one important plot revision resulted from this outlining process. There is still a concern with syphilis and penicillin, as the entries "Wants to help kid sister with Syphillis [*sic*]" and "Daneeka gives advice only," as well as the final entry would indicate.

Another card analyzes the sex theme in the novel with entries relating to caring for the kid sister, Doc Daneeka's experience with the newlyweds, and capricious copulation among nearly everyone. Two cards relate to the "Catch-18" concept, one of them suggesting a Catch-18 "Action Board." These two list various events which apparently fall within the bureaucratic enigma of Catch-18, from "Anyone who wants to be grounded can't be crazy" to "Black's Loyalty Oath Crusade is like Catch-18" to "Drive whores out in compliance with Catch-18."

Most of the notes, however, deal with character analysis, a matter Heller explored with great depth and perception. These cards detail the essential personality and role of each character, indicating both chapter and manuscript page number for each item mentioned. The most extensive scrutiny is given to Yossarian, of course. Here, in chapter by chapter account, are recorded Yossarian's activities and psychological and moral development, from his Assyrian heritage to his symptoms of paranoia, an item followed by the notion: "All he can do to maintain balance." Indeed, these entries stress the "insanity" theme very heavily. Heller records, "Insanity began with Dead Man. Stark naked after Snowden . . ." a matter treated in chapter 9. The following entry contains the comment "Stubbs thinks he's the only sane man left," an issue which now concludes chapter 10 when Dr. Stubbs says "that crazy bastard may be the only sane one left" (p. 109).

Virtually every character in the novel of any significance is covered by Heller in these entries. One card, for example, traces Dunbar's role in the first twelve chapters and shows how he affects Yossarian: they are in the hospital together, Dunbar tells Yossarian there is no God, and he conspires with Nately to get Yossarian out of the officer's club. Another set of cards explores Nately's activities with emphasis on his "sheltered childhood with wealthy parents" and his love for the whore. Several of these entries are intriguing, especially "Becomes a Family man," and the concluding four notations: "Finishes missions," "Volunteer's [sic] for Halfoat's job," "Agrees to fly 75 missions," and "Killed."

In similar fashion the Chaplain, Milo, Doc Daneeka, Clevinger, Orr, Hungry Joe, Aarfy, McAdam (McWatt), Cathcart, and the rest are given scrupulous attention. Some groups of characters are covered together, implying that they may play a single role: so it is with the Majors and, interestingly, with the whores. Nurses Duckett, Cramer, and Hanniball are covered on a single card, as are other pairs of characters: Bleistein and Wintergreen, General Peckenhammer (P. P. Peckem) and General Dreedle, and the Old Folks (a group listed as the old man, old woman, officer's maid, and the enlisted men's maid), although the old man and the old woman are also given scrutiny on a separate card. Another entry covers the Aides (Cargill, Korn, and Moodus) and still another, which lists Whitcomb, Danby, and Stubbs, is labelled simply "Others, Grp." In fact, there are so many cards, so scrupulously thorough, that presumably when Heller got to the end of the analysis and headed a card "Others, Misc." the only significant character left was Scheisskopf.

What emerges from an exploration of these note cards is not so much a new interpretation of the novel as a record of a creative process at work, one that appears, finally, almost entirely at odds with the portrait constructed by the earliest negative reviews of *Catch-22*. What were then frequent charges of faulty construction, illogical structures, chaotic events, must now be measured against the author's record of detailed, meticulous planning and analysis of his novel at each stage of composition. As these notes indicate, the creative impulse behind the novel was not a single conception but one that grew and altered slightly with reflection and revision. The names of many characters were changed; others were subordinated (such as the old woman) or emphasized (Milo). The central motivation of some key scenes was revised, as it was in "The Eternal City." That such changes were made in the course of composition is, of course, in no way remarkable; rather, what is striking is that so much of the novel was planned in advance on note cards and preserved intact throughout the composition. The fact that it was, however, leaves a valuable and fascinating record of the development of one of the most complex, and one of the finest, modern American novels.

Notes

1. These note cards, and all Heller manuscripts referred to, are on file in the Special Collections Division of Brandeis University Library. I am indebted to Joseph Heller for allowing me access to these materials and for reading this essay in manuscript and making many valuable suggestions. I would also like to acknowledge the generous assistance of Mr. Victor Berch, Brandeis University Library, in reviewing these manuscripts. Heller's comments on the note cards are variously in blue, red, and black ink, with occasional pencil notations.

2. Joseph Heller to James Nagel, 13 March 1974, p. 2. A copy of this letter is on file at Brandeis University Library.

3. See, for example, the following reviews of *Catch-22*: J.C. Pine, *Library Journal*, 86 (1961), 3805; William Hogan, "*Catch-22*: A Sleeper That's Catching On," *San Francisco Chronicle*, 3 May 1962, p. 39; Spencer Klaw, "Airman's Wacky War," *New York Herald Tribune Books*, 15 Oct. 1961, p. 8; Richard G. Stern, "Bombers Away," *New York Times Book Review*, 22 Oct. 1961, p. 50; Whitney Balliet, *New Yorker*, 37, 9 Dec. 1961, 247; *Daedalus* (Winter 1963), 155–65.

4. It is now difficult to determine the precise order of the cards and even, in some cases, whether a given card was written before or after the initial draft. All references to numbers and groups of cards are therefore based on my own judgment and on the manner in which the cards are now grouped.

5. This card has ten numbered entries, split vertically after the seventh.

6. All references are to Joseph Heller, *Catch-22* (New York: Simon and Schuster, 1961). The pages referred to are basically pp. 185–92, 206–20. Subsequent references to this edition will be given within the text.

7. For a provocative discussion of this scene, see Minna Doskow, "The Night Journey in *Catch-22*," *Twentieth Century Literature*, 12 (1967), 186–93. Rpt. in James Nagel, ed., *Critical Essays on CATCH-22* (Encino: Dickenson Publishing Co., 1974), pp. 155–63.

8. I have explored the role of the old man, and his relationship to Yossarian, in "Yossarian, the Old Man, and the Ending of *Catch-22*," *Critical Essays on CATCH-22*, pp. 164–74.

9. From what is now p. 407.

10. The name "McAdam," of course, was eventually changed to "McWatt."

11. Two manuscript paragraphs developed from these suggestions were published in my essay "Two Brief Manuscript Sketches: Heller's *Catch-22*," *MFS*, 20 (1974), 221–24. The manuscript seems to suggest that these paragraphs represent a serious attempt at a war novel by Heller rather than a parody written by his characters, as is clear in the note cards. Heller's comment to this point is contained in a letter on file at Brandeis University Library.

Catch–22 and the Language of Discontinuity
Gary W. Davis*

Joseph Heller's *Catch-22*, with its irreverent and bitterly comic description of the last days of World War II, has seemed for many of its readers a frighteningly accurate portrait of the "mentality" behind contemporary social and intellectual institutions.[1] Heller's novel, however, issues more than just a simple challenge to the various commercial, military, and religious organizations which govern the lives of its characters. In the world of *Catch-22*, patients' illnesses always coincide with their doctors' areas of specialization (182–3), fliers disrupt political indoctrination sessions with cries of "Who is Spain?" or "When is right?" (35), and Yossarian, the bombardier, must struggle against the "logic" of the Air Corps if he is to continue to survive. Such situations reveal how society's institutions reflect fundamental discontinuities in language, thought, and behavior.[2] More than this, they suggest that at the heart of such dislocations is that problematic and radical discontinuity which has been the subject of so much critical discussion.

The question of discontinuity and what it represents for language (and hence for culture as a whole, as well as for poetry, fiction, and drama) clearly has been an essential part of major transformations within contemporary discourse. Allied on many levels with the general movement away from the artistic endeavors associated with "modernism" and toward those of "post-modernism," the problem of discontinuity obviously involves more than sweeping changes in the form and style of recent writing. It also is related to those movements which have led much of contemporary thought away from a search for continuities in natural, psychological, or cultural being and toward an acceptance of a discourse which acknowledges linguistic, intellectual, and social discontinuities.

This is evidenced by even the most cursory glance at some of the notions about this question. As various anthologies and symposia have shown,[3] the roots and manifestations of recent conceptions of discontinuity are linked to perspectives ranging from Ernst Cassirer's theory that language is a process of "ever-progressive objectification" to Sartre's portrayal of how "things are divorced from their names," from structuralism's understanding of the essential separation of signifier and signified to Merleau-Ponty's interpretation of language as a labyrinth which can reveal only irreconcilable dualisms.[4] For some (and Sartre's character, Roquentin, would seem an obvious example here) linguistic discontinuity may permit discourse to become so dominant over facticity that authentic action and selfhood can only be restored by a renewed understanding of how "the world of explanations and reasons is not the world of existence."[5] Others, by basing their arguments on Saussure's theory of the arbitrary relation of the signifier and signified, have seen in modern notions of the discontinuity of

*Reprinted, with permission, from *Novel*, 12, No. 1 (1978), 66–77.

the linguistic sign the possibility of a new literary culture. Roland Barthes has thus suggested the emergence of a literature which, in its acceptance of language as an arbitrary and self-sustaining system of signs, might lead us to the core of what he calls the "linguistic pact . . . which unites the writer and the other."[6]

Even more illustrative of the direction of some of the transformations in our conceptions of discourse and discontinuity are such recent endeavors as Jacques Derrida's "deconstructions" of phenomenological and structuralist theories of language and Michel Foucault's analysis of how the modern *episteme* came to view writing as a process inhabited only by words and the interval between words. Along these same lines Eugenio Donato, echoing Nietzsche as well as Derrida and Foucault, finds that much of modern thought has come to see language as a discontinuous process of interpretation. This interpretation, Donato writes, "does not shed light on a matter that asks to be interpreted, that offers itself passively to interpretation, but it can only seize violently an interpretation that is already there, one which it must overturn, overthrow, shatter with the blows of a hammer. . . . Interpretation then is nothing but sedimenting one layer of language upon another to produce an illusory depth which gives us the temporary spectacle of things beyond words."[7]

Such conceptions suggest the extent to which the problem of discontinuity has been seen as characteristic of modern discourse, even when that discourse intends the kind of referentiality or "illusory depth" mentioned by Donato. Indeed Geoffrey Hartman implies in a recent essay on Derrida's *Glas* that an awareness of the problematic boundaries between nature and artifice, events and interpretations, and even texts and commentaries has become an inescapable part of our intellectual order.[8] Ultimately we appear to be confronted by a situation in which words seem to refer only to other words, and thoughts, to other thoughts. This seems to be the case whether one turns to the existentialists' demand for a discourse consistent with human freedom and responsibility, to Barthes' interest in how society transforms ideas and themes into the substance of signifying practices, or to Derrida's vision of the freeplay of interpretation.

It is in this regard that the relations between *Catch-22* and the questions posed by the discontinuities of contemporary discourse assume major significance. In response to this sense of linguistic, intellectual, and social discontinuity, Heller, like many other contemporary writers, turns to language itself for a basic model of these disruptions. This enables *Catch-22* to expose fundamental discontinuities in our discourse and our other systems of exchange. The novel's most vital implications for our literature thus lie in the way Heller's demythologizing of discourse relates to Yossarian's quest for survival and to the question of whether it is possible to discover a more meaningful, "continuous" discourse.

Names serve as the most obvious point of departure for this. In elaborate parodies of long-standing notions about the nature of language, names, in *Catch-22*, often fail to "properly" designate a particular object, person, or concept. While continuing to believe in all the myths of a "proper" relation between names and things, Heller's characters often identify an object or person solely on the basis of a name (or even a label or chart) assigned by the most haphazard methods. Names soon come to be accepted as independent "realities" capable of affecting a person's sense of his own experiences or identity. Yossarian, when he usurps someone else's hospital bed, becomes for that time "Warrant Officer Homer Lumley, who felt like vomiting and was covered suddenly with clammy sweat" (300), while Major Major, when he first entered kindergarten, discovered that he was not, as he had been led to believe, "Caleb Major," but "some total stranger named Major Major Major about whom he knew absolutely nothing" (87).

The opening scene of the novel establishes another important aspect of this linguistic discontinuity. Assigned the task of censoring enlisted men's letters, Yossarian transforms the job into a game that involves more than just a simple parody of its own military context:

> Death to all modifiers, he declared one day. . . . The next day he made war on articles. He reached a much higher plane of creativity the following day when he blacked out everything but *a, an* and *the*. . . . Soon he was proscribing parts of salutations and signatures and leaving the text untouched. . . .
>
> When he had exhausted all possibilities in the letters, he began attacking the names and addresses on the envelopes, obliterating whole homes and streets, annihilating entire metropolises with careless flicks of the wrist as though he were God. . . . (8)

Writing, here, is an activity discontinuous from anything that might be considered "things themselves." Since what happens within this independent world of words is indistinguishable from what happens in "fact," crossing out a name may, in effect, "obliterate" a place. The same logic lies behind Yossarian's attempt to capture the German artillery batteries at Bologna by simply going to the map and moving the red line that indicates the extent of the Allies' conquests (122–3). Once again symbolic forms and expressions have the privileged status usually accorded to "reality." In fact even the Air Corps is briefly convinced that Bologna has been captured.

The process seen in these elementary forms of discourse can serve as a model for other intellectual procedures within *Catch-22*. The clichés and illusions of popular culture, for example, take on much the same status granted to signifiers like maps, charts, and names. With no apparent irony Lieutenant Scheisskopf thinks of his own personal life in terms of the formulae and codes of melodrama: he sees himself as a man "chained to a woman . . . incapable of looking beyond her own dirty, sexual desires to the titanic struggles for the unobtainable in which noble man could become heroically engaged" (74). Elsewhere, the most outrageous fantasies go unchallenged if "verified" by the appropriate forms of the Air Corps' language and logic.

Yossarian's joke about the Germans' "Lepage glue gun" (a weapon which "glues a whole formation of planes together in mid-air") takes on the conditions of a "reality" when it is repeated to him by the squadron's intelligence officer. Yossarian's immediate reaction is to cry out, "My God, it's true" (128–9).

Lieutenant Dunbar's attempts to manipulate time follow the same pattern and lead Yossarian's friend far beyond conventional notions about time's psychological dimensions. "You're inches away from death every time you go on a mission," he tells Clevinger. "How much older can you be at your age? A half minute before that you were stepping into high school, and an unhooked brassière was as close as you ever hoped to get to Paradise. Only a fifth of a second before that you were a small kid with a ten-week summer vacation that lasted a hundred thousand years and still ended too soon" (40). On the basis of such observations Dunbar constructs a private temporal order within which virtually any psychic experience may be granted the status of "reality." The privileged status of this order suggests that, since pleasant experiences make time seem to pass more quickly, the way for him to make his life last as long as possible is to fill it with as many dull, unpleasant, and distasteful conditions as he can (40, 49).

The Air Corps' manner of operation, in *Catch-22*, reveals that this discontinuity extends into all areas of its behavior. At the insistence of General Peckem, the Air Corps has become concerned with making neat "bomb patterns," although, as the General informs Scheisskopf, a bomb pattern is only a phrase "I dreamed up a few weeks ago. It means nothing, but you'd be surprised how rapidly it's caught on" (334). The Army's entire administrative procedure arises from this ability to put purposeless, self-reflexive discourse into action within its field of activity. Ultimately its self-contained organization and action define a closed world whose "illusory depth" becomes its inhabitants' only "reality." Major Major learns this when he discovers that most of the official documents he receives do not "concern him at all. The vast majority consisted of allusions to prior communications which Major Major had never seen or heard of. There was never any need to look them up, for the instructions were invariably to disregard" (94).

As the novel suggests in other scenes, the workings of this language and logic even manage to transform traditional understandings of such concepts as "death," "presence," and "absence." Yossarian's tentmate for much of the time is a "dead man" who had been killed before officially reporting to the squadron. The Army maintains that since the man "had never officially gotten into the squadron, he could never officially be gotten out" (111–2). Yossarian is told to keep sharing his tent with Mudd's personal belongings and official "presence." If this situation reveals how the discontinuities of knowledge can turn what is generally thought of as death's "absence" into the functional equivalent of "presence," Doc Daneeka's final plight presents a telling reversal of this theme. Listed as part of the crew for McWatt's airplane the day it crashes, the doctor is declared "dead" by the Air Corps, though everyone on Pianosa knows that Daneeka was safely on the ground all the while. His physical appearance never can refute the "facts" of official knowledge. When people begin to act as if he really were dead, Daneeka's "life" is transformed into a functional absence.

These famous examples of the novel's peculiar logic illustrate the extent to which Catch-22 exposes the meaninglessness of our conventional understanding of discourse and its processes. Indeed the most familiar expression of this logic shows how signifiers, psychological definitions, and knowledge itself are deployed without reference to any "real" human or natural content. "There was," we learn, "only one catch and that was Catch-22, which specified that a concern for one's own safety in the face of dangers that were real and immediate was the process of a rational mind. Orr was crazy and could be grounded. All he had to do was ask; and as soon as he did, he would no longer be crazy and would have to fly more missions" (47). The "elliptical precision" of this logic (47) reveals that the word "crazy" and the question of Orr's sanity are relevant only to whether he flies combat missions or asks to be grounded. Since both actions are functions of the Army's discontinuous rules, sanity and selfhood are now revealed to be elements of a field of play which is as closed as Yossarian's games with the soldiers' letters. Moreover, by showing that Orr's sanity is to be determined solely on the basis of whether he does or does not agree to fly more missions, Catch-22 demands that we think of the self as unrelated moments of discourse rather than as a continuous or creative entity in itself.

From games with the soldiers' correspondence to rules about a flier's sanity, Catch-22 reveals that the men of the Air Corps must now see as arbitrary and perhaps illusory what they previously accepted as "proper" relations between nature and artifice, things and words, or even events and interpretations. At the same time situations like Orr's challenge the conventional assumption that there is any "proper" relation between such entities; indeed Catch-22 exposes our most fundamental myths about both subjectivity and the possibility of perceiving things in themselves. By bringing to the surface the often hidden workings of our language and logic Catch-22 forces us to recognize that "things" are no different than the perplexing appearances typified by the chaplain's "vision" of a naked man in a tree. It simultaneously reveals the "subject" to be only those interplaying levels of "Optical phenomena," *déjà vu, jamais vu,* and *presque vu,* which Chaplain Tappman experiences as a "subtle, recurring confusion between illusion and reality . . . characteristic of paramnesia" (209–10).

Such disruptions of customary understanding demonstrate how Catch-22's victims are severed from what they had thought of as "existence." Abandoned to a labyrinth of words and appearances, they are elements of a discourse which, referring only to itself, neither comprehends nor controls some "world" beyond. As Yossarian comes to understand, it does not matter if Catch-22 actually exists. "What did matter," he discovers, "was that everyone thought it existed" (418). For this reason words spoken to Yossarian while he is still in cadet school, "We're all in this business of illusion together" (188), project the very essence of Catch-22's reasoning.

Significantly Heller sees these linguistic and intellectual discontinuities reflected in our social systems and institutions as well. Milo Minderbinder can buy eggs for seven cents apiece and still make a profit selling them for five cents (237), while, as the old woman in Rome declares, "Catch-22 says they have a right to do anything we can't stop them from doing" (416). The truly dangerous nature of this discourse is dramatically realized in Colonel Cathcart's attempts to impress his superiors, for his actions and their effects do more than expose the peculiar nature of the language implicit within the most basic concepts of Western philosophy (or even within the idea of "philosophy" itself).[9] Cathcart volunteers his squadron for as many missions as he can, hoping that credit for the men's exploits will result in his own rapid promotion. He therefore sets in motion a grotesque version of Zeno's paradox in which he invariably increases the number of missions the men must complete whenever a flier nears that point at which he can be rotated out of combat duty. Unable to ever finish their combat tours and equally unable to escape from Cathcart's system, the fliers one by one fall victim to German flak and their own commander's zeal for advancement.

As the situation within Cathcart's squadron demonstrates, the Air Corps and its representatives manage to define the "reality" within which their men live simply by setting themselves and their discourse between an individual and any sense he might have of something existing beyond his own words and thoughts. This enables the Army to define the "reality" toward which discourse is directed, regardless of how illusory that "reality" may be or how much these definitions may defy various "normal" conventions. "That's my trouble, you know," Yossarian finally realizes. "Between me and every ideal I always find Scheisskopfs, Peckems, Korns, and Cathcarts. And that sort of changes the ideal" (454). This process allows the Air Corps to blind fliers to what would seem the most obvious situations. Not even Yossarian is able to convince his friends that, as he puts it, "The enemy . . . is anybody who's going to get you killed, no matter *which* side he's on" (127). Heller presents a fitting physical analogue to this general situation in his description of Yossarian's reaction to the compartment which houses the B-25's bombardier. Enclosed within this plexiglass equivalent of the Air Corps' autoletic discourse, Yossarian finds the physical and logical conventions of "normality" significantly inverted. The crawlway leading to an escape hatch now seems only an impediment to escape, while his fellow crewmen have become obstacles to his survival (49–50).

On another level this discontinuity is expressed in the activities of Milo and his ubiquitous M & M Enterprises. In a way which underscores the close alliance between conceptions of language, society, and economics within the modern intellectual order, Milo's power is based upon two general assumptions: that everyone agrees to and has a "share" in his syndicate, and that there is, beneath this, some "proper" relation between the shares and a "reality" beyond. These assumptions help Milo create a mercantile empire which, like the capitalist system itself, holds a controlling interest in many of the combatant armies. The very essence of Milo's endeavor, though, exists solely as discourse. The shares are only the "words 'A Share' written on the nearest scrap of paper" (378) and the syndicate's profits always are as fictional as its shares. Much the same discontinuity is embodied in Milo's physical appearance. "Milo's mustache was unfortunate," we find, "because the separated halves never matched. They were like Milo's disunited eyes, which never looked at the same thing at the same time" (66). More important, however, is the way Milo's manipulations of the language of discontinuity allow him to justify economic victimization of friends, contracts to simultaneously attack and defend the German-held bridge at Orvieto, and bargains to bomb and strafe his own squadron (261–5).

As Milo and M & M Enterprises remind us, violence and the characters' often unusual attitudes toward violence are inseparable from the question of discontinuity. But, in contrast to the worlds of words and administrative procedures, violence never appears to be neatly confined within the Air Corps or any other military or economic organization. Milo's bizarre business deals have vicious effects on others; civilians like Luciana, the mysterious young woman Yossarian meets in Rome, have their bodies mutilated by the bombs of those who have come to liberate them (163); and the inept, internal rivalries of the Air Corps cause the needless bombing of undefended villages (334). In one scene Yossarian discovers that Aarfy, the ambitious, perpetual fraternity boy, has murdered the maid who works in the officers' apartment in Rome:

> Yossarian was aghast. "But you killed her, Aarfy! You killed her!"
> "Oh, I had to do that after I raped her," Aarfy replied in his most condescending manner. "I couldn't very well let her go around saying bad things about us, could I?" (427)

Aarfy's explanation is virtually a paradigm of Catch-22's logical procedures and does more than suggest the fallaciousness of certain kinds of "acceptable" acts and rationalizations. It also reminds us that even when the characters' discourse seems clearly exposed as a manipulation of discontinuous symbolic forms, these activities can have violent effects on others. Aarfy's words thus reveal how the closed discourses of Catch-22 permit the novel's characters to ignore both this truth and the actual physical horrors around them. Clevinger thinks that because the enemy indiscriminately shoots at everyone it is not really true that the Germans are trying to kill Yossarian (17), and Yossarian comes to believe that the hospital, because it makes "a much neater, more orderly job" of death, represents a refuge from the war (170). Thus when the MPs fail to arrest Aarfy and, instead, seize Yossarian for "being in Rome without a pass" (429), they are simply adhering to one of Catch-22's most deeply rooted processes.

On the other hand all of these situations emphasize the difficulties involved in any attempt to "escape" from either the Army or its closed system of logic. The basic direction, however, that such efforts should take seems indicated in the dénouement of Captain Black's Great Loyalty Oath Crusade. Ignoring the oaths, pledges, and performances of "The Star Spangled Banner" which Black has made prerequisite to even the men's meals, Major —— de Coverley neither argues with Black's system nor tries to outwit it. He simply denies its authority by commanding, "Gimme eat" (120). Heller himself focuses on this question in his interview with *The Realist*. "What distresses me very much," he declares, "is that the ethic which is often dictated by a wartime emergency has a certain justification when the wartime emergency exists, but when this . . . ideology is transplanted to peacetime, then you have this kind of lag which leads not only to absurd situations, but to very tragic situations."[10]

In *Catch-22* concern with such conditions is reflected in the way virtually all social and intellectual institutions, from the Air Corps to the language of philosophy, are transformed into parodies of themselves. This does more than display these institutions' basic irrelevance; it discloses how their intellectual foundations are, and perhaps always have been, obstacles and threats to our survival. "The stimulus for a certain action," Heller asserts in the same interview, "justifies an action. If the stimulus is not there and the action exists anyway, then you've got the right to examine why you're doing it."[11] *Catch-22* as a whole, like the scene involving Michaela's death and Aarfy's attempted explanation, exposes a similar and equally crucial aspect of Catch-22's logic. It unmasks foundations and consequences of that long-standing convention that there is some "proper," even "natural" set of names or metaphors upon which are based our language and knowledge, and to which we appeal for our senses of value and justice. The effect is not simply to reveal the characters' isolation from "reality." It exposes how the problematic nature of language has been obscured within the familiar myths of the "proper" relations between "words" and "things."

It often is contact with some form of violence, rather than an intellectual demystification, which reveals this to Yossarian. This is evident relatively early in the novel, when the bombardier succeeds in avoiding the mission to Bologna. Having used a trivial mechanical failure to relieve his crew from what has been rumored to be the squadron's most dangerous assignment, Yossarian goes to the beach, where, ironically, nature itself appears in the form of a frightening, tumultuous process (147–8). Yossarian's walk through the streets of Rome mixes the fantastic and grotesque in a way that further demonstrates to him the distorted violence of experience, the completeness of the physical and spiritual destruction which have been brought about by human imagination and institutions (420–6). And near the very end of the novel Yossarian finally sees through all the confusions surrounding Snowden's death to discover in the gaping wound in the radio-gunner's chest the horror of what Snowden has suffered (447–8).

Such moments seem to suggest the necessity for some kind of direct encounter with whatever "reality" may or may not lie "outside" discourse. This, superficially at least, would seem to be the "meaning" of Yossarian's experience over Avignon. "Man," he discovers in Snowden's suffering, "is matter," a fragile container for "liver, lungs, kidneys, ribs, stomach and bits of the stewed tomatoes . . . eaten that day for lunch." It is a "message," read quite literally in Snowden's entrails, which reminds us that with the "spirit gone, man is garbage. . . . Ripeness was all" (449–50). For this reason Yossarian's recurring vision of what happened that day and the refrain, "Where are the Snowdens of yesteryear," which is such an intimate part of that memory, would seem to demand that we demythologize our closed systems of discourse to confront the apparently "existential" verity of our own mortal and material being. This infers the achievement of a discourse free of the discontinuities exemplified by Catch-22. Its speakers would be able to declare, like Dunbar, that it is not really the "quality" but the mere continuation of one's existence that should be treasured (40). Its "philosophers" would, like the old man in Rome, find civilizations' "ideals" to be clichés which would make more sense when their "logical" sequence is inverted than when they are spoken in their conventional manner (253–4).

Through much of the novel the institution of some such "proper" discourse, on the social as well as the linguistic and intellectual levels, remains one of the few hopes seemingly open to Heller's characters. But, as Catch-22 exposes from the first, neither an arduous process of linguistic and intellectual purification nor the remnants of some "original" speech from which mankind has fallen can lead us to a "natural" discourse in which "matter" and "language" are bound together by some primal "word." This is the import of the events that take place over Avignon, for the scene is marked by the implication of a language of literary allusion (the overtones of *King Lear* and Villon's "The Ballad of the Dead Ladies"), referentiality (Yossarian's reading of the "message" in the entrails), and even metaphysics (the "spirit" without which man is "garbage") into Yossarian's encounter with the physical horrors of Snowden's death.

The bombardier's seemingly "existential" confrontation with Snowden's innards thus discloses that we can no more dwell within some hypothetical order of simple materiality than we can speak in a language free of the self-reflexive discontinuities which make possible Catch-22 and all its variations. It is a scene, therefore, which exposes how discourse and matter are inextricably entwined in human experience. Experience is not a question of oppositions between "matter" and "symbol," "nature" and "art." It is, instead, a question of how "things" and "events" are inseparable, even indistinguishable from "discourse." But they are not made so by that mythic figure of the "proper word," upon which so much of our economic, social, philosophic, and literary language is believed to be based. Matter and discourse, this scene asserts, are doubled, even reversible functions within a world whose "illusory depth" always has been indistinguishable from whatever we have granted the privileged status of "reality."

This, obviously, is why Heller concludes that it is hopeless to try to either master or reform the discontinuities of discourse. As the fates of Dunbar and the old man in Rome remind us (376, 417), our ability to manipulate discourse does not lessen our vulnerability to Catch-22 and mortality. Like Yossarian and his friend, Orr, one can only "flee." When, Heller explains, "the monolithic society closes off every conventional area of protest or corrective action," there is no alternative but "flight, a renunciation of that condition, that society, that set of circumstances."[12]

The difficulties which mark Yossarian's desertion at the end of the novel reveal the extent to which even this alternative is involved in the complex question of discontinuity. On one side Yossarian finds the Air Corps, that institution which, on every level, is a parody of the myths which make possible closed, discontinuous discourses of all kinds. Its offer to make Yossarian a returning "hero" exemplifies its fundamental processes (435–9). On the other side is Yossarian's vision of Sweden as a place of even more than political refuge and physical safety, a land, he thinks, where "the girls are so sweet" and the "people are so advanced" (463). It is a place whose image as a kind of regained paradise reveals that its bases are, like those of Catch-22 itself, founded on the myths of natural experience and a "proper" metaphoric language as the foundation of value. This forces us to question the nature of that act of desertion which concludes the novel, asking whether it is a genuine movement toward a world of continuous discourse and experience (a declaration that, as always, our only recourse is to the ancient myths of a realm of pure, immediate experience) or a recognition about fiction, as an interplay of levels of discourse, which ties *Catch-22* to recent understandings of discontinuity and to the transition from "modernism" to "postmodernism."

It is in this regard that the significance emerges of the alternatives offered at the novel's conclusion. The world of the Air Corps is one which is closed as well as discontinuous. In contrast Yossarian's image of Sweden, even though it is based upon the same discontinuities as Catch-22 and its manifestations, maintains a fundamental openness which makes it neither as autotelic nor as monolithic as institutions like the Army and M & M Enterprises. Heller himself points to this when, discussing the final scenes of the novel, he declares that he no more thinks of Sweden as a real paradise than he believes that Yossarian ever will get there. Sweden and Yossarian's desertion are only images of a "goal," an "objective" for those who seek to renounce the world of Peckems, Cathcarts, and Scheisskopfs.[13] Within the novel itself this openness is maintained by our awareness that "Sweden" is part of Yossarian's imagination and of the imaginations of all those who seek to escape the discourse of Catch-22. In the way that both the characters and the readers of the novel are kept from forgetting the fundamentally "fictional" nature of this "Sweden" we are all reminded of how the world "beyond" is known only in the form of that "illusory depth" which Donato called "the temporary spectacle of things beyond words." If Yossarian's dream of Sweden seems to hold forth that ancient promise of an attainable "proper" discourse, it does so while still reminding us that it is only a simulacrum of all such dreams; it is a fiction whose essential nature exposes both its own fictionality and the myth of the "word" itself.

Yossarian's choice, at the novel's end, is thus between two kinds of fiction and not between two different worlds or between a fiction and some new reality. One fiction, epitomized by the Army, Milo's capitalism, and the closed language of discontinuity, has lost sight of its own fictionality and has come to believe the myths of its own "proper" bases. The other fiction, "Sweden," exposes its own nature, revealing that it is only an image of our longings for some "refuge" or "home," some "origin" or "center" free of that apparently broken discourse within which mankind inevitably finds itself. This is why the novel's "ending" is so problematic, for it seems to leave open the troubling, vital question of which form of fiction *Catch-22* is and what sort of world its hero has chosen. Significantly the novel does not specify whether Yossarian's flight expresses either a preference for the age-old dream of immediate experience or a desire for a discourse of self-reflexively interplaying levels of fiction. Moreover Yossarian's "jump" toward Sweden is taken as much because of his unthinking move away from the descending knife of Nately's whore as it is from any previous decision he may have made (463). Thus, in much the same way as Yossarian is condemned to remain what Heller calls "a spirit on the loose,"[14] forever traversing those invisible yet endlessly marked distances of discourse, the "ending" of the novel is a doubled (non)answer which, like *Catch-22* as a whole, forces us, as it forced Yossarian, back into our own fictions and into the experience of fiction itself.

All of this suggests the position *Catch-22* occupies within the development of our recent literature. On the surface its motifs, characters, and situations would seem to suggest that the novel is heir to all the traditions and perspectives which marked the "existential" novel and the problematic legacy of post-Romantic thought. From this point of view *Catch-22* often seems part of that literature's concern with the self's apparently unending struggle to discover and free its own being. It might even be seen as an illustration of how the workings of those principles of discourse embodied in *Catch-22* constitute a violation of humanity's most fundamental nature.

But the fact that the same discontinuity lies at the heart of both what Yossarian flees and what he hopes will be his refuge must remind us, as do the comments of Barthes, Foucault, and Derrida, that the questions raised by linguistic, intellectual, and social discontinuities have become basic to both fiction, as a genre, and to discourse as a whole. In the works of writers like Borges, Nabokov, or Barth (to name just a few) we find more than just depictions of various kinds and forms of discontinuous discourse. We also see fictions which, recognizing and exposing their freedom from the bonds of representation, use discontinuity for their own ends. The Terra and Anti-Terra of Nabokov's *Ada*, the interplaying systems of myth and fiction in

Barth's *Chimera*, the strange categories of animal life set forth in Borges' famous Chinese encyclopedia (which Foucault declares gave rise to his own work, *The Order of Things*), all suggest an order of signs in which fiction, free of the burden of some myth of a "proper" correspondence to things, can become an open exploration of discourse itself. Likewise the disruptions of experience and discourse seen in *Catch-22* often foreshadow that other, more radical literature of discontinuity whose violent, "schizophrenic" (as it is often called) freeplay has been associated most frequently with writers like Artaud and Burroughs.

In such works, as in *Catch-22*, fiction becomes a medium which reminds us of our longings for a language of continuity and referentiality at the very same time that it exposes the dangerous, closed discourses to which such desires may lead. Such works inevitably draw us away from systems of "proper" discourse and toward the open interpretation and the interaction of different levels of discourse which are at the essence of the experience of fiction. It is in its revelation of the movement toward such fictional forms and of the epistemic transformations of which they are a part that *Catch-22* has played a major role. Heller's novel exposes, on the most obvious levels, the violent absurdities of our commercial, military, intellectual, and literary institutions. More important is its demonstration that the foundations of these institutions lie in those same recurrent myths of the "word" and of a "proper" metaphoric discourse to which we have turned, so often, as alternatives to the kind of discontinuous languages epitomized by Catch-22. In this way *Catch-22* is part of that reorientation within the intellectual configuration which has led us to begin thinking of writing, not as a system of representation closed by some final "meaning," but as the freeplay of interpretation. Like so much of our recent writing Heller's novel thus demands that we ask whether what we might have thought to be "life" must not also be thought of in terms of a freeplay which is inseparable, even indistinguishable, from those processes known as "fiction" and "interpretation."

Notes

1. Throughout, references, included within the body of the text, will be to the following edition: Joseph Heller, *Catch-22* (New York: Dell, 1967).

2. This point has been made, from a wide variety of critical perspectives and with vastly different conclusions, by a number of commentators. In particular, see Robert Protherough, "The Sanity of *Catch-22*," rptd. in *A "Catch-22" Casebook*, ed. by Frederick Kiley and Walter McDonald (New York: Crowell, 1973), p. 210; Tony Tanner, *City of Words* (New York: Harper and Row, 1971), pp. 81–2; and Thomas Blues, "The Moral Structure of *Catch-22*," rptd. in *"Catch-22": A Critical Edition*, ed. by Robert M. Scotto (New York: Delta, 1973), pp. 544–559.

3. The most obvious examples would be Sallie Sears' and Georgiana Lord's anthology, *The Discontinuous Universe* (New York: Basic Books, 1972) and the symposium, *Language and Cultural Discontinuities*, held at The State University of New York at Buffalo, April 15–17, 1970.

4. See, respectively, Ernst Cassirer, *Language and Myth* (New York: Dover, 1953), pp. 35–7; Jean-Paul Sartre, *Nausea* (New York: New Directions, 1964), p. 160; Eugenio Donato, "Of Structuralism and Literature," rptd. in *Velocities of Change*, ed. by Richard A. Macksey (Baltimore: The Johns Hopkins University Press, 1974), pp. 154–7; and Maurice Merleau-Ponty, *Le Visible et l'invisible* (Paris: Gallimard, 1964), p. 17. In regard to the latter, I also am indebted to Donato's perceptive analysis in "Language, Vision, and Phenomenology: Merleau-Ponty as a Test Case," rptd. in *Velocities of Change*, pp. 292–303. Needless to say, when discussing so diverse a group of thinkers so briefly, a blurring of what would otherwise be more clear lines of distinction is perhaps inevitable. But, by focusing my discussion on the changing perception of the processes of signification within Heller's novel I hope to minimize such blurrings.

5. Sartre, *Nausea*, p. 174.

6. Roland Barthes, "To Write: An Intransitive Verb?" in *The Languages of Criticism and the Sciences of Man: The Structuralist Controversy*, ed. by Richard A. Macksey and Eugenio Donato (Baltimore: The Johns Hopkins University Press, 1970), pp. 134, 144–5; also see Barthes' discussion of Michel Butor's *Mobile: Study for a Representation of the United States*, in "Literature and Discontinuity," an essay included in Barthes' *Critical Essays* (Evanston: Northwestern University Press, 1972), pp. 170–83. The change in Barthes' critical position indicated by such recent works as *S/Z* (New York: Hill and Wang, 1974) might suggest a similar change in his attitudes toward this particular question as well.

7. See, in particular, Derrida's analysis in *Speech and Phenomenology and Other Essays on Husserl's Theory of Signs* (Evanston: Northwestern University Press, 1973), *et. passim*, and *De la Grammatologie* (Paris: Minuit, 1967), the second chapter of which recently appeared, in translation, in *Sub-Stance*, 10 (1974), pp. 127–81; Michel Foucault, "Nietzche, Freud, Marx," in *Nietzche, Cahiers de Royaumont, Philosophie VI* (Paris: Editions in Minuit, 1967), pp. 189–190; and, finally, Eugenio Donato, "The Two Languages of Criticism," in *Languages of Criticism*, p. 96.

8. Geoffrey Hartman, "Monsieur Texte: On Jacques Derrida, His *Glas*," *The Georgia Review*, XXIX (Winter 1975), pp. 759–60.

9. See Jacques Derrida, "White Mythology: Metaphor in the Text of Philosophy," *NLH*, VI (Autumn 1974), pp. 49–50.

10. "An Impolite Interview with Joseph Heller," rptd. in *Casebook*, p. 281.

11. "Impolite Interview," p. 289.

12. "Impolite Interview," p. 289.

13. "Impolite Interview," p. 289.

14. "Impolite Interview," p. 289.

Milo's "Culpable Innocence": Absurdity as Moral Insanity in *Catch-22*

Leon F. Seltzer*

The label most frequently adopted in describing the themes and methods of Joseph Heller's contemporary classic, *Catch-22*, is without doubt "the absurd." Study after study of this widely discussed novel has at some point resorted to modern notions of absurdity to account for Heller's frankly

*Reprinted, with permission, from *Papers on Language and Literature*, 15 (1979), 290–310.

impossible, yet almost too real, world. This world—specifically, or rather microcosmically, the American Air Force base at Pianosa during World War II—is as much at battle with itself as with anyone else. It is an irrational, sometimes nightmarish world in which one's superior (and even inferior) officers constitute a greater threat to one's life and sanity than the enemy, and where demonstrating one's patriotism may demand not only the signing of interminable and meaningless loyalty oaths, but also the consumption of chocolate-covered cotton. The outrageous senselessness of most of the book's action has prompted several writers to comment on Heller's grotesque presentation of reality and to relate his underlying philosophical perspective to that of Kafka, Sartre, or Camus, or to dramatists working in the "Theater of the Absurd" tradition.[1]

To view *Catch-22* solely in terms of metaphysical chaos, however, is to ignore the novel's heavily satirical thrust, and most commentators have in fact revealed an awareness that the book's concerns are predominantly moral. What has yet to be revealed is how the novel's absurdities—comic and otherwise—operate almost always to expose the alarming inhumanities which pollute our political, social, and economic system. That is, what now needs most to be explained is how Heller's widely unorthodox fictional methods, routinely interpreted as the technical corollary of his absurdist vision, are also the vehicle for his largely traditional, even orthodox, moral satire. This satire can best be seen as a blistering attack on our capitalistic system, a system that has perverted universally accepted ethic norms by unwittingly encouraging the unscrupulous pursuit of wealth and power.

James Nagel—editor of one of the three critical casebooks available on this obviously seminal piece of contemporary fiction—notes in reviewing the immense body of scholarship already surrounding the novel that many critics have viewed "absurdity," "morality," or "sanity" as the book's essential motif. But considering the patently irrational atmosphere of the book, he seems to regard as unlikely the possibility of ever defining these terms adequately.[2] Granted, the action of the narrative does manage to subvert thoroughly the three concepts, but as long as such irrationality is presented from a viewpoint which is itself rational—a perspective detached and judicious—defining "absurdity," "sanity," and "morality" should be feasible enough. The key is to approach the novel's absurdity not in broad metaphysical terms but in specific moral ones, since the book carries its greatest impact at the moral level; and Heller, despite his appreciation of universal chaos, does acknowledge certain ethical norms. The ultimate horror of the phrase "Catch-22," for instance, is felt when Yossarian hears it, as though a knell, from the lips of the miserably bereft old woman in the Roman brothel. And the words are horrible not because they connote a world in chaos but because they indicate that the system controlling the military is morally mad. The horror of such recognition can only be increased once the reader realizes that this insane system rules far more than wartime behavior. Several writers have by now argued that the novel is not basically about

World War II at all, and even Heller has pointedly remarked: "I deliberately seeded the book with anachronisms like loyalty oaths, helicopters, IBM machines and agricultural subsidies to create the feeling of American society from the McCarthy period on."[3] Elsewhere the author has expressed his agreement with columnist Murray Kempton's observation that the book's morality is so orthodox as to be "almost medieval," adding reflectively: "I suppose just about everybody accepts certain principles of morality."[4]

What all this is meant to suggest is that the morality which informs *Catch-22* is not problematical but almost commonsensical. Its moral commitments are hardly more difficult to discern than conventional allegory, and it is surely significant that Heller himself has referred to the novel as a combination of allegory and realism — a strong indication that the book's absurdity was conceived from the start as a *moral* absurdity.[5] Moreover, as the title of this article attempts to point out, this absurdity is a product not of immorality but of what might be called "moral insanity": a curiously innocent perversion of reason so total as to blind the actor from any meaningful recognition of the moral components of his (or anybody else's) behavior. The title is also meant to suggest that the book does not revolve around problems relating *either* to absurdity, or morality, or sanity, but to all three of these subjects together, as they form humanity's gravest obstacle to intelligent, scrupulous living — in peace as well as in war. And here once again such an outlook has been anticipated not so much by previous critics as by the author, whose many comments on the novel have provided this study with its strongest extratextual support. In one early interview following the book's publication, Heller described *Catch-22* as "a moral book dealing with man's moral dilemma. People can't distinguish between rational and irrational behavior, between the moral and the immoral. . . . It's insane. . . ."[6]

The novel is, if anything, overloaded with examples of moral and rational disability. Lieutenant Scheisskopf lodges imaginary complaints against Clevinger and then, as a member of his Action Board, simultaneously performs the roles of judge, prosecutor, and defending officer. Colonel Cathcart and Colonel Korn criticize Yossarian for his delinquency in twice flying over a bridge at Ferrara on a single mission, not because the desperately successful maneuver unfortunately caused the death of Kraft and his crew — for such a concern the morally insane Cathcart can see only as "sentimental" — but because it will look "lousy" in the report that must be filed with Headquarters.[7] The solution to the problem is Korn's, and it is perfectly calculated to satisfy the moral insanity of the reigning bureaucracy. In Korn's mind, giving Yossarian a medal might be the wisest thing to do, since "a trick that never seems to fail" is "to act boastfully about something we ought to be ashamed of" (143). And because "it's best to play safe" (144), Korn also convinces Cathcart, his superior officer, to file a request that Yossarian be promoted to captain for his unconventional conduct. The promotion, needless to say, is granted.

Of all the characters exemplifying moral insanity in the novel, by far the most prominent of them is the incredibly manipulative black market entrepreneur Milo Minderbinder, the squadron's mess officer. Yet despite the overflow of commentary on the novel, no one has provided a thorough analysis of his character or thematic purpose. This is particularly surprising since Heller has described the book as fundamentally not about the second world war but "the contemporary regimented business society"[8] — and Milo is undoubtedly the most striking and significant representative of that society. This is hardly to say that Milo's role has been overlooked, for while critics have generally given him scant attention as compared to Yossarian, the book's hero, they have in most cases identified his narrative function accurately. They have, among other things, appreciated (or rather damned) him as a "caricature of the American businessman," as embodying "the whole mystique of corporation capitalism," as "the mythic hero of organized greed — of unregulated free enterprise," as "capitalist free-enterprise run amok," as "the symbol of American business and western world capitalism," as "a myopic encapsulation of the Madison Avenue mentality," and as representing "untrammeled private enterprise, a utilitarian business ethic, and the entire moral superstructure of American capitalism itself."[9]

If it can be comfortably asserted that *Catch-22* is a novel harshly critical of our controlling institutions and that the book's absurdity is practically indistinguishable from its satire, then Milo — by forming the bull's eye of the author's satirical targets — deserves to be viewed as quite as important as the more sympathetic protagonist, Yossarian. And perhaps one of the crucial ironies of the book is that Milo is in some ways scarcely less sympathetic than his fellow officer. Although Heller's negative estimate of Milo's mercenary character is never really in question, he does take pains — even while attacking him — to create in the reader a certain qualified positive regard for him. When Yossarian looks distrustingly at Milo early in the novel, we are told: "He saw a simple, sincere face that was incapable of subtlety or guile, an honest, frank face . . . the face of a man of hardened integrity" (65, 66). And Milo's "hardened integrity" — however repellent it may finally be — is real enough. He may sell cigarette lighters, as does Ex-P.F.C. Wintergreen, but whereas Wintergreen's lighters are pilfered from the quartermaster, the lighters which Milo offers for sale — though they may have been obtained deviously — are never stolen outright. He may collaborate with the Germans to defend a bridge against an American attack (an attack which, bizarrely, represents a business deal made with American authorities), but the author must still concede that "the arrangements were fair to both sides" (261). And while he is not above bribery if his Enterprises require it, he confides to Yossarian that he cannot feel safe among people who accept bribes, for "they're no better than a bunch of crooks" (273).

As self-serving and hypocritical as Milo's sentiments may be, there is no doubting their sincerity, so that we cannot dismiss as mere sarcasm Heller's description of his eyes as "liquid with integrity" or his face as "artless and uncorrupted" (263). The problem is that such integrity is completely at the service of moral ideals that cannot, in all sanity, be understood as anything *but* corrupt. As Heller puts it, Milo "could no more consciously violate the moral principles on which his virtue rested than he could transform himself into a despicable toad. One of these moral principles was that it was never a sin to charge as much as the traffic would bear" (66). Another one of Milo's principles is that business contracts must be honored at all costs. And while this may necessitate his purchasing vastly more cotton than he can dispose of (since as a novice in the commodities market he once bought up the entire Egyptian cotton crop), his sacred pledge of allegiance to contracts generally redounds to his fortune — and to the misfortune of everyone else. He defensively argues that the Germans, "members in good standing of the syndicate" over which he presides, are not really enemies, and that he is thus obligated to "represent the sanctity" of his contracts with them (263). But it is he himself who arranges and mercilessly executes the tremendously profitable deal with the Germans to bomb and strafe his own base. And he is able to commit this cold-blooded atrocity with a clear conscience, for he desperately needs more funds to continue buying all the cotton called for in his other inviolable contract. Human impediments are not merely obscured by his morally insane business ethic — they disappear altogether.

Milo also believes in loyalty to his squadron; and Heller, in his heaviest satirical vein, has him pompously rebuke Yossarian late in the novel for his refusal to fly more missions for the insatiable Cathcart. We are told that Milo "shook his head reproachfully and, with pious lips pursed, informed Yossarian in ecclesiastical tones that he was ashamed of him" (413). Such indignation not only points toward Milo's utter insensitivity to death, but anticipates Yossarian's devastating attack on the military police in Rome four pages later. Inspecting with despair the wanton destruction of the whores' apartment in Rome, Yossarian pictures "the fiery and malicious exhilaration with which they made their wreckage, and their sanctimonious, ruthless sense of right and dedication" (417). Milo's own dedication to his country, however, runs a distant second to his devotion to unbridled private enterprise. He has in fact argued earlier that the squadron should be loyal enough to his syndicate to buy its cotton "till it hurts so that they can keep right on buying my cotton till it hurts them some more" — one more indication that his total absorption with monetary gain has dispossessed him of all empathy. He has firmly convinced himself that for the syndicate's well-being the men should be willing to risk theirs and consume his urgently concocted chocolate-covered cotton — even though, as Yossarian wearily pleads with him, "People can't eat cotton" (271). Heller's absurdist brand of allegory should be clear enough: Milo's ruthlessly capitalistic commitments do not, and cannot, support life.

The syndicate that is M & M Enterprises appears at last to be mostly illusory. Milo may proclaim over and over again that "I don't make the profit. The syndicate makes the profit. And everybody has a share" (236). But inevitably the point must arrive at which everybody's having a share is tantamount to nobody's having a share — nobody, that is, but Milo, who is shown throughout as in complete control of the syndicate's multifarious operations. The myth, or meaninglessness, of well-nigh universal ownership is most pointedly suggested in the scene with the rebelliously skeptical Major from Minnesota, who confronts Milo demanding his share of the syndicate. Milo responds to the challenge "by writing the words 'A Share' on the nearest scrap of paper and handing it away with a virtuous disdain" (378). Milo's self-righteous contempt for the Major suggests in turn that he conceives of business as something like a bond that never reaches — nor is *intended* to reach — maturity: it exists for its own compulsive sake and all its profits, like interest payments, go directly back into its ever-expanding self. Heller seems to understand keenly the morally vicious cycle that has so often characterized the heartless striving after material riches. Anything derived from such thorough displacement of feeling is more symbolic than real, so that the final taste of success can be no more savory, or sustaining, than Milo's chocolate-covered cotton.

Despite Milo's self-deceiving protestations that "what's good for the syndicate is good for the country" (238) — a deliberate parody of Charles E. Wilson's famous statement about General Motors — Heller unequivocally demonstrates that Milo's syndicate is basically antagonistic toward his country, and that loyalty to private enterprise and loyalty to one's government are irresistibly opposed. Milo himself remains innocently unaware of this adversative relationship since one of his unquestioned assumptions is that the whole reason for government is to promote such capitalistic undertakings as M & M Enterprises. Such thinking explains how he can consistently act against the government and yet maintain his conviction that his acts serve the country's best interests. For his acts are always within the bounds of the law, and he actually perceives legal loopholes as benign sanctions to encourage creative business ventures. Heller refers to his "rigid scruples that would not even allow him to borrow a package of pitted dates . . . for the food at the mess hall was all still the property of the government" (67). But he nonetheless feels completely at liberty to borrow a package from Yossarian in order to make a profit for himself — or rather for the syndicate, whose continuing growth is the sole criterion dreamt of in his philosophy.

It is obvious that his "rigid scruples" compel him to obey strictly the letter of the law but permit him utterly to disregard the law's spirit. Thus his informing Yossarian, "with a faint glimmer of mischief," that he has "a sure-fire plan for cheating the federal government out of six thousand dollars" (239) does not contradict his expressed obedience to the law, since his venture, we may assume, is not illegal but ingeniously exploitative of legality. He is able to confide in Yossarian because, as Heller very suggestively has had him reflect earlier, "anyone who would not steal from the country he loved would not steal from anybody" (64). By the same token, however, Yossarian's genuine respect for his nation's ideals guarantees his instant dismissal of Milo's offer to make him a partner in his machinations. Milo's legally shrewd (but morally obtuse) mind is also blatantly evident in his rationalizing to the detached Yossarian — throughout the novel Milo's foil and the moral yardstick that enables us to measure his essential dishonesty — that although "bribery is against the law . . . it's not against the law to make a profit. . . . So it can't be against the law for me to bribe someone in order to make a fair [read, "whatever-the-market-will-bear"] profit . . ." (272).

Because, psychologically, Milo's dominant need is to control reality, to bend it to his unruly ego, it follows that he will be opposed to anything that threatens to limit that control. Governmental restraints have always been set on free enterprise, so that Milo, at the same time that he perceives his financial opportunism as licensed by his country's capitalistic ethic, cannot but acknowledge the power of government to restrict his commercial ventures, or to prohibit them altogether. Consequently, his enlarging the scope of his operations to include not only the trading of foodstuffs but the bombing of enemy targets — the enemy determined simply by the country contracting for the bombing — indicates that for Milo the war is actually against government itself. For to Milo the ultimate cause is not freedom but free enterprise, and the battle will be finally won only when war too is controlled not by government but by industrious individuals like himself. When war becomes but one more business to be manipulated by the enterprising, Milo's control of reality — or rather his fantasy of such control — will be complete. As crazy, or morally insane, as this characterization of Milo's unarticulated delusions may seem, it is a reading that derives naturally from Milo's expressed sentiments. After contracting with both American and German authorities to attack — and defend — the German-held bridge at Orvieto, the self-congratulatory Milo explains that "the consummation of these deals represented an important victory for private enterprise . . . since the armies of both countries were socialized institutions" (261).

While such thinking suggests not only Milo's moral myopia but his derangement as well, in the mentally and morally unbalanced world of the novel it escapes condemnation. We learn, for instance, that when Milo raids his own squadron for the Germans the public uproar is stilled once he discloses the enormous profits earned in the deal for the syndicate and convinces everyone "that bombing his own men and planes had therefore really been a commendable and very lucrative blow on the side of private enterprise" (219). Since, as Heller sees it, virtually everyone today needs desperately to believe that he has not been left out — that it is no myth that he owns a share, has a piece of the action, and profits as GM profits — Milo's heinous crimes (and he is quite literally an enemy of the people) are easily enough

rationalized as heroic. Here again an action — and reaction — that is realistically incredible or absurd can be seen as a figuratively — and frighteningly — accurate picture of a people profoundly alienated from a government grown so vast and impersonal as to make them feel powerless. As morally insane as Milo obviously is, his sentiments express those of millions of his
countrymen, who rebelliously, yet somehow innocently, crave membership
in an organization so large and potent as to be beyond the control of the
law. Such "quiet desperation" is betrayed by the public's appallingly un-
critical lionization of Milo and his ruthless exploits. And the painful irony
and ultimate self-victimization of such moral viciousness is poignantly suggested by the author himself, who has commented:

> . . . the content of the book really derives from our present atmosphere,
> which is one of chaos, of disorganization, of absurdity, of cruelty, of bru-
> tality, of insensitivity, but at the same time one in which people, even the
> worst people, I think are basically good, are motivated by humane im-
> pulses.[10]

Since Milo's perverted idealism makes him deplore governmental regu-
lation of business and its virtual "monopolization" of war, it is no surprise
that after attacking his own base he decides not to reimburse his country for
its losses. His hypocritical argument is that since "in a democracy, the government is the people . . . we might just as well keep the money and eliminate the middleman." Then, shifting his rhetorical ground so suddenly that
his glaring self-contradictions may be conveniently overlooked by everyone, he adds:

> Frankly, I'd like to see the government get out of war altogether and leave
> the whole field to private industry. If we pay the government everything
> we owe it, we'll only be encouraging government control and discourag-
> ing other individuals from bombing their own men and planes. We'll be
> taking away their incentive. [266]

This absurd laissez-faire attitude is responsible for Milo's "hawkish" stance
on war, which derives not from any political ideals but from purely economic concerns. War *is* profitable to private industry, and Milo has no desire to see it end. When it suits his purpose, he may profess that he is "willing
to do everything [he can] to win the war" (414), but the pretense and self-
deception of his words is demonstrated by his negotiations calculated ex-
pressly to prolong the combat as long as strategically possible. Heller writes,
for example, of his "selling petroleum and ball bearings to Germany at good
prices in order to make a good profit and help maintain a balance of power
between the contending forces" (377).

Milo's childishly naive conception of his world as something to be manipulated for the best possible gain is of course at the heart of his moral
insanity. And Heller allows the reader no doubt that the radically self-
centered ethic which makes Milo so contemptible is representative — how-

ever hyperbolically—of our culture. Surely it is no coincidence that the author has General Peckem state: "People have a right to do anything that's not forbidden by law" (330) and Doc Daneeka defensively proclaim: "There's nothing wrong with greed" (358). That through the course of American history the ideal of freedom should have become so corrupted as to be popularly construed to mean the right to do anything and everything not strictly prohibited by law is perhaps the deepest tragedy of the book. Yossarian's harsh indictment of the monstrously "principled" opportunism that has too often been the consequence of a capitalistic ethic is eloquently expressed at the novel's conclusion when he observes: "When I look up, I see people cashing in. I don't see heavens or saints or angels. I see people cashing in on every decent impulse and every human tragedy" (455). Milo, mercilessly "cashing in" on the war itself, is the all-too-human predator of good will and bad fortune who best exemplifies Yossarian's profoundly discouraged estimate. It is Milo who tries to persuade him to swallow non-edible cotton, as it is Milo who robs his planes of the carbon dioxide for the life jackets, and their marketable parachutes and medical supplies. And in every instance, Milo's treachery had been innocently motivated by the one principle in which all his mistaken faith resides: namely, "what's good for M & M Enterprises. . . ." The essential falseness of this principle is evident from the falseness of the syndicate's title, since the "&" in "M & M" has been inserted by Milo to avoid the impression that the operation is that of a single individual. But conjunction or not, the abbreviation still spells out to "Milo and Minderbinder" and points, however deviously, to individual ownership and control.

Since Milo's acts are so corrupt, it is only natural to infer that given his popularity and power he is responsible for corrupting others. In fact, the name "Minderbinder" may possibly have been contrived to suggest Milo's amazing "binding of minds" through his steady deluge of self-serving capitalistic rhetoric. It is safest to conclude, however, that Milo does little more than supply the rationalization for his followers' own selfish endeavors to fulfill purely personal ends, and that both Milo and his admirers are best understood as products of a system which has itself corrupted them. For it is the system that has somehow fostered their belief that as free citizens their birthright, indeed their very duty, is competitively to pursue individual interests at every opportunity. Milo merely succeeds in tempting those he deals with to follow inclinations inherited from their culture anyway. Very early in his enterprises, he is able to talk Major —— de Coverly into furnishing him with a plane and pilot to purchase eggs from Malta and butter from Sicily because the Major himself admits to a weakness for fresh eggs and butter. Given the infantile self-indulgence of so many of Heller's characters, the sequel to this action is only to be expected:

> Then the other three squadrons in Colonel Cathcart's group turned their
> mess halls over to Milo and gave him an airplane and a pilot each so that he

could buy fresh eggs and fresh butter for them too. Milo's planes shuttled back and forth seven days a week as every officer in the four squadrons began devouring fresh eggs in an insatiable orgy of fresh-egg eating. [140]

So that this highly specialized egg orgy should not exhaust itself and thereby reduce his influence over the officers, Milo locates plentiful sources for "fresh veal, beef, duck, baby lamb chops, mushroom caps, broccoli, South African rock lobster tails, shrimp, hams, puddings, grapes, ice cream, strawberries and artichokes" (140). His remarkable success in appealing to the officers' oral drives in fact points to their generally infantile stage of development — moral as well as psychological — and hints at their almost total lack of fellow feeling. The widespread passion for eating and obtaining food in the novel seems to have displaced the traditional desire for love and family. At one isolated point we learn that Milo is actually married and has a family, but it is clear that Milo's mind and heart exist elsewhere. The author remarks that "in the spring Milo Minderbinder's fancy . . . lightly turned to thoughts of tangerines" (257), and Milo himself glibly translates the language of parental love to livestock when he describes his black market lamb chops as dressed "in the cutest little pink paper panties you ever saw" (258).

The ultimate hazards posed by Milo's simple-minded transference of interest from people to profit are alluded to by Heller, who has commented of Milo's psychodynamics: "I gave him a mental and moral simplicity that, to my mind, makes him a horrifyingly dangerous person, because he lacks evil intent."[11] Milo's "mental and moral simplicity" enables him to find easy justifications for everything he is impelled to do, so that while his acts may frequently appear hypocritical or deceitful, they are nonetheless executed sincerely and with moral courage. However morally insane his conduct may seem — and however satirically Heller may present it — it always reflects the "purity" of his deeply felt principles:

> With a devotion to purpose above and beyond the line of duty, he . . . raised the price of food in his mess halls so high that all the officers and enlisted men had to turn over all their pay to him in order to eat. Their alternative — there was an alternative, of course, since Milo detested coercion and was a vocal champion of freedom of choice — was to starve. When he encountered a wave of enemy resistance to this attack, he stuck to his position without regard for his safety or reputation and gallantly invoked the law of supply and demand. And when someone somewhere said no, Milo gave ground grudgingly, valiantly defending, even in retreat, the historic right of free men to pay as much as they had to for the things they needed in order to survive. [377]

Such morally perverted reasoning occurs throughout the novel, and it should be recognized that Heller does not at all limit it to Milo. Doc Daneeka lies outrageously to the government in a desperate bid to escape military service, and when inevitably he is found out can only lament that "even the word of a licensed physician is suspected by the country he loves" (41). Chief White Halfoat inveighs against racial prejudice and then adds self-righteously that "it's a terrible thing to treat a decent, loyal Indian like a nigger, kike, wop or spic" (45). And Colonel Cathcart, after making a wholly unscrupulous deal with the glory-hungry Milo to credit him with missions that the other men must fly for him, responds to the mess officer's request that his friend Yossarian be spared from such missions with genuine shock: "Oh, no Milo. . . . We must never play favorites. We must always treat every man alike" (384).

The absurd self-deceptiveness and even the flagrant hypocrisy manifest in these and numerous other incidents, point, though with consummate irony, to the basically "good heart" of Heller's morally mad characters. Moreover, as incredibly callous as Doc Daneeka is portrayed, when his base is bombed (compliments of M & M Enterprises), he freely places his life in peril and works himself to exhaustion striving to save as many lives as possible. As criminally insensitive as Colonel Cathcart is, when General Dreedle is on the verge of having Major Danby shot for an imagined offense, Cathcart yearns to comfort the terrified Major—though he refrains from doing so because he fears looking "like a sissy" (228). Milo's good will is evident in several places, though his finally brutal economic commitments regularly subvert his benign intentions. When Yossarian implores his assistance in locating Nately's whore's defenseless kid sister in Rome, he readily agrees to help and is so moved by the nobility of Yossarian's disinterested search as to exclaim: ". . . we'll find that girl if we have to turn this whole city upside down" (419). Later Milo abandons Yossarian at police headquarters when he accidentally learns of the huge profits to be made in smuggling tobacco; but the author makes it difficult to condemn him, emphasizing that the prospect of such a lucrative venture actually leaves Milo defenseless himself, "as though he were in the grip of a blind fixation, burning feverishly, and his twitching mouth slavering" (420). The passion or "lust" described here is, of course, greed, but since Milo is pictured more as its helpless victim than as its god, and since he is not without attractive personal traits, it is hard to withhold all sympathy from him. Heller himself has spoken of Milo as acting "out of the goodness of his heart" and admitted: "Yossarian is actually fond of Milo, and I am too, as an individual. There's a certain purity of purpose about him."[12]

Still Heller is careful to identify Milo as the one character in the book who "does the most damage."[13] For while Milo's motives may be untainted and his heart undefiled, his conscience—thoroughly pledged to the profit principle dominant in our age—is totally corrupt, compelling him to commit acts cruel and harmful to humanity. Such is the nature of Milo's absurd innocence: a finally pathetic moral deformity that must be judged culpable because of the serious threats it poses to the peace, freedom, happiness, and even the lives of others. Generally the most understanding critical assessment of Milo is one by Wayne Charles Miller:

Milo is not an insidious and conniving power-hungry fascist. In fact, it is testament to Heller's genius that he could create a figure simultaneously so innocent and so destructive as his representative of American business values and perhaps capitalism itself. Milo is frightening precisely because he is such a perfect product of the culture. Industrious, competent, pleasant, engaging, sexually moral or perhaps sexless, he is destined for success. In fact, Milo is the kind of son that most American parents wish their boys to be. . . .[14]

If, then, Milo is not simply a bad seed, it is clearly his culture that has warped his moral growth. The author writes of his "disunited eyes," which "could see more things than most people, but . . . could see none of them too distinctly" (66); and this obviously symbolic description intimates that Milo's vision is hopelessly defective, that he is unable to distinguish between serving his country and exploiting it. A similar situation obtains with the syndicate: he idealistically envisions it as affirming humanity (since "everyone has a share") at the same time that his bedazzled commitment to it leads him systematically to trample on the rights of others. The only standard by which he is equipped to appraise action is monetary, so that his preternaturally shrewd business sense is matched by a moral sense so obtuse, so astoundingly irrational and unaware, that finally we can see it only as insane. Because Milo literally lacks the perspective to see his world whole, or to decipher the moral dimensions of his conduct, blaming him for his perverse adherence to short-sighted morally reprehensible principles may be a little like blaming a deaf man for not listening to what is said to him. Milo's principles do not *prohibit* fellow feeling or empathy, nor is Heller's testifying to his "good heart" a gratuitous assertion. Yet Milo's emotional priorities are such that his genuine compassion for humanity is always overwhelmed by his humanly monstrous passion for money. For example, when he is informed by Yossarian that the funeral he is witnessing is Snowden's, this is his reaction:

"That's terrible," Milo grieved, and his large brown eyes filled with tears. "That poor kid. It really is terrible." He bit his trembling lip hard, and his voice rose with emotion when he continued. "And it will get even worse if the mess halls don't agree to buy my cotton." [270]

This crucial deficiency of feeling is evidenced throughout the novel, and it is most exasperating as it reveals Milo's almost complete absence of moral responsibility, which allows him to contract with the enemy for the deaths of his own men without experiencing the slightest pangs of conscience. For, as he rationalizes to Yossarian, what he undertook for the Germans would have been undertaken anyway; and besides, his business deals with them are very profitable for the syndicate, of which Yossarian himself owns a share. Milo's enduring belief that he is innocent of the deaths for which he has, however unwittingly, made himself morally responsible, underlies his self-righteous protests that he did not start the war, that he is "just trying to put it on a businesslike basis." His absolute denial of any complicity with evil comes in his ensuing question: "Is anything wrong with that?" (262), and suggests a conviction of guiltlessness, or even moral superiority, that perhaps only the most guilty may be capable of feeling.

If Milo's finally culpable innocence stems from his relating to all things as commodities, so does his rampant opportunism — and in the end these two predilections are practically indistinguishable. Together they account for Milo's extraordinary accomplishments as a businessman. Because the author pessimistically views the world as one "in which success was the only virtue" (274), it is no wonder that Milo, the great entrepreneur, becomes something of a world idol in the novel. Stimulating business around the globe, a veritable high priest of commerce, he becomes almost everybody's hero and is showered with adoration and political titles. In one especially parodic chapter, "Milo the Mayor," we learn that in recognition of his having brought the Scotch trade to Sicily he has been elected Mayor of Palermo, Carini, Monreale, Bagheria, Termini Imerese, Cefali, Mistretta, and Nicosia; that for bringing the egg trade to Malta he has been named its Assistant Governor-General; that he is Vice-Shah of Oran, Caliph of Baghdad, Imam of Damascus, and Sheik of Araby; and that in parts of Africa he is the reigning corn god, rain god, and rice god. In America, Milo fares equally well, being a paragon of corporate know-how and success. The thinly veiled acerbity of Heller's satire against the almost universal acceptance of free enterprise and the inhumane values so carelessly authorized by it is conspicuous in the lines: "Milo had been caught red-handed in the act of plundering his countrymen, and, as a result, his stock had never been higher" (378). The admiration and respect accorded him betrays the American worship of material success over all else and its need to identify with individual accomplishment by assiduously cultivating the illusion — created initially by the business tycoons themselves — that "everyone has a share" and that "what's good for M & M Enterprises is good for the country." Heller finds various ways of generalizing this heedless pursuit of material well-being, just one of them being Nurse Duckett's casual abandonment of Yossarian because she "had decided to marry a doctor — any doctor, because they all did so well in business . . ." (372).

Exemplifying in caricature form the monetary drives of most of the populace, Milo is driven by the same socially divisive but culturally endorsed quest for wealth and power. He is therefore not identifiable in the novelistic context either as amoral or immoral. For his morality, rooted firmly in the laws of modern economics, does not really run counter to that of his culture. The crucial point is that Milo is moral according to the absurd, morally insane, standards which prevail; but viewed from any traditional set of ethical norms he is corrupt — exactly as corrupt as the culture whose unofficial but universally practiced ethic he embodies and whose madly utilitarian vindication of his lucrative but literally murderous bombing of his own base carries its own condemnation. If Milo's country allows such outrageous misbehavior to go unpunished (and Heller has admitted that its doing so can only be understood allegorically[15]), it is because Milo's acts are in essential conformity with his country's institutional framework. Its gross insensitivity to the lives of its average citizens is an outcome of its wildly discriminatory power structure.

Again, the evil that Milo and others depict is not the result of something peculiarly sinister about them but the outcome of their lacking what in the novel is referred to as "character," a deficit that allows them to take advantage of their bureaucratic positions to pursue worldly success as their culture implicitly advocates. If they pervert the original meaning of freedom, it is because the capitalistic system to which they owe their greatest allegiance has in its evolution *already* perverted it. All they have done has been to react with "moral and mental simplicity" (i.e., innocently) to its apparent message and, in a most "democratic" spirit, compete relentlessly to achieve more than their fellow man.

Such opportunism stems from a curiously willful innocence and grows into the full-fledged moral insanity that best defines the absurdity everywhere present in *Catch-22*. It is a world in which even the dull Major Major eventually learns that, practically, sinning and lying are good for him. Such an insight does not really come as a surprise, we are told, "for he had observed that people who did lie were, on the whole, more resourceful and ambitious and successful than people who did not lie" (100). Much later in the novel the singularly virtuous chaplain must admit, after he has told his first lie, that the results are "wonderful." Deliberately parodying Genesis in language identical to that used to describe Major Major's unholy discovery, Heller writes, "The chaplain had sinned, and it was good," adding in a now famous passage:

> . . . everyone knew that sin was evil and that no good could come from evil. But he did feel good; he felt positively marvelous. Consequently, it followed logically that telling lies and defecting from duty could not be sins. The chaplain had mastered, in a moment of divine intuition, the handy technique of protective rationalization. . . . It was almost no trick at all, he saw, to turn vice into virtue and slander into truth, impotence into abstinence, arrogance into humility, plunder into philanthropy, thievery into honor, blasphemy into wisdom, brutality into patriotism, and sadism into justice. Anybody could do it; it required no brains at all. It merely required no character. [372]

While the chaplain has enough character to resist giving way to his demonic conclusions, events quickly make him realize just how widely the military bureaucracy has been seduced — or rather, corrupted — by them. In one of the novel's most terrifying scenes, he is taken to a cellar and brutally questioned by a group of officers about violations he has not committed. His interrogators "handily" find him guilty of everything they charge him with, including "crimes and infractions" which, they readily confess, they "don't even know about yet" (395). After this travesty of justice is completed, the chaplain's alarm is replaced by "overwhelming moral outrage" (396); and more daring than ever before, he confronts Colonel Korn with his righteous protests — only, once again, to be confounded by the "immoral logic" (397) of the colonel's unfeeling response.

This "immoral logic" is clearly the logic of opportunism, and it consists of all the "protective rationalizations" that hopelessly pervert all meaningful moral standards. The moral insanity that results from such reasoning is abundantly evident throughout the book, and it is perhaps most blatant in Korn's incongruous reasoning with Yossarian at the end of the novel, when he and Cathcart craftily attempt to remove the threat to their authority created by the bombardier's insubordination by returning him home a hero. Korn offhandedly discloses to Yossarian that his not really deserving to be exempted from further combat is one of the reasons he does not mind exempting him. Similarly insane is Cathcart's rationalization for raising the men's missions: the pilot McWatt's accidental mutilation of Kid Sampson and McWatt's own consequent suicide. And so, of course, is his raising them again once he learns from an official flight form that Doc Daneeka has been on board the fated plane. The fact that Doc Daneeka has not actually been on the flight does not affect the colonel's decision, for the written document is all his debased moral sense requires to justify his determination to make his men fly more missions than anyone else, in the hope of attaining the professional advancement he craves. His thinking, however moral he may self-deceptively consider it, is purely opportunistic and closely resembles that of the power-seeking Captain Black, whose "Glorious Loyalty Oath Crusade" is motivated not by any genuine patriotic feeling (despite what the Captain himself might think) but by the desire to become "a man of real consequence" (121) in the squadron and maybe even replace Major Major (who is not permitted to sign the oaths) as squadron commander.

The crowning symbol of all this uncontrolled opportunism is "Catch-22," which is most meaningfully defined by the forsaken old woman in Rome, who tells Yossarian (echoing the old "might makes right" idea) that "Catch-22 says they [here specifically the MP's but in essence most people everywhere] have a right to do anything we can't stop them from doing" (416). In this late scene we learn that Catch-22 is not merely the label for all the morally crazy double binds in the novel but the summary explanation of these binds — namely, that to achieve recognition, assert power, or attain wealth most people can, and will, do almost anything they think they can get away with doing. Given any social, political, or economic system designed primarily to safeguard individualism and only secondarily to safeguard individuals, moral chaos must be the result. The horrible irony of this situation is that this humanly unaccountable law of opportunism was never intended as a law at all, was never meant by those who founded government, particularly *our* government, to become a national creed. Yossarian reveals an awareness of this tragic misinterpretation of the nation's original purpose in his pained reflection that "Catch-22 did not exist . . . but it made no difference. What did matter was that everyone thought it existed, and that was much worse . . ." (418). Yossarian has a glimpse of the awful truth which is Catch-22: not only that a corrupt American officialdom has been confused with America but that the entire nation is helplessly victimized by accepting as official, written law all the unscrupulous power ploys that seem sanctioned by a democratic government. Or, to put it somewhat differently, unwritten loopholes in the laws have become confused with the laws themselves, enabling those in positions of authority to trespass freely on the rights of others. In addition, "freedom from" has been misconstrued as "freedom to," so that almost everyone regards himself as "bound" to be in opposition to everyone else in pursuing life, liberty, and happiness.

Such a circumstance accounts for the fact that the real enemy in the novel is not the other side but our own. General Peckem's remarks that "Dreedle's on our side, and Dreedle *is* the enemy" and that "General Dreedle commands four bomb groups that we simply must capture in order to continue our offensive" (332) sharply expose the destructive competitiveness that identifies us as a country fundamentally at war with ourselves. Quite literally in the novel, we are our own worst enemy. Milo's freely appropriating the morphine from the squadron's planes to market it as he deems fit provides further symbolic testimony of how individualism, degraded in practice to mere opportunism, can only increase our suffering.

It should be stressed that the object of Heller's attack is not America per se but those people whose greedy exploitation of it compromises the peace and freedom of others — though, to be sure, this distinction is at times extremely difficult to maintain. For those who control our various systems and institutions ultimately make our country what it is. Still, both Heller and Yossarian insist on the distinction; and it is right that they do so. When Colonel Korn asks Yossarian, "Won't you fight for your country? . . . Won't you give up your life for Colonel Cathcart and me?" Yossarian shows his final comprehension of all that has transpired by retorting: "What have you and Colonel Cathcart got to do with my country? You're not the same" (433). However indirectly, this climactic scene has been anticipated almost from the very beginning when the author, speaking in his own voice, notes: "All over the world, boys on every side of the bomb line were laying down their lives for *what they had been told* [emphasis added] was their country . . ." (16).

Catch-22 itself is not intended to symbolize America but what those in command have reduced it to. And it is the moral wickedness which Catch-22 stands for that constitutes the greatest threat to Yossarian's existence. Most significantly, it is Catch-22 that forces him to go on flying missions after he should have been recognized as fulfilling his obligations. At one point, Doc Daneeka tells Yossarian that "Catch-22 . . . says you've always got to do what your commanding officer tells you to." And when Yossarian protests that Twenty-Seventh Air Force Headquarters states that he can go home after forty missions (he now has forty-eight), Doc Daneeka counters irresistibly: "But they don't say you have to go home. And regulations do say you have to obey every order. That's the catch" (60). At another point, Yossarian gets Doc Daneeka to concede that if he fills out a medical form testifying to his unfitness he can have him removed from combat status. But once again Catch-22 renders this action worthless since Group must approve the form and, as Doc Daneeka very well knows, "Group isn't going to" (179). Yossarian is effectively stripped of all his rights not so much by the law as by a bureaucratic system that is at base totalitarian. In this system all men are not created equal, so that Yossarian is in fact a captive held by his own side. That the higher authority to which he must submit is as immoral as it is irrational is shown by the fact that he is kept on active combat status even when replacements for him are readily available and the Allies are virtually assured of victory.

The deviousness of the peremptory nonlaw which is Catch-22 is best suggested by the "innocently" authoritative Milo. For Milo's specifically economic ideals are at bottom almost synonymous with the ideals of all the other systems attacked in the novel. His charging whatever the traffic will bear for his goods and services (in the name of free enterprise) is hardly different, for example, from Cathcart's endlessly raising the number of missions his men must fly (in the name of patriotism). The true motive in each case is opportunism, or, on a more basic level, the need or compulsion to assert one's will over others. And the sanction for such tyrannical assertion is Catch-22, since in essence it *means* the right to do whatever one can manage to do with impunity. When Milo tells Yossarian that "he was jeopardizing his traditional rights of freedom and independence by daring to exercise them" (414), the context suggests that Milo's hypocritical warning is inspired by his subliminal awareness that should Yossarian continue to revolt by, ironically, affirming his rights — and prompt others to follow him — the system itself, of which Milo is metaphorically the leader, would crumble. To survive, the system depends on the cooperation of the oppressed with the oppressors, and once the oppressed remonstrate against the Catch-22 framework which dehumanizes them, the system — supported by the most tenuous legal foundations in any case — cannot but disintegrate. But Heller, a most sober realist, really has no such expectations that Catch-22's supremacy will ever be effectively challenged, for so long as the masses never recognize its existence as a fabrication of ambitious individuals to achieve and preserve personal power, they must remain impotent to resist its dubious authority.

Dr. Stubbs, one of the novel's most positively handled characters, says of Yossarian: "That crazy bastard may be the only sane one left" (114), and his paradoxical appraisal helps point out Yossarian's difficulties. Because Yossarian refuses to submit, robotlike, to the system and persists in his efforts to defy it, he is perceivable as insane, incapable of adapting to the social and moral norms of his time. But because he alone seems capable of appreciating the sanctity of life and its desecration by all the spiritually void authorities who would gratuitously rob him of it, he is ultimately to be perceived as the novel's "hero" of sanity. He has, however, little in common with the traditional hero, since while he may offer minor frustrations to the enemy (the villain-system of opportunism) he cannot begin to alter its morally insane structure. His only alternative, then, is not to fight but to flee, and the novel's romantic-realistic conclusion attests to Yossarian's unvanquishable humanity — as well as to the tragic untenability of this humanity. But although his impassioned effort to leave all the Milo's of the modern world behind him and locate an area where sane moral commitments prevail may indeed be futile, there is no denying its integrity and courage. And here, for one last time, it is fitting to bring in the comments of the author:

> Now, in Yossarian's situation — his environment, his society, the world; and it's not just America, it's the world itself — the monolithic society closes off every conventional area of protest or corrective action, and the only choice that's left to him is one of ignoble acceptance in which he can profit and live very comfortably — but nevertheless ignoble — or *flight*, a renunciation of that condition, of that society, that set of circumstances.
>
> The only way he can renounce it without going to jail is by deserting it, trying to keep going until they capture him. I like to think of him as a kind of spirit on the loose. You know, he is the only hope left at the end of the book. Had he accepted that choice. . . .[16]

Notes

1. See, for example, John W. Hunt, "Comic Escape and Anti-Vision: Joseph Heller's *Catch-22*," *Adversity and Grace: Studies in Recent American Literature*, ed. Nathan A. Scott, Jr. (Chicago, 1968), pp. 91–98; Jean Kennard, "Joseph Heller: At War with Absurdity," *Mosaic* 4 (1971): 75–87; Vance Ramsey, "From Here to Absurdity: Heller's *Catch-22*," *Seven Contemporary Authors*, ed. Thomas B. Whitbread (Austin, 1968), pp. 99–118; Howard J. Stark, "The Anatomy of *Catch-22*," *A Catch-22 Casebook*, ed. Frederick Kiley & Walter McDonald (New York, 1973), pp. 145–58; and Brian Way, "Formal Experiment and Social Discontent: Joseph Heller's *Catch-22*," *Journal of American Studies* 2 (1968): 253–70.

2. *Critical Essays on Catch-22* (Encino, Calif., 1974), p. 4.

3. "Playboy Interview: Joseph Heller," *Playboy*, June 1975, p. 61.

4. "An Impolite Interview with Joseph Heller," *A Catch-22 Casebook*, p. 273. Originally published in *The Realist* 39 (1962): 18–31. Page citations for this interview are to the *Casebook* reprint.

5. Ibid., p. 281.

6. *Newsweek*, 1 October 1962, pp. 82–83.

7. Joseph Heller, *Catch-22* (New York: Dell, 1962), p. 142. All future references are to this edition and are cited in the text.

8. "Joseph Heller Replies," *The Realist* 50 (1964): 30.

9. See, respectively, Joseph J. Waldmeir. "Two Novelists of the Absurd: Heller and Kesey," *Contemporary Literature* 5 (1964): 193; Robert Brustein, "The Logic of Survival in a Lunatic World," *The New Republic*, 13 November 1961, p. 12; Jess Ritter, "What Manner of Men Are These," *Critical Essays on Catch-22*, p. 56; Donald Monk, "An Experiment in Ther-

apy: A Study of *Catch-22*," *The London Review* no. 2 (1967): 17; Wayne Charles Miller, "Joseph Heller's *Catch-22*: Satire Sums up a Tradition," *An Armed America: Its Face in Fiction* (New York, 1970), p. 215; James Nagel, "*Catch-22* and Angry Humor: A Study in the Normative Values of Satire," *Studies in American Humor* 1 (1974): 100; James M. Mellard, "*Catch-22: Déjà vu* and the Labyrinth of Memory," *Bucknell Review* 16 (1966): 37.

    10. "An Impolite Interview," p. 276.

    11. "Playboy Interview," p. 64.

    12. "An Impolite Interview," pp. 282, 290.

    13. Ibid., p. 290.

    14. "*Catch-22*: Joseph Heller's Portrait of American Culture — The Missing Portrait in Mike Nichols' Movie," *A Catch-22 Casebook*, p. 385.

    15. See "An Impolite Interview," pp. 279, 281, 282.

    16. Ibid., p. 289.

Something Happened

Something Happened   Kurt Vonnegut, Jr. *

The company that made a movie out of Joseph Heller's first novel, "Catch-22," had to assemble what became the 11th or 12th largest bomber force on the planet at the time. If somebody wants to make a movie out of his second novel, "Something Happened," he can get most of his props at Bloomingdale's — a few beds, a few desks, some tables and chairs.

Life is a whole lot smaller and cheaper in this second book. It has shrunk to the size of a grave, almost.

Mark Twain is said to have felt that his existence was all pretty much downhill from his adventures as a Mississippi riverboat pilot. Mr. Heller's two novels, when considered in sequence, might be taken as a similar statement about an entire white, middle-class generation of American males, my generation, Mr. Heller's generation, Herman Wouk's generation, Norman Mailer's generation, Irwin Shaw's generation, Vance Bourjaily's generation, James Jones's generation, and on and on — that for them everything has been downhill since World War II, as absurd and bloody as it often was.

Both books are full of excellent jokes, but neither one is funny. Taken together, they tell a tale of pain and disappointments experienced by mediocre men of good will.

Mr. Heller is a first-rate humorist who cripples his own jokes intentionally — with the unhappiness of the characters who perceive them. He also insists on dealing with only the most hackneyed themes. After a thousand World War II airplane novels had been published and pulped, he gave us yet another one, which was gradually acknowledged as a sanely crazy masterpiece.

Now he offers us the thousand-and-first version of *The Hucksters* or *The Man in the Gray Flannel Suit*.

There is a nattily-dressed, sourly witty middle-management executive named Robert Slocum, he tells us, who lives in a nice house in Connecticut with a wife, a daughter and two sons. Slocum works in Manhattan in the communications racket. He is restless. He mourns the missed opportunities of his youth. He is itchy for raises and promotions, even though he despises his company and the jobs he does. He commits unsatisfying adulteries now and then at sales conferences in resort areas, during long lunch hours, or while pretending to work late at the office.

He is exhausted.

He dreads old age.

Mr. Heller's rewriting of this written-to-death situation took him 12 years. It comes out as a monologue by Slocum. Nobody else gets to talk, except as reported by Slocum. And Slocum's sentences are so alike in shape and texture, from the beginning to the end of the book, that I imagined a man who was making an enormous statue out of sheet metal. He was shaping it with millions of identical taps from a ball-peen hammer.

Each dent was a fact, a depressingly ordinary fact.

"My wife is a good person, really, or used to be," says Slocum near the beginning, "and sometimes I'm sorry for her. She drinks during the day and flirts, or tries to, at parties we go to in the evening, although she doesn't know how."

"I have given my daughter a car of her own," he says near the end. "Her spirits seem to be picking up."

Slocum does his deadly best to persuade us, with his tap-tap-tapping of facts, that he is compelled to be as unhappy as he is, not because of enemies or flaws in his own character, but because of the facts.

What have these tedious facts done to him? They have required that he respond to them, since he is a man of good will. And responding and responding and responding to them has left him petrified with boredom and drained of any capacity for joyfulness, now that he is deep into middle age.

Only one fact among the millions is clearly horrible. Only one distinguishes Slocum's bad luck from that of his neighbors. His youngest child is an incurable imbecile.

Slocum is heartless about the child. "I no longer think of Derek as one of my children," he says. "Or even as mine. I try not to think of him at all. This is becoming easier, even at home when he is nearby with the rest of us, making noise with some red cradle toy or making unintelligible sounds as he endeavors to speak. By now, I don't even know his name. The children don't care for him, either."

Mr. Heller might have here, or at least somewhere in his book, used conventional, Chekhovian techniques for making us love a sometimes wicked man. He might have said that Slocum was drunk or tired after a bad day at the office when he spoke so heartlessly or that he whispered his heartlessness only to himself or to a stranger he would never see again. But Slocum is invariably sober and deliberate during his monologue, does not seem to give a damn who hears what he says. Judging from his selection of unromantic episodes and attitudes, it is his wish that we dislike him.

And we gratify that wish.

Is this book any good? Yes. It is splendidly put together and hypnotic to read. It is as clear and hard-edged as a cut diamond. Mr. Heller's concentration and patience are so evident on every page that one can only say that *Something Happened* is at all points precisely what he hoped it would be.

The book may be marketed under false pretenses, which is all right with me. I have already seen (British) salespromotion materials which suggest that we have been ravenous for a new Heller book because we want to laugh some more. This is as good a way as any to get people to read one of the unhappiest books ever written.

Something Happened is so astonishingly pessimistic, in fact, that it can be called a daring experiment. Depictions of utter hopelessness in literature have been acceptable up to now only in small doses, in short-story form, as in Franz Kafka's "The Metamorphosis," Shirley Jackson's "The Lottery," or John D. MacDonald's "The Hangover," to name a treasured few. As far as I know, though, Joseph Heller is the first major American writer to deal with unrelieved misery at novel length. Even more rashly, he leaves his major character, Slocum, essentially unchanged at the end.

A middle-aged woman who had just finished *Something Happened* in galleys said to me the other day that she thought it was a reply to all the recent books by women about the unrewardingness of housewives' lives. And Slocum does seem to argue that he is entitled to at least as much unhappiness as any woman he knows. His wife, after all, has to adapt to only one sort of hell, the domestic torture chamber in Connecticut, in which he, too, must writhe at night and on weekends, when he isn't committing adultery. But he must also go regularly to his office, where pain is inflicted on all the nerve centers which were neglected by the tormentors at home.

(The place where Slocum works, incidentally, is unnamed, and its products and services are undescribed. But I had a friend of a friend of an acquaintance ask Mr. Heller if he minded naming Slocum's employers. Mr. Heller replied with all possible speed and openness, "Time, Incorporated." So we have a small scoop.)

Just as Mr. Heller is uninterested in tying a tin can to anything as localized as a company with a familiar name, so is he far above the complaining contests going on between men and women these days. He began this book way back in 1962, and there have been countless gut-ripping news items and confrontations since then. But Heller's man Slocum is deaf and blind to them. He receives signals from only three sources: his office, his memory and home.

And, on the basis of these signals alone, he is able to say, apparently in all seriousness: "The world just doesn't work. It's an idea whose time is gone."

This is black humor indeed — with the humor removed.

Robert Slocum was in the Air Force in Italy during World War II by the way. He was especially happy there while demonstrating his unflagging virility to prostitutes. So it was also with John Yossarian, the hero of *Catch-22*, whose present whereabouts are unknown.

There will be a molasses-like cautiousness about accepting this book as an important one. It took more than a year for *Catch-22*, to gather a band of enthusiasts. I myself was cautious about that book. I am cautious again.

The uneasiness which many people will feel about liking *Something Happened* has roots which are deep. It is no casual thing to swallow a book by Joseph Heller, for he is, whether he intends to be or not, a maker of myths. (One way to do this, surely, is to be the final and most brilliant teller of an oft-told tale.) *Catch-22* is now the dominant myth about Americans in the war against fascism. *Something Happened*, if swallowed, could become the dominant myth about the middle-class veterans who came home from the war to become heads of nuclear families. The proposed myth has it that those families were pathetically vulnerable and suffocating. It says that the heads of them commonly took jobs which were vaguely dishonorable or at least stultifying, in order to make as much money as they could for their little families, and they used that money in futile attempts to buy safety and happiness. The proposed myth says that they lost their dignity and their will to live in the process.

It says they are hideously tired now.

To accept a new myth about ourselves is to simplify our memories — and to place our stamp of approval on what might become an epitaph for our era in the shorthand of history. This, in my opinion, is why critics often condemn our most significant books and poems and plays when they first appear, while praising feebler creations. The birth of a new myth fills them with primitive dread for myths are so effective.

Well — I have now suppressed my own dread. I have thought dispassionately about *Something Happened*, and I am now content to have it shown to future generations as a spooky sort of summary of what my generation of nebulously clever white people experienced, and what we, within the cage of those experiences, then did with our lives.

And I am counting on a backlash. I expect younger readers to love Robert Slocum — on the grounds that he couldn't possibly be as morally repellent and socially useless as he claims to be.

People a lot younger than I am may even be able to laugh at Slocum in an affectionate way, something I am unable to do. They may even see comedy in his tragic and foolish belief that he is totally responsible for the happiness or unhappiness of the members of his tiny family.

They may even see some nobility in him, as an old soldier who has been brought to emotional ruin at last by the aging process and civilian life.

As for myself: I can't crack a smile when he says, ostensibly about the positions in which he sleeps, "I have exchanged the position of the fetus for the position of the corpse." And I am so anxious for Slocum to say something good about life that I read hope into lines meant to be supremely ironical, such as when he says this: "I know at last what I want to be when I grow up. When I grow up I want to be a little boy."

What is perhaps Slocum's most memorable speech mourns not his own generation but the one after his, in the person of his sullen, teen-age daughter. "There was a cheerful baby girl in a high chair in my house once," he says, "who ate and drank with a hearty appetite and laughed a lot with spontaneous zest: she isn't here now; and there is no trace of her anywhere."

We keep reading this overly long book, even though there is no rise and fall in passion and language, because it is structured as a suspense novel. The puzzle which seduces us is this one: Which of several possible tragedies will result from so much unhappiness? The author picks a good one.

I say that this is the most memorable, and therefore the most permanent variation on a familiar theme, in that it says baldly what the other variations only implied, what the other variations tried with desperate sentimentality not to imply: That many lives, judged by the standards of the people who live them, are simply not worth living.

Joseph Heller's Milk Train: Nothing More to Express
Joseph Epstein*

Although novelists, unlike railroads, do not operate on timetables, the history of novelistic production turns up expresses, good steady locals, and an occasional milk train. Dostoevsky, an express running under the steam of immense gambling debt, produced four major novels (*Crime and Punishment, The Idiot, The Possessed* and *A Raw Youth*) and several lesser works (lesser for Dostoevsky, major for almost anyone else) within a nine-year span, James Joyce put eight years into the creation of *Ulysses*, then 17 more into the astonishing verbal filigree work involved in *Finnegans Wake*. Among contemporary American novelists, Saul Bellow produces a new novel at roughly five-to-seven-year intervals, marking, for those who keep charts on such things, a straight upward line of increased mastery. The late John O'Hara churned out novels and stories at so furious a clip that an Evelyn Wood speed-reading course was nearly required to keep up with him. At the opposite extreme, there is Ralph Ellison, who, after *Invisible Man* (1954), surely one of the finest American novels of the last 50 years, continues, two decades later, to chug away at his second novel, one of the great milk trains of American or any other literature.

Like Ralph Ellison in these if in no other respects, Joseph Heller is notable for being a slow worker as well as for being one of the few American novelists able to sustain a reputation on the basis of a single book. With hindsight, it is possible to see that *Catch-22* (1961), Heller's first and only other novel, was a well-aimed bomb. To cite works only in its own direct line, the novel has clearly been the intellectual sire of the film "Dr. Strange-

*Reprinted, with permission, from the *Washington Post Book World*, Oct. 6, 1974, pp. 1–3. © 1974 the *Washington Post*.

love" and, more recently, of the movie and now television series, "M.A.S.H." It brought comedy to the essentially grim subject of war, and thereby demonstrated its utter absurdity. Before the appearance of *Catch-22*, anti-heroism in American fiction was well on its way to being established; it took things a step further, however, and can be read as a mass over the death of heroism itself. It held that, in the mad, impersonal killing of modern warfare, heroism was a joke, and only seeing after one's own survival made sense: in an insane world, only the man who pretended to insanity can be judged sane. Beginning as a cult novel, *Catch-22* spread in popularity to the point where, along with Paul Goodman's *Growing Up Absurd* and the novels of Kurt Vonnegut, it has to be accounted one of the key books to understanding the fashionable nihilism of the past decade.

There was a catch in *Catch-22*, as the novel's more perceptive critics pointed out. The catch is that Heller, till nearly the end of his novel, does not mention the Nazis, and thus nowhere suggests that, absurd though modern warfare most truly is, there really was no alternative, except the unthinkable one of knuckling under to Hitler's Third Reich. Evil is the missing component in *Catch-22*, and if one is to go all the way with one's nihilism, as Heller was not in this novel, then one must proclaim World War II to have been an outright fraud, which Heller was not prepared to do. Still, it took a certain courage for Heller to use World War II as the background for *Catch-22* — Korea was then available, and of course today Vietnam would be an absolute patsy for demonstrating his argument. On the other hand, it may come down to no more than the fact that Heller's own experience was of World War II, and he is not a writer who works well outside the boundaries of his own experience.

Despite the flaw running up the center of *Catch-22*, the novel had a winning exuberance and a wealth of comic invention. Between its energy and its comedy, Heller was able for the better part of 400 pages to sustain interest in the grotesquely mad world he set before his readers. More than with most novelists, the universe of Heller's novels is a self-enclosed one. Accept his assumptions and his conclusions inevitably, sometimes hilariously, follow. The assumptions of *Catch-22* are that courage, bravery, liberty, love of country, and other human virtues are all a joke, a hideous cover-up for the urge toward self-advancement, the will to power, and simple craziness. Interestingly, in its assumption *Catch-22* is a precursor to much of the fiction that arose out of the past decade, but with an even deeper skepticism about conventional explanations of human character and how the world works. In the fiction of Donald Barthelme, Leonard Michaels, Thomas Pynchon, and Robert Coover, among others, this skepticism slices to the bone: character counts for nothing; plot is a laugh, since cause can no longer be held to explain effect; and language itself is no more than the stick of a blind man, a thing which we use to grope our way around in the dark but which really lights up nothing. A curious symbiosis is at work here; as Heller's first novel, directly or indirectly, fed the fiction of these younger writers of the generation following his own, so Heller's second novel seems to feed off their work.

Something Happened is the title of Joseph Heller's new novel, and it is intended in the questioning sense of "What Happened?" Heller's narrator, Bob Slocum, is in part in the situation described by the European novelist Manes Sperber who, in *Journey Without End,* has written: "At those crossroads of one's life, when one ceases to ask 'What is still to happen to me?' and begins instead to wonder: 'What has happened to me? What have I done with my life?' — that is a time when it is easy to panic." Something has happened, all right, but it is in the nature of the kind of novel Heller has written that we never learn what, specifically, it is. The quality of life is less good than it once seemed, relationships between husbands and wives and parents and children are impossible, the country is going to hell in a handwagon. "The world just doesn't work. It's an idea whose time has gone." All these points are duly, even repetitiously and dully, noted, but what exactly has happened to bring about the malaise that constitutes the only emotional climate of *Something Happened* is never pinpointed beyond this.

As a novelist, in *Catch-22* as in *Something Happened,* Joseph Heller's method is never to explain but to let description suffice. "Description," wrote Wallace Stevens, "is revelation." Instead of an analysis of the malaise, then, we get a description of it. In the nearly 600-page monologue provided by Bob Slocum, there is no attempt to understand what is going on, but only to describe what it feels like to live under the malaise. Much as if he were talking to a tireless and well-paid psychoanalyst, Slocum rambles on confessionally, formlessly, repetitiously. Anxieties slide into fantasies, fantasies into terrors, terrors into nostalgia. It is almost as if we, the novel's readers, are in the psychoanalyst's chair, notebook on lap, a decanter of hot coffee on the desk, patiently awaiting the completion of the analysand's tale, so that we might then return to the quiet of our study, reassemble the data, and offer an answer to what exactly has happened.

What are the basic data? Bob Slocum is in his 40s, a middle-echelon executive of a large corporation, a suburbanite living on a quarter-acre in Connecticut, a husband, and a father of three children: a teenage daughter, with whom he falls into ceaseless argument, a younger son whom he loves but feels slipping away from him, and a second, still younger son who is hopelessly retarded. Things are complicated from the outset by the fact that Slocum is a good bit more of a bastard than Everyman. (Or is it one of the assumptions that, if the truth be known, we are now all a good bit more of a bastard than Everyman?) He is a womanizer, and a man who has sex, as they say, in the head, but not only in the head: he traffics in prostitutes, fits in nooners during the working day, has ladies everywhere, and when not doing it is thinking about it. (Everyman again?) But crimes of the bedroom seem the least of his offenses.

William Maxwell, a writer who shares with Heller the English language and almost nothing else, has a character in a recent story in *The New Yorker*, "Over by the River," about whom he writes: "With his safety razor ready to begin a downward sweep, George Carrington studied the lathered face in the mirror of the medicine cabinet. He shook his head. There was a fatal flaw in his character: nobody was ever as real to him as he was to himself. If people knew how little he cared whether they lived or died, they wouldn't want to have anything to do with him." Maxwell, in his story, leaves it at that; the whole of *Something Happened* is taken up with elaborating upon how little Bob Slocum cares about anyone. At his corporation, he toadies to those above him, is cavalier to those beneath him — is strictly and wholeheartedly the corporate operator. He can scarcely wait for his troublesome daughter to grow up and leave him. If he could do it without losing face — which, apparently, he cannot — he would prefer to install his retarded son, who is a trial and an embarrassment, in an institution. As he watches his mother, who toward the end of her life *is* installed in an institution, grow closer to death, he feels one principal emotion: revulsion. He abhors a mess, is squeamish, doesn't really mind if people break down or die but prefers they have the good grace to do so while he isn't on the premises. In short, he is a swine. But a swine with a difference — and the difference is that throughout the novel he is the one who is telling us what a swine he is.

Does awareness count for anything? Not in a Joseph Heller novel it doesn't. For all his awareness, Slocum's days are empty and sour. He is besieged by anxieties, has a full-blown Cassandra complex: everywhere he sees doom. He knows how small are the rewards he has to look forward to — advancement at his office, more money, a larger house — but wants them anyway. He makes bitter little jokes and puns in parentheses, followed by the words "ha, ha," irony being his only defense mechanism. His wife defrays part of the expense of the emptiness of their life together by becoming an afternoon tippler. He would like to leave her before she breaks down — it would be awkward to do so after she breaks down — but fears a divorce. "More and more things seem to be slipping into a state of dissolution, and soon there will be nothing left." Still, he goes through his paces: fornicating, operating, playing out the game. "Apathy, boredom, restlessness, free-floating, amorphous frustration, leisure, discontent at home or at my job — these are my aphrodisiacs now."

If Captain Yossarian's purpose in *Catch-22* is survival, Slocum is as tenacious in his less clear purpose. He wants to get on, to "get his" before it — cancer, heart attack, arteriosclerosis, whatever — gets him. Slocum is not, to be sure, Yossarian in mufti. If he resembles anyone in *Catch-22*, it is the character named Dunbar, who cultivates boredom because boredom makes time pass more slowly and thereby lengthens his life. But here the resemblance to *Catch-22* ends. *Something Happened* has none of the joyous energy of *Catch-22*, nor much of its comic invention. It is a novel of bleak landscapes and shadowy characters. It begins in anxiety and ends in despair. Nothing happens in *Something Happened*.

This is by deliberation. The nature of Slocum's work remains unknown. Most characters are not described, except for their deformities: a limp on one, a bit of spittle on the corner of the mouth on another, the overweight of a third. Like so much fiction of its kind, physical description is kept arid and abstract; concretion, interestingly enough, is lavished only on sex. Slocum's wife's buttocks, breasts, and other parts are described in detail; nothing is said about her face. Perhaps this is not surprising; perhaps it comes down to no more than a technical problem. If a novelist has no interest in plot, if he has no interest as well in character, if he cannot believe in the first and is bored by the second, then drama, the twists of plot out of which character is formed or revealed in fiction, is denied him also. This, if one wishes to write at novel length, leaves sex.

A filthy mind, says La Rochefoucauld, is a perpetual feast. Joseph Heller writes: "I wonder what I *would* feel like if my wife came home smelling of another man's semen." La Rochefoucauld is wrong. Or at least his remark ought to be revised to read: A filthy mind dines best alone. Pornography is a dead end in literature; it is better portrayed, if we must have it, in the movies. But given the loss of credence in character and in plot that is part of Heller's novelistic equipment, pornography is all that is left him, or any other writer who works under what is called the post-Modernist sensibility. Under this sensibility, despair is assumed, defeat is assumed, hopelessness is assumed. (Oddly, an ample audience for all this bad news is also assumed.) What results is, in effect, Kafka with screwing — which, as anyone who has looked into Kafka knows, isn't Kafka at all. It is merely writing about screwing under the guise of higher purposes.

If *Something Happened* turns out to be of slight interest in itself, it is of wider interest in demonstrating that fiction written under the assumptions of the post-Modernist sensibility cannot sustain itself over the length of a large novel. A Donald Barthelme can float a story or sketch under these same assumptions for eight or ten pages on sheer brilliance. But at greater length, things tend to flatten out — the literature of exhaustion itself in the end proves exhausting to read. In Joseph Heller's case there is an irony here that an ironist such as himself might perhaps appreciate. Thirteen years in transit, when the milk train of his second novel finally arrived at its destination, the cargo had gone sour.

Joseph Heller: Something
Happened to the American Dream   Nicholas Canaday*

In *Something Happened* (1974), Joseph Heller gives us Bob Slocum, the Willy Loman of the 1970's, who says ironically about his characterizing name that it "means nothing that I know of and I don't know where it came from" (*Something Happened*, New York: Alfred A. Knopf, Inc., 1974, p. 32). Slocum is no longer low, as Willy Loman was always to be; Slocum has arrived, made it, become one of the managers of corporate America. For Willy the American society was on the way to becoming the corporate state — acquisitive, ruthless, cruel, but impersonal and framed within an order with rules seemingly apparent to all. But Slocum's world is a bizarre and distorted version of what America has become in our time. Slocum's own irony operates on several levels: as a sloganeer he finds it easy to outrage the conventional mind ("America the beautiful isn't," p. 481), and for the intellectuals he invokes Walt Whitman ("I hear America singing fuck off," p. 481). Most damning of all, America is no longer even functional: "The world just doesn't work. It's an idea whose time has gone" (p. 506).

Slocum is not, like Willy Loman, stupid and confused; he is bright and clear sighted. Nor is he in the least well intentioned; instead, Slocum is malicious with almost everyone. While Willy was in part motivated by guilt because he had not succeeded, Bob Slocum is motivated by the fear of losing what he has, and at the same time he understands that success is a kind of madness. Slocum has in fact succeeded in achieving Willy's dream, and he is, mostly, well liked by his business associates. Bob Slocum now desperately seeks protection against loss, escape from vulnerability. Early in the book Slocum speaks of his fears and reveals the significance of the title of the novel: "Something did happen to me somewhere that robbed me of confidence and courage and left me with a fear of discovery and change and a positive dread of everything unknown that may occur" (p. 8).

The book is essentially a monologue, an interior ordering of Slocum's perceptions about his work and his family; and it is largely static. The structure, however, frames Slocum's conscious emotional achievement, which is a determined response to his fear of vulnerability. The narrative is the story of Slocum's efforts to screw down his life so tight that discovery and change and the unknown cannot possibly threaten him. He succeeds. "I get the willies," he says in the first line, and it is explicated soon thereafter by "I really don't trust myself anymore in any tight situation whose outcome I can't control or predict" (pp. 3, 8). Whatever striving or risk-taking, whatever sense of adventure may have once been part of Slocum's life, something has happened to it. To Slocum the dream of material success, once achieved, is not a nightmare; it is simply not satisfying. Yet he is desperately determined to hold fast to what he has achieved. The last line of the novel announces

*Reprinted, with permission, from the *CEA Critic*, 40, No. 1 (1977), 34–38.

confidently: "Everyone seems pleased with the way I've taken command" (p. 565).

As narrator, Slocum's attempts at humor — sometimes successful, more often not — serve to characterize his nervous insecurity. The comedy is a mask for alternating impulses of hostility and fear, as well as boredom, frustration, and discontent. The frequent ironic comments about his own telling of his story suggest a skittering across a surface, a texture shimmery and superficial. Little is deeply felt, and no attitude is deeply held. The narrative voice, like the structure of the novel, is a function of character.

The office is the most important part of Bob Slocum's world — surrealistically rendered and characterized by fear, frustration, and boredom within strong lines of power. Since there is no work being done, energy goes out and comes back across a taut web of power and sexual connections. Responsibility is much less clear than the power relationships: Who runs the company? Green, White, Brown, Black, or the twelve elderly men at the top who founded and built it? Slocum's immediate superior, Green, is "the only person in the company with courage enough to behave badly" (p. 40), yet his behavior is purposeless and erratic. What might have been creative energy in Green has become only impetuousness; strong principle, only abrasive belligerence.

Bob Slocum has some power (six of the people in his department are afraid of him); he even has security. His fear of being fired, which he continually expresses, is irrational because he knows the company always takes care of its mistakes. But when work is trivial, relationships become unreal. If there is anywhere any substance, anything being done, in the company, it is never described by Slocum. Of course he is ambitious: he wants more power and the attendant money and approbation. The ambition is a defense against loss, because his acquisitiveness is an antidote to the fear of losing.

Much of the section of the novel about the office is devoted to Slocum's reminiscences about his lecherous pursuit of a woman named Virginia in a company where he worked before he went off to World War II. Her name is ironic: she had remained virginal to Slocum while teasing him with stories of past and ongoing sexual encounters. Although she had allowed him various sexual liberties, in fact had encouraged them, she had always finally eluded him. Virginia represents no youthful romantic ideal; she simply is a girl he could not get, and she had committed suicide before he had returned from military service. She stands in contrast to Jane, another young woman who works for the company at present. Slocum is now older, has more experience and more power, but with Jane he is satisfied with fantasy. Thus the older man fears precisely that intimacy that had escaped the younger. Although Slocum feels he can do whatever he wants with Jane, their relationship consists mainly of "the lascivious banter that tickles and amuses and encourages [them] both" (p. 25). Ironically, this same relationship had satisfied Virginia years before when the adventurous young Slocum was imprudently taking risks trying to get her. To complicate one's life with a real relationship with anyone, Slocum now senses, makes a person exposed and vulnerable.

Fear and power, the opposites of love and caring, characterize Slocum's family relationships. His feelings for his wife range from lust to pity to disgust. While complaining about his alienation from her, he observes that his wife has become a compliant, eager sexual partner. She drinks in the afternoon and flirts broadly at parties; and Slocum, characteristically, likes most to make love to her when she is not in the mood. Nor does he have any better relationship with his children. He characterizes his daughter as "nervous, spiteful, embittered, and vindictive" (p. 137). The retarded son Derek, his youngest, is a burden and an embarrassment. The other son, Bob, who fears him and has stopped talking to him, is killed in the climactic scene of the novel. When the boy is struck by an automobile running out of control over a sidewalk in a shopping center — a freak accident — Slocum suffocates him in a moment of panic. The sudden and sparsely detailed episode of his son's death stands in contrast to the verbose, repetitive quality of most of the narrative because it reflects genuine feeling. The son is the only person in Slocum's world with whom he might have had a meaningful relationship. Once that possibility is gone, and despair is reinforced by anguish and shame, what is left of Slocum's life is a hard, satisfying kernel of invulnerability.

All relations of dependence in Bob Slocum's life are thus either abandoned or warped grotesquely. In the company, too, the people are all relatively strong and independent — most of them are bright, attractive, and young. The one exception is Martha, a rather mysterious typist who symbolically represents the weak, stupid, ugly, and old. So everyone avoids her, hoping not to become involved. Martha illustrates that dependency is something to be taken care of by the system; on a personal level it is an embarrassment and makes one vulnerable. Martha is slowly going crazy, it is said, although there is no attempt to communicate with her. She merely sits alone, typing. She was hired by mistake on the recommendation of someone who hires all the secretaries, and no one has the courage to confront her, let alone fire her. When she finally goes into a catatonic state, Slocum demonstrates his newly acquired authoritative manner, directing that Medical, Personnel, Security, and Travel Sections be called immediately to take her away, taking charge "like a ballet master" (p. 565).

This novel is deliberately not about the crisis of the intellectual in our time. As Everyman in the 1970's, Bob Slocum is much closer to Archie Bunker than to Moses Herzog. Despite occasional insights into his own condition, Slocum has no intellectual dimension in his life. Neither literature nor any other art — nothing we usually refer to as "cultural" — is relevant to him. Although he speaks vaguely about being more "liberal" than his friends, and he especially condemns his hated reactionary sister-in-law, he has no real concern for economic, social, or political issues. That the time of the novel is never pinned to contemporary events — as, for example, is common in the novels of Updike, Bellow, and others — is of course a part of Heller's impressionistic, non-representational technique; but it also reflects Slocum's perceptions. Such matters are not what engage him. Religion is absent from the novel; nor is Slocum interested in any pseudo-religion, cause, or movement. There is neither depth nor transcendence in this particular life.

Nor is there any sense of community in Bob Slocum's life. Just as with his family and at the office, so his wider world contains no possibility of mutual support within a group. When other parents of retarded children, for example, make sympathetic overtures to the Slocums, he rejects them harshly: "I detest clannishness of every kind. It boxes me in claustrophobically. Or shuts me out. I don't like to feel boxed in" (p. 511). What might be community is immediately exaggerated into clannishness, and the nervous remark about being boxed in while simultaneously being shut out reveals a neurotic distaste for and fear of human relationships. The social life of the Slocums reflects the same impulse: "We prefer large, noisy gatherings at which public conversation is impossible; we are on guard at smaller, formal groups in which the discussions at any time might take an unpredictable turn to zero in on us" (p. 527). To be guarded against desperately is the chance that a group of people in a public conversation, and the word *public* points to a significant aspect of relationships within a community, might seek to know who Bob Slocum is, because in fact he has no identity. Furthermore, he is incapable of relating to people except as a superior or a subordinate. Both his personality and character make devastatingly apparent this incapacity, and the wider implications for social, economic, or political life are that Bob Slocum can never be a part of a cooperative venture of any kind.

A one-dimensional life cannot sustain a rebellion. Slocum thinks about what he calls malicious and obvious disobedience, but he believes all aberrant acts would simply be absorbed by the system: "Any act of rebellion would be absorbed like rain on an ocean and leave no trace. I would not cause a ripple" (p. 19). His conception of an act of rebellion is significantly some kind of atypical behavior like tearing up a machine-processed check. A radical re-structuring of his world or even his life style is never a conscious alternative, and his sense of defeat springing from his belief that one person can make no difference is a cliché of modern American life. It is interesting that Slocum also says: "I have lost the power to upset things that I had as a child; I can no longer change my environment or even disturb it seriously" (p. 19). The rebellion of a child would, of course, be absorbed by the environment even more efficiently than that of an adult, but in fact the remark about childhood represents a yearning for an imagined vigorous past. Slocum may think he is talking about his own youth, but we know from the details of his past that he was no more rebellious then. What Heller is portraying here is a nostalgic yearning for youthful energy and confidence before something happened, for what is thought of as a younger America. And this backward view toward an imagined better time is, as Heller knows, still another cliché.

At the end Bob Slocum finally copes with his world — efficiently, technically, managerially. Perhaps his typical dream, which he describes as involving "bitter frustration and humiliation and insurmountable difficulty" (p. 31), does recur, but at least consciously he believes that the world he confronts is all of reality. In this fictional portrait of the Watergate mind, Bob Slocum believes that the world is controlled by the smart and the tough. (In fact, the narrative line of this novel might be thought of as a long monologue spoken to a tape recorder.) Desperately motivated by a fear of discovery and change, dreading everything unknown but imagined — some possible assault by a possible antagonist — Slocum at last believes himself to be no longer vulnerable. He has taken command.

Immunity for Bob Slocum, however, is purchased at great emotional cost, including the suppression of all traces of any sense of collective responsibility. One moment of insight comes to him near the end: "Who *am* I? I think I am beginning to find out. I am a stick: I am a broken waterlogged branch floating with my own crowd in this one nation of ours, indivisible (unfortunately), under God, with liberty and justice for all who are speedy enough to seize them first and hog them away from the rest" (p. 303). During the entire action of the novel Slocum has been nearing the end of a process that has been a turning away from the real world, away from community — that crowd he floats with hardly qualifies — to the inner exclusivity of self. Such self-centeredness, paradoxically, means the loss of self, because only through relation and reciprocity can the self be sustained. Therefore Slocum has, as he puts it, ascended "while falling to pieces." And he adds, using still another ironic allusion, "Only in America is it possible to do both at the same time" (p. 523). Thus, as Jospeh Heller reminds us in this novel, whatever happened to Bob Slocum has also happened to America.

"A Permanent Game of Excuses": Determinism in Heller's *Something Happened*
Susan Strehle*

Joseph Heller's long-awaited second novel, *Something Happened*, puzzled and disappointed many reviewers. In a particularly sensitive piece, Kurt Vonnegut, Jr. summed up some of the central problems the novel poses for its critics: narrator Bob Slocum appears to be "morally repellent and socially useless"; evidently, "it is his wish that we dislike him. And we grat-

*Reprinted, with permission, from *Modern Fiction Studies*, 24 (1978–79), 550–56. *Modern Fiction Studies*, © 1979 Purdue Research Foundation, West Lafayette, Indiana 47907.

ify that wish."[1] Even more important, the novel seems extremely pessimistic: it "is so as astonishingly pessimistic, in fact, that it can be called a daring experiment. . . . Heller is the first major American writer to deal with unrelieved misery at novel length."[2] In both of these qualities, the novel demonstrates an abrupt departure from *Catch-22*, whose protagonist, Yossarian, engaged our sympathy by defining a morality for the absurd world and whose conclusion suggested an optimistic hope for escape.

But the pessimism of *Something Happened* and the repellence of its narrator find their source in Slocum's determinism. In contrast to Yossarian, whose rebellious stance implied an existential faith in human freedom, Slocum maintains a deterministic belief that man is the helpless and irresponsible pawn of fate. Compounding the difficulties of critical interpretation, Slocum's viewpoint dominates the novel; we are almost completely restricted to his version of reality. If we are intended to accept his deterministic vision, the novel is indeed simply a pessimistic reflection on contemporary American ills; but if we are encouraged to judge Slocum an unreliable narrator, then the novel becomes a more subtle exploration of a consciousness resisting its own freedom and responsibility.

Slocum begins his narrative with "the willies," a state of non-specific anxiety which existentialists consider an authentic mode of being: "I get the willies when I see closed doors. Even at work, where I am doing so well now, the sight of a closed door is sometimes enough to make me dread that something horrible is happening behind it . . . I wonder why." But Slocum's response to anxiety is decidedly inauthentic; he continues, "Something must have happened to me sometime."[3] This statement, the first invocation of the novel's title, implies a deterministic belief that human responses are conditioned by undefinable environmental and psychological factors. Human will is irrelevant because we have no freedom of choice; we are molded by forces we cannot control. Moreover, we cannot be held responsible for our actions since they do not result from our volition. Slocum's anxiety, his actions, and his identity are founded on an external "something" which happened to him.

I want to suggest that Heller undermines Slocum's credibility throughout the narrative and presents an existential view of determinism. Such a view finds clear expression in Sartre's *Being and Nothingness* in a passage that anticipates Slocum's narrative precisely:

> Psychological determinism, before being a theoretical conception, is first an attitude of excuse, or if you prefer, the basis of all attitudes of excuse. It is reflective conduct with respect to anguish; it asserts that there are within us antagonistic forces whose type of existence is comparable to that of things. It attempts to fill the void which encircles us, to re-establish the links between past and present, between present and future. It provides us with a *nature* productive of our acts, and these very acts it makes transcendent; it assigns to them a foundation in something other than themselves

by endowing them with an inertia and externality eminently reassuring
because they constitute a permanent game of *excuses*.[4]

In his "reflective conduct with respect to anguish," Slocum refuses to confront his dread of freedom in a void by blaming that dread on something
external. He reifies the antagonistic forces within himself; one is a "crawl-
ing animal flourishing somewhere inside me that I try to keep hidden," and
one is a "desolate lost little being I yearn for," the innocent child he used to
be (pp. 111, 305). His whole narrative comprises an effort to re-establish
links, as he leafs through his own past and that of his family and forms pre-
dictions for the future, always seeking a vision of continuity that will allevi-
ate his dread of time. His most strenuous effort to evade anguish occurs in
his habitual externalization of his own actions and decisions; he claims they
always have their foundation in "something" other than themselves. But
while Slocum plays this "permanent game of excuses" throughout the novel,
Heller exposes the game as a bankrupt evasive strategy. Moreover, the climactic action of the book invalidates determinism and reaffirms an existential world view. This reading implies a belief that *Something Happened* is
not a radical and pessimistic turning away from the attitudes of *Catch-22*
but a more complex and equally successful presentation of similar attitudes.

The assertion that "something happened," recurring throughout the
novel, represents a massive effort by Slocum to justify his failures, his mediocrity, and his disappointment with himself by locating their origin in external forces rather than in his own internal character and decisions. If Slocum
begins with the comforting excuse that "something did happen to me somewhere that robbed me of confidence and courage" (p. 8), he moves quickly
to identify some specific sources of his grief. First, he blames his wife, who
drinks during the day, flirts outrageously at parties, and has become "as
lustful and compliant as one of Kagle's whores or my girl friends." His wife
tells him, proudly, "You did it. . . . You made me this way," but he denies
responsibility: "I can't believe it was all my fault" (p. 125). He prefers to
explain the changes in his wife and himself with his usual evasion: "What
happened to us? Something did. I was a boy once, and she was a girl, and
we were both new. Now we are man and woman, and nothing feels new
any longer; everything feels old." His explanation locates the source of
change in the simple passage of time. But, during that time, he has treated
his wife as an object: "I didn't care whether she enjoyed it or not; just as
long as *I* got *mine*," and "I probably enjoyed her terror and my violence"
(pp. 119–120). If "something happened" to turn Slocum's wife crass and
insatiable, the reader begins to believe it was Slocum himself.

Slocum's children provide another source of anguish. His disagreeable
and contentious daughter is moving toward disaster; her "die is cast . . .
although I don't know when her dice were rolled or who did the throwing.
(I know I didn't)" (p. 183). Her unhappiness is not Slocum's fault if it has
been predetermined in a cosmic dice game rather than bred under his own

roof. For his other children, an unnamed, painfully timid nine-year-old son and a younger boy named Derek, who is hopelessly brain-damaged, Slocum also predicts fatal disasters which he cannot seem to avert. He mourns, "Something happened to both my children that I cannot explain and cannot undo. I can't be good to them, it seems, even when I want to" (p. 177). Again, this external, vague something has inexplicably caused harm, and Slocum is helpless. His will to be good to the children is rendered impotent by that same force, so he is not responsible when, often, he is not good. But the reader witnesses too many of these failures to accept the excuse. Slocum ignores Derek as completely as he can; he competes with his daughter when he talks to her at all; and he pushes and browbeats his son. Slocum does condemn himself occasionally: "What a prick I was," he remarks, but he goes on excusing himself: "I plead guilty, your honor, but with an explanation, sir" (p. 282).

Though he extends implicit blame for his disappointments to specific people—his wife, his children, his parents, the people in his office— Slocum's largest indictment is reserved for the cultural climate of contemporary America, in which decay and deterioration form the most conspicuous features. While *Catch-22* described a world of anarchic energy, culminating in a *Walpurgisnacht* realization of nightmares in "The Eternal City," *Something Happened* presents a world of entropic decline. Slocum suggests a vision of America as both corollary and source for his own loss of energy and dissipation of ideals:

> Smut and weaponry are two areas in which we've improved. Everything else has gotten worse. The world is winding down. . . . From sea to shining sea the country is filling with slag, shale, and used-up automobile tires. The fruited plain is coated with insecticide and chemical fertilizers. Even pure horseshit is hard to come by these days. They add preservatives. You don't find fish in lakes and rivers anymore. You have to catch them in cans. . . . "America the Beautiful" isn't: it was all over the day the first white man set foot on the continent to live. . . . People between rich and poor radiate uneasiness. They don't know where they belong. I hear America singing fuck off. (pp. 480–481)

Slocum's problems must not be of his own making, for if "the world is winding down," how can a single man resist? But here, again, Slocum's complaints about his environment conceal his own responsibility. This passage describes forms of ecological waste caused by corporations, yet Slocum never considers the validity of his own corporate allegiance. The modern American businessman has manufactured the automobile tire, added preservatives, and flushed chemicals into the rivers; Slocum, however, displaces the source of the problem from his own generation to the Pilgrims. He turns his own class, the people between rich and poor, from accomplices into victims of the disaster; they radiate uneasiness, as he does, because of a situation somebody else created.[5] Slocum evades any recognition of his complicity in America's problems while blaming a personified, profane American for his own distress.

If Slocum's exploitation of the deterministic game of excuses undermines his credibility for the reader, the climactic action of the book finally invalidates his deterministic vision. Near the end of the novel, Slocum rises on the corporate ladder by taking Andy Kagle's job, and his nine-year-old son dies, apparently by accident. Throughout the novel, this son has served as the locus of a set of existential values which the reader and Slocum find more attractive than Slocum's own values. Slocum must choose between the son's code, which rests on an assumption of radical freedom and responsibility, and his own deterministic vision. This choice becomes synonymous with a choice between warning and helping Kagle or taking Kagle's job with its increased money, power, and prestige. Slocum decides to take Kagle's job, and I want to suggest that he then deliberately murders his son. In doing so, he finally succeeds in convincing himself that he is the helpless victim of accidents. Ironically, it is just at this point that the reader is convinced of Slocum's culpability and, implicitly, of an anti-deterministic human responsibility for choice and action.

Slocum's nine-year-old son is the most compelling character in the novel; he is the unacknowledged hero. Unlike almost all of the others, he is not competitive. When he is winning a race at school, he starts laughing and slows down to wait for the other runners to catch up. When the members of his family begin competing in destructive arguments, he tries to stop them with a joke. In our first glimpse of him, he works at defusing family tensions around the dinner table: " '*Olé*,' says my boy, and we all smile" (p. 110). Slocum realizes that the boy unites the family by calling its members to consciousness and affection: "this angelic little boy of mine . . . [draws] us together again by reminding us who we are and what we know of each other . . . by evoking and recalling to us the great need and capacity for affection each of us has hidden away very deep inside." He calls them to a sense of responsibility for their actions, prevents them from "mangling each other willfully, brutally, and irreparably," by making them aware of a better choice in affection (p. 165). Though the boy does not voice philosophical theories, his acts reveal an instinctual notion that people are free to choose and that good choices make other people happy, while bad ones hurt.

The boy also opposes his father's belief, which will prove important in the decision to take Kagle's job, that money brings happiness. In one of the most memorable scenes in the novel, the little boy deliberately gives away a nickel in the face of his father's displeasure. He explains why he does it, revealing an innocent good nature and simple generosity:

"I was happy," he states with a shrug . . .
"Yeah?"
"And whenever I feel happy," he continues, "I like to give something away. Is that all right?"
"Sure . . . Why were you happy?"

". . . Because I knew I was going to give it away." He pauses a moment to giggle nervously. "To tease you," he admits. "Then when I knew I was happy about that, I wanted to give the nickel away because I was happy about wanting to give the nickel away." (p. 300)

The boy's explanation echoes *Catch-22* in its circular but sensible reasoning. He is happy because he is generous and senses that is good, and when he is happy he wants generously to share that happiness with others.

In the repeated confrontations between father and son, Slocum frequently reveals a sense that his son is better than he is. Just as the son calls the family to consciousness and responsibility, he evokes in the father an awareness of his failures and a sense of guilt. After Slocum has created a particularly ugly scene, he sees the little boy "standing docile and repentant (as though he were to blame) . . . I have never before or since in all my life felt so totally cruel, so rotten, depraved, and inhuman." Slocum apologizes, promising to be kinder, and the little boy forgives him readily: "You're the best daddy in the whole world." But Slocum knows better and admits guilt: "I am the worst daddy in the whole world . . . I broke my promise to him many times. He continued to love me anyway" (pp. 335–336). By demonstrating the superiority of an affectionate nature, the child evokes an alternative which Slocum has rejected. Faced directly with this alternative in the form of his son, Slocum's determinism falters; he cannot simply excuse his actions, but must acknowledge the "rotten, depraved, inhuman" nature of his behavior.

Focused by the vision of his son's superiority, Slocum's longing for a better identity takes the shape of a little boy. He sees his best self as a trapped, lost little boy who somehow receded inside as Slocum matured. He wonders, "What happened to the lovely little me that once was?" He recalls a few scenes from his youth that support his sense of having been better than he is now; as a child, he had the same instinctual values as his son. In the first pages of the novel, Slocum remembers walking as a child into a coal shed where his big brother was joined in sex with a girl from his own class in school. Though the young Bob Slocum doesn't understand what happened in the coal shed, he makes an intuitively sound judgment when his big brother and the girl emerge: "He walked with a swagger I had never seen before and knew at once I did not like" (p. 5). That swagger is part of the adult world that Slocum has come to inhabit; the company he works for "is in favor of getting laid if it is done with a dash of élan, humor, vulgarity, and skill, without emotion" (p. 66).

Slocum wishes he could recapture the lost little boy inside him and become innocent, generous, and loving again. Throughout the book, he wonders, "Where are those scattered, ripped pieces of that fragmented little boy and bewildered young man who turned out to be me?" (p. 134). He mourns the loss of the "lovely little me": "The little boy is missing; I don't know where he came from; I don't know where I went; I don't know all that's happened to me since. I miss him" (p. 205). In a particularly sensitive use of language, Heller implies that Slocum both regrets the loss of and fails to match up to the little boy he is "missing." His regret and longing crystallize in the scene where his son gives away money because he is happy. Directly afterwards, Slocum realizes: "I know at last what I want to be when I grow up. When I grow up I want to be a little boy" (p. 338). He wants, in short, to reject the adult's stultifying determinism and regain the child's responsible freedom.

As a result of the son's crucial dual role in Slocum's consciousness, of both symbol for all he wishes he were and reminder of how far he "misses" that goal, Slocum identifies closely with his son. "When I think of him, I think of me," Slocum notes; "Our minds are very much alike, his and mine, in our humor and our forebodings" (pp. 159, 163). Slocum comes to see the lost little boy hiding inside himself as a form of his "angelic" son: "hiding inside of me somewhere, I know (I feel him inside me. I feel it beyond all doubt), is a timid little boy just like my son who wants to be his best friend and wishes he could come outside and play" (p. 229). The equation of the two little boys in Slocum's mind leads him to feel a physical closeness with his son. He suspects that "I identify with him too closely . . . When he's scared, I'm scared, even though I'm not scared of what he's scared of. . . . When he quivers, I quake. My nose runs when he's got a cold; I sneeze too and my throat turns sore. When he has a fever, my temples burn" (pp. 337–339). This literal physical identification with his son suggests that, for Slocum, his son has become the little boy inside him.

The merger of the two little boys coupled with Slocum's being offered a job that involves sacrificing both boys' values for money and prestige, results in tragedy. In making his choice between keeping his own job and taking Kagle's, Slocum is also choosing between recovering and abandoning his boy. That Slocum has a clear choice between these alternatives emphasizes his freedom for the reader. True to his established adult identity, Slocum chooses the better job; true to his deterministic vision, he denies he has chosen at all. He presents himself as the passive recipient of fate's latest twist: "It is God's will. . . . 'I was promoted today' " (p. 536).

Slocum has decided to abandon the little boy, who is both his son and the child inside that does not fit into the corporate scheme. The section in which Slocum takes Kagle's job begins with an ostensible reference to getting rid of Derek by sending him to a home; however, the statement refers even more strongly to the other little boy: "I've got to get rid of him. There's no getting away from it. (He is so sweet. People who meet him tell us how sweet he is. They are being sweet when they say so)" (p. 499). Derek is never called sweet by anyone, least of all by Slocum himself, who admits that "I'm not sure I like Derek" and comments that he "is not especially good-looking, and we do not love him at all" (pp. 275, 357). It is, instead, the nine-year old son who is sweet and who is universally liked by the people who meet him: "He is a good-looking son, kind and inquisitive, and everyone likes him (or seems to)" (p. 228). Even Derek's nurse, "who is considerate to none of us . . . not even to Derek anymore, I suspect, singles my boy out periodically for loud flattery" (p. 259). Thus, when Slocum remarks that "I've got to get rid of him," his seeming reference to Derek contains an even more pointed reference to the other little boy.

Inevitably, then, Slocum enacts an ostensible "accident" in which he gets rid of the boy. Immediately prior to the tragedy, he says, "I want my little boy back too. I don't want to lose him. I do" (p. 557). With intentional ambiguity, Slocum reveals his hidden desire to be rid of the two little boys who have merged; he doesn't want to lose "him," but he does lose him — and, more significantly, he does *want to* lose him. When he finds the boy bleeding from superficial wounds, he acts at last: "I have to do something. I hug his face deeper into the crook of my shoulder. I hug him tightly with both my arms. I squeeze" (p. 558). Though Slocum has convinced himself that the boy is already dying in agony, it is clear that this hug is not meant to comfort but to suffocate. It recalls, with heavy irony, an exchange of hundreds of pages earlier when the son asks: " 'If you do want to get rid of me, how will you do it?' 'With hugs and kisses,' I answer in exasperation" (p. 233). Fulfilling his own prophecy, Slocum succeeds in ridding himself of the poignant reminder of his freedom and responsibility.

In the final reference to the novel's title, Slocum convinces himself of the truth of his deterministic vision while Heller finally destroys its validity for the reader. Slocum is called to the scene of his son's accident by a youth in his early teens who runs by, shouting, " 'Something happened!' " (p. 557). Slocum is sure that this is the fated disaster he has predicted for his son throughout the novel. He acts to finish off the boy because he tells himself that death has already come from the outside, from the environment, from the car that crashed into the store window. But the reader understands, though Slocum is unable to face it himself, that nothing simply happens by itself: people make things happen. The youth's cry of " 'Something happened!' " becomes richly ironic in retrospect since nothing much had happened until Slocum arrived on the scene to make something happen. For the reader, this last evocation of the title exposes the deterministic vision as a refusal to cope with the evident responsibility we all bear for our actions and the corresponding freedom with which we choose them.

If this reading of the novel has merit, *Something Happened* is not a pessimistic departure from *Catch-22*, but a more subtle exploration of similar themes. While Yossarian represented Heller in his affirmation of freedom and of responsibility, Slocum does not. But the book urges those same affirmations by implication. While an omniscient persona for the author guided the reader through *Catch-22*, *Something Happened* challenges us to interpret a limited and unreliable narrator. What Heller often said explicitly in his first novel, he suggests obliquely in his second. Slocum resists and denies freedom in his deadly deterministic game, but the reader is freed from the narrow limits of his faulty perspective to a broader vision of Heller's imaginative triumph.

Notes

1. Melvin Maddocks also terms Slocum "A weightless figure with no pull of gravity morally or emotionally," in "Boring from Within," review of *Something Happened*, *Time*, 14 October 1974, p. 87.

2. Kurt Vonnegut, Jr., review of *Something Happened*, *The New York Times Book Review*, 6 October 1974, p. 2. Other reviewers who note the book's pessimism include Nelson Algren, review of *Something Happened*, *The Critic*, 33 (October 1974), 90, and Pearl K. Bell, review of *Something Happened*, *The New Leader*, 28 October 1974, p. 18.

3. Joseph Heller, *Something Happened* (New York: Alfred A. Knopf, 1974), p. 3. All citations refer to this edition. Ellipses throughout are mine.

4. Jean-Paul Sartre, *Being and Nothingness*, trans. Hazel E. Barnes (1943; rpt. New York: Washington Square Press, 1966), pp. 78–79.

5. Though Slocum might seem wealthy by many standards, with his "choice country acre in Connecticut," he does not perceive himself as rich. His daughter asks, "Will we ever be rich?" and he responds, "No" (p. 115).

Joseph Heller, *Something Happened*, and the Art of Excess

Thomas LeClair*

In *The Pleasure of the Text*, Roland Barthes distinguishes between the text of pleasure, "the text that contents, fills, grants euphoria; the text that comes from culture and does not break with it, is linked to a comfortable practice of reading," and the text of bliss, "the text that imposes a state of loss, the text that discomforts (perhaps to the point of a certain boredom), unsettles the reader's historical, cultural, psychological assumptions, the consistency of his tastes, values, memories, brings to a crisis his relation with language."[1] While Barthes insists that bliss comes "only with the *absolutely new*" (p. 40), American novelists in the 1970s demonstrate that the text of bliss can also be produced by excess. If recent books by Joseph Heller, William Gaddis, Robert Coover, John Barth, Thomas Pynchon, and Joseph McElroy lack the militant originality of the *nouveau roman*, they do have an unsettling massiveness or multiplicity of implication that exceeds the norms of conventional fiction — the text of pleasure. For the American novelist who writes for a large audience or publishes with a commercial press, a work of excess has the rhetorical advantage of soliciting conventional responses which are then overturned because excess forces the reader to reconsider such notions as proportion, propriety, quantity, and value. Unable to consume the excessive text, the reader feels that "state of loss" and crisis in "his relation with language" that Barthes rather ironically calls bliss.

The strategy of excess Heller employs in *Something Happened* can be usefully contrasted with the method of Pynchon's *Gravity's Rainbow*. In

*Reprinted, with permission, from *Studies in American Fiction*, 9 (1981), 245–60.

the terms of information theory, *Gravity's Rainbow* is overloaded, *Something Happened* is redundant. The multiplicity of events, characters, discourses, and codes of meaning in Pynchon's book creates a diversity, an informational improbability, that readers cannot process into some familiar configuration. Despite its apocalyptic sentiments, the novel itself is an open system. Its excess of information suggests plentitude, possibility. *Something Happened* is by comparison decidedly closed. By imposing strict imaginative and linguistic constraints on his narrator, Heller creates a redundant text, one in which clearly limited elements — characters, actions, words — are combined, recombined in probable ways, and even repeated. As reviewers noted, not always with sympathy, this redundancy was a large artistic risk for Heller. If an overloaded novel resists its reader, the reader of *Something Happened* may resist being under-informed, under-stimulated; he may feel "a certain boredom," Barthes remarks. The novel succeeds because its repetitiveness is wholly functional, creating a double effect: one mimetic, one metaphysical. Coming late to the corporate man in the exurbs, as he came late to war in *Catch-22*, Heller uses excessive familiarity to defamiliarize a social experience often treated by other novelists; he uses redundancy to renew. Once redundancy has created a memorable character to ride the 5:45 of his readers' imaginations, Heller presses it further to create a sense of futility that he makes instructive by implicating readers in it and by making that futility metaphysical and not just Bob Slocum's personal despair. A set of disturbing thematic and aesthetic paradoxes arises from the novel's excess. In the world of Bob Slocum and in the fictional system that is *Something Happened*, fullness is emptiness, largeness is smallness, motion suggests stillness, and articulation implies silence. These reversals in turn contribute to Heller's most important accomplishment in the novel; demonstrating the ultimate futility of quantitative and causal thinking. Thinking of himself as trapped in a job and in a family, Bob Slocum is most surely and instructively trapped in a mode of thinking and in the language of that thinking. It is Heller's realistic portrayal of Slocum's "realistic thinking" that makes *Something Happened* a profound, as well as an observant, work of representation.

The distinction between causal thinking and cybernetic thinking is made by Gregory Bateson in *Steps to an Ecology of Mind*.[2] Rooted in the mechanistic science of the nineteenth century, causal thinking assumes closed systems and makes all phenomena subject to a unitary method concerned with measuring quantities and forces, with energy transfer between entities, and with creating lineal chains of efficient causes. Cybernetic thinking posits open systems and focuses on the kinds of relations among phenomena, on structures and context, on exchange of information (rather than energy), and on circular systems incorporating final causality. When employed to analyze human consciousness, causal thinking reifies and atomizes the self, creates a strong opposition between identity and world. Cybernetic thinking is holistic, preserving an ecological complementarity of self and other. Causal thinking leads to what Bateson and R. D. Laing after him call the "double bind," a situation in which a person feels trapped between two contradictory injunctions.[3] If the person in the bind accepts the either/or basis of causal thinking, he cannot see the bind as a both/and situation, as an intersection of two systems rather than an internal contradiction of one. No amount of precision of causal discrimination will solve the double bind, and it may make the bind stronger, massively insoluble. What breaks the bind is recognition of the different categories or contexts in which the seemingly contradictory, binding propositions exist. Because the assumptions of causal thinking are embedded in common discourse, cybernetic thinking, as Wittgenstein said of philosophy, "is a battle against the bewitchment of our intelligence by means of language."[4]

"It was after the war that the struggle began," says Heller.[5] In *Catch-22*, the struggle is for physical survival and, in Yossarian's case, for preservation of a minimal moral code. In *Something Happened*, the struggle is psychological and epistemological: Slocum's search for certainty and purpose. While both novels are full of double binds, the binds in *Catch-22* are imposed by the superior force of the military bureaucracy. One of the last definitions of "Catch-22" makes this clear: "Catch-22," explains the old woman in Rome, means "they have a right to do anything we can't stop them from doing."[6] If the characters cannot see through the paradoxes of power logic, the reader can. The binds of *Something Happened* are familial and linguistic, imposed by the self, complicated by love, and more difficult for both characters and readers to dissolve. This resistance makes *Something Happened* a better novel, a book that shows considerable artistic growth. The shifts from satire to irony, from external to internal, partially account for this growth, but more significant in *Something Happened* is Heller's full exploitation and testing of his medium: the conventions of confessional narration, the norms of realism, the limits of common language. He manipulates impossible materials—exhausted situations and used-up language—into a simultaneous dramatization of, and mockery of, limits. Like Nabokov and Beckett, Heller makes failure artful. And Heller preserves verisimilitude: a child in gym class, men at a convention, conversation on the ride home from church. As it examines itself and the conventions it adopts, *Something Happened* also examines *Catch-22*. In abstract but important terms, the struggle in *Something Happened* partially results from Bob Slocum's mapping of the quantitative assumptions of *Catch-22* onto his own consciousness and life.

There is a faith in *Catch-22* that more is best, both in the composition and in the system the novel is about. The model for the military is the production line. Material and labor are entities; work proceeds through a chain of causes governed, in the military, by a chain of command. Value is quantity: the size of a command or corporation, how much profit M & M Enterprises turns, how many missions are flown. As General Peckem says: " 'While none of the work we do is very important, it is important that we do a great deal of it' " (p. 330). This quantitative logic is internalized by the characters down the chain of command. For Captain Black, "the more loyalty oaths a person signed, the more loyal he was" (p. 117). Dobbs's plan to murder Cathcart turns into "a blood bath" (p. 233) that includes McWatt. The wisdom of the old man in Rome is living 107 years. Dunbar's schemes for extending time are quantitive desperation. Orr, in his patience with multiple small objects and repeated failures, is the saintly contrast to Dunbar. More complex are the responses to quantity of Cathcart and Yossarian. Cathcart creates what Heller calls an "arithmetical world" (p. 193) by splitting his life into "black eyes" and "feathers in his cap," which he lists, adds up, and measures against one another. This quantitative analysis of personal experience is "unstable" (p. 193), as well as trivial, because Cathcart cannot keep his categories mutually exclusive: Yossarian keeps popping up on both sides of his split. Not as analytical as Cathcart, Yossarian enjoys his "Gargantuan appetites" (p. 136) and his numerous sexual conquests. But Yossarian is also beset by numerous anxieties which are not directly war-related. He lists the diseases he could get, the accidents he might suffer, and is terrified by the "necrotic profusion" (p. 147) and the "ungovernable mutative mass" (p. 148) of mushrooms sprouting in the forest.

Despite the destructiveness of quantitative values in *Catch-22*, despite the inefficiency of the quantitative method and the primal terror quantity stimulates, Heller has Yossarian find certainty in quantity, discover a message in mass. In the Eternal City chapter, the repeated sufferings Yossarian witnesses lead him to speculate about the numbers of victims and the numbers of injustices in the world. After a long series of questions beginning with the phrase "how many," Yossarian computes the state of goodness in his world: "When you added them all up and then subtracted, you might be left with only the children, and perhaps with Albert Einstein and an old violinist or sculptor somewhere" (p. 422). In the Snowden episode, quantity yields a message, not just a result. Repeated until Yossarian can fully remember the "God's plenty" (p. 449) of Snowden's spilled guts, the episode suggests there is a secret in quantity: "The spirit gone, man is garbage" (p. 450). The faith implicit here is that a large quantity of experience, especially repeated experience, produces a qualitative, conclusive recognition that changes behavior. Enough relatives produce an absolute. After he understands the secret, Yossarian departs from the rule of quantity to save a child. In *Something Happened*, Heller does not have knowledge add up to a transcendent conclusion. When Bob Slocum brings to his experience a similar faith in the collection of data, in repeated examination, and in the existence of a unitary meaning to direct him, no secret appears. Quantity and futility are in direct proportion. Slocum does not save his child.

The conclusive message Yossarian receives is reflected by the form Heller gives the ending of *Catch-22*. In the first two-thirds of the novel, Heller establishes a disorienting and satiric fullness through fragmented time, associative ordering, repetition, and a language marked by superlatives. Words such as "endless," "largest," "worst," "best," "every," and "always" appear on most of the pages of the book. In the last third of the novel, as Yossarian moves toward the single secret, Heller funnels materials into a unitary form: time is linear, causality banishes the gratuitous. Out of many comes one. There are good artistic reasons for a hero's discovering a meaning and for the suspense a narrowed focus gives. After the excess does its satiric work, it can be ruled and ordered into an edifying conclusion, a climax of knowledge. But this conceptual and formal funneling reinforces rather than questions cultural assumptions about the relation between quantity of data and important knowledge. Despite its surface resistances to reading, *Catch-22* is what Barthes would call a text of pleasure.

In *Catch-22* the reader's expectations are confuted in the beginning, restored in the end. In *Something Happened*, Heller sets up initial expectations that he both strengthens and finally confutes with excess. The novel has a traditional structure for confessional narration: it moves from the external world of the present (the office) to Slocum's family, his past, and private memory, and returns to the external present. But this structure, which has a privileged status from psychiatry, is hollow. Despite the mass of detail and Slocum's persistent analysis, the growth of knowledge usually dramatized by this structure is absent. Bob Slocum cannot know what he wants to know, and the reader who shares Slocum's expectation and method must share his futility. Slocum appeals to his reader's curiosity and gains his confidence by revealing a privacy rarely breached. While the anxieties, desires, and ambivalences Slocum admits may be common, the attention he gives to the minutiae of his life — the details of pettiness, phobias, and quotidian experience — exceeds the requirements of verisimilitude, defamiliarizes his ordinariness, and achieves a "reliability" that far outweighs the distaste such revelations may create. Slocum is the naive narrator whose excessive artlessness evidences his truthfulness, whose confessed evasion of certain truths proves his commitment to a larger truth-finding. The faults he reveals also help Heller implicate the reader in Slocum's intellectual method. Morally and even analytically superior to the Slocum of the first sections, the reader is invited to prepare a causal explanation for Slocum's behavior — as Slocum himself is doing in a rather haphazard and not very penetrating way. At first the redundancy of Slocum's account underlines his purposiveness, but as he continues to repeat his experiences, recapitulate his fantasies, and elaborate his analyses, the redundancy suggests to the reader following Slocum's causal search that he, the reader, has been implicated in a futile methodology. Other contemporaries, most notably Pynchon and Barth, have attacked the notion of mechanistic causality with novels about absurdly ambitious intellectual projects — Stencil's historiography in *V.*, Andrews' account of his father's suicide in *The Floating Opera*. What makes *Something Happened* original, as well as poignantly persuasive, is Heller's location of that ambition in ordinary life and his use of redundancy to register the futility of that ambition.

Power is the theme that unifies the recognition that *Something Happened* works toward and the life it presents: power of explanation, power
over people and things. The desire for power exists in both the family and
the corporation, but the structure of the novel implies that corporate value
poisons private life. In Slocum's family, power is occasionally mediated by
love; in his company power is an end in itself. Production, leadership, responsibility, pride — none is as important as the imposition and consolidation of power. The people Slocum allows to emerge from the corporate
warren represent various kinds of power: Brown physically threatens
Slocum, Green has a social and verbal "whammy" on him, Baron can fire
him at any time, and White can fire Baron. Slocum's work and socializing,
his compassion and aggression, the meaning of closed doors, and even his
lunch-time lays are all measured in terms of power. When a bind arises between friendship with Kagle and the chance for Kagle's job, Slocum relies
on the principle of most power: he takes Kagle's job.

Slocum brings home his power principle and its attendant paranoia. At
the beginning of his narrative, Slocum seems to have more power at home
than at the office. He possesses his family: wife, daughter, and son are "my
wife," "my daughter," "my son." They have no names. But if he possesses,
then he must protect, which creates a bind between power and responsibility. Possession also means, for Slocum, explanation. He never considers why
the corporation is as it is, but the power he thinks he holds in his family
requires him to explain to himself what makes them unhappy and, if he has
this power, what makes *him* unhappy. This relationship of power, possession, and explanation is not explicitly recognized by Slocum. The occasion
for his mid-life account is quite ordinary, a set of transitions: his shift in
jobs, his daughter's passage into maturity, his son's beginning adolescence.
But the reader sees that Slocum's absorption in power is not just the trace
element in the torturing binds of his domestic life but also a source of his
obsessive need to explain and a reason for the kind of explanation he attempts. Fearful of physical assaults, wary of social embarrassment, always
looking for psychological advantage and verbal superiority, Slocum projects his present atmosphere back over his life, attempts to understand his
life as a power series of events tripping off one another like switches in a
circuit: "Somebody must have set me off in this direction, and clusters of
other hands must have touched themselves to the controls at various times,
for I would not have picked this way for the world" (p. 307). Many of the
reasons that psychologists and sociologists have advanced for contemporary
malaise — loss of religion, lack of purposeful work, family breakdown, surburban separation, sexual license — are manifested in the novel, even directly articulated by Slocum; but he cannot be satisfied with a composite
explanation. He wants the single-gauged certainty of mechanistic science;

he seeks a first cause or, at least, the fateful intervention that sent him, like a billiard ball, to his present position: "Somebody pushed me," says Bob Slocum (p. 307).

Slocum's assumption that his life is a chain of efficient causes can be seen as a defense, a way for him to deny his own responsibility: "What decided to sort me into precisely this slot? (What the fuck makes anyone think I am in control, that I can be any different from what I am?)" (p. 210). But his conception of his life gives him more anxiety than comfort. There is much Slocum does not want to know and much about his present he would like to avoid, yet his obsessional returning to events of his earlier life and to dreams or fantasies he thinks may reveal the past bespeak a commitment to knowledge and solution that tortures rather than releases Slocum. As Slocum works toward the solution that eludes him, his pain increases; he begins to doubt his sanity; he worries more and more about language. Slocum's daily life and his frustrating attempt to understand it combine to make his present unbearable and, finally, destructive. Early in the novel Slocum summarizes his intellectual problem: "I am lacking in sequence for everything but my succession of jobs, love affairs, and fornications" (p. 135). He wants that sequence and believes it can be found. Reflecting on his daughter's life, Slocum defines what he seeks in sequence: "There must have been a break somewhere, an end and a starting point, a critical interval in her development of some breadth and duration that I cannot remember or did not notice (just as there must certainly have been a similar start of metamorphosis somewhere back in my own past that I took no notice of then and cannot remember now)" (p. 205). Seeking "the critical interval," the exact moment of change, Slocum repeatedly examines episodes he thinks may give away the secret. He isolates his daughter's early birthday party and forages his memory for dramatic change in his son's development. He returns again and again to his last conversation with his mother, each time remembering, like Yossarian, a few more details. He divides up experience into smaller and smaller units, makes his memory into a film:

> Nearly every time I search back I come upon myself standing still inside some memory, sculpted there, or lying flattened as though by strokes from the brush of an illustrator or in transparent blue or purple chemical stains on the glass slide of a microscope or on the single frame of a strip of colored motion picture film. Even when the film moves, I am able to view the action only in arrested moments on single frames (p. 427).

Despite this frustration, Slocum holds faith in his method. "And yet," he says "I must have moved from where I was to where I've come" (p. 427). His search goes on for the critical frame between the frames and for the first cause. He pushes back to the earliest event for which he has evidence: "I was born, I was told, with a mashed face and red and blue forcep bruises on my shoulders and arms but felt not one message of pain because I had no nervous system yet that could register any" (p. 559). It is to this unsatisfactory end, a physical event without measurable effect, that Slocum's method brings him. Still he does not repudiate his method: the reader has to measure it against Slocum's expectations and the results it gives. Slocum's desire is to explain himself as an entity rather than as a person: to account for his life as matter in a sequence of energy transfers. When he falls back on psychological causality, his notions are naive. Slocum alludes to Freud and uses several psychoanalytic terms, but his conception of Freudian psychology is from what Anthony Wilden calls the "bio-energetic Freud," the early Freud whose ideas of drive and force came from mechanistic science.[7] The kind of causal sequence, whether material or psychological, that Slocum tries to find does not lead — it cannot lead — to the reductive certainty he desires and assumes. Instead his method generates an analytic atomization of experience and a temporal regress that could be infinitely extended. These natural limits of the causal method are made obvious when Slocum uses it to analyze a life that is more exchange of information than exchange of energy. Searching his past for what happened and waiting for something to happen in the future, Slocum loses his present. His frustration with his impossible task contaminates his life and his relations with others.

Slocum's equation of power and happiness and his causal method are called into question by two characters nominally under his power — Martha, the typist going crazy at the office, and Derek, Slocum's brain-damaged son. Though powerless over others and even themselves, Derek and Martha are happy, or so they finally seem to Slocum. He begins to identify with them, wonders if he talks to himself as Martha does, and wonders too if fearless Derek might be the lucky one in his family. Derek also exemplifies the bind of possession and explanation mentioned above. Having helped create Derek, Slocum feels he must explain what happened. After he has given a chapter to his wife, daughter, and normal son, Slocum considers Derek. This order and the increased digressiveness of Derek's chapter illustrate the evasion of Derek's condition that Slocum willingly admits. But the placement also points up the futility of Slocum's thinking. Because Derek is more a phenomenon than a person, Slocum's mechanistic method should be able to explain what happened to Derek. Slocum gathers data and conclusions from a variety of scientific experts, but they can agree on neither etiology nor prognosis. Derek is an accident that Slocum tries to forget, not just because of the sorrow and inconvenience Derek brings, but also because he is walking proof that the certainty, even necessity, that Slocum seeks in causal chains is unavailable, illusory. As a youth working in the insurance company, Slocum recognized the overwhelming quantity of accidents in life: "What impressed me most was the sheer immensity of all those dead records, the abounding quantity . . . that vast, unending sequence of unconnected accidents that had been happening to people and cars long before I came to work here, were happening then, and are happening still" (pp. 20–21). But Slocum cannot accept accident in his own life; he tries to connect the dead records of his past into sequence.

Corollaries of causal thinking, according to Bateson and Wilden, are the self's splitting and reifying itself and the existence of double-bind situations created by either/or logic. Slocum thinks of himself as a collection of "1,000 me's" (p. 399), miniature selves and split selves occupying him as though he were a city. He also sees himself in others — Kagle, his daughter, Derek, and most fully, in his nine-year-old normal son. Atomized and redoubled, Slocum thinks of these selves as things, as real substances that "scratch and stick" him (p. 399). These objectified selves, often earlier versions of the present Slocum, struggle for power within. They contradict one another, create tense ambivalences. To accept these ambivalences as natural or essential would be to deny the possibility of the single causal chain Slocum works toward, so he denies his internal evidence that experience is "both/and" and inflicts his faith in "either/or" upon his family and himself. Ambivalences and contradictions thus become destructive double-binds. Because Slocum loves and identifies with his normal son more than any of his other family members, the binds in that relation are most complex. The episode in which Slocum chastizes the boy for giving away money is one small, clear example of the double-binds and Slocum's characteristic "solution." Given money by his father, the boy understands two injunctions: be generous and do not be generous. Father and son go around and around this contradiction without seeing that the two directives exist on two different levels of meaning, in two different contexts. Slocum finally uses power — "a lame and dogmatic Because" (p. 281) — to put an end to the discussion but not the confusion. As the boy increasingly distances himself from his father — closes his door, becomes silent — Slocum experiences the binds of contradictory wishes: he wants his son to be independent and he wants his son to be dependent; he wants to protect his son from suffering and he wants to not have to protect his son from suffering. Unable to fruitfully analyze and dissolve these binds, Slocum suffers what Wilden calls "oscillations": he alternates between extreme responses to each of the contradictory desires.[8] As the book nears its happening, Slocum fantasizes desperate protection of his son and fantasizes destroying him. When the auto accident does happen and Slocum feels he has "to do something" (p. 562), extremes unite in one response: Slocum clasps — binds — his son to him in a killing embrace.

Thinking of his life as a necessary sequence of events, Slocum is unprepared for accident. Anxiously strung between contradictions his mode of thinking can neither accept nor resolve, he destroys what he most wants to save. But the final irony of *Something Happened* is that the accident and Slocum's act end the atomization, binds, and lack of sequence that have tortured him. In the last chapter, the self is solidly and simply "I," no contradictions bother the new Bob Slocum, and life now approaches the orderliness of the list he keeps: "Systematically, I am putting my affairs in order. I tick them off my list" (p. 566). Now Slocum is in control; he is a "ballet master" (p. 568) with power over people in the corporation and his family. But this is only a parody of the conclusion in *Catch-22*, for Slocum is in his last chapter a dead man. His ambivalences indicated a reciprocity with other humans, a concern and vulnerability. Now pure cause without concern for previous causes, Slocum becomes what he had hoped to find, a thing bumping other things, the product of his method.

While cybernetic thinking is not a therapeutic solution to the conditions Heller presents, *Something Happened* dramatizes the destructive misapplication of causal methodology that cyberneticists and the cybernetics-influenced R.D. Laing have analyzed. Slocum's experience in his company, in his family, and in the past he reports is essentially the experience of information exchange, which by its nature is reciprocal and complex. Both the sender and the receiver of messages "cause" the exchange; efficient and final causality combine. Because information is a relation and exists at different levels of abstraction, treating information exchanges as if they were energy exchanges — as Slocum does — simplifies and distorts man's fundamental experience. A method used to predict the processes of entities will not only fail to understand the processes of information but can also interfere with the continued work of those processes. As Slocum chases his causal chain, he imposes the harmful corollaries of causal thinking and inflicts his frustration on his family. The cybernetic definition of man as locus of information emphasizes participation in multiple ecological systems, his reciprocity with others, and a goal-seeking futurity. Slocum's causal thinking substitutes for these qualities a closed system, a powerful opposition between self and world, and temporal regression. Neither mode of thinking can ground man in some absolute certainty, some Snowden's secret, but relativity is admitted by cybernetics while the causal method, naively accepted, holds some promise of a single answer, an irreducible element. Slocum fails to find this answer, fails to see the limits of his method, and fails his family as he fails himself. In this novel about Oedipal relations, Slocum echoes Oedipus as adult king: searching for the cause of malaise, he uncovers himself.

Heller allows Slocum's failure to be complete and self-enclosed. He furnishes no alternatives to Slocum's mode of thinking, makes no measuring allusions behind Slocum's back. The reader must learn the nature of Slocum's failure by participating in it. While the events Slocum reports document his day-to-day failure as husband and father, the more significant failure of his mode of thinking is manifested through the redundancy of selection and language that is the novel's excess. In information theory, redundancy is defined as the probability of a message, the degree to which the text of a message can be anticipated. Repetition is, of course, the ultimate redundancy. In *Something Happened*, the associative jumps and mutations of Slocum's narration produce what first seems to be an improbable text, a text difficult to anticipate. But as the novel progresses, the shifts in time and the digressions come to be only superficially significant because Slocum so often returns to previously described episodes, reviews the small number of characters, or articulates reveries and analyses familiar from earlier pages.

Although the chapters are increasingly digressive and fragmented, until the very end when Slocum imposes an obviously arbitrary and false order, the materials of these chapters are like the stones in the pockets of Beckett's Watt: finite permutations. "Self-indulgence," said some reviewers of *Something Happened*, and Slocum certainly is narcissistically indulgent. But his combination and recombination more significantly reveal an attempt to make his account a closed system, the kind of system in which causal thinking is supposed to work. Bob Slocum fears others' closed doors but closes his whenever possible. *Something Happened* is his attempt to close out experience he would deny and close in experience he believes will reveal the secret of his life. The more Slocum repeats materials within his closed system, the more desperate and ineffectual his closure and causal method seem to the reader. Redundancy thus prepares the reader for Slocum's final failure.

There are, as well, proximate uses of redundancy. The utterly familiar life, repeated, loses some of its familiarity; this is the *déja vù* effect Heller notes and uses in *Catch-22*. The boredom Slocum feels in his repetitive office tasks, in his affairs, and in his conversations at home is best made palpable by Heller's risking the reader's boredom. Even Slocum recognizes this effect: "I begin to perceive what a stereotype I am only when I realize how often my daughter and my boy can predict and mimic my remarks with such verbatim precision" (p. 287). But redundancy does its most important work when Heller uses it to confute Slocum's and the reader's assumptions about quantity and causality, cumulative knowledge, close inspection, and conclusion. The episode with Virginia, one of the most redacted in the novel, supplies an excellent example. Slocum wonders why nothing ever happened between Virginia and him at the insurance company. He tells over and over, adding a few details each time, what she did, what he did, what others in the office did, what men did to Virginia before, what he stopped men from doing, what Virginia did to herself, and what he did afterwards; but this mass of detail, repeatedly considered, coughs up no satisfying conclusion, though Slocum does begin to realize that his failure was verbal, not knowing the right things to say. It was verbal failure then, verbal failure as he writes. Repeatedly attempting to manage a situation of information exchange as a situation of power, Slocum failed to have intercourse with Virginia. When he analyzes the experience, Slocum repeats the original failure by doggedly examining and re-examining the episode for cause rather than for information.

Like business, sex, and fatherhood, language is power for Bob Slocum: if language can push around other people, it should be able to name the critical cause, reduce his life to a definitive sentence. As a Market Researcher, Slocum has been successful "collecting, organizing, interpreting, and reorganizing statistical information . . . converting whole truths into half truths and half truths into whole ones" (pp. 28–29). He uses his wit to make political and sexual conquests at the office, to battle his daughter, and to please his son. In an environment of few physical demands, talk is important action and is a subject that pervades the book. Slocum yearns to address the company convention but fears his slight stammer. He is obsessed with stillness: motionlessness and silence seem the same. His dying mother's silence and Derek's inability to speak haunt him; his most frightening dreams and fantasies have him paralyzed and silent, still as a stone. Because the power of speech is so crucial to Slocum, his oscillations between anxieties over language and fantasies of verbal impotence are a primary index of his growing desperation amidst his life's materials. Near the end of his account, Slocum worries that soon he will "be repeating myself with everyone everywhere and be shunned as a prattling old fool" (p. 429). He fears that he talks to himself and to strangers. Yet he also admits enjoying the babble to which he is reduced by Penny's sexual skills; he envies Derek's freedom from sense, he thinks he might want to stutter: "What a liberating release it might be from the lifelong, rigorous discipline of speaking correctly" (p. 437). Speech does not just reveal binds; it is itself a bind and yet another source of irony for the novel's climactic event. Slocum is wounded by the silence of his boy, who worries what his parents would do with him if he could not speak. When he cries for help after the accident, Slocum acts rather than speaks, wordlessly suffocates his son. Then he asks for silence: " 'Don't tell my wife' " (p. 562). The last chapter doubles up the irony: told in a thoroughly affectless prose, it reports Slocum's directing others "with an authority that was almost musical" (p. 568).

Speech as action fails dramatically; Slocum's inability to summarize what happened to him in some satisfying, original sentences is progressively revealed by the linguistic redundancy that duplicates the larger rhythms of redundancy. From Slocum's fear of killing a mouse "completely" (p. 10) to his admission "I could not prove I was me" (p. 292) to his imagined deathbed "muttering 'Ma! Ma! Ma! Ma!' to the end" (p. 327), the reader is reminded of the fused vitality and futility of Beckett's fiction, silence feared and filled at any cost. By imposing strict constraints on Slocum's language, Heller creates a primer style that is an analogue of Slocum's naïveté about causal sequence. While the question "what happened" is natural at a primer stage of language, an obsession with this question limits the kinds of sentences the speaker will generate, thus increasing the redundancy that the limited lexicon and paratactic structures of a primer style produce. Limited language and limited thinking are reciprocal in effect. If common sense encourages causal thinking, common talk reveals its limitations. Lacking concrete precision and conceptual sophistication, Slocum's lexicon exists in a mid-range that is both vague and repetitive. His talk is full of familiar sludge-like abstractions (" 'Everybody is something' " p. 204), clichés and euphemisms, tautologies, filler and periphrasis. In his naming prose, abstractions are often reified: "I have this thing about authority, about walking right up to it and looking it squarely in the eye, about speaking right out to it bravely and defiantly, even when I know I am right and safe" (p. 15). *Something Happened* has few allusions, several metaphors much repeated, only occasional shifts in register (formal and vernacular), and some tonal shifts — hyperbole, exclamations, questions — that make the words used no less redundant. Without resources for variety, Slocum combines and repeats the words he has. His syntax is also repetitive. Though Slocum searches for causal sequence, there is surprisingly little causal subordination in his sentences. Statements of condition and reports of action become discourse by simple addition or opposition. Compounds — subjects, verbs, modifiers, and sentences — produce a sense of fullness but within the same basic structure, the text seems a collection of raw data awaiting Slocum's analytic reduction into conclusive statements. When they are delivered, they are locked into the agent-action syntax his causal method dictates.

The following passage articulates Slocum's purpose and illustrates the motions of his language: "There are blurred histories of myself inside requiring translation and legibility. There is pain — there is so much liquid pain. It never grows less. It stores itself up. Unlike heat or energy, it does not dissipate. It all always remains. There's always more than before. There's always enough near the surface to fuel a tantrum or saturate a recollection. Tiny, barely noted things — a sound, a smell, a taste, a crumpled candy wrapper — can mysteriously set off thrumming vibrations deep within" (pp. 533–34). "Translation" and "legibility" are his reductive purpose: lucid explanation. Pain is his condition; it builds up and repeats like the sentences. The repetition emphasizes that pain, but the redundancy of diction and syntax in the middle of the passage also suggests Slocum's difficulty in doing more than naming the condition. Then pain changes from condition to active agent: "fuel" and "saturate." The next step is identifying entities causing the pain, which leads into a temporal regress. The "things" here are too tiny to be named and too numerous to be translated into legible conclusion. They and all the other things, along with all the actions, can be reduced only to the empty title sentence. Repeated or transformed into equally vague formulae, "something happened" is a refrain summarizing the ultimate futility of causal thinking.

Slocum is trapped within his prose. Though superficially conscious of his language, he cannot imagine through to a different way of speaking and thinking. He is fussy about punctuation, agreement, and case; he comments on words and jokes about banalities; and he recognizes that he acquires others' vocabularies (as he acquired another's handwriting). But his prose remains in what David Lodge, after Roman Jakobson, calls the "metonymic mode," the mode of contiguity and combination.[9] The alternative, the "metaphoric mode," sees similarities and analogues, a simultaneity of systems that also characterizes cybernetic thinking. Slocum attempts to do with quantity and repetition what can be managed only by a change in perspective, a new way of thinking about his life. Thus the fullness of *Something Happened* is finally empty, its largeness proof of Slocum's smallness. Despite its numerous shifts, it seems motionless. Redundant articulation tends toward silence. Because Slocum's language is the common tongue, the reader who sees its failure and sees his own complicity is brought to that "crisis [in] his relation with language" that Barthes says marks the text of bliss. *Something Happened* "imposes a state of loss." Heller's art of excess "discomforts" and "unsettles the reader's historical, cultural, [and] psychological assumptions." The reader learns not what happened or why but learns instead to consider the more important questions: how he conceives his life, how he speaks it.

Notes

1. Roland Barthes, *The Pleasure of the Text*, trans. Richard Miller (New York: Hill and Wang, 1975), p. 14; subsequent references in parentheses.

2. Gregory Bateson, *Steps to an Ecology of Mind* (New York: Ballantine, 1972); Anthony Wilden, *System and Structure* (London: Tavistock, 1972) further develops this distinction.

3. R. D. Laing, *The Politics of Experience* (New York: Ballantine, 1967).

4. Ludwig Wittgenstein, *Philosophical Investigations*, trans. G. E. M. Anscombe (Oxford: Blackwell, 1953), p. 47.

5. Joseph Heller, "Interview: Art of Fiction LI," *Paris Review*, 15 (Winter, 1974), 142. The actual quote from *Something Happened* is: "It was after the war, I think, that the struggle really began" (New York: Knopf, 1974), p. 87; subsequent references in parentheses.

6. Joseph Heller, *Catch-22* (New York: Dell, 1974), p. 416; subsequent references in parentheses.

7. Wilden, pp. 132–38.

8. Wilden, pp. 103–05.

9. David Lodge, *The Modes of Modern Writing* (Ithaca: Cornell Univ. Press, 1977).

The Dark Stranger in Heller's *Something Happened*

Joan DelFattore*

Joseph Heller's second novel, *Something Happened*, is an unusually long and complex work because its protagonist-narrator, Bob Slocum, is less concerned with describing external events than with considering his fears, desires, memories, and lack of control over many of his own actions, including the apparently accidental smothering of his nine-year-old son. Not surprisingly, in view of the novel's complexity, reviewers and critics have approached *Something Happened* in several ways: William Kennedy, Robert Scholes, and Kurt Vonnegut, for example, address the question of whether Slocum, a middle-aged executive in an unspecified corporation, is Heller's depiction of Everyman, while Molly Haskell interprets the novel from a feminist perspective, Edward Grossman identifies Jewish elements in it, Robert F. Lucid considers its implications as a novel about an Ameri-

*This essay was written specifically for this volume and is published here by permission of the author.

can businessman, Wilfred Sheed defines it as a variant form of the novel of manners, and Richard Hauer Costa and George Sebouhian place it in the context of similar literature by other authors.[1]

Despite their differences, however, almost all discussions of *Something Happened* have one point in common: their recognition of the emphasis that the novel places on thoughts, attitudes, and motivations Slocum does not understand and cannot control. Shorter pieces, such as reviews, tend to approach this issue by stressing the compulsive quality of his thoughts and actions, and longer critical articles discuss such topics as his close identification with his older son, his tendency to reify internal forces to define his own fragmentation, and the significance of his "inner" narrative voice, expressed in parenthetical asides. Nevertheless, despite this widespread recognition of the importance of mental activity that Slocum does not fully understand or consciously control, no one has done more than mention the fact that he is subject to dreams; yet these dreams, frequent and in many cases recurrent, not only clarify and refine the most important motifs which appear in his waking thoughts but also suggest associations, fears, and desires of which he remains entirely unaware or about which he is confused and ambivalent.

Slocum mentions a number of recurrent dreams, several of which are complex, convoluted, and fragmented. It is clear, however, that one of the most prominent and important dream figures in the novel is a dark stranger with a concealed knife whose identity and purpose entirely elude Slocum. By considering the two recurrent dreams in which this dark stranger appears, and taking into account the contexts in which they occur and the stimuli which lead to Slocum's recounting them, it is possible to demonstrate how they bring together some of the disparate threads of his seemingly chaotic narrative into a coherent pattern based on a single overwhelming psychological drive: his terror of powerlessness, which arises from his tendency to equate self-worth with the ability to dominate others. Further, because of the symbolic significance of the dark stranger, the dreams in which he appears clarify Slocum's apparently inappropriate reactions to some of the people around him, including two upper-level executives in his company, his wife, his teenage daughter, his normal nine-year-old son, and his retarded younger son.

Slocum associates the idea of power with two physiological functions, sexual performance and the ability to speak. He regards sexual encounters primarily as opportunities to assert dominance, and he uses speech as a means of persuading women to have intercourse with him and as a source of influence over bosses and co-workers.[2] His overall fear of powerlessness is expressed accordingly, in individual fears of symbolic castration through various types of sexual failure and speechlessness. He is not conscious of some aspects of these individual fears and never identifies them as parts of a single pattern, but the dream figure of the dark stranger unites them all and connects them with hidden aspects of his own personality associated with his need to dominate by means of sex and speech.

Slocum's tendency to regard sex primarily as an opportunity to exercise power is evident throughout the novel. He delights in insisting that his wife have intercourse with him when she does not want to, is displeased when she or one of his many mistresses seems to enjoy it, and avoids women, even his wife, when they take any kind of sexual initiative or respond too readily to his. He also regards his sexual activity as a means of taking revenge on the female population for what he perceives as humiliations inflicted on him by certain women, especially a bossy middle-aged woman named Mrs. Yerger, who was his superior in the insurance company in which he worked when he was seventeen. He associates Mrs. Yerger with his wife's mother and sister, who compete with him for dominance over his wife, and he responds to their competition with displays of promiscuity and near-rape intended to re-establish his sense of ascendancy over her. In addition to using sex to bolster his feeling of superiority over women in general and his wife in particular, he uses it to exercise mastery over women co-workers whose positions in the company are inferior to his. He repeatedly indulges in sexual banter with a young subordinate named Jane, for example, because he enjoys knowing that he could have her whenever he wants to, and the fact that he does not want to makes her availability particularly attractive to him.

In thus regarding sex as an opportunity to assert power, Slocum is motivated by more than simple *machismo*. He associates sexual dominance so strongly with self-respect and success that it becomes those things in his mind, taking on an importance far beyond its objective value. The best illustration of this is his repeated use of the expression "to fit in" in such a way that it becomes a pun linking sexual penetration with winning a place for himself at home and in the office and being accepted as a worthwhile human being. When he reluctantly accompanies one of his bosses to a whorehouse, for example, he thinks, "Once I'm there I'm all right (I fit right in),"[3] and, later in the novel, when he has taken that boss's job and is apparently successful in his work and accepted by important executives, he describes scenes in which they praise him in these terms:

> "I like the way you've taken control."
> "I'm glad to see you're fitting in."
> (I am fitting in) (p. 568).

Throughout the novel, Slocum's use of word plays like this one, his obsessive repetition of certain material, and his reactions to events make it clear that, to him, sexual power is more than a physiological function; it is a means of asserting his essential self-worth.

Slocum's preoccupation with sexual power underlies his first mention of the dark stranger, which occurs in his description of a recurrent dream which synthesizes several points connected with his need to dominate.

> When I sleep away from home with my wife, I will have a nightmare the
> first or second night, usually the same one: a strange man is entering ille-
> gally through the door, which I have locked, and drawing near, a burglar,
> rapist, kidnapper, or assassin; he seems to be Black but changes; I think he
> is carrying a knife; I try to scream but can make no sound. I have this same
> bad dream at home often, even though I carefully lock all my doors before
> going to sleep. I have had it dozens and dozens of times. I have always had
> it (pp. 168–69).

The content of this dream and the fact that it is so closely associated
with Slocum's wife that it does not occur in her absence suggest that one of
the issues with which the dark stranger is associated is Slocum's fear, expressed repeatedly in the narrative, that his wife might commit adultery
with one of his colleagues. On this level of interpretation, the locked doors
through which the stranger passes represent the safeguards with which Slocum surrounds his wife, including his assiduous attendance to her at parties
and his attempts to convince her that she is incapable of making a life without him. His remark that the dark stranger "seems to be Black" is a pun that
helps justify his suspicion of his colleagues, one of whom is named Black, by
linking it with racial prejudices which appear throughout the novel in his
repeated use of the term "nigger" to describe any male whom he perceives as
a threat to his manhood. Further, since Black is an upper-level executive in
whose presence Slocum is unable to feel dominant, he is an appropriate
dream symbol for the imaginary seducer of Slocum's wife who thereby symbolically emasculates him.

It is clear elsewhere in the novel that Slocum's wife gives him no reason
to believe that she has any sexual interest in Black or in any of Slocum's
other colleagues, and his doubt about the dark stranger's possession of a
knife illustrates his uncertainty about the real existence of this type of castration threat in his waking life. On this level of interpretation, therefore,
this dream represents not only Slocum's dread of his wife's infidelity and of
his own consequent loss of power and status in the office and at home, but
also his recognition that that dread is probably irrational.

In his description of the dark stranger, Slocum says that he "seems to be
Black but changes." Here he is suggesting, without consciously understanding the import of what he is saying, another aspect of the dark stranger's
identity and another level of meaning in the dream. The dark stranger, who
appears to be someone else — a black man or a colleague — shades into an
embodiment of Slocum's own obsessive need to dominate. In his relationship with his wife, he himself is "burglar, rapist, kidnapper, [and] assassin."
He robs his wife of self-confidence to fulfill his need for her dependence; he
regards sex as something he does to her for his own satisfaction; he removes
her as far as possible, psychologically if not physically, from anyone he regards as a threat to his dominance over her, including her mother and sister;
and he destroys as much of her self-esteem as he can for the sake of his own.
Although he occasionally feels guilty about certain aspects of his treatment

of his wife, he does not recognize the exploitative quality of his behavior, and he does not consciously realize that he is sacrificing her welfare to his overwhelming need for dominance, represented by the dark stranger.

Because this dream is so closely connected with Slocum's wife, he might have been expected to recount it in the section of the novel devoted to her. Instead, he does so in the section entitled "My daughter's unhappy"; moreover, he recalls the dream while speculating on whether his fifteen-year-old daughter is still a virgin. Elsewhere in this section, he toys with the idea of seducing one of his daughter's teenage friends, and he often associates his daughter with his mistresses and with Virginia Markowitz, a deceased young woman whose sole purpose in the novel is to represent the object of Slocum's unfulfilled and unfulfillable sexual longing. All of this suggests that Slocum, who never consciously considers seducing his daughter, is subject to incestuous urges which appear in his dream of the dark stranger, who is undeterred by the locked doors of conscious censorship.

Like his other sexual impulses, Slocum's incestuous urges are dominative rather than romantic. His relationship with his daughter is based almost entirely on conflict and is characterized by frequent arguments in which he treats her as an adult rather than as an adolescent, thinking of nothing but vindicating his own superiority by outwitting her. Because he habitually regards sex as a means of asserting dominance, he naturally reacts to his daughter's insubordination by wanting to have intercourse with her and thus reduce her to what he regards as her proper place, but, because she is his daughter, he censors that inclination, which appears only in his dreams. The dark stranger therefore represents yet another aspect of Slocum which does not emerge in his waking thoughts: his image of himself as the seducer, and thus the master, of his daughter.

Taking into account all of these levels of interpretation, it is clear that the dark stranger fulfills two functions in this dream. First, he embodies not only Slocum's sexual fears and desires but also their source: his preoccupation with dominance. More importantly, because all of this is combined in his single being, the dark stranger confirms the existence of relationships among issues whose interdependence is only implied in the main body of the narrative. It is obvious in the context of the dream that Slocum's groundless anxiety about the possibility of his wife's infidelity, his exploitation of his wife, and his incestuous desires are parts of a single pattern based on his irrational view of sexual power, but, in the rest of his rambling narrative, these associations are less clear. Although he is very explicit about behavior and attitudes which appear to be highly unacceptable by conventional standards, such as his unfilial and unjust treatment of his dying mother and his verbal abuse of his daughter, internal censorship sends him off on tangents whenever he approaches, in his waking thoughts, realizations or associations which are unacceptable to Slocum himself. Including dreams like this one in the novel thus allows Heller to introduce in symbolic form topics that the character of Slocum, if he is to remain consistent, cannot discuss otherwise, and to show relationships among issues that Slocum discusses separately because he cannot consciously admit that they are connected.

Slocum's references to dreams involving the dark stranger do not deal exclusively with his concept of sex as power; they also reflect his tendency to associate facility in speech with sexual dominance and thus with power and self-esteem. His narrative includes numerous examples of this tendency, such as his obsession with the memory of Virginia Markowitz, who, when he was seventeen and she was twenty-one, routinely allowed him to kiss and touch her for brief periods before she pulled away abruptly, leaving him flushed and frustrated. He perceives his failure to have intercourse with her as having been verbal as much as sexual: he simply could not say the right words. Similarly, when he associates the idea of castration with his retarded younger son, comparing him with Faulkner's Benjy Compson, he assumes that the boy faces the threat of castration not because he is retarded but because he cannot speak. Slocum's association of castration with speech impairment is also evident in his obsessive memories of tonsillectomies, particularly his own and his older son's. He makes over twenty references to them, ranging in length from a few words to a page and a half, and invariably associates them with helplessness and deep fear. Although he never explicitly connects them with the idea of speech impairment, the associations are clear: the anesthetic renders the patient incapable of consciously controlled speech, and the surgical procedure produces temporary difficulty in speaking and entails the risk of accidents leading to permanent loss of speech. It is also clear that he associates tonsillectomies with symbolic castration; in connection with the removal of his son's tonsils and adenoids, for example, he tells one of his mistresses that adenoids are undescended testicles and makes a Shandyesque reference to the fact that adenoids dangle behind the nose.[4]

Slocum's association of tonsillectomies with sexually traumatic experiences may have begun with a very early episode in his life, which he recalls on the first page of the novel. "Maybe it was the day I came home unexpectedly with a fever and a sore throat and caught my father in bed with my mother that left me with my fear of doors, my fear of opening doors and my suspicion of closed ones." The fact that this is a primal scene experience, and the sexual significance of the reference to doors, have already been discussed by Michael Hoyt and Michael Moore, respectively.[5] The salient point of this episode as it relates to the present discussion is that Slocum came home "with a fever and a sore throat." His references to his tonsillectomy make it clear that he recalls it as a punitive experience involving pain, thirst, darkness, and abandonment, and it is at least possible to speculate that his excessively emotional memory of this event may be rooted in a childhood belief that his tonsillectomy was a punishment for having observed his parents in bed, a circumstance which uninstructed children typically regard as an act of violence associated in some poorly understood way with the genitals.[6]

The dark-complexioned doctors involved in the tonsillectomies that Slocum obsessively recalls are the only dark strangers with unseen knives whom he encounters in his waking life, and the dark stranger not only resembles them in appearance but also fulfills the same function: representing the threat of symbolic castration. The dark stranger's similarity to the doctors thus suggests that, in addition to embodying other aspects of Slocum's fear of powerlessness, he is associated with the fear of speech impairment. This is borne out when Slocum says of the dark stranger, ". . . I think he is carrying a knife; I try to scream but can make no sound" and when he moves from describing this dream to describing memories of his own tonsillectomy, his daughter's, and his older son's.

Although Slocum's association of the dark stranger with the fear of speech impairment is evident in the first dream, it is more central to the second dream in which that figure appears. Appropriately, this dream is recounted in the section of the novel which deals with Slocum's retarded and speechless younger son, Derek, who also appears as a character in the dream. Slocum's recollections of this dream ramble on for three pages, but the dark stranger appears in only one section of it:

> Horace White strolls into my dreams often with his nearly featureless face, hangs around awhile, and turns into florid, fleshier Green, who fumes and glares scathingly at me as he starts to make a cutting remark and then clears out as rapidly as I'd like to as soon as the menacing, dark stranger enters and draws near with his knife I never see, either waking me up moaning in primordial fright or quitting the scene graciously to make way for someone like my wife's mother or sister, Forgione, or Mrs. Yerger. Or my daughter, boy, and/or Derek. Or someone else I haven't invited (p. 400).

In this dream, the dark stranger appears in conjunction with individuals who are part of Slocum's waking life or memories, each of whom represents one of the censored issues associated with the composite figure of the dark stranger. For example, Slocum's memories of Mrs. Yerger, his emasculating former boss, and his feelings toward his wife's mother and sister, who compete with him for his wife's regard, have already been defined as factors which help to sting him into the attitude of sexually oriented exploitation which is among the qualities personified by the dark stranger. Similarly, Slocum's daughter's rebelliousness has been mentioned as the basis of incestuous urges which are also personified by the dark stranger. By thus juxtaposing the composite figure of the dark stranger with characters representing his component parts, this dream, like its predecessor, reveals not only attitudes of which Slocum is partially or entirely unaware but also associations which are only implied in the main body of the narrative.

The first character mentioned in his dream is Horace White, an upper-level executive in the unnamed company which employs Slocum. White, whose lack of personal distinction is represented in the dream by his "nearly featureless face," occupies a privileged position in the company because of his relationship to its founders and directors, his wealth, and the fact that he owns stock. He functions in the novel as an authority figure who forces Slocum to stand motionless and speechless while pretending to be fascinated by White's newest desk toy from Brentano's, and, when he demands changes in Slocum's work, Slocum is unable to speak effectively in reply because of White's superior position. The dream associates White with another authority figure, Green, who stands out in Slocum's mind because of his refusal to allow Slocum to make a speech at the company convention and because of his insistence that Slocum display an attitude of craven obedience which includes limiting his speech to the types of language and phrasing that please Green. In the main body of his narrative, Slocum expresses feelings of hatred and fear toward these two men which are so excessive that they puzzle him, especially in the case of White, who is comparatively inoffensive in his manner. The dream reveals Slocum's association of White with Green, who is deliberately offensive ("florid, fleshier Green, who fumes and glares scathingly a me"). It also reveals his association of both men with the dark stranger, who consistently represents issues connected with Slocum's irrational and obsessive fear of powerlessness. These associations make it clear that his hostile reactions to White and Green, which he consciously believes to be unconnected with one another and with everything else in his life, are part of a coherent pattern based on his fear of powerlessness and his tendency to associate power with the ability to speak effectively, which White and Green inhibit.

The dark stranger with the unseen knife, who enters immediately after the departure of White and Green, introduced by a pun ("cutting remark"), functions throughout the entire dream segment as he does with reference to these two men; that is, the presence of this composite figure with his multiple associations helps to clarify the relationships among all of the other, apparently unconnected, figures in the dream and to place them in an overall pattern of meaning. Moreover, Slocum's desire to escape when the stranger appears and his use of the terms "menacing" and "primordial fright" illustrate his dread of the associations attached to that figure. It is because of the intensity of this dread that his reactions to the persons to whom he transfers this emotional energy seem so thoroughly out of proportion. As this dream illustrates, these persons include not only dominative bosses and competitive women but also other figures who have not yet been discussed, such as Forgione, who enters the dream at this point.

The three women who are named with Forgione have already been defined as being, in Slocum's view, emasculating females; Forgione, Slocum's older son's physical education teacher, is an emasculating male. During a long discussion with Forgione on the subject of the boy's dread of gym class, Slocum conceives an irrational loathing for him which is based on his size, strength, and power over Slocum's beloved son, all of which make Slocum feel inferior, ineffectual, and unable to speak effectively.

Later in his narrative, Slocum acknowledges an unreasoning fear of Forgione and speaks of him in connection with the anesthetist at his son's tonsillectomy, the doctor who told him that his mother had had the stroke which impaired her speech, and the doctor who announced that Derek would never learn to speak. The appearance of Forgione in this dream in conjunction with the dark stranger is, therefore, another illustration of Slocum's irrational reaction to anyone who makes him feel threatened for such relatively minor reasons as Forgione's size and position, Mrs. Yerger's bossiness, and Green's petty tyranny. He does not see such individuals as individuals but as parts of an overwhelming series of events and possibilities designed to undermine his assertion of power through sex and speech, and he reacts accordingly, with an emotional intensity which is entirely out of proportion to the external events which appear to occasion it.

The last individuals whom Slocum mentions in connection with the dark stranger in this dream are his daughter and his two sons, the nameless nine-year-old he eventually smothers and the retarded younger child, Derek. Throughout the novel, Slocum expresses extreme reluctance to think about Derek; in fact, the section of the novel most directly concerned with him is entitled "It is not true" and consists of a series of apparent digressions, one of which is Slocum's description of this dream. Like other episodes in this section of the novel, this dream is only an apparent digression from the subject of Derek because it is concerned with the aspects of his disability which Slocum tries hardest to forget: speechlessness and helplessness.

Slocum's reluctance to consider the details of Derek's condition is based not on fatherly concern but on a deep-seated dread of recognizing speechlessness and helplessness as attributes of anyone belonging to him. Nevertheless, despite his attempts to dissociate himself from Derek, he sees the child not only as a reminder of a speechless condition which might in some way come upon him but also as an embodiment of qualities of his own which he would prefer to deny. Shortly before recounting this dream, for example, he visualizes Derek as a grown man, "slobbering, a thickset, clumsy, balding, dark-haired retarded adult male with an incriminating resemblance to a secret me I know I have inside me and want nobody else ever to discover, an inner visage. (I think I sometimes see him in my dreams)" (p. 391). He also refers to himself in the same terms he uses to describe Derek, particularly when he is relating some failure which occurred because of his inability to dominate by means of speech. In discussing his failure to have intercourse with Virginia Markowitz, for example, he describes himself as "a dumb, shy, frightened, and idiotically ingenuous virgin little boy" (p. 361) and exclaims "what a feeble-minded idiot: I could have had her then" (p. 362). Numerous examples like these make it clear that Slocum identifies Derek with an ineffectual, tongue-tied, nondominative quality which he wants to disown but reluctantly recognizes as part of himself.

Since Derek, like the dark stranger, embodies Slocum's fear of loss of power through speechlessness, his presence in this dream is not surprising. The reasons for his brother's appearance in conjunction with the dark stranger, however, are less immediately obvious because Slocum loves his older son dearly and identifies him with a part of himself which he envisions as a little boy hiding inside him: a little boy who represents the promise of self-determination, honor, and personal fulfillment which Slocum believes was once extended to him and is now inexplicably lost. Several critics have commented on the strength of Slocum's identification with his older son; Susan Strehle Klemtner, for example, writes, "Slocum comes to see the lost little boy hiding inside himself as a form of his 'angelic' son. . . . [His] literal physical identification with his son suggests that, for Slocum, his son has become the little boy inside him."[7] Klemtner suggests that Slocum cannot bear being so strongly reminded of seemingly desirable qualities which he does not really want to possess because they would interfere with his material advancement, and that his apparently accidental smothering of his son occurs because, in order to retain his deterministic belief that whatever he does is beyond his own control, he must eliminate the embodiment of alternative values whose existence he wishes to deny. Klemtner's argument is convincing, but outside the scope of her essay there is another aspect of the relationship between Slocum and his son which is also part of his complex motivation for killing the boy: his association of his older son with Derek and, through him, with the entire range of his fears of powerlessness.

Although Slocum loves his older son, he is exasperated almost to the point of violence by the boy's occasional episodes of speechless helplessness. On a summer day at the beach, for example, the boy stands petrified and silent while another boy in his play group bullies him; later, he stands on the boardwalk screaming wordlessly until his parents arrive, although he should have been able to find his own way home. Because of episodes like these, Slocum associates his older boy with Derek, an association which is underlined by his observation that in some of his dreams, "my staring, waiting nine-year-old boy becomes staring, speechless Derek" (p. 401). When recalling the older boy's speechless episodes, and at no other time, Slocum uses such expressions as "I could have strangled him" (p. 329), although he does not realize that he means it. Further, when he finally does kill his son, he does so in a way that resembles a daydream in which he murders Derek: "Derek I smother with a huge hand over his mouth to stifle his inarticulate noises and hide his driveling eyes, nose, and mouth" (p. 392). It is therefore clear that Slocum's association of his older son with Derek, which is suggested in this dream and supported by episodes in Slocum's waking life, is one of the factors which contribute to the act and manner of killing his son.

As the diversity of critical responses to *Something Happened* suggests, this highly complex novel can be interpreted by means of many different approaches, most of which are not mutually exclusive. No matter what approach is used in analyzing the novel, however, and no matter how many valid interpretations it has, to understand *Something Happened* in any sense it is necessary to understand the character of Bob Slocum. For this reason, the dreams of the dark stranger make a significant contribution to the meaning of the novel. They clarify ideas that Slocum mentions and then suppresses, and they help to explain his irrational and excessive responses to such individuals as White, Green, Forgione, and Slocum's wife's mother and sister. They also confirm the existence of fears and desires which are strongly implied by events in the narrative but of which Slocum himself is unaware, such as his incestuous urges and the specifically exploitative quality of his relationship with his wife. Most importantly, they reveal a pattern of association among his ideas of sex, speech, and power which underlies many of his internal and external responses. By considering the significance of his dreams it is possible to understand areas of his character which are otherwise obscure: those areas in which he is, to himself, a dark stranger.

Notes

1. William Kennedy, "Endlessly Honest Confession" [review of *Something Happened*], *New Republic*, Oct. 19, 1974, pp. 17–19; Robert Scholes, "Heller's World: Is It Ours?" [review of *Something Happened*], *Chronicle of Higher Education*, Dec. 9, 1974, p. 9; Kurt Vonnegut, [review of *Something Happened*], *New York Times Book Review*, Oct. 6, 1974, pp. 1–2; Molly Haskell, [review of *Something Happened*], *Village Voice*, Oct. 24, 1974, pp. 33–34; Edward Grossman, "Yossarian Lives" [review of *Something Happened*], *Commentary*, Nov. 1974, pp. 78, 80, 82–84; Robert F. Lucid, "The Major Novelists View the American Businessman," *New York Times*, June 29, 1975, Sec. 2, p. 14; Wilfred Sheed, "The Good Word; The Novel of Manners Lives," *New York Times Book Review*, Feb. 2, 1975, pp. 2–3; Richard Hauer Costa, "Notes from a Dark Heller: Bob Slocum and the Underground Man," *Texas Studies in Literature and Language*, 23 (1981), 159–82; George Sebouhian, "From Abraham and Isaac to Bob Slocum and My Boy: Why Fathers Kill Their Sons," *Twentieth Century Literature*, 27 (1981), 43–52.

2. In "Joseph Heller, *Something Happened*, and the Art of Excess," Thomas LeClair places Slocum's association of language with power in another context. LeClair focuses on Slocum's attempts to assert control over his life by verbalizing "in some satisfying, original sentences" (p. 257) the "something" that has defined his destiny, as if the universe were a closed system of fixed and identifiable cause-and-effect relationships. See *Studies in American Fiction*, 9 (1981), 245–60.

3. Joseph Heller, *Something Happened* (New York: Knopf, 1974), p. 76. All references are to this edition.

4. Sigmund Freud's theory of dream symbolism includes the idea of "upward transference," which suggests that a dreamer may represent castration in the form of such injuries to the head as having the teeth pulled and the hair cut (*The Interpretation of Dreams*, Second Part, Vol. 5 of *The Standard Edition of the Complete Psychological Works of Sigmund Freud*, ed. and trans. by James Strachey et al., [London: Hogarth, 1953] pp. 385–87). Slocum's references to adenoids as testicles seems to be an extension of this idea. Although Freud's theories are by no means universally accepted by contemporary psychologists dealing with real-life patients, it is appropriate to use a Freudian viewpoint in interpreting Slocum's dreams because they are literary artifacts created by Joseph Heller for the purpose of clarifying certain points in the novel, which is demonstrably Freudian in orientation. Heller himself has undergone lengthy psychoanalysis, and *Something Happened* is filled with explicit references to Freud himself and to such ideas as the Oedipal complex, penis envy, id and ego, castration anxiety, infant sexuality,

and the relationships among sex, money, and feces. All of these ideas are not exclusively Freudian, of course, but their frequent use does suggest a bias in that direction.

5. Michael F. Hoyt, "On the Psychology and Psychopathology of Primal-Scene Experience," *Journal of the American Academy of Psychoanalysis*, 8, (1980), 311–35; Michael Moore, "On the Signification of Doors and Gates in the Visual Arts," *Leonardo*, 14 (1981), 202–05.

6. See, for example, Freud, "On the Sexual Theories of Children," in Vol. 9 of *Complete Psychological Works* (1959), 220–22.

7. " 'A Permanent Game of Excuses': Determinism in Heller's *Something Happened*," *Modern Fiction Studies*, 24 (1978–79), 555.

Something Happened: The Imaginary, The Symbolic, and the Discourse of the Family

James M. Mellard*

Joseph Heller took a tremendous risk in *Something Happened*. He has spoken of the risks in his *technique*, the manner in which the "first and third person," he says, "are fused in a way I've never seen before, and time is compressed into almost a solid substance."[1] But one may suggest that the greater risk lies in the novel's psychological subtlety of content, structure, and theme. Though the psychological dimensions of *Something Happened* are evident from the outset, readers are perhaps thrown off the track by an overt invocation of the Oedipus complex as an explanation of those psychological disturbances suggested in the narrator's—Bob Slocum's—fear of closed doors and in other features of behavior. Slocum seems to imply that since he actually invokes an outmoded Freudian etiology, one must look elsewhere for the "real" causes of his neurotic behavior. In truth, one does well by the novel by merely shifting toward a *post*-Freudian interpretation, one found in the linguistic and semiotic approach of Jacques Lacan.

Lacan's version of Freudian psychology entails what one commentator calls a "classic narrative" pattern operating through the discourse of the family. Its stages or phases begin with birth and then move "in turn through the territorialization of the body, the mirror stage, access to language, and the Oedipus complex. The last two of these events belong to what Lacan calls the symbolic order, and they mark the subject's coming of age within culture."[2] These stages in turn operate within a dialectic Lacan calls the *Imaginary* and the *Symbolic*. The "mirror stage," initiating the movement into language, is essentially egocentric and thus caught up in the secondary narcissism of the Imaginary. Ordinary psychological growth, culminating in the cultural "coming of age," involves one's moving from the Imaginary to the Symbolic. If Bob Slocum is to grow psychologically, he must move from the earlier to the later phase; as long as he remains within the Imagi-

*This essay was written especially for publication in this volume and is included here by permission of the author.

nary, he will retain an essentially neurotic psychological disposition. Caught up in the Imaginary, the neurotic is defined by the belief one can recapture an initial plenitude or fullness of meaning and being. All neurosis, in Lacanian psychology, is therefore dominated by the terms of the Oedipal complex—castration, desire, the forbidden, sacrifice, the Father. Fredric Jameson has said that "neurosis for Lacan is essentially a failure to accept castration, a failure to accept the primal lack which is at the center of life itself: a vain and impossible nostalgia for that first essential plenitude, a belief that one really can in one form or another repossess the phallus."[3] For Lacan, genuine—rather than neurotic or nostalgic—forms of desire entail a recognition that human fate is "incompleteness" and that desires, unless one comes to terms with them, will inevitably be repeated in time. There is no "ultimate satisfaction" (p. 172) of desire available in reality, and neurosis itself is manifested for Lacan in one's attempts "to achieve ultimate certainty" (pp. 172–73).

Plenitude belongs to a symbolic order, and within that order it is identified as the Phallus. The Phallus exists as a *function*, not as a thing (least of all an actual penis). Thus it will always be known through a signifier, through something that stands for it, rather than through the "thing" itself. Phallic plenitude thus really belongs to language. It will find its place in the order of signification where the "denominator" stands in Lacan's formula: S/s. Because the virgule here represents a bar, forever impassable, between signifier (S) and signified (s), it also defines the structure of desire: just as the signifier represents the effort to recapture the signified, so the *objects* of desire represent the subject's efforts to recapture the original fullness of being that underlies desire. Thus the structure of desire is observed in the structure of language; it operates in the two main axes found in language: the paradigmatic (or axis of similarity) and the syntagmatic (or axis of contiguity). These two axes of language provide the two tropological modes— metaphor and metonymy—by which literary texts are ordinarily expanded or developed, but they are also related to Freudian psychological concepts of condensation and displacement, as well as the linguistic concepts of the synchronic and diachronic. According to Kaja Silverman, "metaphor and metonymy respond to similarity and contiguity as the basis for the *temporary replacement* of one signifying element by another. . . . Within metaphor and metonymy the primary and secondary processes find a kind of equilibrium, one which permits profound affinities and adjacencies to be discovered without differences being lost."[4]

In Lacanian terms, one can make two important points about technique and narrative structure in *Something Happened*: first, Heller's text is largely the result of Slocum's many linguistic displacements of desire as he searches the labyrinth of memory for the ultimate signifier (the Phallus), that representation of the source, origin, essence of his primal self, being, identity. Second, the *histoire* or story of the novel, which is almost swallowed up in the massive volume of those displacements, finally produces a narrative structure displaying Slocum's movement from a desire to achieve ultimate completeness, certainty, plenitude to a realization that these can never be achieved. At the novel's end, following Slocum's resigned acquiescence to the terms of the Oedipus complex, Heller shows his subject coming of age within his culture by moving out of the narcissism of the Imaginary into the objectivity and indeterminacy of the Symbolic. *Something Happened* thus has the *structure* of comedy, but it is surely without the festive mood that often accompanies comedy. In that absence of festivity lies Heller's most damaging critique of American mercantile culture.

If readers are to grasp the *unconscious* underlying the signifiers of Slocum's consciousness, that consciousness will have to be read as a language. Lacan suggests that the unconscious, like language, operates largely through the processes of metaphor and metonymy, forms of distancing through substitutions based on similarity or on displacement toward other objects associated within a context. The "profound affinities and adjacencies" of metaphoric and metonymic displacement characteristic of the entire novel are bountifully illustrated in the first chapter. They become visible in the very first sentence: "I get the willies when I see closed doors."[5] Heller's protagonist, like any reader, wonders why he dreads "that something horrible is happening behind" closed doors. He says that "something must have happened to me sometime" (p. 3), and he even offers potential explanations developed in a combination of metonymic and metaphoric displacements that ordinarily would gladden the heart of any Freudian analyst. "Maybe it was the day I came home unexpectedly with a fever and a sore throat and caught my father in bed with my mother. . . ." This metonymic association, however, is just the beginning of a series of other associations closed by a metaphoric substitution for that primal scene. He offers, for example, four alternative explanations for his fear of closed doors: [1] "Or maybe it was the knowledge that we were poor. . . . [2] Or the day my father died and left me feeling guilty and ashamed. . . . [3] Or maybe it was the realization . . . that I would never have broad shoulders and huge biceps. . . . [4] Or maybe it was the day I did open another door and saw my big sister standing naked . . ." (pp. 3–4).

Any one of these might have been sufficient as an explanation for Slocum's fear, but he offers them less to explain, it seems, than to mask its real cause or causes. Lacan suggests that the unconscious operates through the same means of signification as language, but language can never fully recover the signified through the agency of the signifier. Thus, the subject-consciousness (Slocum's here), in his discourse about himself, will be "caught up in an order of symbols" and therefore will move "progressively away from the truth of his essence."[6] Such progressive distancing from the Oedipal "truth" is precisely what one confronts in Slocum's narration. After the series of alternative causes for his fear of closed doors, he launches into the first dramatized scene of the novel. That scene is simply a metaphoric substitution, with greater metonymic detail, for the parental primal scene mentioned first. "I remember also," he says, "with amusement now, because it happened so long ago, the hot summer day I wandered into the old wooden coal shed behind our redbrick apartment building and found my big brother lying on the floor with Billy Foster's skinny kid sister . . ." (p. 4). Slocum is never able or willing to provide details of what he observed in his parents' bedroom, but he does give readers considerable information about the substitute "primal" scene in which his older brother is involved. The language he uses suggests he has stepped upon a snake, or, perhaps, a mouse. When he had first "heard a faint, frantic stirring" upon entering "the dark place," he felt as though he "had stepped on something live." Thus, he was momentarily relieved to discover it was only his "brother lying on the floor with someone" (p. 4). But after his brother yelled at him and threw a lump of coal, the prepubescent Slocum "bolted outside," feeling "too guilty to escape," he says, "and almost too frightened to stay and take the punishment I knew I deserved — though I didn't know for what" (p. 4). Slocum's question, upon the couple's exit from "the yawning blackness behind" the "enormous wooden door," will be the one that haunts the novel: ". . . What was happening in there, Eddie? Did something happen?" (p. 5).

Slocum's ambivalent desire to know what "happened," his generalized pursuit of knowledge, sexual and otherwise, thus, by a process of displacement, becomes associated with doors. The closed door is thus the bar between exterior and interior, known and unknown, signifier and signified, in Slocum's personal "language" of images. Inevitably, the signified is readily transferred to other large gaps in Slocum's knowledge where desire and fear are mingled. It is rather abruptly shifted in Slocum's discourse from the domain of sex toward the domain of death as a result of metonymic associations with his brother. He is reminded that his big brother is now dead, as is his father, so Slocum cannot ever ask what he was "never bold enough to ask" while Eddie was alive (p. 6). Thus, he admits, "today, there are so many things I *don't* want to find out" (p. 6). He does not want to visit hospitalized friends, he says, because "I might open the door of the private or semiprivate room and come upon some awful sight for which I could not have prepared myself" (p. 6). And he will not phone hospitals to inquire after his friends "because there's always the danger I might find out they are dead" (p. 6). But he is never satisfied with any stance he takes. Thus he admits to a ghoulish episode when he did phone a hospital after he knew of someone's death, but he says he wanted merely to know how the hospital would handle the issue. The question, for Slocum, thus had been shifted, metonymically, from one of death to one of "technique": "Would they decide he had died, passed away, succumbed, was deceased, or perhaps even had expired?" (p. 7). What he really wants to know are the words by which the death would be signifed. *He* was surprised when the woman on the phone said that the person "is no longer listed as a patient." But the *reader* is surprised at Slocum's reaction to the episode, for it generates the same emotional affect in Slocum as his *sexual* inquiries: "Certainly, my heart was pounding with great joy and excitement at my narrow escape" (p. 7), he says, as if the approach to knowledge of sex and death is of the same order as his escape from *discovery* of what he is actually doing, as if escape from the embarrassment of being found out in one's morbid or erotic inquiries is tantamount to escaping one's mortality or sexuality.

One final representation of Slocum's psycho-sexual concerns makes up the bulk of the brief first chapter's remaining two pages. If it were not for the fact, as Lacan sees it, that metaphor and metonymy are the primary means to knowledge of the subject, one would surmise that Slocum has strayed totally away from "the truth of his essence" in his recounting the episode of the mice. The mice would seem to function, in the language of the unconscious, in the place of the signified, and thus in the place of the Phallus, for they are quite as unapproachable as the "s" is beyond the bar separating it from the "S": "I didn't know what to do about those mice," he says. "I never saw them. Only the cleaning lady did, or said she did, and one time my wife thought she did, and one time my wife's mother was almost sure she did. After a while the mice just disappeared" (pp. 8–9). Slocum admits that he is not certain they were ever really there, but like any unknown, yet somehow desired object, they nonetheless made his life miserable for a time. They inevitably brought back the other significances represented in doors. "I never knew what I would find when I opened the doors to inspect my traps" (p. 9), he says, not sure whether he most feared *catching* or *not* catching the mice. He is sure, however, that he dreaded he might "open a door in the kitchen and find a live mouse crouching in a dark corner" (pp. 9–10), and he would have to kill it. "The possibility of finding a live mouse behind every door I opened each morning filled me with nausea and made me tremble. It was not that I was afraid of the mouse itself (I'm not that silly), but if I ever did find one, I knew I would have to do something about it" (p. 10).

Clearly, the live mouse has come to have a powerful symbolic function in Slocum's imagination. As a metaphor, it will have (Lacan would say) significance as a symptom of what ails Slocum. What ails Slocum is his inability to come to terms with the duality of the Oedipus: *desire* to possess the phallic plenitude forever lost at the separation from the mother, and *fear* of the consequences of possessing that which will represent the plenitude. Thus, by way of the processes of metaphor and metonymy operating through the first chapter, one is led back to the concerns expressed in the novel's initial sentence, which has produced the metonymical image representing the duality of Slocum's major theme: *eros* and *thanatos*. In its positive aspect, this theme is the *Phallus*; in its negative, it is *Castration*. "Lacan will say," according to Lemaire, "that what corresponds in the unconscious to any possible imaginable form of sexual relation is an individual 'lack,' an original and chronic state of self-insufficiency. He will say that it is in this that the universality of the castration complex lies."[7] The closed door thus becomes the object in Slocum's imagination representing the absence or lack that defines his life, as well as the bar separating him from the fulfillment he seeks.

Robert Slocum is a man caught in the grip of a neurosis, and it is expressed in the facility with which he fills the void through those metonymic and metaphoric expansions. These tropological moves project into the world his own contradictory fears, thus creating an environment in his own image. On the one hand, for example, every door in Slocum's life will be identified with every other; on the other hand, his every experience or feeling contradicts itself: "I've always been afraid I was about to be fired. Actually, I have never been fired from a job" (p. 15); "When I grow up I want to be a little boy. . . . When I grow up, I want to be someone dignified, tasteful, and important . . ." (pp. 340–41). His world may indeed be just exactly as he says it is, but there is no perspective upon it except his. The "reality" of the world Slocum projects is inconsequential to any analysis of *Something Happened*, however, for readers are forced to regard all his utterances as symptoms of his ailment. In Lacan's terms, Slocum has become fixed at the stage of the Imaginary, precisely that stage which works through identification and duality just as do metaphor and metonymy.

Slocum's "confession" thus rather clearly illustrates the functioning of the Imaginary: "Lacan defines the essence of the imaginary as a dual relationship, a reduplication in the mirror, an immediate opposition between consciousness and its other in which each term becomes its opposite and is lost in the play of the reflection. In its quest for itself, consciousness thus believes that it has found itself in the mirror of its creatures and loses itself in something which is not consciousness."[8]

The etiology for his fears concerning doors that Slocum provides in the first few paragraphs of the novel focuses largely upon the "classical narrative," *histoire*, or story underlying the family romance, the Oedipal drama structuring the discourse of the family. If, that is, the Oedipus complex is the "cause" of Slocum's problems, then it seems likely it will be displayed repeatedly in those displacements of metonymy and substitutions of metaphor produced within his discourse. What Slocum will not do, presumably, is talk directly about his father and mother as sexual beings. What he might well do, however, is push them aside for others who can replace them as less threatening objects. He seems clearly to do such substituting in his recollections concerning his brother and Billy Foster's kid sister and in other rather clearly sexual memories. A few others occur occasionally. Several are brought together, symptomatically, in one passage in the chapter entitled "It is not true." He relates all the images to his reasons for self-hatred. "I can even hate myself — me — generous, tolerant, lovable old Bob Slocum . . . for staying married to the same wife so long when I've had such doubts that I wanted to, molesting my little girl cousin once in the summertime when no mothers were looking . . ." (p. 360). The memory here of the "molesting" of the girl cousin is paired with another passage relating the same incident. In the earlier recollection, he recounts that "once in my early teens, I paid a younger cousin of mine, a girl, a dime to pull it for me and was terrified afterward that she would tell my mother or my brother or someone in her own family" (p. 339). In the later account, he says, "I can still recall her vacant, oblivious little girl's stare. I didn't hurt or frighten her. I only touched her underpants a moment between the legs, and then I touched her there again. I gave her a dime and was sorry afterward when I realized she might mention that. Nobody said anything. I still keep thinking they will" (p. 360). In the first account, he says "she made me happy. For only a dime" (p. 339); in the second, "I didn't get my dime's worth" (p. 360).

The other recollections that float up during this second passage involve the same frustrations and self-accusations. They clearly manifest Slocum's entrapment at the stage of the Imaginary, with its identifications and oppositions. He says, "I can kick myself for fumbling all those priceless chances I had with Virginia at the office for more than half a year, and with a couple of Girl Scout sisters I knew from high school earlier" (p. 360). He can even hate himself, he says, for "seeing my big brother with his fly open on the floor of that shadowy coal shed beside our brick apartment house with a kid named Billy Foster's skinny kid sister . . ." (p. 360). And he can feel self-disgust at his lack of sexual knowledge or experience in comparison to the girl's, Geraldine Foster's: even though she was not "as smart" as he, she "was going all the way already with guys as old and big as my big brother. While *I* wasn't even jerking off yet!" (p. 360). He can feel disgust, moreover, for his cravenly reactions to all those powerful, domineering women in his life who evoke those fears of interdiction, discovery, and rebuke associated with sexuality: his mother-in-law, his sister-in-law, Derek's nurses, and "broad and overbearing unforgettable Mrs. Yerger in the automobile casualty insurance company, who towered over me then, it seemed . . . when she hove into view like a smirking battleship" (p. 361).

Slocum's adult behavior suggests the obsession with sex and sexual fulfillment associated with neurotic desire. His behavior reflects the anxieties that emerged in his childhood and youth. Though any of the varied memories may locate the site of his "problem," the one memory that most insistently returns and is most strikingly elaborated is the one concerning Virginia—"Virgin for short, but not for long" (p. 14). Since Mrs. Yerger evokes all those figures of authority who preside over Slocum's feelings of sexual guilt, frustration, and hostility, the usual conjunction of Mrs. Yerger and Virginia in Slocum's mind suggests something of the nature of his problem: "I remember Mrs. Yerger, and I remember Virginia. . . . What a feeble-minded idiot: I could have had her then. She was hot. I was petrified. What in hell was inhibiting me so long, strangulating me? No wonder when I finally tore free it was with a vengeance" (pp. 336–37). What readers confront here (though it is not clear that Slocum himself understands) is the classic castration complex. In its unresolved form, according to Lacan, it will remain fixed in the Imaginary phase, whereas a "cure" would involve translation into the phase of the Symbolic. "In the castration complex," writes Anika Lemaire, "the Imaginary is the insatiability with which roles and modes of being are sought to compensate, together with sex, for the profound ill of human incompleteness. It is also the uninterrupted rotation of reflex adaptations to styles and functions of being which prove themselves by experiment to be adequate to the unconscious wish which produces them. In short, the Imaginary is everything in the human mind and its reflexive life which is in a state of flux before the fixation is effected by the symbol, a fixation which, at the very least, tempers the incessant sliding of the mutations of being and of desire."[9]

The memories of his relationship with Virginia in the office of the automobile casualty insurance company are both metaphoric and metonymic in relation to the material they displace. The structure of the memory is metaphoric because it imitates the basic pattern of the other sexual memories, beginning with the primal parental scene (A observes B engaged sexually with C). Its structure can thus substitute for all the others, but especially for the more threatening primal scene. But the structure also allows movement from point to point around the triangle of signification formed by the S, the s, and the bar between: S/s. The memory in its metonymic power provides *syntax*, a syntagmatic chain of signifiers that begins to take the form of a discursive structure. If one follows out the chain, in other words, one can begin to understand the *statement* Slocum is making to readers — and perhaps to himself as well.

Paradigmatically, the office situation replaces the family situation because it can produce substitutes for the authority of the father (here it is the *figure* of authority, the commanding presence of Mrs. Yerger, who in Slocum's mind represents all authority), the mother (represented by Virginia, an "older woman," who is both innocent and seductive, nurturing and threatening), and of course the "child" (seventeen-year-old Bobby Slocum). The office also provides substitutes for the sibling relationship and the representation of the violation of the interdiction against incest. Slocum's "brother" is twenty-one-year-old Tom Johnson and another "mother/lover" is twenty-eight-year-old Marie Jencks; "tall, blond, buxom," "striking and attractive," Marie Jencks "was humping" Slocum's friend "whenever she wanted to" (p. 80), and the relationship amazed him, Slocum says, more "than I'd been to find my big brother on the floor of that wooden coal shed with Billy Foster's skinny kid sister" (p. 80). Syntagmatically, the office situation also provides a connected plot, a story that eventually puts young Slocum inside a room, on the *other* side of a closed door, with an apparent opportunity to engage Virginia sexually. Slocum crosses the bar, moves to the side of the other, replaces father-brother-friend in the embrace of the desired object, only to find he cannot possess that which he seeks. Each day, often several times a day, Slocum and Virginia would sneak off to a file storage room for "swift, incredible trysts" (p. 370) but they always ended, their desires unconsummated, with Virginia's invariable, transparent lie, "Someone's coming" (p. 370).

Ultimately, Slocum has his chance to ravish Virginia in that storage room and discovers that she is no more possessable through seizure than seduction. In the company of two older boys, teased into going there with Virginia, Slocum is more daunted than ever, no more able to consummate the act than before. He is fearful of exposure, fearful of being displayed as sexually lacking, fearful of the potential violence of the whole scene. So, seeing Virginia's taunts turn to terror, he changes from would-be-rapist to would-be-hero, and, despite a tumult of contradictory sexual feelings, manages to drive the other boys away. Until this episode of the near-rape, the scenes Slocum performs with Virginia are essentially rehearsals for both—for young Slocum, an opportunity to work through his adolescent Oedipal conflicts; for Virginia, an opportunity to break out of her own Oedipal entrapment (she seduces fifty-five-year-old Len Lewis, a married co-worker; she had once been gang raped, she claims, by the Duke University football squad; and her father had committed suicide while she was in college). Virginia has given Slocum the chance to act out his Oedipal fantasies, but, he feels fortunate to admit, he never had to act *on* them with her in any conclusive way. Thus, never having had her, he can forever dream of her as the object that would provide him complete satisfaction to his desires.

Just as the casualty company office forms a structure that can substitute, metaphorically, for the family, the company for which Slocum works now also forms a family structure. Slocum's adventures at the casualty company seemed to focus upon incest through the maternal/female aspect of the Forbidden in the Oedipal triangle; his work nowadays seems more clearly focused upon the paternal aspects of the interdiction of incest. The twelve directors at the top of the company represent a paternal force that seems to reside in the realm of Lacan's Symbolic, the locus of the Dead Father. "In the domain of social symbolism," says Lemaire, "the third term which mediates between the living will be the Ancestor, the Dead. God, the Sacred Cause, the Institution, Ideology, etc."[10] The directors, Slocum says, "seem friendly, slow, and content when I come upon them in the halls (they seem dead) and are always courteous and mute when they ride with others in the public elevators" (p. 13). Slocum has little contact with *them*, but he does have contact with their apostle, Arthur Baron, "who is boss of us all in this division" (p. 37). Arthur Baron serves in their stead as the Symbolic "father," the Absent Father whose power to reward and punish mediates Slocum's relationship with his horde of rivals, his primitive "brothers." Those rivals, potentially innumerable in the company, are reduced to just one: Jack Green. Green serves as the chief competitor for a job Baron holds out to Slocum, though Slocum fears others, too.

The new job becomes the object that replaces the mother in the yet further displaced Oedipal family structure. Andy Kagle, who already is wedded to that job, becomes the figure in the realm of the Imaginary who most readily substitutes for the father against whom Slocum must struggle. Slocum is as ambivalent about Kagle and his job as he would have been over replacing his real father. After Arthur Baron has told Slocum to begin preparing in secret to take it over, Slocum even warns Kagle to shape up, do all the things he knows he must do in order to save his job: "Grow up, Andy," he says. "You're a middle-aged man with two kids and a big job in a pretty big company. There's a lot that's expected of you. It's time to mature. It's time to take it seriously and start doing all the things you should be doing. You know what they are. You keep telling me what they are" (p. 65). But Kagle is unable or unwilling to "grow up," and Slocum realizes that, despite all, he wants that "better job" himself (p. 67). That job thus becomes the virtually sexual "object" Slocum seeks — as he sought after women — in order to appease his desire.

Slocum clearly stands in relation to Kagle as the male child to the father. But Kagle resides in the Imaginary for Slocum, not in the Symbolic where Baron stands, for he is an other who merely duplicates Slocum. Like Kagle, Slocum has two (normal) children and a responsible job in a big company. The two are "comfortable" (p. 49) with each other, as a father and son might be, and Slocum admits that Kagle "has been good to me from the day I came to work here. . . . He makes my job easier. He relies on my judgment, takes my word, and backs me up in disputes I have with his salesmen. Many of his salesmen . . . hold me in some kind of awe because they sense I operate under his protection" (p. 50). But, in addition to the identifications associated with the Imaginary realm, there are also oppositions, for contradictions in Slocum's feelings toward Kagle will also mark the Oedipal relation. Slocum knows that "Kagle trusts me and knows he is safe with me" (p. 49), but Slocum translates Kagle's feelings into weakness and thus no longer *fears* Kagle. "In fact," Slocum says, "I feel that I would scare him whenever I chose to, that he is weak in relation to me and that I am strong in relation to him" (p. 49). Worse yet, Slocum acknowledges a "hideous urge every now and then while he is confiding in me to shock him suddenly . . . or to kick his crippled leg. It's a weird mixture of injured rage and cruel loathing that starts to rise within me and has to be suppressed" (p. 49).

Slocum says he does not know where this urge comes from or whether he will be able to control it, but the source of the urge is distinctly Oedipal. Heller makes no mistake about this source, for that limp he gives Kagle is the metonymic connection to Oedipus one might most readily expect in this context. Moreover, on days that Slocum has been with Kagle, he too takes on the Oedipus impediment: "If I'm with Andy Kagle, I will limp" (p. 75). But if Slocum is to be "cured," he must transcend such merely immediate, mirror relationships. As much as he may like Kagle, Kagle cannot be the father-figure to Slocum who will signify the *place* of the father in the symbolic or perform the role of the symbolic Law that effectively prohibits the child's union with the figure of the mother in the Oedipal configuration.

Kagle, in short, does not have the power of interdiction where Slocum's relation to the position of the mother (that is, the job) is concerned.

The company for which Slocum works may substitute for the family structure, but there is also the actual nuclear family within which Slocum must play his role. One may assume that the biological family — at least in a novel — is never *just* a family. It will reveal important aspects of the character of the main subject, too. "Psychoanalysis has shown the family, like language," writes Kaja Silverman, "to be a vital relay between the various territories that make up subjectivity and the larger cultural field."[11] With his actual family, however, Slocum remains just as much within the mirror stage of the Imaginary as he does within the company. He feels just as contradictorily toward his wife as he does Kagle and others at work. "We are no longer close enough for honest conversation," Slocum says, but adds, parenthetically, "we *are* close enough for frequent sexual intercourse" (p. 119). When they were young their sexual endeavors were largely replays of Slocum's relationship with Virginia, with the significant exception that he does make it with his wife, whose frightened response was as skittish as Virginia's. "I think we liked each other once," he says. "I think we used to have fun; at least it seems that way now, although we were always struggling about one thing or another. I was always struggling to get her clothes off, and she was always struggling to keep them on" (p. 119).

Nowadays, Slocum says that he lays "girls . . . that are as young as she was then, and much more nimble, profligate, and responsive, but it isn't as rich with impulse and excitement and generally not as satisfying afterward" (pp. 120–21). Moreover, nowadays, his wife is just as nimble, profligate, and responsive as the young women, but Slocum laments, "I'm not sure I like her this way, although I would have liked it back then, but I'm not sure about that, either. I'm really not sure I *want* my wife to be as lustful and compliant as one of Kagle's whores or my girl friends, although I know I am dissatisfied with her when she isn't" (p. 125). What neither Slocum nor his wife knows is that they are simply caught up in the syntax of Slocum's desire, she being just one more element in a chain that includes countless unnamed sexual partners of Slocum as well as many who *are* named: Penny, Jill, Rosemary, young co-eds, various prostitutes. If Slocum is to overcome his problem, he will have to demonstrate that he can break this chain of apparently unappeasable desire anchoring him in the Imaginary.

Slocum also manifests his entrapment at the realm of the Imaginary in his relations with the other members of his family — the three children. Each of the children seems to represent for Slocum a stage along the way to the development of a normal "self." Derek, the mentally retarded child and the only family member ever named, seems associated in Slocum's mind with himself as a linguistic or sexual or social "idiot." He also represents Slocum's fear of the absence of love, for he feels that no one in his family (except perhaps for the other son) now really cares for Derek. And Derek also represents Slocum's speechlessness in the face of authority. By a process of metonymic linkages, Derek comes to stand in relation to his nurses as Slocum had stood to Mrs. Yerger, back in the casualty company office. He says of the nurse they have now, "she reminds me of Mrs. Yerger. I want to yell dirty things at this nurse now for the debasement Mrs. Yerger made me suffer then" (p. 129). But, then, one of the problems the idiot child brings with him is that he evokes the Oedipal range of Slocum's anxieties concerning himself through the metonymic sequences he initiates: "Every older woman I find myself afraid of reminds me of Mrs. Yerger. Every feeble old woman I see reminds me of my mother. Every young girl who attacks my pride reminds me of my daughter. No one reminds me of my father, which is okay with me, I guess, since I don't remember a father for anyone to remind me of. Except Arthur Baron. I think I may feel a little bit about Arthur Baron the way I might have felt about my father if he had lived a little longer and been nice to me" (pp. 129–30). Derek represents for Slocum the double-sidedness of his problem, for on the one hand he wants, much of the time, to return to the condition of somatic, speechless immediacy *vis à vis* "reality" Derek represents, but on the other that condition of idiocy is precisely the image of human vacancy most contrary to the plenitude Slocum seeks. Thus Derek's existence is a physical plenitude marked by mental vacancy, just as Slocum's life is a material largess marked by spiritual emptiness.

Slocum's daughter represents a stage of development much closer to psychosocial maturity than that attained by either Derek or the other son. She of course invokes the threat of Oedipus from a second side, the side opposite that of the maternal relations (mother, Virginia, Marie Jencks, Mrs. Yerger). The relationship of father and daughter is marked by the expected pattern of love/hate. Their favorite game is what Eric Berne calls "Uproar," in which the two engage in verbal sparring and the daughter ends by stalking into her room and slamming the door after her. "She still has power to wound me," he says. "I have power to wound her (so maybe we have not really written each other off entirely yet. Maybe that's why we want to, we are dangerous to each other. My wife can't hurt me. My daughter can)" (p. 187).

But trapped with him in the Imaginary, his daughter reminds Slocum invariably of his relation to himself. His reflections on her turn into reflections upon his own past. "I also think I may have been *more* unhappy than my daughter when I was young, and felt even more entrapped than she does in my own sense of pathless isolation," he says, upon shifting toward a long passage concerning his childhood and youth that culminates in a description suggesting the extent of his dissociation from a coherent self:

> There must have been a second person who grew up alongside me (or *inside* me) and filled in for me on occasions to experience things of which I did not wish to become a part. And there was even a third person of whom I am aware only dimly and about whom I know almost nothing, only that he is there. And I am aware of still one more person whom I am not even

aware of; and this one watches everything shrewdly, even me, from some
secure hideout in my mind in which he remains invisible and anonymous,
and makes stern, censorious judgments, about everything, even me (p.
135).

The passage had begun with the lament that "there are long gaps in my past
that remain obscure and give no clue" (p. 134); it ends, equally lamentably,
"I am lacking in sequence for everything but my succession of jobs, love
affairs, and fornications; and these are not important; none matters more
than any of the others; except that they do give me some sense of a connected past" (pp. 135–36). But, obviously, all these do matter, for they are
all he has so long as he is locked in the Imaginary phase of psychological
development.

Slocum's other, "normal" son is the one who stands in the most problematical relation to Slocum. Slocum suspects that his daughter has already
escaped him for her own personality beyond his, and he knows his idiot son
will never ascend to the level of personality, consciousness, language — that
is, the Symbolic. But he still has hope for "my boy." His son is good, kind,
thoughtful, generous, loving — everything that one hopes he will retain
even after absorption into his culture, but everything that is almost inevitably to be lost. This son is involved in his own rite of passage, the conflict
with his own father-substitute — Forgione — at school, a passage into that
heart of darkness known as civilized life. But at the outset he is clearly that
puer aeternis Slocum feels must reside deep down inside himself somewhere. He *is* Slocum's pre-Oedipal self: "He is probably the only person in
the world for whom I would do almost anything I could to shield from all
torment and harm. Yet I fail continually; I can't seem to help him, I do seem
to harm him. . . . In my dreams sometimes he is in mortal danger, and I
cannot move quickly enough to save him. . . . He perishes, but the tragedy,
in my dreams, is always mine" (p. 159). The son is representative of that self
Slocum longs to regain but which Slocum is perhaps also responsible for
having destroyed. "I am still a little boy," he says. "I am a deserted little boy
I know who will never grow older and never change, who goes away and
then comes back. . . . He never goes far away and always comes back" (p.
158). But as for his son and that self Slocum once had been, "between us
now there is a cavernous void" (p. 158). That void becomes infinite when,
just as Slocum had feared, his son does die — and not just in his arms, but
also, finally, and accidentally, at Slocum's hands.

Something Happened is a novel that moves forward so glacially it
hardly seems to move at all. But there is forward progress in its plot: Slocum
does change, there is growing intensity of emotional affect, and several
complications are resolved or goals achieved (as in any well-made plot).
The plot kernel embedded within Slocum's work focuses on Kagle's job.
Slocum gets it. Slocum is not entirely happy that he "won" it, and his wife
gives him a hard time about it, for which he seems to assume Kagle's limp

(see p. 540). Slocum also gets to make his speech at the company convention; he heads the convention, but the speech, "at Arthur Baron's suggestion, was kept short" (p. 565), while Kagle and Green both get to speak at great length, much to Slocum's chagrin. With Kagle's job come other problems that Slocum has to solve: he retires those friends who are thought to be detrimental to his job or the company's success, including Ed Phelps, Red Parker, and Kagle; he transfers the feared Johnny Brown to another company and handles Martha the typist (who has slowly been going crazy) when she has her expected breakdown, but he feels that Jack Green still has "the whammy" on him, though Slocum now is his superior. Within his family, Slocum manages to settle several complications. "I have told my wife I love her," he says; he had been unable to do so since he had found out about the possibility of his getting Kagle's job. He and his wife have "decided to keep Derek longer (he may get better. They may be wrong. They're finding new things out every day)." And finally, he reports, "I have given my daughter a car of her own," and he has given his wife a new convertible ("We are now a three-car family," he says [p. 566]) and permission to shop for the new house they need because of his promotion.

If Slocum's problem, the cause of his neurosis, were material it would surely be resolved along with these other complications. His success at the company certainly has brought the material plentitude. But the plenitude he has sought has been more primal than that. It has been the plenitude Lacan associates with the symbolic role of the Phallus, that really androgynous signifier which locates the original fullness of being one found first at the breast of the mother, and, secondarily, in the authority of the father. But the lesson of psychoanalysis is that such primal undifferentiated being is lost at the accession to language and cannot be regained. Slocum, toward the end of the novel, begins to recognize that fact, and the emotional intensity of the narrative escalates rapidly. All the elements in the discourse of the family begin to coalesce. Toward the end, following a description of his very birth trauma, Slocum says, "Fear. Loss of love, loss of the loved one, loss of love of the loved one. Separation. We don't want to go, we don't want them to go, we can't wait for them to leave, we wish they'd return. There seem to be conflicts" (p. 559).

The items, the contradictions, the feelings are precisely those associated with the Oedipal theme of castration and the fixation at Lacan's Imaginary stage. Slocum realizes that the apparent solution for the lack he suffers lies in his past: "I was in need of whatever nipple succored me," he says, "and whatever arms lifted me. I didn't know names. I loved the food that fed me—that's all I knew—and the arms that held and hugged and turned me and gave me to understand, at least for those periods, that I was not alone and someone else knew I was there" (p. 559). But the plain fact is, and Slocum has begun to realize it, that he will never regain that place (virtually) inside the mother, she who has, he believes, reinforced his fears of inadequacy to replace the father in her dying words, "You're no good. . . .

You're just no good" (p. 545). Nor will he ever *regain* the father who died when Slocum was very young, the father who, Slocum's dreams tell him, is missed as desperately as the brother, Eddie, who also died young, and the son who has begun to slip away from Slocum and who, like the father and brother, dies young too.

> Oh, my father — why have you done this to me?
> I want him back.
> I want my little boy back too.
> I don't want to lose him.
> I do.
> "Something happened!" . . . (p. 561)

If there were any question that the death of Slocum's boy were not the most important event in this novel, the congruence of the novel's title and the exclamation announcing the accident leading to the death surely would inform readers. The death of Slocum's son is the climactic event that causes the critical changes in Slocum suggesting he has moved out of the mirror stage, that is, from the Imaginary into the Symbolic. Lacan has written that the moment in which the mirror-stage comes to an end is the moment in which the *I* becomes linked to "socially elaborated situations." "It is this moment," Lacan says,

> that decisively tips the whole of human knowledge into mediatization through the desire of the other, constitutes its objects in an abstract equivalence by the cooperation of others, and turns the I into that apparatus for which every instinctual thrust constitutes a danger, even though it should correspond to a natural maturation — the very normalization of this maturation being henceforth dependent, in man, on a cultural mediation as exemplified in the case of the sexual object, by the Oedipus complex. [12]

His psychological victory is ironic, not to say Pyrrhic. Since the Symbolic is very closely tied to a specific culture, one may not particularly like what Slocum has become after his "cure." Anika Lemaire has summarized the problem as Lacan sees it:

> If symbolism [that is, the Symbolic phase] is . . . a human dimension or even a positive human condition in that it socializes and organizes man, it also presents the disadvantage of formalizing the vital individual experience. What is more, symbolization is human, it is the work of human minds, which implies from the start: imperfection, reduction, arbitrariness, submission to external constraints and a partial failure to recognize its own mechanisms. The impossible task of symbolization in the broadest sense of the word is to organize at its own level the multiplicity of "vital human conditions." Each type of social organization has only been able to respond to these necessities in a partial way, accentuating certain aspects of life at the expense of others and therefore effecting repression. [13]

One may not like what Slocum has become at the end, but it seems evident he has at last internalized the values of his culture and assumed *his* place in the Oedipal structure not as the child but as the father. His boy has represented the desired opportunity to remain in the place of the child. Slocum had felt a powerful identification with the boy, and through him had hoped to cling to the pre-Oedipal innocence of the child. It would seem that the boy, rather than Derek, should be "a product of [his] imagination." "I never think of Derek in danger; I only think of my boy or myself" (p. 533). The boy represents the innocence *vis à vis* the Symbolic that Slocum wishes to protect forever. Thus, it seems, finally, that the death — the killing, really, since apparently Slocum accidentally smothers the boy while trying to comfort him after the accident, which would not, the doctor says, have been fatal — is almost more a figurative or allegorical sacrifice than real.[14] It *had* to happen, it was the something that had to happen, if Slocum was to come to terms with his life — the Oedipus structure — within his culture.

Joseph Heller was assumed a very difficult technical risk in *Something Happened*. Given the limitations of the first-person, confessional narration, he has to find some way to suggest that Slocum has indeed changed as a result of the great mental rift the boy's death causes. For better or worse, he has to show that Slocum is wedded to the values his culture associates with the role of the Father. Heller does that in the final, very brief chapter in several ways. First, he reduces the amount of parenthetical qualification in which Slocum engages, and along with that almost totally eliminates the identifications and contradictions associated with the stage of the Imaginary. Second, he shows that Slocum's focus has shifted entirely to the external complications in his business and family life, demonstrating that he is "putting [his] affairs in order" (p. 566). Third, he gives Slocum new "voices" to hear, voices of approbation representing the symbolic authority of the Father, which of course is the company:

> "You're a good administrator, Slocum."
> "You've done a good job, Slocum."
> "I liked the way you stepped right in and took over."
> "You've got the department really humming, Slocum."
> "You got Kagle out pretty smoothly, didn't you, Slocum? Ha, Ha" (p. 568).

Fourth, he shows that Slocum has taken up the company game — golf — and meets a "much higher class of executives at Arthur Baron's now when he has us to dinner" (p. 568). And, finally, Heller dramatizes Slocum's taking "command" in the handling of Martha the typist's breakdown. Martha has been mentioned occasionally throughout the narrative, and she comes to stand for the psychological catastrophe Slocum himself becomes aware he is facing but cannot acknowledge publicly: "(The company takes a strong view against psychotherapy for executives because it denotes unhappiness, and unhappiness is a disgraceful social disease for which there is no excuse or forgiveness)" (p. 534). Martha's psychological problem is also no doubt associated with those Slocum finally realizes he had not recognized in Virginia, whose sexual teasing and quirky behavior masked the deep emotional troubles that led her to suicide, by the same method her father had used. Martha's problem thus has almost incalculable range for Slocum, so when she "went crazy for [him] finally at just the right time in a way he was able to handle suavely," taking "charge like a ballet master" (p. 568), she provides Slocum with the means to display his "coming of age" within the company, his accession to the role of Authority, the Law, the place of the Father: "Everyone seems pleased with the way I've taken command" (p. 569). He still misses his boy, but he seems to know what his mature place must be. He may not be whole now, but he does "fit in."

Notes

1. "An Interview with Joseph Heller," *Playboy*, 22, No. 6 (June 1975), 74.

2. Kaja Silverman, *The Subject of Semiotics* (New York: Oxford University Press, 1983), p. 150. Silverman's chapter on Lacan and Freud (pp. 126–93) is excellent. See also Jacques Lacan's *Speech and Language in Psychoanalysis*, trans., with notes and commentary by Anthony Wilden (Baltimore: Johns Hopkins University Press, 1981). Other writings of Lacan are included in *Ecrits: A Selection*, trans. Alan Sheridan (New York: Norton, 1977). Lacan is an especially difficult writer, so one is likely to find the commentators very helpful, particularly some of those who attempt to show Lacan's place within the structuralist, post-structuralist, and deconstructionist movements. For Lacan's relation to Freudian concepts, one will find useful J. Laplanche and J. B. Pontalis, *The Language of Psycho-Analysis*, trans. Donald Nicholson-Smith (New York: Norton, 1973). For those interested in other uses of Lacan for literary interpretation, see also *The Fictional Father: Lacanian Readings of the Text*, ed. Robert Con Davis (Amherst: University of Massachusetts Press, 1981).

3. Fredric Jameson, *The Prison-House of Language: A Critical Account of Structuralism and Russian Formalism* (Princeton: Princeton University Press, 1972), p. 172. The quotations following are also from this text.

4. Silverman, p. 109.

5. Joseph Heller, *Something Happened* (New York: Knopf, 1974), p. 3. All further quotations from the novel will be cited parenthetically within the text. There are several interesting essays on the novel one might want to see in conjunction with the present essay: the best lengthy analysis available is Thomas LeClair, "Joseph Heller, *Something Happened*, and the Art of Excess," *Studies in American Fiction*, 9 (1981), 245–60; other good essays include Walker Percy, "The State of the Novel: Dying Art or New Science?" *Michigan Quarterly Review*, 16 (1977), 359–73; George J. Searles, "*Something Happened*: A New Direction for Joseph Heller," *Critique*, 18, No. 3 (1977), 74–82; Nicholas Canaday, "Joseph Heller: Something Happened to the American Dream," *CEA Critic*, 40, No. 1 (1977), 34–38; Susan Strehle Klemtner, " 'A Permanent Game of Excuses': Determinism in Heller's *Something Happened*," *Modern Fiction Studies*, 24 (1978–79), 550–56; and George Sebouhian, "From Abraham and Isaac to Bob Slocum and My Boy: Why Fathers Kill Their Sons," *Twentieth Century Literature*, 27 (1981), 43–52.

6. Anika Lemaire, *Jacques Lacan*, trans. David Macey (London: Routledge and Kegan Paul, 1977), pp. 6–7. Lemaire's is an excellent study.

7. Lemaire, p. 59.

8. Lemaire, p. 60.

9. Lemaire, p. 61.

10. Lemaire, p. 60.

11. Silverman, p. 130.

12. *Ecrits*, pp. 5–6.

13. Lemaire, p. 58.

14. One should note that the way in which Slocum's son is run down by a car in a shopping center is foreshadowed in the imagination of Chaplain Tappman of *Catch-22*, where the Chaplain's "wife's trim and fragile body [is] crushed to a viscous pulp against the brick wall of a market building by a half-witted drunken automobile driver." See Joseph Heller, *Catch-22* (New York: Simon and Schuster, 1961), p. 266.

Good as Gold

The Deceits of Black Humor

John W. Aldridge*

In an essay published ten years ago I made certain impious pronouncements about the literary movement known as black humor or dark comedy, then just passing the peak of its quite meretricious popularity.

What troubled me most about black humor was that in too many instances it cut itself off from the vital source of effective satire — the close observation of the social and political world — and it evidently did so because it was too easily horrified by the grotesqueness and complexity of that world and found it less painful to retreat into cuteness (as does Kurt Vonnegut) or fabulation (as does Thomas Pynchon) than to endure and create the genuine dark comedy of contemporary experience. The result was that the living reality of the object or condition being satirized was too obliquely suggested in the work of these writers, or was altogether absent.

In the years that have passed since I made these observations, the world has moved on, but black humor on the whole has not. Its formerly innovative attitudes and artistic devices have been absorbed into the public domain and become institutionalized there as part of the official convention of discourse through which, not only in fiction but also in poetry, drama, journalism, and film, we habitually register our bafflement or outrage at the insane discontinuities and seemingly gratuitous malevolence of contemporary life. They are available now, like processed food in a supermarket, to any artist or social commentator in need of a jar of pickled Angst or instant Doom, and these ingredients had better be abundantly present in any work with pretensions to being taken seriously as an honest statement about the larger unrealities of our time. But to the extent that black humor has substituted buzzwords and stereotypical formulations for fresh, imaginative perceptions, it has conditioned its audiences to respond in certain prescribed ways to experience without really providing them with the experience. If one finds the conditions of contemporary life deranging, one can take comfort from the fact that black humor has identified derangement as the only sane response, has classified it as the prime symptom of entropy, anomie,

*Reprinted from *Harper's*, 258 (March 1979), 115–18. ©1979 by *Harper's* Magazine. All rights reserved. Reprinted from the March 1979 issue by special permission.

157

atomization, and other derivatives of the Second Law of Thermodynamics, and has perfected certain highly stylized modes of dramatizing it in fictional form. Thus, one knows that whenever the characters in a novel do not resemble human beings, it is because they have been dehumanized by the entropic forces that are fast dehumanizing us all. Whenever a fictional landscape seems fragmented or nightmarishly surreal, so that it is impossible to tell precisely what is going on, one knows that it is intended to function as a metaphor of the disorientation of the psyche when confronted with the bizarre arbitrariness of events. If the experiences and people portrayed in a novel seem trivial or empty, one can be sure they seem so because they represent the exhausted sensibility of the age.

In short, black humor has provided us with a number of analogical or parabolic evocations of the psychological disturbances of contemporary life, evocations that are sometimes so compelling we are almost persuaded that they actually do reveal reality rather than merely a set of stock responses to it. Yet over and over again in black-humor fiction the problem is that while the responses may be powerfully rendered, the concrete events and specific social circumstances that induced them are seldom identified or objectified. That essential dimension of fiction that Hemingway once described as comprising "the exact sequence of motion and fact which made the emotion" is almost always missing, leaving the emotion afloat in a causeless void.

It is one of Joseph Heller's several virtues as a black humorist that he has been able to avoid this problem and dramatize his steadily darkening vision of contemporary life through an evocation of the experiences responsible for it. In the fiction of Pynchon and Donald Barthelme, for example, virtually everything and everyone exists in such a radical state of distortion and aberration that there is no way of determining from which conditions in the real world they have been derived or from what standard of sanity they may be said to depart. The conventions of verisimilitude and sanity have been nullified, and the fiction itself stands as a metaphor of a derangement that is seemingly without provocation and beyond measurement.

Heller, by contrast, derives his materials from the actualities of the observable world, portrays them with much greater fidelity to realism, and achieves his effects through comic exaggeration and burlesque rather than hallucination — which is perhaps to say that he descends from Dickens rather than Beckett. His characters are almost always grotesques, but they are presented as grotesques, and with no suggestion that grotesqueness is the natural and universal state of being. One is always certain, furthermore, precisely to what degree they and their situations are absurd or insane, because his narrative point of view is located in an observer with whom we can identify and who is rational enough to be able to measure the departures from rationality in the people and situations he encounters.

Yossarian's problem in *Catch-22*, for example, is that he is hopelessly sane in a situation of complete madness. The high comedy of the novel is generated by the fact that military life, when viewed satirically — which is to say, rationally — becomes ludicrous and, in wartime, malevolent. But there is nothing in *Catch-22* that a person of Yossarian's perpetually affronted sensibility would not have perceived in the same circumstances. The boundaries of the normal and predictable are never exceeded, but they are extended satirically to the point where, as happens in wars, all kinds of idiocy, cruelty, obsessive self-interest, and the most inhumane bureaucratic exploitation are made to seem normal and predictable, hence altogether horrifying. The big joke of the "catch" itself — that the men cannot be grounded for reasons of insanity because they are sane enough not to want to fly the required missions — is a particularly sick joke because it might so easily have been a reality. Colonel Scheisskopf, who ponders various ways in which his men might be wired or nailed together in order to produce a perfect marching pattern; the general who orders his squadrons to bomb a village that has no strategic significance whatever because he wants photographs showing a perfect bombing pattern; Milo Minderbinder, who creates a massive syndicate involved in the exchange and sale of goods to both the Allies and the Axis powers, and who for a fee will arrange the bombing of his own men; Doc Daneeka, who, because he was scheduled to be aboard a plane that crashed, is declared officially dead, even though he is standing there protesting that he is alive — all are cartoon figures made plausible because they are extensions of the cold logic of wartime insanity. But in their comic extravagance these characters and others serve to dramatize Heller's altogether uncomic hatred of a system, supposedly consecrated to high patriotic service, that could so easily become diabolical because it views people as inanimate objects to be manipulated and destroyed for inane reasons. In such a situation Yossarian clearly has abundant provocations for his paranoia. There are real enemies out there, whether on our side or theirs, and, as he repeatedly complains, they are trying to kill him. But the vastly more frightening concern is that if he has no identity as a human being, then his death will have no significance.

In his second novel, *Something Happened*, Heller faced the opposite problem. The paranoia of his protagonist, Bob Slocum, is seemingly without provocation, yet it must somehow be dramatically justified. If Slocum has enemies, he can only suspect or imagine that they are out there, but he cannot locate them. The danger, moreover, is not that they will kill him but that in some mysterious way they will not allow him to discover and live a meaningful life. In the conventional view Slocum has all the advantages that make for meaning: a secure position with a large corporation; an excellent income; a big house in Connecticut; an attractive wife with whom he has regular and good sex; and at least one child, his elder son, whom he deeply loves. Yet such things do not constitute the sum of his life, and his difficulty — which is also a large technical one for Heller — is that he must locate and make real the sources of his anguish in a situation characterized precisely by the absence of difficulty.

The environment in which Slocum lives and works has, in fact, been quite deliberately engineered by the various bureaucratic agencies of the new mass dystopianism so that it will contain no conflict or contingency, so that it cannot be engaged, affirmed, or denied by anyone within it. It has been created in conformity to the dogma most reverenced in the technocratic era: that the freedom to take risks in an adversary environment has been abolished in favor of a secure function within an environment that has been happily sanitized of both freedom and risks — the system rewarding the dutiful performance of one's function with a guarantee that nothing will happen to anyone ever again.

Slocum's voice drones in an interminable monologue out of a void in which the only sound is the sound of itself. It ranges obsessively over the past and present, trying to articulate the incomprehensible, seeking always to talk its way out of what is for Heller the ultimate, terrifying helplessness: the inability to identify or confront the forces that are destroying one's life and preparing one's death. But the deeply lodged suspicion in both *Catch-22* and *Something Happened* is that there is no one at all in charge, that Kafka's castle is in fact empty, that there is no crime for which one eternally stands condemned, no order behind organization, no system behind bureaucratic structure, no governing principle behind government, that what is happening is happening for no reason, and that there is absolutely nothing to be done about it because the causes responsible cannot be located and the very idea of responsibility may have lost all meaning.

This is the radically nihilistic perception behind Heller's new novel, *Good as Gold*. Yet in spite of it he has been able to generate what is at times an almost joyous comedy out of the depths of apocalypse and to identify and engage some of the specific social conditions that have caused the vision of apocalypse to become a defining feature of the present. Heller has accomplished this through his particularly effective use of two seemingly different kinds of narrative materials — the Jewish family experience (his first attempt in fiction to draw on this experience) and a wildly phantasmagoric rendition of the Washington political scene. His protagonist, Bruce Gold, is a minor Jewish intellectual, academic, and essayist who plans to write an "abstract autobiography" based on the history of Jewish life in America, a book that is never written, but which the novel, in effect, becomes.

Gold moves back and forth between Washington and various dreadful meetings with his relatives in New York, seeing no connection between the two except that Washington promises to be a glamorous escape from the wretchedness of the family. Yet it is one of the central brilliances of the novel that although they are never explicitly paralleled, the Washington and the family experiences finally assume a portentous similarity. Both represent aspects of the same condition: the collapse of those values that once made humanity and rationality necessary.

As Heller portrays it, the trashed and decaying environment of South Brooklyn becomes an objectification of the devolving history of Gold's second-generation immigrant family. The neighborhood in which he grew up had at one time been a community held together by ties of blood relationship, ethnic tradition, and loyalties growing out the shared experience of struggle and privation. Now the area has become a jungle and a battlefield, where teenage gangs roam the littered streets "murdering old people casually in the course of their youthful depredations," boarded-up shops are vandalized, and there seem to be no places left where people can "buy food, have their suits and dresses mended and dry cleaned, their shoes and radios fixed, and their medical prescriptions filled." As Gold drives up Mermaid Avenue, he does not see a single drugstore or Jewish delicatessen:

> There was no longer a movie house operating in Coney Island: drugs, violence, and vandalism had closed both garish, overtowering theaters years before. The brick apartment house in which he had spent his whole childhood and nearly all his adolescence had been razed; on the site stood something newer and uglier that did not seem a nourishing improvement for the Puerto Rican families there now.

And Gold, like Tiresias brooding upon the wasteland devastation, concludes:

> Every good place has always been deteriorating, and everything bad is getting worse. Neighborhoods, parks, beaches, streets, schools were falling deeper into ruin and whole cities sinking into rot. . . . It was the Shoot the Chute into darkness . . . the plunging roller coaster into disintegration and squalor. Someone should do something. Nobody could. No society worth its salt would watch itself perishing without some serious attempt to avert its own destruction. Therefore . . . we are not a society. Or we are not worth our salt. Or both.

Like the old neighborhood, Gold's family once had a communal integrity founded on the need to survive in an environment that was harshly adversary — not because of crime and violence but because times were hard, jobs were scarce, and too many immigrant families were competing to make a life in a new country. Gold's brother and five sisters all made large sacrifices, the brother quitting school early and going to work to help support the family, while the father lost job after job. It could hardly be said that they were happy picturesquely toiling together or even that they deeply cared for one another. They were and remained the sort of people who are caring only so long as circumstances require them to be. Now that they are middle-aged and affluent, they have disintegrated into a group of bickering malcontents who come together only because they are tyrannized into it by their maniacal eighty-two-year-old father. At family gatherings their prime concern is to persuade him to cut short his annual visit with them and return to Florida. But the father has no intention of doing so because he knows it would give them pleasure. He finds his own pleasure in abusing Gold unmercifully because Gold is an intellectual and writes articles that nobody in the family can understand and that do not make money.

All these people have long been displaced from the realities that formed them and gave them some sense of common purpose, and now they have become abstracted into caricatures of hostility and self-interest. Having survived the need to deal aggressively with their environment, they have turned their aggressions against one another, while around them what is left of their old environment is being destroyed by new generations of displaced people to whom it has no relation whatever and whose aggression against it is a means to nothing.

In the Washington sections of the novel this effect of derangement from conditions of order, sanity, and meaningful causality is achieved through a masterful burlesque of government bureaucracy. The people in these sections are shown to be as divorced from reality as Gold's family is displaced from South Brooklyn. Political figures have lost all sense of the principles, causes, issues, and human interests they have been elected to work for and represent, and the result in their case is not aggression but a kind of psychotic arbitrariness. In the absence of clear and unavoidable imperatives that fix the nature of reality and control one's perception of it, reality can become anything one wishes it to be or decides it is. Titles of official positions have no relation to any specific function, and any office can be filled by anyone, since no one knows what qualifications are needed for what office. Therefore, any qualifications will do for any office. The language of government is similarly unrelated to the ideas or experiences it is supposed to describe. Words are used not to communicate but to obscure meaning, because all meaning is provisional and conjectural.

Gold hopes to be chosen for an important political position in Washington, and in an effort to win favor has written a flattering review of the President's book *My Year in the White House*. The President, who is a pointedly unnamed successor to Gerald Ford, has evidently spent much of his first year in office writing about his first year in office. "Yet," Heller observes, "nowhere in the book does he say anything about being busy with writing the book." He is delighted with Gold's review, especially with a phrase from it, "Nothing succeeds as planned," and instructs Ralph Newsome, an old friend of Gold's now serving as an "unnamed source" in the White House, to sound him out about his interest in a government appointment. Newsome offers Gold several possible choices ranging from Ambassador to the Court of St. James, head of NATO or the CIA, unnamed spokesman, Secretary of Defense, the Treasury, HEW, or the country's very first Jewish Secretary of State (Henry Kissinger, according to Gold, has lied about being a Jew and is really a German). Newsome assures him that whichever job he decides to take, he will be able to do anything he wants "as long as it's everything we tell you to say and do in support of our policies, whether you agree with them or not. You'll have complete freedom." When Gold asks for time to think all this over, Newsome tells him that "we'll want to move ahead with this as speedily as possible, although we'll have to go slowly. . . . We'll want to build this up into an important public announcement, although we'll have to be completely secret."

Gold's time in Washington is spent in repeated sessions with Newsome, during which they discuss the possible jobs he might want to hold, and in trying to arrange for Gold to meet the President. But it turns out that the President actually nevers sees anyone, and sleeps during his office hours because, as Newsome explains, "he is a very early riser. He is up at five every morning, takes two sleeping pills and a tranquilizer, and goes right back to bed for as long as he can sleep."

As he did in *Catch-22*, Heller tends here to ring too many changes on what is essentially one good joke. And the satire much of the time is so light-heartedly outlandish that it very nearly neutralizes one's awareness that the kind of insanity Heller makes laughable has also in the real world had the most destructive consequences. Yet there is more than an edge of anger in Heller's portrait of the Washington political scene, just as there are extremely ominous implications in his vision of American culture. His novel is indeed comic, often hilariously so, but it is also comedy of the bleakest and blackest kind. It is all about a society that is fast going insane, that is learning to accept chaos as order, and unreality as normal. The horror is that the time may soon come when the conditions Heller depicts will no longer seem to us either funny or the least bit odd.

[Review of *Good as Gold*]   Jack Beatty*

Joseph Heller has written an exuberantly funny saga on "the Jewish Experience in America." If you're wondering *whose* Jewish experience, then you're in the same quandary as Bruce Gold, Heller's 48-year-old protagonist. Gold, however, a professor of English at City College and a man with an eye for the main chance, does not let his ignorance of the Jewish experience in America, or even his doubts about the metaphysical status of such a thing, stop him from contracting to do a book on the subject for an editor friend of his, who may stand for one of New York's leading literary impresarios, nor from agreeing to run chapters from his book in a small intellectual monthly edited by yet another of his old Columbia classmates, Maxwell Lieberman. When we learn that Lieberman has already written his autobiography we can have no doubt about *his* identity: he plainly stands for a celebrated intellectual of the neo-conservative persuasion, and his neo-conservatism is so patently the philosophy of the courtier, slavering

*Reprinted from the *New Republic*, 180 (March 10, 1979), 42–44. Reprinted by permission of the *New Republic*, © 1979 The New Republic, Inc.

to be heard in Washington and on Wall Street, that he is nearly the most repellent character in a novel full of naked egotists.

Lieberman's philosophy is of a piece with the nickname he has adopted—the quintessentially goyish cognomen "Skip." "Skip" Lieberman has abandoned all dignity in his rush to be assimilated, and Bruce Gold holds him in contempt for this. But Bruce sacrifices nearly as much himself when another of his Columbia friends, Ralph Newsome, a close adviser to the president, hints that he might have a job high up in a post-Nixon administration. Gold, it seems, wrote a favorable review of the president's book, *My Year in the White House;* the president was flattered. More decisively, he was impressed with Gold's gift for the empty phrase, and in the Washington pictured in this novel there can be no stronger qualification for high office than that.

The plot involves Gold's descent on Washington where, after abandoning his Jewish wife for a propitiously lean Protestant princess named Andrea Pugh Biddle Conover, after enduring the antisemitic vituperation of Andrea's dotty father, a member of the Virginia gentry with political influence, and after serving on a committee that meets only to adjourn—after this education in the sinuosities of Washington politics Gold is surprised at "how much lower he would have to go to rise to the top." The top, Ralph Newsome hints, might even be the job of secretary of state, and, according to a theory Gold has worked out with the help of his father, that would make him, Bruce Gold, the first Jewish secretary of state.

And what of Henry Kissinger? Julius Gold has a theory about that. After reading the notorious Oriana Fallaci interview with Kissinger—it appeared in *The New Republic*—in which Kissinger compared himself to a lone cowboy, the old man has come to the conclusion that Kissinger could not possibly be a Jew:

'No siree. He said he was a cowboy, didn't he? A lonesome cowboy riding into town to get the bad guys, didn't he? All by himself. Well no cowboy was ever a Jew.'
    'Not,' said Gold's stepmother, 'on your life.'
    'Show me one,' challenged Gold's father.
'Shepherds, maybe. No cowboys.'

The risk Gold runs in trying to become the first real Jewish secretary of state is that he will be forced to act like Henry Kissinger, and that would mean his moral destruction.

For Bruce Gold hates Henry Kissinger. He refers to him familiarly as "that fat little fuck." Heller's use of obscenity is a deliberate rhetorical strategy, an effort to rescue Kissinger from the obsequious politesse of Joseph Kraft and James Reston, to put this low character in a low verbal context. It is an act of radical moral imagination, equivalent to the Freudian method of referring to sexual matters in the most explicit way possible so as to strip them of their spurious mystery and power. But Heller does not rely on obscenity alone to take Kissinger's proper measure: Gold is accumulating notes for a devastating book about Kissinger (it will prove, among other things, that Kissinger is not a Jew) and Heller has him ruminate on his subject in sentences studded with Yiddish words, as if to oppose the simple values of the immigrant generation of Jews to Kissinger's arrogance and opportunism. And Heller's animus is nothing if not informed. He has searched through the rich record of Kissinger's vanity and callousness and has filled the novel with Kissinger's more damning utterances as well as with adverse comment on Kissinger from such sources as Anthony Lewis, Woodward and Bernstein, and this journal. Those who hold Kissinger in high esteem will find this book impossible to read. Those, on the other hand, who are of Gold's conservative opinion that —

> Kissinger would not be recalled in history as a Bismark, Metternich or Castlereagh, but as an odious *shlump* who made war gladly and did not often exude much of that legendary sympathy for weakness and suffering with which Jews were regularly credited

— these readers will take perverse delight in every scarifying page. *Good as Gold* is a cultural event. A major novelist has taken on our greatest celebrity with all the power of wit and language at his command, and perhaps not since Tolstoy eviscerated Napoleon — Solzhenitsyn's Lenin is too mild to be in the comparison — has a central historical figure been so intimately castigated by the Word. Score one for literature.

Good as Gold works as a series of contrasts between Washington and New York, Gentile and Jew, the nihilism and opportunism of politics and the viciousness and strangled love of family life. The Washington scenes are brilliant political satire, but the scenes of the Golds at dinner belong to the heights of comedy. Gold's family includes: "four older sisters who seemed like 450 when they flocked around him with their questions, solicitudes and advice"; Julius Gold, a despotic narcissist who hates Gold and who keeps discovering new Jewish holidays to postpone his annual winter retreat to Miami; and Gussie Gold, Julius's second wife, who adds a touch of real insanity to the prevailing amiable dementia. Gussie is the kind of bitter loony Heller fans will recognize from *Catch-22:*

> Often she called him to her side just to tell him to move away. Sometimes she came up to him and said, 'Cackle, Cackle.'

Gussie is forever knitting, and it is a measure of what Gold has to put up with from his family that when he asks her *what* she is knitting, his father tells him not to ask *personal* questions.

These family dinners are torture for Gold. Yet underneath the casseroles of kugel and noodle pudding, the platters of potato salad and the endless bowls of matzoh balls, beneath the practiced taunts, the feverish intimacy of the Gold family, there are some abiding values at work which Heller wants us to recognize and, I think, celebrate. Gold's brother Sid is the best example of what these values entail.

Sid, a prosperous businessman, is no hero; he's just a good man. He hated his father, yet bailed the old man out of his last business, and still pays the bills for his Florida retirement. He resented his smarter kid brother but paid his way through Columbia nonetheless. Sid has done his duty. In a scene as delicately naturalistic as the rest of the novel is manically stylized, Bruce gets Sid to talk about his life, and inevitably, he is self-deceived. How else could he have made those sacrifices?

> 'Sid, you must have resented me a lot back then, didn't you?'
> 'Oh no Bruce,' Sid said. 'Why would I do that, I was always very proud of you.'
> 'I had such an easy time of it after you had such a hard one, I got those good marks in school and was able to go to college.'
> 'I'm glad we were able to send you,' said Sid. 'No, I didn't mind that.'
> 'Didn't you mind having to take care of me?' Gold asked softly. 'I was the youngest boy and the family made such a fuss over me. Sid, it's OK to say yes. People in families often dislike each other for much less than that.'
> 'No, I didn't mind.' Sid spoke with his face partially averted from Gold's fascinated gaze.

Sid has been caught with strange women in hotels all over North America, yet he hasn't divorced his wife, and the check of this merely formal morality is one of the salient differences between the Jews and the Gentiles in this novel. "Golds don't get divorced." "We have deaths sometimes, no divorces," declares old Julius. *They* are the ones who go in for adultery. *They* get the divorces: "I've been married to Ellie ever since my divorce from Kelly," one of them, Ralph Newsome, says to shocked, suggestible Gold. "There was the legal problem of my annulment from Nora, but Nellie. . . ." It is Newsome who suggests that Gold get rid of Belle, his Jewish wife, and marry Andrea Biddle. Gold is tempted. He and Andrea even get engaged. But to his distress, he discovers that she plans to continue her adulterous career even after they are married. That might be OK for Biddles but not for Golds — unless, that is, Bruce can somehow cease being a Jew. One night, while asleep in Andrea's arms, he approaches that charmed state. He dreams that he is Van Cleef and Arpels. He is that glittering 5th Avenue store and all the well-bred people enter him and say nice things about him: "You are not a listener anymore," they whispered. "You are not," they lullabied, "even a Jew." This dream shows clearly enough where he's headed. It's the classic path of the hero of romance, down into the underworld where metamorphosis and the loss of identity threaten and allure. Gold is recalled to New York and to himself, however, by Sid's death. The novel ends with Bruce sitting *shivah* for Sid, having refused Newsome's final cryptic offer to be the first Jewish secretary of state.

On the way home from Sid's funeral, Gold beholds an amazing and, we can't but feel, symbolic sight. In the schoolyard of a Brooklyn yeshiva some boys in skull caps and sidelocks are playing baseball. Gold stops his car and walks over for a closer look just as an argument breaks out among the players:

> As Gold watched, the catcher, a muscular, redheaded youth with freckles and sidelocks and a face as Irish or Scottish or Polish as any Gold had ever laid eyes upon, moved wrathfully toward the pitcher with words Gold for a minute had trouble believing.
> "*Varf!*" shouted the catcher. "*Varf* it already! *Varf* the fucking ball!"

Baseball and Yiddish, they make an unlikely synthesis, but at least it is a synthesis, not an assimilation. I take it as one of the meanings of this rich and finally very traditional novel that all of us need the values that rise out of the Jewish experience in America to keep us human — to prevent us from becoming Kissingers of the personal or the public life.

Bruce Gold's American Experience   Leonard Michaels*

In his diary Kafka asks, "What have I in common with Jews?" Immediately he answers, "I have hardly anything in common with myself and should stand very quietly in a corner, content that I can breathe." Thus, failure to identify with his people inspires a joke about failure to identify with himself. The same failure, and the same joke extremely elaborated, describes much of Joseph Heller's third novel, "Good as Gold."

As the title boasts, "Good as Gold" is a dazzling commodity. It is in fact another big book about Jews — literally about a Jewish professor, Bruce Gold, who has an idea for a book about the Jewish experience in America. He sells the idea to friends of his in publishing, two sleazy, conniving opportunists. One is Lieberman: a "fat, round, vulgar face" with "tiny eyes." He edits a small intellectual magazine. The other is Pomoroy, a grimly serious, intelligent editor at a "faintly disreputable" publishing house. Both see the Jewish book as potentially lucrative, but while Lieberman wants it to be sensational, containing such things as what it feels like for a Jewish man to have sexual intercourse with "gentile girls," Pomoroy wants Gold to write a book "useful to colleges and libraries." In any case, Gold's idea for the Jewish book, which occupies him through the first chapter, is never realized because he does too many other things.

He goes to family dinners and parties, he jogs, he visits his doctor, he has love affairs, he converses with friends, he travels between Washington and New York, he teaches a class at his college, he eats frequently and thinks much about food, his life, marriage, careers of famous men in government,

*Reprinted from the *New York Times Book Review*, March 11, 1979, pp. 1, 24-25. © 1979 by The New York Times Company. Reprinted by permission.

and the novel climaxes in a nightmarish flurry of adulterous activity. Though Gold never writes his book, we finally have the book he lives, "Good as Gold." It is indeed about Jews and a lot more, and it satisfies the requests of vulgar Lieberman and grimly serious Pomoroy, for it is both high and low in comic spirit. It contains much truth as well as gross, slap-stick lunacy.

While the title speaks ironically about Bruce Gold's intention to make money on the Jewish experience, it also mocks him with paradox, suggest-ing in his very name problems of identity and value. How good is Gold? Is Gold good? (As for Bruce, a Gaelic name, what is a Jew doing with it?) Beyond all this doubleness, the novel has a double plot that reflects its deep-est subject, alienation—being what you are not, feeling what you don't feel, thinking what you don't think, living a life that is not yours. Essen-tially, then, "Good as Gold" is about some American Jews, their bastardized existence, their sense of congenital inauthenticity. Kafka's agonies of per-sonal identity are brought up to date by Heller and remade American— bold and commercial.

Virtually everything about his hero is ambivalent or inconsistent. Gold is a middle-aged Jew, bored by his professorial duties, who yearns for a glamorous job in Washington among politicians he finds contemptible. Though he is the author of books, essays, stories, poems and reviews, he knows that none of them is distinguished by moral character, personal depth, brains or talent; and, for this reason, he can be said to consider him-self contemptible. Despite his deficiencies—or, as Heller suggests, because of them—he wins invitations to speak before groups of university students and businessmen. Gold is married to a decent, dumpy, obedient, all-endur-ing Jewish woman named Belle, who "would never fight or say anything wrong at home or do anything wrong outside," and was always "kind and practical and so good to the children and family." Of course, Gold is contin-ually adulterous and he wants to marry a tall Gentile blonde whose charac-ter is defined by robotlike promiscuity, fast cars and horses.

Most important to the description of Gold is his oppressive family. Much of the time in the novel is spent with them, mainly at the dinner table in scenes that are delightfully theatrical and funny; they probably could be staged with little change. The family characters tend to be hilariously ob-noxious, especially Gold's father—a narcissistic tyrannical fool—and Gold's older brother, a goodhearted ignoramus who infuriates Gold with displays of smug, idiotic erudition. For example:

> " 'It's really one of the great miracles of nature, isn't it? The way vul-
> tures, or gizzards, as they sometimes are called—'
> " 'Buzzards,' growled Gold, without looking up.
> " 'What'd I say?'
> " 'Gizzards.'
> " 'How strange,' said Sid. 'I meant buzzards, of course—how vultures

are able to locate dying animals from five or ten miles away — even though all of them, from the moment they're born, are always totally blind.' "

There are also several doting sisters; one beloved debauched younger sister; three enervating children; and an insane stepmother who may live forever as a possession of the English language. Here Gold meets her for the first time:

> " 'And what,' he said in his most courtly manner, 'Would you like us to call you?'
> " 'I would like you to treat me as my own children do,' Gussie Gold replied with graciousness equal to his own. 'I would like to think of you all as my very own children. Please call me Mother.'
> " 'Very well, Mother,' Gold agreed. 'Welcome to the family.'
> " 'I'm not your mother,' she snapped."

Along with Lieberman, Pomoroy and other amusing, revolting Jewish friends from his youth in Coney Island, the family determines one plot of the novel that is exquisitely realistic — that is, grotesque, witty, lugubriously banal. Its Jewish characters are comically limited, but they suffer, they have pasts, they have interior lives, and they constitute the roots, trunk and branches of Gold's inescapable, basic identity. He wants, nevertheless, to escape it. Given his family and friends, it is hard to blame him for this, but only death can make it possible. At the end of the novel, when someone close to him dies, he sinks into a sort of ambiguous reconciliation with himself.

The Protestant characters in the novel, in contrast to the Jews, are essentially unproblematic and mechanical. They determine most of the other plot, which is mainly fantastic but includes an astounding vision of our leaders in Washington. Astounding because, while fantastic, it doesn't seem incorrect. Among these characters is Ralph Newsome, who went to college with Gold and now works for the President. He is the purest, least problematic Protestant in the novel. Here he tempts Gold toward Washington, the stronghold of American venality and blond power:

> " 'All of us want you working with us as soon as possible after the people above us decide whether they want you working here at all.'
> " 'As what?' said Gold, who already knew the answer was ardently yes.
> " 'Oh, I don't know,' said Ralph. 'We probably could start you right in as a spokesman.'
> " 'A spokesman?' Gold was abruptly doubtful. It sounded like something athletic. 'What's a spokesman?'
> " 'Oh, Bruce, you must know. That's what I've been when I haven't been doing something else. A government spokesman, an unnamed source. . . . In a month or two, we can move you up.'
> " 'To what?'
> " 'Well, if nothing else, to a senior official.' "

These temptations are offered several times, always with greater intensity, and eventually Newsome sees no reason Bruce Gold can't be Secretary of State or head of NATO. Given Heller's picture of Washington — full of lazy, unprincipled, prurient careerists — there is no reason Gold couldn't be Secretary of State. Indeed, it is one of Heller's triumphs in the novel that he makes this observation convincing and perhaps more valuable to our understanding of our Government than a library of Presidential papers. In this respect, "Good as Gold" is certainly "useful to colleges and libraries."

In contrast to Gold's ambivalent character, there is at least one figure in the novel who is absolutely who he is, a man of ultimate authenticity: Hugh Biddle Conover, an old dying Protestant of infinite wealth, father of the woman Gold wants to marry. Father and daughter, Gold imagines, can be instrumental in getting him a job in Washington, in the President's inner circle. The realistic-Jewish-plot and the fantastic-Protestant-plot, as separate from each other as Gold is from himself, come together with concentrated ferocity when Gold visits Conover's immense estate (seven acres under the roof of one house) to ask for the hand of his immensely tall, blonde daughter. Conover refers to Gold with various Jewish names. He doesn't discriminate, you might say, regarding Jews:

> " 'How does it feel, Dr. Gold, to know you've already failed your children and probably your grandchildren as well — to realize you've already deprived these innocent descendants of yours of the chance to enter good society?'
>
> "Gold echoed him with disdain. 'Good society?'
>
> " 'Yes, Shapiro, you know what I mean. I'm in it and you're not. My family is and yours isn't. You have aspirations and regrets and feelings of inferiority and I don't. What are you doing in here with me?' "

Here and elsewhere, Conover's speeches are too flatly punishing to be terribly funny. Long, detailed, precise, full of venomous hatred, they are not only impossible in reality, but the hatred seems finally to exceed the comic situation. This happens again in an extended comment Gold makes on the career of Henry Kissinger. In both cases the satirical animus is focused on loathsome qualities of Jews, but the book is essentially about Jews, especially those like Gold, who wants to escape his identity while exploiting it, particularly by making a lot of money on a big book about Jews. Heller himself is implicated, but only insofar as "Good as Gold" is about such books and the people who write them. He exploits the exploiters. He has his cake and eats it, too. Indeed, the novel self-consciously comments on itself in the title and in other places, and thus seems literally to feed on itself.

Conover's denunciation of Gold is echoed by many other people: Gold's stepmother says he has a "screw loose"; his father introduces him as "the brother of my son Sid"; his daughter tortures him in small mean ways; his doctor teases him sadistically about his decrepitude; his lover says he has middle-aged attitudes toward sex; the narrator describes him as a scheming mediocrity, a disillusioned, deeply compromised, mealy-mouthed fraud; and Gold thinks less of himself than anyone else does. He is perhaps the most exposed, humiliated hero of our day.

What distinguishes Conover from Gold's other detractors is that his comments are based on the contrast between Gold and himself, but we understand that he is finally only a noise named Conover, the product of Gold's fears and self-hate. The same is more or less true of other Protestants in the novel, including Conover's daughter, whose immense height, beauty, blondeness and blithely brainless promiscuity are so exaggerated as to guarantee her unreality and allow the treatment she receives. For example, during the visit to Conover's estate, she pleads with Gold not to use her sexually, thus suggesting what he wants — revenge against her father and sexual-social violation. The point is that, just as Conover's racism comes from the mind of Gold, so does the pleading of his daughter specify Gold's own desire to ravish and soil. Later, she tells him he can tie her up and do whatever he likes to her, as if she fancies herself the creature of his masturbatory Jewish imagination. The narrator describes Gold, in relation to her, as "rapacious and calculating," but he seems also sadistic, impotent and slimy.

Father and daughter, comic Protestants of Gold's imagination, play the same role Jews once played in the Protestant imagination. The reversal is much apparent in contemporary movies and novels, but Jewish artists can be trusted to balance attacks on Protestants with lots of anti-Semitism. For these satirists the truth of our American life lies between ugly and funny. In Lenny Bruce, Woody Allen and others, a powerful satirical convention has been established, and it is just what Heller says, ironically: good as gold. His novel comments on itself constantly, and the merciless denunciation of his scapegoat hero is the price Heller pays for his artistic conscience.

It's a little embarrassing to confess that I was not tough enough to laugh always at such vile objects as Conover, his daughter, Gold's friends and others who represent us to ourselves in a morally degenerate society. "Look too long into the abyss," says Nietzsche, "and the abyss will look into you." Anyhow, the self-conscious complexities of the novel make it inconsistently funny and sometimes tiresome.

However Protestants are conceived and treated, it is one of the themes of "Good as Gold" that Jews violate themselves in their relations with such unreal creatures of their own minds, especially when Jews yearn for tall blondes and jobs in Washington, where successful Jews are "slaves." The chief example, for Gold, is Kissinger, about whom Gold plans to write a book called "The Little Prussian." He is so obsessed with Kissinger that, among the great variety of scenes, we find a long, detailed account of Kissinger's career, written by Gold. It is full of Yiddish name-calling and so rich in moral revulsion as to seem like a voodoo incantation intended to make the real man sicken and die. Kissinger is described by Gold, with evidence taken from newspapers, as self-demeaning, sycophantic, sanctimonious, incompetent, self-seeking, power-crazy, murderous and like a Nazi.

According to Gold's father, it is possible Kissinger isn't a Jew. This is relevant to the novel's paradoxical, ironical character, because it gives the final twist to the relations between Bruce Gold, an imaginary hero, and the real living Kissinger, a non-Jewish Jew married in fact to a tall blonde. In brief: Bruce Gold yearns to escape what he is so that he can become what he isn't, which is precisely what he hates. He nearly succeeds, nearly becomes a Washington non-Jewish Jew, a rich, powerful slave with a tall blonde wife.

The way Heller plays with this psycho-physical transmogrification of his hero is remarkably impressive, and I suspect that Bruce Gold is a uniquely original hero. Has there ever been one who is the self-despising alter ego of a world-famous person? A hero who exists, in his very essence, relatively? At the core of its satirical vision, "Good as Gold" seems to have combined Einstein's theory of relativity with Kafka's agonies.

Heller's Gold and a Silver Sax   Benjamin DeMott*

Bruce Gold, hero of Joseph Heller's third novel, *Good As Gold* (Simon & Schuster, $12.50), is a forty-eight-year-old English professor with problems. Unable to cover his children's tuition bills on academic pay, he has been piling up debts in the form of advances for unfinishable book projects ("a study of the contemporary Jewish experience in America"). He also suffers intermittently, from doubt about his professional worth. The published cultural commentaries and political observations that support his modest reputation seem to him cheesy stuff (he "thought much less of his work than even his fussiest detractors"), and lately his opportunism has bothered him. Audiences of pious elderly reactionaries love him, but so do fire-eating teen-aged Maoists, and the reason for this isn't pretty: Gold shifts his pitch according to the sympathies of whatever crowd is at hand. (He once exploited, in two different ways, within twenty-four hours, a news story about a Texas official who had escaped trial on some counts for which he had been indicted. First he used the story "to confirm the suspicions of an audience of millionaires that the federal government had it in for all rich Texans, [second] to insinuate convincingly the next afternoon to an assembly of college students just thirty miles away that justice, in the presence of rich politicians, was not blind but merely looking the other way.")

Finally, there's some trouble with his close relatives — a status problem. Gold's father, stepmother, older sisters, brothers-in-law, even his own younger daughter, all see him as a loser. "Whatever he does is wrong," is his father's contemptuous assessment.

Hard times, but comes a chance to break out. Gold reviews, in the waf-

*Reprinted from *Atlantic Monthly*, 243 (March 1979), 129–31. © 1979, by The Atlantic Monthly Company, Boston, Mass. Reprinted with permission.

fling manner he has made his own, a volume by the incumbent Chief Executive (the title is *My Year in the White House*), and in doing so hits upon phrases that entrance the not undim presidential eye. A White House aide named Ralph, known to Gold from graduate school, suggests he consider joining the Administration, probably with Cabinet rank. There are catches in the invitation — so many, indeed, as it turns out, that the hero's effort to cope with them becomes the main narrative business of the tale. But Gold's optimism is unfaltering and his pliancy matchless, at least for a while. The Pennsylvania Avenue inner circle decides that, stylewise, he would do well to divest himself of dumpy Belle, his wife of twenty-odd years. Gold takes steps. The inner circle decides he ought to pursue, as a substitute for Belle, a tall millionairess with Potomac Establishment connections and a startlingly promiscuous nature. Further steps. The inner circle recommends sucking up to a famous anti-Semitic Washington fixer who has lied under oath to Congress fourteen times. Gold sucks up.

So it goes, for a time. At length, though, the hero notices a certain lack of movement. He's grateful for compliments and continues to snap up unconsidered trifles. White House staffers revere his standard idioms ("boggles the mind," "I don't know"), and he's granted a place on a presidential commission run by a Connally-like Texas governor. But the governor proposes quick adjournment so that the group can accomplish "in just two meetings what [has] taken [other presidential commissions] as long as three years: nothing." And in addition, the governor is rude to Gold ("Gold, you a Jew, ain't you?").

Slights begin accumulating. Appointment after appointment at the Oval Office is canceled. Gold's sponsor, Ralph, grows steadily more equivocating. Gold is stimulated to recall his hostility to a former Secretary of State, Henry Kissinger (State is the post Gold covets), and the memory diminishes his awe of the office. Potomac fever, in short, is wearing off, and in the end Gold returns to Belle and the contemporary Jewish experience in America.

As a send-up of Capital conventions and clichés, *Good As Gold* is sometimes funny. The hero asks a White House aide what jobs are open and learns there's a spot for a "spokesman" from which one would move up in a month "to a senior official . . . free to hold background briefings, any time you want, every time we schedule them." The presidential commission that adjourns upon formation resembles a thousand such executive bodies — assemblages of token blacks, widows, football coaches, ambassadors, mayors, doctors, English professors, token everybodies. And Heller casts a rightly cold gaze on the "organizations with Brobdingnagian names [that are] sprouting like unmanageable vines and spreading like mold with sinecures and conferments for people of limited mentality and unconvincing motive" — such real-life enclaves as the American Enterprise Institute for Public Policy Research or the Hoover Institution on War, Revolution and Peace.

The representation of Jewish family life in *Good As Gold* isn't bare of stereotype, but several episodes achieve a likable zaniness—for example, a crazily heated family debate on the meaning of the term "north" in relation to the term "up." And there are moments of refreshingly straight talk, as when Gold's baby sister, Joan, who has renamed herself "Toni," answers Gold's question about the meaning, in her mind, of their common heritage: "If you want to know what my Jewish experience is, I can tell you. . . . It's trying not to be. We play golf now, get drunk, take tennis lessons, and have divorces, just like normal Christian Americans. We talk dirty. We screw around, commit adultery, and talk out loud a lot about fucking. . . ."

Yet despite all this I found *Good As Gold*, billed as a "major American classic," unsatisfying, and I believe I know why. It's this simple: the author can't decide how disturbed he is (or whether) by his hero's troubles and the world's, hence can't make the troubles consequential to the reader. Bruce Gold appears persuaded most days that the country is finished: ". . . he knew there was no longer anything legal to be done under the American system of government to discourage crime, decrease poverty, improve the economy, or nullify the influences of neglect. . . . [he] knew that the most advanced and penultimate stage of a civilization was attained when chaos masqueraded as order, and he knew we were already there." He finds proof of collapse in the continuing eminence of Henry Kissinger: ours is a "society in which . . . a blundering, blathering, shoddy hypocrite [is] honored as a celebrity instead of shunned and despised. . . ."

But the author himself is at pains to assure the reader that Gold is completely of a piece with his contemporaries—meaning he's a coward, a lazy, exploitative teacher, an envy-ridden competitor, and a match for Kissinger at doubleness (Gold "realized also that he was not just a liar but a hypocrite"). The hero's characteristic response to the collapse of civilization is unembarrassed pleasure at being furnished with an article idea:

> Multitudes witnessed the avalanching decline. Gold's spirits were improving tremendously as this vocabulary of degeneration and decay coursed through his head. It was the Shoot the Chutes into darkness and dissolution, the plunging roller coaster into disintegration and squalor. Someone should do something. Nobody could. No society worth its salt would watch itself perishing without some serious attempt to avert its own destruction. Therefore, Gold concluded, we are not a society. Or we are not worth our salt. Or both.

Gold had his article. Yet he's never raked over by his creator for this cynicism: as the title hints, in these pages none but the Gold standard applies.

Would this count if high levels of novelistic energy were sustained in the book? Conceivably not. Good fiction, dark views, and judgmental ambiguity often coexist. But the case is that in *Good As Gold* ambiguity infects, inhibits, and ultimately depletes the energies of creation—wears things down. An example is the treatment of Secretary Kissinger. For a novelist this figure presents opportunities seemingly too rich to waste. Agility, slyness, persuasiveness, vanity, humorous self-awareness, plus the evident condescension to ordinary folk who bring only uncosmopolitan American-ness to the conduct of foreign affairs — these features of character beg for imaginative penetration. What is such a human being to himself? In this book we're offered — instead of an answer — a section of direct quotations from lifeless, objective newspaper dispatches about the former Secretary of State, excerpts from columns by Anthony Lewis, and the like. Nothing in the lot is freshly imagined.

It's the same story with the presentation of life in the executive bureaucracy. We smile when the author points mockingly at familiar outward behaviors, expecting a probe that will show the insides of the deeds and talk, thereby demonstrating, incidentally, the difference between a first-rate novel and a first-rate Russell Baker column. But the probe doesn't come. This novelist seems to have concluded that the essence of life at the bureaucratic top can be delivered by repeating several dozen times a single oxymoronic gesture as a symbol of administrative inaction:

> We'll want to move ahead with this as speedily as possible, although we'll have to go slowly.

> We want everyone in government to read it, although we've stamped it secret so nobody can.

> He [the President] probably wants you here as soon as you can make the necessary arrangements, although he probably doesn't want you making any yet.

Internationally renowned, Mr. Heller stands forth just now as the author of only three books, therefore overviews of his oeuvre aren't yet in order. Even so, it's perhaps worth recording that his career thus far has helped to clarify the limits of comic apathy, or stylized unresponsiveness, as a resource for writers whose subject isn't war. At some moments in history — the *Catch-22* moment was among them — the tones and gestures of indifference are, paradoxically, energizing; they light up, by shocking, hellish, absurdist strokes, the conditions that quicksilver phrases such as "consciousness dulled by horror" can only obscure. But at other moments indifference and related postures lack dimension, adding up to little beyond themselves. The themes of *Good As Gold* are by no means negligible, and it's possible that the author conceived the novel as an ambitious cultural inquiry into the state of America now. But the finished production struck me, I'm afraid, as a rather listless and dispirited piece of work.

Talking with Joseph Heller

Charlie Reilly*

Q: My congratulations on *Good as Gold*. It's a remarkable book. In fact, I think it has that harmony between humor and subtle profundity that you handle as well as anyone writing today.

HELLER: I'm glad you liked it. I'm pleased you enjoyed the humor too because I was just reading a very perceptive review by a professor named John Aldridge who called *Good as Gold* the bleakest of my three books. I think he used the phrase, "an extension of Heller's darkening vision." The more I thought about it the more I could see what he meant.

Q: You're kidding? Bleaker than *Something Happened?*

HELLER: Bleaker than *Something Happened* and *Catch-22* — the bleakest and most biting despite the, I think he used the word, hilarity. He focused largely upon the Washington episodes and speculated that what Heller is imagining today may well be happening tomorrow. He also commented upon what I have in there, perhaps unconsciously, about the decline of the contemporary family.

Q: That's a sensitive response. I guess I was groping in that direction when I talked about the book's subtlety and profundity.

HELLER: Here we go! *Inquiry* is probably hoping for some political views and we seem to be moving again toward an intellectual literary column. I mean that respectfully; *Inquiry* is a good magazine.

Q: I'm sure *Inquiry* is hoping for your thoughts about the novel, period. As I collect myself now, I realize that I meant to say the pace and tone of the novel reminded me of what was best about *Catch-22*. There were at least a dozen portions where I put down the book and laughed out loud — and how often does that happen in a book? But as I came to the final passages, as the protagonist's life becomes so frenetic, I got the same eerie feeling I did with both of your other novels. I found what I had dismissed as "fun" sneaking up on me, and I found myself being absorbed with, well, the moral undercurrents of the book.

HELLER: I should stress I was very conscious of the similarities between *Good as Gold* and *Catch-22*, and I was vigilant not to repeat the same comic techniques too often — techniques like sudden shifts in time and place. In the final sections I make extravagant use of such techniques, but that was the result of a conscious decision. I wanted those seven days when

*Reprinted, with the permission of the author, from *Inquiry Magazine*, May 1, 1979, pp. 22–26.

they're sitting shivah to move quickly. But, on the whole I tried hard to avoid the types of aphoristic and verbal humor that I used in *Catch-22*.

Q: Although *Catch-22* was set during World War II, you directed a lot of its satire against the then-current excesses and evils of McCarthyism. I wonder if there isn't something complementary in *Good as Gold*. This novel supposedly concerns the "Jewish Experience," but at the same time it intensely, ferociously, comments on Kissinger, Vietnam, and post-Vietnam politics.

HELLER: The answer to your question is yes. There's a review I've seen that closes with the thought that Gold is Jewish only in his symptoms. The implication, and it's sensible, is that he's representative of the entire country at this time. *Good as Gold* does focus upon the Jewish experience, but ultimately Bruce Gold finds his experience is not particularly more Jewish than, well, mine. I feel that many people my age, people who went to college after the war and became involved in academic or literary activities, have had experiences that are not materially different from those of people who aren't Jewish.

Q: A couple of people asked me after our first interview whether you're Jewish and I had to say I didn't know because it never occurred to me to ask you. You haven't written about Jewish protagonists or themes before, in other words. But, are you from a Jewish family, similar to Gold's?

HELLER: Well, yes, I'm Jewish. But, no, I didn't have a large family like Gold, nor did I become involved in dinners similar to the Gold family's. To tell you the truth, I'm not sure where the idea came from for those dinners in the novel. My wife has a large family and, of course, we all gathered for Thanksgiving and whatever. But there was nothing like the, well, uproar and anger you find in Gold's dinners. What I was trying to do there, at least in part, was to point out incongruities — to suggest that even though Gold was being considered for the position of secretary of state, inside the home he was still the youngest brother, the kid who didn't know enough to use a handkerchief.

Q: So the fact that this novel came well along in your writing career does not reflect that you have been brooding about, perhaps building toward, a novel about the Jewish experience?

HELLER: No, emphatically not. I got the idea for this book immediately after giving a reading from *Catch-22* and *Something Happened* in Wilmington, Delaware. Afterwards, in a small question group, a woman asked me why I had never written about the Jewish experience. I answered that I had had only two ideas for a novel in twenty-one years, so I certainly wasn't excluding it. And then I said, I wasn't at all sure I was qualified to write about the topic, I wasn't sure I was that much in touch with the experience as the writers who had already handled it so wonderfully, writers like Bernard Malamud and Philip Roth. But while I was going home on the Metroliner, I began musing about the possibilities and began making notes. By the time I got off the train, I had the idea for the novel; a book about a guy who got an advance for a book about the "Jewish Experience" and then realized he hadn't had any such experience.

Q: But, by the end of the novel, doesn't the reader at least perceive Gold has a more profound and important "Jewish Experience" than Gold himself realizes?

HELLER: I suppose, but Gold is correct in perceiving his "Jewish Experience" is far removed from, say, Dubin's, in Malamud's new book, or from any character in Malamud's work.

Q: One character in *Good as Gold*, Gold's father Julius, especially fascinated me: Despite his cantankerous, sarcastic, patriarchal, egocentric nature, I wound up liking Julius Gold enormously.

HELLER: Good. If I may immodestly say so, I think that's one of the achievements — I don't have the nerve to say triumphs — of the novel. I had originally decided to depict him as an almost stock character — a nasty, vile-natured, old tyrant — but about halfway through the writing I decided I'd do that, but also try to persuade the reader to feel sorry for him at the end. Julius is right and the children are right too. When he complains that he took care of his parents and now his children don't want him, he's addressing something that's prevalent throughout the country. We don't want our old people with us. It's similar to a line in *Something Happened* where the text says something to the effect that Slocum's aged mother became a burden to him as soon as he no longer needed her.

Q: You've done something in *Good as Gold* with narrative point of view that is unprecedented, even for you. I must confess that the effect of *Catch-22*'s order out of chaos and the "Beckettean" voice of *Something Happened* had an enormous impact upon me. But, in this one, the unnamed third-person-omniscient narrator actually shows up in the text, concedes he could have served Gold better, and predicts what will happen later in the tale. Then, a couple of pages later, a reference is made to an author named "Joseph Heller." Now, you've never done this before. Had you planned it from the start?

HELLER: Yes. From the start I planned injecting the first-person pronoun into the novel fairly regularly, and doing so in a way that would incline the reader to infer that that first-person voice belonged to me, Joseph Heller. I wanted very much to have some kind of sustained, perhaps disconcerting, reminder to the reader that this *is* only a story, that it shouldn't be taken too seriously. What happened was, as I wrote the book, I began to worry that the effect might be too precious — I had even conceived at one point of having dialogues between a character and "me" — and I was worried it would prove too jarring upon the reader. What I ultimately decided to do was include a number of lines here and there that would have the same effect but that would not stand out. For example, in addition to the passages you mentioned, there was the occasion when Gold was musing, first, upon the extraordinary situation of awaiting a high government appointment while hustling a book, and then upon the fact that this was exactly what Kissinger was doing. The next sentence says, "in a novel, no one would have believed it." That sort of thing happens often. I don't know if you noticed the way the allusions to Dickens operate. On one occasion the phrase occurs, and it's a borrowed simile, "as solitary as an oyster." In ensuing passages there are a number of criticisms that seem to apply to Charles Dickens but have also been applied to *Something Happened* and *Catch-22*: too long, too many characters, too many improbable events. But, to answer your question, I finally decided in that one chapter, and only in that one, to introduce formally the "I" narrator. I suppose it was almost an attempt to disarm criticism and, in a humorous way, do something integral to the sense of the novel.

Q: This intrusion of the narrator, this confronting the reader with a tension between narrated event and "realistic" fact, reminded me of Laurence Sterne's eighteenth-century novel, *Tristram Shandy*. Are there "Shandyean" influences on your novel?

HELLER: Oh yes, I had *Tristram Shandy* very much in mind for this book. That's the reason I refer to it so often.

Q: And, am I correct in thinking *Good as Gold* Shandyean in a special sense: specifically, in that Sterne's novel, to a significant extent, is a book about the composition of the book *Tristram Shandy*?

HELLER: Yes.

Q: So, to an extent, *Good as Gold* is a book about the composition of the book *Good as Gold*?

HELLER: It is, except that by the time it's over, Gold himself still hasn't started it.

Q: At least he seems a lot better off for having gone through all the events and scrapes in the novel.

HELLER: He is. He's not necessarily a better man, but he has shaken off those ambitions that are presented in the book as ignoble. He's resolved not to use public service, for instance, as a camouflage for personal and social advancement.

Q: And despite his announced contempt for Kissinger, he has finally stopped becoming, in effect, a Kissinger.

HELLER: Oh yes. Kissinger was not simply a target of Gold's envy; he was a model for what could be achieved.

Q: I have to admit that I can recall very few major satirists who deal as directly and vigorously with real figures — people like Kissinger, Helms, Haig, Kleindienst — as you do in *Good as Gold*. I wonder if working with real people makes the writing more difficult, or more nerve-wracking, or easier?

HELLER: It's not as major a departure as it may seem. *Catch-22* was originally going to deal with some well-known figures, but by the time the book was ready for publication most of them were dying or losing power. In this particular book, I felt it worked well. But, no, it wasn't easier or harder to work with specific public figures. In fact, I suspect that if I were regularly employed as a satiric columnist, I would probably find it much easier to work with specifically identified figures. And keep in mind that most of the direct references take the form of verbatim quotations of newspaper pieces.

Q: Another thing that interested me was the effect that writing about the Vietnam War had upon you. It seemed apparent in *Something Happened* that you felt a sense of moral outrage over our role in the war, and in this one Gold seems to boil in rage at some aspects of it. Was it difficult to write about an issue that is so enraging and draining?

HELLER: No, and this is true of *Catch-22* as well. When I'm writing, I am only interested in writing. Now when I'm not writing, I confess I can hear something that will make me boil over. A phrase that really gets to me, for instance, would be one of those neoconservative references to Vietnam as a national tragedy, but only because we lost. That thought fills me with ire. To begin with, the person who says it is typically untouched by tragedy; like me, he has not lost a son or a job. In addition, the implication is that if we had won, the war would have been somehow less tragic. People with that mentality, I have to admit, impress me as being the scum of the earth.

Q: But when writing you don't find yourself consumed with savage indignation, as Swift put it? When you were creating Gold's abject fury over what was done and said during the Vietnam era, you weren't churning inside?

HELLER: No, and the same was true of *Catch-22*. One of the most stirring portions of *Catch-22*, and I know this because I've read it to audiences, is the passage that describes Snowden's death. When I wrote that, I recall having finished it and then sitting back and wanting to smile. It's not that I was dismissive or callous. But I knew it was done well. I knew it was right. At the moment of composition I felt no sympathy for Snowden, none for Yossarian, none for Gold. It's not that I'm devoid of such emotions. But many people don't realize the degree of detachment, the intensity of concentration, required in serious writing.

Q: And yet I hope you would agree that all of your works are intensely moral. In others words, you're not simply playing games with the issues you're working with.

HELLER: Oh yes, definitely.

Q: I guess what I'm trying to say is that what Gold says about Kissinger seems to me to be so right and moral and profound.

HELLER: But keep in mind that Gold is not that much of an idealist. If you want to talk about a character who can, well, denounce Kissinger, I think the President's unnamed source, Ralph Newsome, might be a better candidate. Ralph uses invective against Kissinger far more effectively. To me, his terms for Kissinger are far more impressive than Gold's since Gold's are largely spoken in anger.

Q: Perhaps I'm not prepared to admit Ralph's virtues since I found him so dislikeable.

HELLER: That's interesting. Most people I've spoken to so far have liked him.

Q: Really?

HELLER: They like him as a character. There's a candor to him. After the book was finished, he began to remind me of Milo Minderbinder in *Catch-22*. He is willing to say what is actually so. He is genuinely embarrassed when Gold advises him his definition of a friend is someone who would hide him. If you'll recall, after Gold does ask Ralph to hide him, Ralph apologizes and says — and he's genuinely contrite — "Oh God, Bruce, I'm not your friend; I'm sorry if I said anything to give you that impression." Then again, I may be the wrong person to ask. I wound up more or less liking Conover, the bigot, and even the Texas governor — who to a degree resembles John Connally. It's similar to what happened in *Catch-22* with General Dreedle and Milo. Conversely, I have to admit that I have a hero who was intended to be an unsympathetic figure. Morally, Gold is an ignominious person. He wound up the way Bob Slocum of *Something Happened* started out to be.

Q: Maybe I was forewarned by *Catch-22*, but when I was barely into *Good as Gold* and when I realized you were raining characters down upon me, I grabbed a pencil and scribbled a family tree of sorts. At the end, when you again managed to bring all the characters and subplots together, as you did in *Catch-22*, I was filled with admiration. What I wonder is, when you wrote it did you compose it the way I read it, that is, in an episodic way? Did you have an elaborate master plan from the start?

HELLER: I wrote it largely the way you read it. This book required very little in the way of outlining, almost none in fact. In the instance you cited, I decided to make a virtue out of necessity. I knew I wanted to handle a large number of people and I knew it was going to be virtually impossible to linger over each and define each character without killing the pace of the book. So what I did was have Gold react in the book to this swarm of people the way the reader would. If you'll recall, Gold occasionally will forget the names of the people to whom he's talking and will begin improvising names arbitrarily—sometimes it's a name from Dickens, sometimes from Greek mythology. I think this is an unavoidable problem in the modern novel. Perhaps in a Russian novel you could afford the luxury of a couple of hundred pages of character delineation. But modern readers don't have the patience for that sort of thing.

Q: What about characters who don't show up until late in the novel, characters like Linda Book?

HELLER: I had thought through all the major characters, and she's a good example, right from the start. At least, I did it as soon as I decided this was going to be a major novel. When I began *Good as Gold*, my intention was to dash off a short, frivolous book. I felt that, after the years and years I spent on *Something Happened*, it would be pleasant to concentrate on something that would be short and quick. At least, I finished it in three years.

Q: That's true. The others took seven and fourteen years.

HELLER: Believe me, I'll settle for three for the next one.

Q: Do you have an idea for the next one?

HELLER: None at all. Maybe I should go back to Wilmington and give another reading.

Ethnic Identity as Moral Focus: A Reading of Joseph Heller's *Good as Gold*

Wayne C. Miller*

"If you ever forget you're a Jew," said Gussie Gold in a tone of stately rebuke, "you can rest assured that a gentile like Conover will remind you."

"They know it, for God's sake," Gold replied to her, "and they accept me there for what I am."

"Yeah?" said his father. "And what are you? You going into government with them? As what?"

"As secretary," said Gold, in a voice falling lower with embarrassment, "of State."

The old man wound his face up into an expression of disgust and asked, "What kind of job is that for a Jewish boy?"[1]

In all three of his novels — *Catch-22* (1961), *Something Happened* (1974), and now *Good as Gold* (1979) — Joseph Heller has explored the moral landscape of American culture during that period in which the United States emerged as the dominant nation in the Western world and fully adopted the principles and activities of power politics on a global scale. His heroes — Yossarian, Slocum, and Gold — all deal with the tangle of temptations that America, at the time of its ascendance, presents. All try to come to terms with themselves in a system wherein the power morality of the nation-state, that web of shifting alliances based on self-interest, has filtered down through the corporate order to family and individual relationships as well. In *Catch-22* Heller dealt with the basic values of the profit system and presented the war as the inevitable product of an insane culture that valued material gain more than human life and whose morality was based on the impact of power and the operation of the free market, a combination that defines human beings as commodities among other commodities. In *Something Happened* he portrayed the moral and psychological dilemmas of a protagonist living within that culture at the pinnacle of its power — within a cocoon that both protects and deadens, permitting the hero many possessions and pleasures but denying him any sense of vital human connection, even within the family.

Catch-22, a satirically distanced "outside narrative," allows Yossarian the hope of a political alternative, an ideological ameliorative, in his final gesture of setting out for socialist Sweden, a neutral state. *Something Happened*, a relentless "inside narrative" and a *tour de force* creation of consciousness, permits no such illusion of escape. Slocum, defined primarily by his place in the economic order, is confined within the system that produced him. An upper-middle class consumer of goods and people within a culture whose affluence encourages waste, he is limited to corporate definitions of

*Reprinted, with the permission of the author, from *MELUS*, 6, No. 3 (1979), 3–17.

success and failure: "I must remember not to smile too much. I must maintain a facade. I must remember to continue acting correctly subservient and clearly grateful to people in the company and at the university and country clubs I'm invited to who expect to find me feeling humble, eager, lucky, and afraid. I travel less, come home more. (I'm keeping myself close to home base, which isn't home, of course, but the company.)"[2] In short, Slocum's values have been created by the technological state in which he functions. His life belongs to the company, the corporate order that Heller defined in *Catch-22* and explored in *Something Happened;* Slocum is "successful" within it.

Bruce Gold, the hero of Heller's third novel, is apparently on the verge of a success even greater than Slocum's—in his case within the upper reaches of governmental power—when his father asks, "What kind of job is that for a Jewish boy?" For Gold, a particularly bright and upwardly mobile Jewish boy from Brooklyn, the answering question is "What else is there?" Besides, the myths of America, supported by the nation's dominance of world markets and economic growth in the post-World War II period, apparently promised the fulfillment of ascendance to the "elect" for many second generation white ethnics. Yet, Gold, in some of his more lucid moments, has doubts. During one of them he gives himself up "to the contemplation of what it would be like to work with Ralph for the President, marry Andrea, share her apartment in Washington, fuck her richer and even more attractive friends, serve on a Presidential Commission on education, and be an overpaid professor of Urban Studies. It was to die" (p. 140).

Within a pattern that calls to mind the structure of a Morality Play in which the hero, in the face of death, chooses between various representatives of good and evil, Gold vacillates between, on the one hand, the moral death of public success with its power and pleasures and, on the other, the possibilities of a personal alternative that he hardly understands. The temptations are great. The decisions are not easy. In tone, *Good as Gold* is closer to *Catch-22* than it is to *Something Happened*, but Heller, writing this book in the 1970s, is not able to offer his hero the hope in a political solution; indeed, in the decades since the creation of *Catch-22*, the socialist states that have generated enough economic strength to enter the arena of global power politics have proved themselves to be as morally bankrupt as their capitalist counterparts. Despite the bleakness of the political landscape, particularly for those who have equated personal morality with political position, Heller, ever the moralist, remains interested in ethical alternatives in the contemporary setting. It is the contention of this essay that the notion of ethnicity, particularly as an alternative to the values of the corporate order of the modern nation-state, is at the heart of the moral vision of *Good as Gold* and that the hero finds a salvation of sorts in the personal commitment to family, to friends, and, finally, to the composite of values that grow out of the American Jewish experience as he accepts his personal past. In the face of his brother's death Gold chooses family, the ultimate connection of shared history, shared rituals, shared survival through time. He chooses the morality of his ethnic minority as an alternative to the power morality that is the province of the ruling class in American society, a class comprised primarily of White Anglo-Saxon Protestants.

In *Good as Gold* members of the ruling class are the villains of the piece, at least insofar as they would tempt the hero to deny his essence in exchange for their acceptance and for a place in the hierarchy of power that they control. The only characters in the novel who surpass the WASPs in their villainy are those non-WASPs who crave acceptance by the elite to the point of adopting their ways and their values. Hence, Henry Kissinger, the Jewish professor who, as Secretary of State, provides rationalizations for the international power politics of the ruling class, emerges as the ultimate villain, particularly the Kissinger who could engineer massive bombardments in Southeast Asia and also get on his knees to pray with Nixon. The ever-taller Harris Rosenblatt and the ever-aspiring neoconservative Maxwell Lieberman — he who would be Kissinger — are comic variations within the novel's galaxy of American Jewish aspirants. During most of the narrative Gold is an aspirant as well, and it is his moral dilemma, his temptation, his vacillation among his various possibilities that provide the central focus for the development of the fiction. It is no wonder that he lowers his voice with embarrassment when he reveals to his father that he could become Secretary of State, for he knows what Julius Gold's response will be: " 'You tell me what business a Jew has in government here. You name me one Jew who ever went into government who was any good' " (p. 383).

Good as Gold is not an easy novel to categorize, particularly since Heller mixes within it elements of several fictional and dramatic traditions, and seems to have in mind as well the inclusion of character types, themes and narrative situations from the variety of materials within the tradition of the American Jewish novel. The major tone of the work and the key to its structure and meaning is that of ambivalence, a psychological state essential to the central figures of the Morality Plays and *the* psychological state, according to Heller, of Jews in America. In an approximation of the abstraction of a Morality Play, various characters in *Good as Gold* are caricatured to the point of appearing as Virtues and Vices as the hero vacillates among choices.[3] A journey motif is present as Gold moves between the mostly realistic depictions of the family situation in Brooklyn and the often highly stylized, overly extended presentations of national leadership in Washington. Heller contrasts the landscapes effectively throughout: Washington as an illusory Eden where, apparently, Gold, at the top, can be sheltered from the harsher realities of American life; Brooklyn as the concretization of those realities, a place of racial strife, prejudice, crime, violence, a place that Gold knows because he grew up there. Against the symbolic moral landscaping there is much of the traditional novel of maturation except for the catch that the hero is forty-eight years old and matures by traveling backward to the rediscovery of self in his boyhood in Brooklyn.

Along the way, his ambivalence is not only central to the structure of this novel concerned with the American Jewish experience; it also suggests patterns of behavior and adjustment in the general ethnic and racial minority experience in America. Gold is a man between — capable of reaching toward an identity determined by the values of the dominant culture but divided in his attitudes toward such success, recognizing the achievement of it as death even while compelled to pursue such achievement.

In fact, as the narrative unfolds, it reveals that Gold has been pursuing such success ever since he chose to attend New York City's version of the Ivy League, Columbia University. The importance of his choice is not lost on his father, Julius, who exclaims: " 'It's a good thing his mother never lived to see the day he was born' " (p. 34). The father knows full well that his first wife died when Bruce was a high school student, still living in Coney Island, still in his ethnic environment. It was at Columbia where the ambivalent, unsure Bruce was born as he took his first significant step into "mainstream" America. It is there that he met Ralph Newsome, the college acquaintance now on the White House staff who emerges as both tempter and panderer in the service of the system, promising both the possibilities of power and concurrent possession of the Protestant princess. Since Gold has placed both his sons one step further on the track of apparent assimilation — one is at Yale, one at Choate — he understands that a position close to the center of political power is viewed as the ultimate mark of distinction, yes, even for intellectuals, yes, even for teachers of literature. If the degrees at Columbia made possible Gold's right of passage into the land of the Gentiles and into the system dominated by White Anglo-Saxon Protestants, the position in Washington could provide the setting for Gold's final attempt at denying his family, his past, his ethnic roots as he pursues the way to wealth and a new identity. For instance, he finds himself agreeing with Newsome's explanation of his latest divorce: " 'Well Bruce, to put it plainly, I couldn't see much point in tying myself down to a middle-aged woman with four children, even though the woman was my wife and the children were my own' " (p. 51). The escape from responsibility and the possibility of promiscuity have their appeal. In fact, Heller suggests in *Good as Gold* that all too often movement toward public success at the center of power bears a direct relationship to movement away from responsibility to other human beings, even those to whom one should feel some emotional commitment. It is a signal of the war between Gold's conditioned desire for such success and his horror at the possibility of its fulfillment that after informing Newsome that he would come to Washington he crawls into bed with Belle, his wife who "was no dope" and who absolutely refuses to leave New York (pp. 78–79).

Nevertheless, the Capitol tempts Gold. During his first visit to Newsome's office, Heller's entranced hero envisions official Washington as a technologized Eden:

> Gold was not certain, but never in his lifetime had he felt more sanguine about his prospects. He glanced out the window at official Washing-

ton and caught a glimpse of heaven. Through the doorway, the view of the open office space was a soothing pastoral, with vistas of modular desks dozing tranquilly under indirect fluorescent lighting that never flickered; there were shoulder-high partitions of transclucent glass, other offices across the way as imposing as Ralph's, and the dreamlike stirrings of contented people at work who were in every respect impeccable. The women all were sunny and chic — not a single one was overweight — the men wore jackets and ties, and every trouser leg was properly creased. If there was a worm at the core of this Garden of Eden, it escaped the cynical inspection of Gold, who could find detritus and incipient decay everywhere. (pp. 121–122)

His critical facilities momentarily destroyed, Gold nods in assent to Newsome's instruction that experience and knowledge do not count in government and that the only useful lesson from the past is " 'to grab what you want when the chance comes to get it' " (p. 120). In order to get his share all Gold must do is to write empty phrases for the President and become one of the administration's men of integrity who will agree to anything the administration wants to do.

As part of the deal he also gets, or seems to get, Andrea Conover, the kind of WASP princess idolized by ethnic writers as diverse as John Fante, Piri Thomas, Eldridge Cleaver, and, among a host of others, F. Scott Fitzgerald. Ironically, it may be proof of the recognition of the death of the American dream of assimilated upward mobility that Heller's hero, unlike Gatsby, does not die in the pursuit of this version of Daisy. Like Gatsby, Gold dreams of the orgiastic future, in this instance life with "some languorous, exquisite, young blond Englishwoman of noblest birth . . . a floating seraph of ageless and ethereal beauty who brought him tea with sugar cubes on a tray" (p. 54). Indeed, Andrea is blond, tall, attractive, rich, well-connected. She is willing to do anything in bed Gold wants. In fact, there are times when she seems to realize that her role in life is to be the embodiment of the sexual fantasies of American aspirants, and, in playing out that role, she too is victimized. Willing to perform sexual acrobatics, she rarely comes, and, in fact, this Ph.D. in Home Economics seems to work at sex about the same way she works at riding horses, while getting more pleasure from the latter activity. To his amazement Gold wonders why he finds this embodiment of his dreams so boring. At an important juncture in the novel — at the culminating point of Section VI, "You Will Hurt Your Foot," a point which brings Gold to the intellectual conclusion that becomes the title of Section VII, "Invite a Jew to the White House (and You Make Him Your Slave)" — the hero is in bed with Andrea, theoretically the key to his sexual and cultural fulfillment, but finds himself thinking about the people of his actual past: his father, the boys from Brooklyn, and particularly, his brother Sid. Indeed, the character of the older brother, Sid, is developed in Section VII as an alternative role model for Gold — an alternative to the role that he has been pursuing in his quest for public success as the aspiring Jew who would be Kissinger.

In Sections VII and VIII, "We Are Not a Society *or* We Are Not Worth Our Salt," Gold rids himself of Kissinger with a series of incantations filled with Yiddish invective. It is not easy. Once again, the temptations are great. For Kissinger seems to have all those things young boys in America are trained to want: Kissinger, the man of power as Secretary of State; Kissinger, the intellectual as advisor to the Rockfellers; Kissinger, the money-maker as consultant to NBC and the Chase Manhattan Bank; Kissinger, the fucker of many WASP women and the husband of one of the tallest; Kissinger, the connoisseur as (good grief!) the selector of metal *Portraits of Greatness* for mass public consumption. The last is a clue to the self-satisfied self-aggrandizement that Gold finally sees as selling-out; in fact, even the even-tempered Belle finds the former secretary's selling of coins contemptible. In Gold's mind Kissinger becomes the dumb *putz*, the *grubba naar*, the *schnorrer*, the odious *shlump*, the portly *trombenik*, the noisy *balaboss*, the bustling *bonditt*, the *klutz*, the *nebbish*, the clever *shaygetz*, the *gonif*, the *shlemiel*, the self-satisfied *behayma*, and, among other similar terms of Yiddish endearment, the *punim*. It is Kissinger who could joke about brutalizing the Vietnamese with massive bombings as a face-saving gesture as we accepted their terms. It is he who could see no moral issues in the invasion of Cambodia. It is he who comes to embody the very nature of the power politics of the modern nation state. "For the very life of him Gold could not recall such rakish and jocular contempt for the victims of massive bombardment as ever coming from a Jew, or from many Christians since Adolf Hitler, Heinrich Himmler, Joseph Goebbels, Herman Goering, Hjalmar Schacht, and Joachim von Ribbentrop" (p. 352). In fact, Gold considers writing a biography of Kissinger, tentatively entitled *The Little Prussian*, instead of the book on the American Jewish experience. In comtemplating the biography he enforces his father's lesson, " 'He [Kissinger] ain't no Jew' " (p. 42).

In order to avoid any possible dismissal of his treatment of Kissinger as the figment of a novelist's imagination, Heller intersperses direct quotes from newspapers in building his case. At the close of his longest Yiddish-filled diatribe against the former Secretary of State, Gold refers to a clipping that describes Kissinger's denial by silence of United States responsibility to a specific ethnic group, the Kurds, who were fighting a war in Iraq that had been fomented and financed by this country. The rebel leader, Mustafa Barzani, had pleaded: " 'Our hearts bleed to see the destruction of our defenseless people in an unprecedented manner. We feel, your Excellency, that the United States has a moral and political responsibility towards our people who have committed themselves to your country's policy. Mr. Secretary, we are anxiously awaiting your quick response' " (pp. 357–358). Gold then states that "The only response to this betrayal of an ethnic group was a profound silence, although his Excellency Kissinger, a fellow of sensitive nature who showed he could *kvetch* and *krechtz* like a *kronkeh bubbeh* when his tender feelings were hurt, defended himself more loquaciously in London later against accusations of something squalid and obscene in the usurious passion with which he appeared to be exploiting his former government position for money" (p. 358). Thus, Gold, who aspires to be Secretary of State and who simultaneously wonders how low he will sink in order to rise to the top, finds in Kissinger the perfect object for the slings and arrows of own self-hatred as Kissinger becomes for Gold the embodiment of an unauthentic existence as an imitation WASP.

It is no accident that Heller has Gold refer specifically to the Kurds as an ethnic group. For almost immediately following this ethnic referencing—interrupted only by the quoting of Lawrence Eagleburger's statement to Kissinger, " 'Henry, you're full of shit,' " and William Watt's " 'Fuck you, Al' " to General Haig—Gold thinks of the ways in which members of another ethnic group, the Jewish kids from Coney Island, would have dealt with members of the Nixon circle:

> Gold was entranced.
> "Fuck you, Al"?
> "Henry, you're full of shit"?
> *Azoy zugt men* to such *machers* as a General and a Secretary?
> The boys from Brooklyn could have handled that. With mother's milk they'd imbibed the good sense to think realistically of such *monzehrem* in government from Tsar Nikolai in St. Petersburg to the *chozzerem* in City Hall and the *scutzem* in the social establishment in Washington, D. C. (p. 359)

Thus, the boys from Coney Island, the place where Gold as a youth thought everybody was Jewish, become a touchstone for his evaluation of his situation and his attempt at self discovery. Just previous to Gold's main diatribe excoriating Kissinger he had discussed his youth in Coney Island with one of the boys, Spotty Weinrock, and had been told: " 'We're all very proud of you every time we read your name in the paper. But we still think you're a *schmuck*' " (p. 315). Thus, with straightforward simplicity, Spotty voices the ambivalence present throughout much of the Jewish community, the ambivalence at the very center of Gold's character. It is after having drinks with Fishy Siegel and Spotty in an Italian Bar, the last refuge for Jews in Coney Island, that Gold arrives at the knowledge that marks an end to the immigrant dream. While walking the ravaged landscape of the city streets, he concludes: "Assimilation was impossible, upward mobility a fantasy" (p. 326). In his own case he has been promised the position of Secretary of State if Andrea marries him. The catch is that Andrea will marry him if he becomes Secretary of State. Her father, Pugh Biddle Conover, the essence of WASPitude and a powerful figure because he has lied under oath for both Republican and Democratic administrations, has informed Gold on his prospects as a potential member of the family: " 'The fact is that I want nothing to do with any Jews but my doctor, lawyer, dentist, accountant, bookkeeper, secretary, broker, butcher, travel agent, tailor, business partner, realtor, banker, financial manager, best friend, and spiritual advisor. One thing I like about all you Jews but Kissinger is that you've kept out of foreign policy because we wouldn't let you in' " (p. 370). Appraising Gold as a potential son-in-law, the ever-honest Conover announces: " 'A middle-age Jew is better than a nigger, I guess, and not much worse than a wop or a mick. Or somebody bald!' " (p. 238). While, to Conover, a Polish son-in-law would be probably the worst of all (p. 240), it is clear that Gold is bad enough. On the possibilities of Gold's attaining a cabinet position, Conover offers another honest evaluation:

> "Frankly, I don't much care about these appointments or even what hap-pens to the country, as long as my capital is safe. I've been able to sell off two of the serious-Vice-Presidential-candidacy-considerations recently, one of them, I believe, to a wide receiver for the Houston Oilers, whatever that is. Would you like to have yourself mentioned six times as a prospect for the Vice Presidential nomination in the next Presidential election cam-paign, Rappaport, as a going-away present, if you'll only go away? As God is my witness, I pray you will not let being a little sheeny inhibit you, you kike. I hear they're giving mentions to coons, Greeks, dagos, spics, and women. Would you like to go in public like a beggar with your hat in your hand merely to appear to be under consideration for the Vice Presidential nomination with a long line of other humble mendicants, or for a Cabinet job you'll be leaving in disgrace or disgust in two years?" (p. 374)

In fact, the preserved-in-alcohol Conover gives Gold the final advice that propels the vacillating hero once again back to Brooklyn: " 'If I were you, Goldilocks, instead of trying to ape me I would make it a point always to present myself as Jewish since you'll never get by as anything else' " (p. 367). As Spotty had said, "we're all very proud of you . . . but we still think you're a *schmuck*."

With the possible exception of his father, Julius, no one in Bruce Gold's family would call him a *schmuck;* nevertheless, as a group they do share some of Spotty's ambivalence. Heller structures the family in order to com-municate the impact of the American experience on several generations. There is a definite demarcation in collective character between the children closest to the actual immigrant experience: Sid, Esther, and Rose, and those born later: Ida, Muriel, Bruce, and Joannie. Heller does not present the older women in any great detail except to let the reader know that they have defined themselves in terms of traditional marriages, suffered the stings of anti-Semitism, still pride themselves on their cooking, and still find comfort in the presence of the whole family. In the midst of encroaching old age, Esther, who lost her first husband, Mendy, to cancer, has a suitor, Milt; Rose, worried about two children who never appear but who are referred to in terms that define them as drug-addicted, aimless American casualties, fears losing the job she has held for forty years and clings to her husband, Max, whose claim to fame is that he was one of the first Jews in the Post Office. Both women know that they should be proud of Bruce even though they do not quite understand what he does. Esther knows just enough to ask her younger brother: " 'If you go to Washington, you wouldn't ever do anything to make us ashamed, would you?' " (p. 115). Ida, despite the physical threats she now faces as a teacher, still has the air of a first generation American woman grateful that she was allowed to be trained in any profession. While there is nothing but affection between the two older women, there is a competitive edge between Ida and Muriel, particularly in terms of which one has prospered more economically. Muriel, the youngest of the sisters to participate in family gatherings, is the one least in touch with traditional values: amidst hints that she engages in the game of suburban adultery, she emerges as a bad example for her children, and, even worse, within the frame of one of Heller's ethnic references, she does not cook traditional meals well. The youngest, Joannie, who has left the East for L. A. and married a man who changed his name from Finkleman to Fink, describes her life to Gold: " 'We spend a lot of time in California trying to get each other to forget we're Jewish' " (p. 83). Facing the possibility of divorce, she says: " 'You can add that to my Jewish experience. I just know I'll wind up living with some kid with a motorcycle who plays the banjo and wants to be an actor. Oh, Christ, I'll be smoking dope with nitwits again, won't I?' " (p. 288). In the midst of the same conversation, Bruce and Joannie, the two youngest children, marvel at the heroic quality of the immigrant experience. Gold, in amazement, says: " '—leaving with children from a small town in Russia more than sixty years ago and coming all the way here. How did they do it? They knew they would never go back. I can't go anywhere without hotel reservations and I can't go out of town two days without losing some laundry or having a plane connection canceled. . . . How did they know where to go? Where did they sleep? The trip must have taken longer than Columbus. What did they think and talk about, what did they eat? They were just kids. They had Sid, remember, and Rose was just a baby' " (p. 287).

It is clear that Heller uses the women in the family to trace the processes of Americanization and that he intends such Americanization as a reflection of one of the section titles in *Good as Gold*: "Every Change Is for the Worse." From the courage of uneducated people embarking on a dangerous journey to an unknown land, then descending to Joannie's situation and the condition of Rose's children, Heller traces moral decline as each generation loses contact with the source of their ethnic identity.

Yet, despite the fact that Gold marvels at the heroism of the migration and at the courage it took to face life in an unknown land, throughout the novel his attitudes toward his family are, naturally, ambivalent. His "distaste for family dinners" and his "aversion . . . toward all forms of domestic sentiment" date from the time he entered Columbia. He cannot stand the thought of attending Belle's surprise party for Rose, yet fills up with tears when he sees his sister's happiness; in fact, it is relatively early that he tells Ralph that he can't fly immediately to Washington because his "big sister" is having a birthday, and at the very moment he thinks of Julius as "his fucking crackpot of a father," his throat knots with a lump of nostalgic grief. In Washington, in the crucial scene in bed with Andrea, apparently on the verge of the public success that would somehow transform him, Gold worries about the possibility that Sid has rejected him and then dreams the nightmare that he is no longer a Jew.

In one of the most effective and realistically depicted exchanges in the novel, Sid, in conversation with Bruce over lunch, relates his own Jewish experience in America. It is an account of loneliness and alienation. It is an account of prejudice, and, in the face of prejudice, some financial success. He reveals to Bruce the facts of their mother's death, the responsibilities foisted upon him because of the father's lack of success in the American business world, and, no matter what, the necessity of maintaining the close human connections that family provides, particularly in the face of death. Again, the lessons are hard for Gold, for if Washington seems to offer a glimpse of the orgiastic future, his family connections root him in the past, burden him with responsibilities, and provide proof of his own mortality. What Gold seems most reluctant to finally face is that the Sid who arranged family finances in order for the father to live in some dignity, the Sid who cares about the sisters and, generally, about his family, the Sid who distrusts abstractions and who plays with rationalizations: this Sid is a far better role model than Kissinger, the ersatz Jew in the game of power politics, rationalizing the interests of the Conover class. There can be little doubt that the older brother's talk about vultures, particularly in conversational contexts in which discussion of Bruce's going to Washington is prevalent, relates directly to the members of the ruling class and their power brokers in government. In his subtle, indirect way, Sid echoes Fishy Siegel's reference to politicians: " 'They know they're crooked?' " (p. 318).

Within the frame of Heller's juxtapositioning of contrasting events, it is important that Sid's death coincides with the hero's possible meeting with the President at the Embassy Ball, for Sid's death calls his younger brother back from the pursuit of public success to the facts of his family, even as Gold cries, with tears in his eyes, " 'He does this to me every time. He'll ruin my whole day, my whole weekend' " (p. 433). It also calls him back to the authenticity of his own experience and to the necessity of taking on the responsibilities that grow out of his past. Throughout the novel Heller introduces intimations of death and usually presents his hero as recoiling from any mention of it. Comically, Julius and his second wife, Gussie Gold, revel in their longevity as they poke fun at the now dead movie stars given life on late shows and other television movies. But Gussie, the stepmother, is often serious on the subject, mentioning the inevitability of death a number of times, usually to her husband's horror. In the face of death, he, Julius the non-believer, is using every possible Jewish holiday imaginable to stay with his family and informs them that when he dies he wants them to put him in the kitchen under the table (p. 277): " 'In my day, we didn't push people away from their children and their grandchildren when they began to be old. They died near their homes and their families. Like your mother did. And your mother's mother, she died in my house, and my own mother, in my brother Meyer's house she died when we brought her here. Today you wouldn't even bring me here, would you?' " (p. 276). It is significant that Gold — who worries that as he grows older he looks increasingly like his older sisters and who shudders as he sees his beautiful younger sister, Joannie, showing signs of age — is the only member of the family in the East who has not made plans for his own death; he is the only one without a burial plot. When Gussie attacks him for being unauthentic, not even Jewish, she tells him he wastes his time whenever he visits his mother's grave. The fact is that Gold never visits. This stepmother, whom Gold dismisses as crazy, chastises him in ways that question his very identity: " 'You admire money and you idolize the people who have it. You crave success. Wouldn't it be funny,' she went on, and cackled at him with a gleam of satanic wickedness in her eye, 'if he isn't even your real father and you've been taking all this criticism from him for nothing all these years? Wouldn't it be funny if you aren't even Jewish? You don't even know the language and the holidays, do you?' " (p. 302). Thus Gussie Gold, who once turned down Pugh Biddle Conover and who keeps knitting a seemingly unending and purposeless piece of goods that connects past and present, instructs Gold: Consider death.

With Sid gone, he must. His first act is to organize the *shivah;* his second is to arrange to begin meeting his classes again; his third is to begin thinking about actually writing the book on the Jewish experience in America, the book that Heller is just completing. Lieberman, theoretically the intellectual editor of a serious journal, had told him to put in lots of sex to make it sell; Pomoroy, an editor for a slightly disreputable publishing house, and a figure who emerges early in the book as a potential moral guide — suffering both from love of family and growing success — had urged him to do something serious. *Good as Gold* is that serious book — yes, yes, filled with wacky humor and even funnier sex, the stuff that Heller knew would make it sell in order to reach a wide audience with its moral dilemmas and lessons.

Heller's achievement in this novel is monumental not only because he captures some of the levels and intensities of ambivalence that characterize the members of minority groups in their relationships to the ruling class. In addition, through his treatment of at least three generations of Jews in America, he seems to have consciously evoked aspects of the fiction written by American Jews throughout their presence in this culture. Certainly, *Good as Gold* includes the kind of specifically Jewish alienation and loneliness present in Abraham Cahan's *The Rise of David Levinsky* (1917), particularly in terms of the difficulties encountered in actually achieving success. The novel contains elements of mixed feelings toward family present in Anzia Yezierska's *Children of Loneliness: Stories of Immigrant*

Life in America (1923). When Gold rejects the possible union with Andrea, he follows a path already established by Arthur Levy in Ludwig Lewisohn's *The Island Within* (1928), and when he juggles a wife (Belle), a mistress (Andrea) and a "whore" (Linda Book), he resembles the hero of Ben Hecht's *A Jew in Love* (1931). Esther and Rose's story of job hunting and persecution conjure up any number of Jewish proletarian novels of the Thirties, and Sid's account of economic privation and sexual degradation call to mind works of fiction as different as Michael Gold's *Jews Without Money* (1930) and Henry Roth's *Call It Sleep* (1934). In the caricatured figures like Conover, *Good as Gold* evokes characters from the work of Nathan Wallenstein Weinstein (Nathanael West); in fact, some of the desperate humor may owe a great deal to West's work, particularly in this case of the *Dream Life of Balso Snell* (1931). There are characters that seem straight out of some of the assimilationist novels of the fifties — for instance, one can imagine Herman Wouk's Greenwald and Heller's Harris Rosenblatt frequenting the same club. More recently, Philip Roth's Portnoy, performing sexual acrobatics with his WASP Monkey, in *Portnoy's Complaint* (1969), may represent the prototype of Andrea's expectations for Gold. The theme of Bernard Malamud's *The Assistant* is morality rooted in ethnicity, and Malamud's Sy Levin, in *A New Life* (1961), is a somewhat more naive Jewish-English-teacher-aspirant although Levin finds "success" by "saving" a WASP woman and her children. Saul Bellow's Elya Gruner, in *Mr. Sammler's Planet* (1970), is a character, like Sid, who knows the terms of his contract, and, like Sid, he serves as an instructor to the more intellectual protagonist. In any case, it seems clear that Heller is aware of working within an American Jewish tradition in fiction, and he is as much aware of that tradition as writers as different from him as Jay Neugeboren and Isaac Bashevis Singer.

Like some of Malamud's and Bellow's characters, Heller's hero in *Good as Gold* finds refuge in ethnicity, specifically the composite of inherited Jewish practices which no longer have real religious meaning for him but do serve as sources of moral strength and continuity. For those who have viewed Heller as an absurdist writing existential comedy, his latest novel may seem a departure from, or even a partial denial of, his earlier work. Actually, there is a fairly straight path from Milo Minderbinder's "What's Good for M&M Enterprises Is Good For the Country" in *Catch-22* to Lyndon B. Johnson's "I've Got His Pecker in My Pocket" in *Good as Gold*. In both novels Heller analyzes the effects of the operation of power morality, one during wartime in Italy, one during peacetime in Washington. In both novels Heller presents most thought as mere rationalizations of power positions. Yossarian, an Assyrian whose own ethnic group once experienced a holocaust, almost makes the deal with Cathcart and Korn just as Gold almost makes the deal with Newsome. In fact, there are many moments when Gold echoes Yossarian's desire to simply be left to make love to beautiful women, enjoy the good life, and not be responsible for any of his actions — seemingly, the results of striking a bargain with those who control the system. In *Catch-22* Yossarian is directly prevented from making the deal by the intervention of Nately's Whore and indirectly by the knowledge provided by Snowden's death. Gold is directly prevented by the fact of Sid's death and indirectly by his growing responsibility to family. Yossarian may want to save Nately's Whore's kid sister; Gold has his own daughter to worry about. In addition, Gold is an older hero than Yossarian. And, importantly, he is an intellectual. It is his observation, not that of a third person narrator, that "history was a trash bag of random coincidences torn open in a wind" (p. 74). It is his contention that "the American economic system was barbarous, resulting, naturally, in barbarism and entrenched imbecility on all levels of the culture" (p. 73). It is his conclusion that the major ideological alternative available in the modern world, Communism, "was a drab, gray, wintry prison at the end of a cul-de-sac from which no turning back was imaginable" (p. 74). The youthful Yossarian takes off for Sweden; the more mature Gold returns home. In *Good as Gold* the rituals out of the past, however irrational they may seem, provide an organic form created by members of a culture through centuries of time. In existentialist terms, the novel presents the possibilities of the achievement of authenticity through a commitment to one's personal, familial, and cultural past. In short, Heller suggests that the ethnic dimension can provide an alternative to simply functioning as a cog in a corporate or bureaucratic machine — living a life such as Slocum's. The odds of escaping the power of corporate, national or even global homogenization may be as slim as Yossarian's reaching Sweden, but Heller, in *Good as Gold*, seems convinced that it may be the good flight. In any case, he seems clear in his conviction that Gussie Gold's *"Cackle, Cackle"* is as viable as any of Newsome's rationalizations and double talk.

Notes

1. Joseph Heller, *Good as Gold* (New York: Simon and Schuster, 1979), p. 383. (Further references to *Good as Gold* will be made parenthetically within the text.)

2. Joseph Heller, *Something Happened* (New York: Knopf, 1974), p. 407.

3. Quite an improbable character, equipped with all the apparently preternatural qualities that technology can provide, Greenspan, the Jewish FBI Agent, resembles characters like Good Angel (*The Castle of Perseverance*) or Good Deeds (*Everyman*) in his urging Gold toward goodness, frequently with the exclamation, "You're a *shonda* to your race." Also, the character of Newsome suggests Bad Angel (*The Castle of Perseverance*) or Mischief (*Mankind*).

Something Jewish Happened: Some Thoughts About Joseph Heller's *Good as Gold*

Melvin J. Friedman*

> As a Jew, I am a descendant of the tribes accurately called People of the Book. Our very metaphors for reality are taken from the usages of the written word. (From Morris Philipson's acceptance speech of the PEN Publisher Citation.)

It is well known that Joseph Heller's original title for *Catch-22* was "Catch-18."[1] In a sense he has written his Catch-18 in his latest novel, *Good as Gold*. Eighteen is something of a mystical number for Jews. *Chai*, which means living, is the eighteenth letter of the Hebrew alphabet, and Jews have traditionally made charitable contributions in denominations of eighteen. The *Mishnah* speaks of eighteen as being the ideal age for Jewish men to marry. And it is probably no accident that James Joyce, who was well-acquainted with Jewish practice and belief, divided his *Ulysses*, that life-affirming, Jewish book, into eighteen chapters.

Good as Gold marks Heller's first elaborate flirtation with the American Jewish fictional scene, dominated for so long by the triumvirate of Saul Bellow, Bernard Malamud, and Philip Roth. Two of the three, in fact, published novels in 1979, the year *Good as Gold* appeared.[2] Malamud's *Dubin's Lives* and Roth's *The Ghost Writer* have shifted the Jewish scene to rural New England while Heller's most recent novel offers the more familiar urban contours and rhythms of New York and Washington, D.C. While Malamud's William Dubin and Roth's Nathan Zuckerman negotiate Wordsworthian terrains, Heller's Bruce Gold confronts the usual Jewish family and guilt problems. Indeed, on the surface, *Good as Gold* seems to mark a return to an innocently ethnic time in the 1960s when novels like Bruce Jay Friedman's *Stern*, Philip Roth's *Letting Go*, and Wallace Markfield's *To an Early Grave* were the expected fare. A number of reviewers responded to this possibility, such as Gene Lyons, who suggested rather flippantly that "Heller should give Woody Allen a cut of the take, who should pass most of it on to Philip Roth. With a couple of minor changes of particulars, many of the book's passages could be inserted into *Letting Go*, *Portnoy's Complaint*, *My Life as a Man* or *The Professor of Desire*. . . . Heller's latest is too much of the time like the transcript of a twelve-hour Henny Youngman routine, so that even his truly effective lines are smothered under one's sense of *déjà vu*."[3] Charles Berryman, writing two years after the publication of *Good as Gold*, takes a quite different position on its Jewishness:

*This essay was written especially for this volume and is published here by permission of the author.

Heller recognizes the competition, and succeeds by turning the conventional genre into a comic parody. If the typical Jewish protagonist often feels threatened by the anxious counsel of his immediate family, the hero of Heller's novel is inundated by the contradictory advice of no less than fifteen close relatives. If the family meal is supposed to be a ritual of the Passover feast, the dinners of the Gold family rival the banquets in the *Satyricon* for headache and heartburn. If the heroes of Roth and Bellow often seem to live in a world invented by Kafka, the protagonist of *Good as Gold* is haunted by shadows of persecution that even appear as messages in his Chinese fortune cookies. . . . Much of Heller's comedy depends upon outrageous multiplication.[4]

Berryman has the advantage of distance from Heller's novel—a luxury denied reviewers who must meet pressing deadlines—which helps make his stance more plausible than that of Lyons or that of other early commentators who typically complained that it is "a rather listless and dispirited piece of work"[5] and that it "achieves only tastelessness."[6]

Good as Gold, in support of Berryman's position and that of a number of reviewers who found it to be vintage Heller,[7] holds up remarkably well under rereading and close scrutiny. Parody and satire are clearly the controlling ingredients. The building blocks are sturdily fashioned on incongruities of language and situation. Put simply, *Good as Gold*, published twenty years after Philip Roth's first book, *Goodbye, Columbus* (1959), casts a knowing and exaggerated glance at a vast body of Jewish American fiction; it successfully caricatures many of the recipes offered by Jewish writers of the past two decades. *Good as Gold*, one might say, stands to this post-*Goodbye, Columbus* literature much as *Don Quixote* did to the tales of chivalry, "The Rape of the Lock" to the Homeric and Virgilian epic, and *Gulliver's Travels* to the preposterous travelogues of discovery.

Among the first things to be noted about this art of exaggeration and "outrageous multiplication" is the lexical performance of Bruce Gold, the main character of Heller's novel. The phrasemaking urgencies, with their clichéd rhythms, of this Jewish La Rochefoucauld makes the White House interested in his talents. Gold is prepared to leave his professorship of English and even his marriage for the right kind of appointment in Washington. His liaison with the president (whom he never meets) is a former graduate school friend, Ralph Newsome, who speaks in contradictory sequences and at one point legitimizes this verbal habit: " 'Maybe I do seem a bit oxymoronic at times. I think everyone here talks that way. Maybe we're all oxymoronic.' "[8] *Good as Gold* is a novel in which language is all-important. Words explode ridiculously on the page. Large doses of incoherent dialogue fill virtually every chapter.

Gold negotiates three geographies: the university, the family, political Washington, D.C.[9] They are all verbal constructs, with their own special grammars. The university, perhaps the least visible presence in the novel, is the springboard for his various activities. As a graduate student in English at Columbia, he was involved with the non-Jewish Ralph Newsome as well as three Jews, Lieberman, Pomoroy, and Rosenblatt, who move in and out of Gold's narrative. (The Jewish foursome of Gold, Lieberman, Pomoroy, and Rosenblatt may recall the four Jewish Volkswagen riders, who also had Columbia connections, in Wallace Markfield's *To an Early Grave*.) All predictably deal in words: Newsome collects them for the president of the country; Lieberman edits a magazine; Pomoroy serves as "executive editor in a thriving, faintly disreputable, commercial book-publishing house" (p. 15); Rosenblatt repudiates the Jewishness of his childhood, especially its Yiddish vocabulary; Gold supplies Newsome with *bons mots* for White House consumption, publishes articles in Lieberman's periodical, and owes Pomoroy a book on the Jewish experience in America — all while continuing his professorial career.

It is this life as a university don which is the silent partner in Gold's transactions. He devotes little time to his classroom obligations, waits in the wings "for an endowed chair in the Urban Studies Program that would double his salary while halving his course load" (p. 137), and always has his bags packed in readiness for the call to Washington, D.C. His verbal dexterity is of little value to his students, whom he barely tolerates; a Jewish member of one of his classes, who expresses disappointment at the direction things are taking, produces the twisted reaction: "Gold was praying hard that Epstein would drop his course before he had to read his essay" (p. 137). Gold, who has an enviable way with words, uses them to curious and circuitous ends within the academy — as weapons of deception rather than enlightenment. "Gold was the architect of an illicit and secret policy of détente that permitted members of the German Department to give courses in remedial English to Hispanic and Oriental students in exchange for votes on critical issues at faculty council meetings" (p. 137).[10]

Jews have traditionally been known as the People of the Book and teaching has always been regarded among them as an honored profession. Anti-Semitism, alas, long kept them from university posts, especially in the Humanities. The poet Theodore Weiss once commented in conversation that during his tenure at Yale (1944–46) he was one of only two Jewish faculty members there teaching humanistic disciplines. Diana Trilling speaks quite openly of anti-Semitism in the English department at Columbia in the 1930s in her "Lionel Trilling: A Jew at Columbia."[11] The situation fortunately turned around dramatically in the decades following the Second World War. Theodore Weiss now teaches at Princeton and the Yale and Columbia literature departments are graced with scholars of the eminence of Geoffrey Hartman, Harold Bloom, Steven Marcus, and Michael Riffaterre.

Jewish writers responded to this change by invading a territory which had long been jealously guarded by novelists with names like Theodore Morrison, May Sarton, Robie Macauley, Stringfellow Barr, and Randall Jarrell — the academic or campus novel. Philip Roth has contributed a number of Jewish professors to the gathering, including Gabe Wallach and Paul

Herz (*Letting Go*) and David Kepesh (*The Breast* and *The Professor of Desire*), but has not yet written a pure example of the academic novel. This was left to Bernard Malamud who wrote a worthy successor to *The Groves of Academe, Pictures from an Institution, The Stones of the House,* and *The Disguises of Love* in his *A New Life*. Malamud took his alliterative, Anglo-Saxoned epigraph from Joyce's *Ulysses*, "Lo, levin leaping lightens in eyeblink Ireland's westward welkin!," and indeed the last name of his protagonist, S. Levin, is buried in this quotation. Bellow also went to *Ulysses* for the naming of his professor ("he had a farm in the county Down off a hop of my thumb by the name of Moses Herzog over there near Heytesbury street"), although his *Herzog* is more the unraveling of a tormented professorial mind than it is a campus novel.[12]

But it is clear from these examples and others that when Jews were finally admitted freely to university posts fictional chroniclers of their vagaries also entered these restricted playgrounds. Bruce Gold belongs to the second generation of these literary offspring; he does not understand the uncertainties of his "fathers." Unlike Paul Herz, S. Levin, and Moses Herzog, Gold feels quite secure in the academy. His aggressive presence in Heller's novel seems a mockery of the anxieties experienced by fictional and nonfictional Jews who tried to make their way on the faculties of universities. Heller devotes relatively few pages to Gold's academic chores because of their insignificance in his *Weltanschauung*.

Many more pages are given over to the family culinary gatherings, which offer the second of the geographies. Charles Berryman rightly conjures up the banquets in the *Satyricon* to express their immensity and overpowering qualities. The Rabelaisian catalogues of dishes prepared by Gold's sisters and sister-in-law are breathtaking. Each performed an exacting task and insisted on the integrity of her assignment:

> Harriet excelled at baking and was forever miffed upon arriving with two or three of her cheesecakes, moist chocolate cakes, or coffeecakes to find a deep-dish fruit pie, cookies, and a high whipped cream or chocolate layer cake already purchased or, at Muriel's or Ida's, two specially ordered gâteaux St. Honoré, alongside which all other efforts necessarily paled. Esther specialized in stuffed derma and noodle puddings; living alone now, she was expanding into potato and cheese blintzes and experimenting with dishes other than derma, unaware that with chopped liver and stuffed cabbage she was encroaching upon Ida's traditional territories and that with chopped herring she was transgressing against Rose, who was unmatched in the family with all edible things from the sea, as well as with soups, matzoh balls, and other varieties of dumplings. Rose suffered the unintended affront in silence, Ida chafed vocally, Esther shuddered in repentance (pp. 98–99).

This all sounds like a leaf torn out of Stephen and Ethel Longstreet's *The Joys of Jewish Cooking*. It is not quite what proponents of *cuisine minceur* have in mind. The detail is splendid, the satirical edge sharp. Family gatherings have become a staple of American Jewish fiction of the past quarter century, but nowhere are they more realized than in *Good as Gold*. The finest comic moments are dinner parties that honor such Hellerian events as the "sixth-and-a-half wedding anniversary" of Gold's father and step-mother. This particular gathering begins with Gold's stepmother asking her husband the seemingly innocuous question, " 'where would you like me to put you?' " (p. 272). This sets off the anger of Gold *père*, who at the age of eighty-two is uncomfortable with any talk of burial. A crescendo of family voices respond. Gold listens with his usual incredulity. The thought crosses his mind that "in other families relatives quarreled over cash and bibelots; here they bickered over burial plots" (p. 275). He copes with this no better than with the oxymoronic sequences of Ralph Newsome. Gold has a sense, along with the Roman poet Horace, of *concordia discors rerum*.

Gold is emphatically "caught" in his Judaism during these baroque gatherings. They offer painful reminders of his Jewishness, what Wayne C. Miller in a valuable article calls his "ethnic identity." Miller goes on to say: "Like some of Malamud's and Bellow's characters, Heller's hero in *Good as Gold* finds refuge in ethnicity, specifically the composite of inherited Jewish practices which no longer have real religious meaning for him but do serve as sources of moral strength and continuity."[13] Gold finally falls back on these resources of Judaism when he makes his decision to leave the Embassy Ball and return to New York for his brother Sid's funeral. While he maintained an embarrassed and uncomfortable presence at earlier gatherings, he plays an assertive part here at this last family function in the novel. The roles to be filled fell increasingly upon Gold . . ." (p. 434). He organizes the ritual of "sitting *shivah*" at Esther's house and arranges the formation of a ritual of "sitting *shivah*" at Esther's house and arranges the formation of a *minyan*. He visits his mother's grave and on the way home "he came upon a softball game in a schoolyard played by boys wearing *yarmulkas*, and he left the car to watch. Athletes in skullcaps? The school was a religious one, a *yeshiva*. Some of the teen-agers had sidelocks, and some of the sidelocks were blond. Gold smiled" (p. 447). Jack Beatty, in his *New Republic* review, rightly views this as a "symbolic sight." This final scene of *Good as Gold* clearly echoes the baseball game at the beginning of Chaim Potok's *The Chosen*.

Indeed, by the end of the novel, Gold has been wondrously transformed. If there is such a thing as a Jewish epiphany he has experienced it. Tommy Wilhelm's final moments in the chapel, mourning a deceased person he has never met, at the end of Bellow's *Seize the Day*, offer some of the same vibrations. These last few pages of *Good as Gold* may act as a kind of echo chamber as familiar sounds are heard from two decades of Jewish American writing. But Gene Lyons' assessment of everything being "smothered under one's sense of *déjà vu*" (p. 727) is not quite fair to Heller's considerable accomplishment in awakening Bruce Gold to his Jewish heritage. The vitriol seems to have deserted Heller's pen and turned into redemptive, affirmative soundings. The sense appears to be that those boisterous, gas-tronomic family gatherings, which appeared at the time to unsettle and even outrage Bruce Gold, were responsible for his renewal.

It is interesting to note that while words were essential to his success as a university professor—in the classroom, in his published books and ar-ticles, in his zany, alliterative contributions to the college catalog ("Through Hell and High Water with Hemingway, Hesse, Hume, Hobbes, Hinduism and Others: A Shortcut to India" [pp. 137–38])—they seemed to fail him in family situations. Gold was tongue-tied in the face of the irratio-nal onslaughts by his father, stepmother, brother, and sisters. The violence they did to logic, language, and the bases of scientific fact invariably left him without suitable response. He seems to gain a respect for silence which serves him handsomely in the final pages of the novel. The role of observer or listener replaces that of wordsmith.

This wordsmith aspect of Bruce Gold is what tempted him for so long to confront that third geography, the political life of Washington, D.C. Gold's contributions here were to be largely verbal. Heller situates the most surreal moments, the most preposterous encounters, in these Washington sections of *Good as Gold*. Jewish American writers of Heller's generation have usually avoided political satire. Philip Roth tried it out in *Our Gang*, which revealed the chicanery of the Nixon administration several years be-fore Watergate was uncovered. One reviewer of Heller's novel even saw a connection: "As it winds on and on, *Good as Gold* views the leaders of this land with the sort of perversity and disdain expressed by Philip Roth in *Our Gang*."[14] Heller, unlike Roth, meshed the Jewish with the political.[15] He concentrates much of his attention on the anti-Semitism of establishment government circles. Gold encounters it at every turn, in a subtle way from his former classmate Ralph Newsome, in a more blatant form from several mainstays of the Washington scene, one of whom calls him by every con-ceivable Jewish name but his own. Gold draws attention to his own Jewish-ness through his aggressive hatred of another Jew, Henry Kissinger. He is a collector of Kissingeriana and plans a book on his *bête noire*. This book and the other one on the Jewish experience somehow become intertwined. It is only at the end of the novel, when Gold renounces his political aspirations, that he gives up on the former secretary of state: "With Kissinger gone, he was stuck only with the book on the Jewish experience in America he owed Pomoroy and Lieberman" (p. 443).

Kissinger acts as a kind of Jamesian *ficelle*, which helps tidy up the arrangement of parts. As a former college professor, as a Jew, and as a part of the Nixon cabinet, he brings together the various strands of the novel. As a number of commentators have accurately remarked, Kissinger is both the object of Gold's hatred and a mirror image of him. The more strenuously Gold verbally assaults him the more he comes to resemble him. It is only when he gives up on his Kissinger project in favor of his Jewish book that he rids himself of his *dybbuk*.

Kissinger as *dybbuk*[16] inspires on Heller's part a dozen pages about "the little Prussian" (the title of Gold's proposed book on him), liberally sprinkled with Yiddish invective. One strong Yiddish word which does not appear in this section is *shonda*. This word, which means scandal or disgrace, is part of almost every comment of an unlikely Jewish FBI agent, Greenspan. Stephen W. Potts accurately characterizes him "as Gold's Jewish conscience in the latter parts of the book."[17] Greenspan is something of an anti-Kissinger who helps Gold exorcise his demon and return to the fold. Indeed he is present at the end when Gold is able playfully to hurl his favorite word back at him: " 'Shame, shame, Greenspan. You're a *shonda*' " (p. 444).

Outrageous word plays of every variety and the indulgences of Yiddish are strong components of the Washington, D.C. parts of *Good as Gold*.[18] Heller has clearly caught the rhythms of the verbal dishonesty of the nation's capital. He could not have known of course that Ronald Reagan, in an inspired gesture, would one day name as his deputy press secretary someone with the name Larry Speakes; and he could not have known either that Speakes suitably would play the role of White House spokesman and remark revealingly to the press: "You don't tell us how to stage the news and we don't tell you how to cover it" and "He [Reagan] didn't mean what you thought he said."[19] Nature has once again imitated the work of art as it seemed to do following the publication of Roth's *Our Gang*.

Political chicanery is revealed in *Good as Gold* through language, especially through its abuse. Promises are made and withdrawn in a single verbal gesture. Jews are especially susceptible to the ambiguities of the word, from Henry Kissinger to Bruce Gold. Gold's friend Harris Rosenblatt, who has too easily adjusted to the vagaries of the Washington scene after his failures at Columbia Graduate School, can make the slight concession " 'I used to be Jewish, you know' " after insisting " 'I don't understand Yiddish' " (p. 380). He has given up his heritage and the diaspora language of his people for admission to the Harvard Club. When Gold asks " ' How can you be a member of the Harvard Club . . . when you went to Columbia with me?' " Rosenblatt uses the twisted reasoning he has mastered: " 'I'm a millionaire, Bruce . . . and every millionaire is a Harvard man. Although not every Harvard man, of course, is a millionaire. There's really only one outstanding university in the country, Bruce, and I'll never regret that I went to the Harvard Club for lunch today' " (p. 442).

This language of chicanery seems finally to wear down Gold. This as much as anything else may account for his return to his brother's funeral and his subsequent embracing of the resources of his religion. If "Catch-18" is indeed a plausible subtitle for *Good as Gold* it is because Bruce Gold who was once "caught" in his Judaism finally begins to "live" it. He has played out his Jewish role of stand-up comic[20] (his first name may well offer an allusion to Lenny Bruce) in favor of more abiding concerns and values. Heller has managed to bring Gold to this point by multiplying incongruities of language and situation and by echoing and even outdistancing in his techniques contemporaries who have been writing Jewish fiction since the 1950s. *Good as Gold* performs duty on many fronts; a great deal Jewish happens.

Notes

1. Indeed he also published a short story, "Catch-18," in *New World Writing* in 1955. Two short manuscript sketches, quoted and discussed by James Nagel in his "Two Brief Manuscript Sketches: Heller's *Catch-22*," *Modern Fiction Studies*, 20 (1974), 221–24, reveal Heller's preoccupation with the Jew during the early work-in-progress period of *Catch-22*. See also Daniel Walden's " 'Therefore Choose Life': A Jewish Interpretation of Heller's *Catch-22*," in *Critical Essays on Catch-22*, ed. James Nagel (Belmont: Dickenson Publishing Company, 1974), pp. 57–63.

2. See my "The American Jewish Literary Scene, 1979: A Review Essay," *Studies in American Fiction*, 8 (1980), 239–46. Pearl K. Bell reviews the Heller and Malamud novels together in her excellent "Heller & Malamud, Then & Now," *Commentary*, June 1979, pp. 71–75.

3. Gene Lyons, "Contradictory Judaism," *Nation*, June 16, 1979, p. 727; hereafter cited parenthetically in the text.

4. Charles Berryman, "Heller's Gold," *Chicago Review*, 32 (Spring 1981), 110–11; hereafter cited parenthetically in the text.

5. Benjamin DeMott's words in his "Heller's Gold and a Silver Sax," *Atlantic Monthly*, March 1979, p. 131.

6. Words from the unsigned "Briefly Noted" dismissal in the *New Yorker*, April 16, 1979, p. 158.

7. See, for example, John W. Aldridge's "The Deceits of Black Humor," *Harper's*, March 1979, pp. 115–18; Jack Beatty's "*Good as Gold* by Joseph Heller," *New Republic*, March 10, 1979, pp. 42–44; and Leonard Michaels' "Bruce Gold's American Experience," *New York Times Book Review*, March 11, 1979, pp. 1, 24–25.

8. Joseph Heller, *Good as Gold* (New York: Simon and Schuster, 1979), p. 122; hereafter cited parenthetically in the text.

9. Other critics also view *Good as Gold* in a triadic way. Charles Berryman, for example, sees it as "a mixture of three different kinds of fiction: a Jewish family novel, a political satire, and the story of superman [Henry Kissinger] demythologized" (p. 110). Thomas R. Edwards insists "Heller seems to have put together themes for three different books. . . ." See "On the Gold Standard," *New York Review of Books*, April 5, 1979, p. 10.

10. For an excellent discussion of these matters, see James Nagel, "Joseph Heller and the University," *College Literature*, 10 (1983), 16–27. See also the suggestive and wide-ranging essay by Frances K. Barasch, "Faculty Images in Recent American Fiction," which follows the Nagel piece in *College Literature* (pp. 28–37). Barasch's essay offers some useful perceptions of *Good as Gold* and touches on matters I discuss below.

11. *Commentary* (March 1979), pp. 40–46.

12. From the time of Henry Roth's *Call It Sleep* (1934), *Ulysses* has been a central and charismatic work for Jewish American writers. Joyce's depiction of the inner life of a Jewish sensibility, Leopold Bloom, directly influenced such inward turning novels as *Herzog*; a novel like Markfield's *To an Early Grave* seems to be a modest revival of Bloomsday, with the setting moved from Dublin to Brooklyn and with the "Hades" chapter of *Ulysses* acting as central text. *A New Life* depends less on *Ulysses* than these other books, but the fact that Malamud has chosen to go to it for his epigraph and for the last name of his hero is obviously noteworthy.

When Joyce uses the word "levin" in the passage Malamud quotes from the "Oxen of the Sun" chapter, he may have been offering an archaism which means "lightning" or else he may have been playing on the Hebrew world *lev* which means "heart."

13. Wayne C. Miller, "Ethnic Identity as Moral Focus: A Reading of Joseph Heller's *Good as Gold*," *MELUS*, 6 (Fall 1979), 16.

14. Lee Eisenberg, "Jewish Questions," *Esquire*, February 27, 1979, p. 18.

15. It should probably be mentioned, though, that two Jewish figures make an appearance in Roth's book: "The two men who resigned from the Supreme Court were Mr. Abe Fortas and Mr. Arthur Goldberg" (*Our Gang* [New York: Random House, 1971], p. 99). However, Jewish matters are not especially crucial to the novel.

16. One of Leo Rosten's definitions of *dybbuk* in his *The Joys of Yiddish* (New York: Pocket Books, 1977) fits the present situation: "A demon who takes possession of someone and renders the mortal mad, irrational, vicious, sinful, corrupt" (p. 104).

17. Stephen W. Potts, *From Here to Absurdity: The Moral Battlefields of Joseph Heller* (San Bernardino: Borgo Press, 1982), p. 57.

18. A number of reviewers of the novel have apparently succumbed to the word games. Note the following, for example: Thomas R. Edwards' "On the Gold Standard" (*New York Review of Books*, April 5, 1979); Raymond A. Schroth's "I wonder who's Kissinger now?" (*Commonweal*, May 11, 1979); Morris Dickstein's "Something Didn't Happen" (*Saturday Review*, March 31, 1979). I admit to a slight case of the illness myself; the title of the present essay, much like Dickstein's, plays on the title of Heller's second novel.

19. "Speakes Speaks," *Milwaukee Journal*, March 16, 1983, Part 1, p. 14.

20. An example of a stand-up comic routine in *Good as Gold* is the following: "Shunning the literary magazine in high school because of Lieberman, Gold mailed ten of his short poems to the *Saturday Review of Literature*. Six came back with rejection slips and four were accepted, at a price of ten dollars each. Lieberman turned blue. He swore he would never forgive Gold for acting alone instead of sharing his initiative. To teach Gold his place, Lieberman mailed twenty-five of *his* poems to the *Saturday Review of Literature*. Thirty-nine came back" (p. 63).

Films and Plays

Playwright-in-Anguish

Elenore Lester*

A sharp November blue sky blazed like a pennant above Harkness tower and the Yale campus was a dazzle of noontime sun. But Joseph Heller, the playwright-in-anguish, emerging from the drama school, was at odds with the picture postcard setting. Heavy-set, dark and brooding, looking un-chic and un-Ivy League in his spanking new sheepskin jacket, he lumbered along, weighed down on one side by an overloaded briefcase.

Rehearsals for Heller's play, "We Bombed in New Haven," which opens tomorrow night at the Yale Repertory Theater, had just passed the halfway mark, and the playwright, author of the long-term best-selling novel, "Catch-22," was feeling a little frayed around the edges as a result of his first excursion into the theater. He had just gotten word that Mike Nichols, Barbara Harris, Paul Newman and Walter Kerr were planning to attend the opening and he wasn't entirely overjoyed.

"I thought we were going to have a good time putting on a play at Yale, but this way . . ." he shrugged. "You have all the stresses of a Broadway opening without its actually being Broadway."

He sighed heavily as we set out for an off-campus restaurant. "So it's like I was telling my psychiatrist," he said in the down-to-earth, sour-cream-and-pot-cheese Brooklyn accent carefully nurtured by many New York sophisticates successful in the arts, "It's not that I'm trying to dominate the director; it's just that I want the director to know what's in my mind and have the same thing in his mind so that he'll do what I want him to do without my trying to dominate him."

Having summed up for all time the problem of playwright-director relations and having done it in terms reminiscent of "Catch-22," where simple logic always collides with an absurdly structured universe, Heller seemed to feel a little better and was able to muster a smile. "You want to know the real truth?" he asked. "The real truth is that things have been going beautifully. Larry Arrick, the director, and the actors have been a revelation to me — the way they've gotten hold of his thing. After the first week they understood the play better than I did. They've seen things in it, psychological

*Reprinted from the *New York Times*, Dec. 3, 1967, Section 2, pp. 1, 19. ©1967 by The New York Times Company. Reprinted by permission.

meanings, I never thought of. Now I see that actors are real creative artists. They've brought so much imagination and enthusiasm. They're really wonderful, only . . ." he paused and nose-dived back into his Dostoevskian mood. "The only thing is I'm not happy."

So what's wrong?

Two things, Heller indicated, carefully, lovingly hanging up his sheepskin ("it's not really very expensive and I hear they last forever") and sliding into a booth.

"It's my nature to be suspicious. I just don't trust people. I know it's not right, but that's the way I am. I'm trying to be flexible and I think I have been so far. I don't mind making changes — as long as they're on minor matters. But I'm concerned about my literary personality. I don't want Joseph Heller distorted. I don't want anything on stage I wouldn't like to see as a member of the audience, and up to this point we've had no serious problems. Only — well, I am the way I am, and I'm biting my nails. And the second thing is I just don't like the theater."

YOU DON'T LIKE THE THEATER!!!

"No. And I'm not kidding." He shook his head sadly, "I think it's a very limited medium. I hardly ever go. Even the few times you see something good it's never really that good. Drama critics are too generous. They overpraise things."

But how come this play?

"Boredom. What's there to do in the evening if you don't go to the theater?" he offered reasonably. "You certainly can't watch TV. I had been working on my new novel — it's about a middle-aged man caught in a sterile, monotonous, regimented existence, very different in style and content from 'Catch-22,' and I found I had a few hours for meditation every evening, so I started to play around with the idea of dramatizing 'Catch-22.' After a while I found myself with a new set of characters and new ideas and I started getting really excited about it."

The play, which resembles "Catch-22" insofar as it concerns a group of men who go on bombing missions, is somewhat abstract. Its setting is any theater and city in which the play is given. The time is always the present. The stage illusion is constantly broken by the characters' efforts to break out of their roles. ("They told me it was something like Pirandello's 'Six Characters in Search of an Author,' " said Heller. "But I had never seen or read the play. I finally read it and I don't think much of it.") The Yale drama school publicity office describes the play as a "surreal comedy of war" — a description that raises Heller's hackles.

"War is no comedy; it's a tragedy. The play is a drama with a tragic ending. And by the way, I don't like the cuteness and archness in the title. It just happens that it's an accurate one. The men really do bomb in New Haven. I realize I'm considered a humorous fellow, but the truth is I wouldn't bother writing comedy," he said. "People find things to laugh at in 'Catch-

22' and probably they will in the play, but that's just because laughter is part of life. The things I write are funny only up to a point. Actually I am a very morbid, melancholy person. I'm preoccupied with death, disease and misfortune." He cast a long look of unutterable pain over his hot roast beef sandwich.

"No, don't classify me as a writer of black comedy either," he continued. "I don't want to be grouped with those writers." The writers he really loves, Heller explained, are Shakespeare and T. S. Eliot. And if the Heller humor is to be compared with anyone else's, he'd like it to be Nathaneal West, or Nabokov, or maybe Aristophanes. The modern dramatist he most enjoys is Beckett, "but I'd rather read him than see him staged."

Heller doubts whether he'll do much more serious writing for the theater although he thinks he might like to try a musical. He has interrupted work on the novel to handle a few Hollywood "polish" jobs, among them "Sex and the Single Girl," and to write "We Bombed in New Haven," which took him four or five months. And now the 44-year-old author is involved in a teaching schedule that takes him to the University of Pennsylania one day a week and to Yale another day for courses in fiction and dramatic writing.

In the past seven years Heller's reputation as a novelist has assumed the legendary proportions that Salinger once claimed on campus. Heller's regular-guy manner and apparently offhand teaching technique have reinforced his popularity among Yale students.

"We can't go on with our regular discussion today," he announced to his students as I entered the dramatic writing class with him. "You know, about whether —————— is really a fairy. The New York Times is here." Then he slumped in his seat and asked for the latest gossip about the progress of his play (drama school students may observe all rehearsals). They chatted and Heller mentioned that he had asked to have a bit of stage business taken out. "I found it offensive," he said. "You see, I'm a Puritan." The students looked a little shocked, but they relaxed and smiled indulgently when he continued, "I don't like to see things on stage that seem to expose an actor or actress to any indignity." (He later amplified this and told me he doesn't like any character in fiction, even contemptible ones, treated with contempt. "I always come to sympathize deeply with my villains.") Finally Professor Heller was ready to deal with the subject of the day — Aristotle's Poetics.

In the classroom the playwright and students discussed Aristotle's theories of drama and in a nearby rehearsal hall the "We Bombed in New Haven" company wrestled with the problems of bringing a play to life. Director Larry Arrick, formerly associated with the Second City company and most recently director of Murray Schisgal's "Fragments," took a break and slipped into a luncheonette for a bowl of pea soup. He had the intense look of a man in the throes of creation and clearly would have preferred to be left alone with his pea soup, but was willing to talk between sips.

"This is the best company I've ever worked with anywhere," said Arrick. (It includes students and professionals, among the latter Anthony Holland and Ron Leibman, both Second City alumni, and Stacy Keach, who created the title role in Barbara Garson's "MacBird.") "And the play is marvelous — its subject is war, but its theme is not. War is a metaphor here for a game these people are playing. We are all playing a kind of game in this country today, you know. We go to the theater or we look at Picasso's *Guernica* in the Museum of Modern Art and we say, 'Yes, war is terrible' and then we go and have some coffee. We aren't changed at all. We go to be moved, yet we aren't changed. This is a self-serving thing that gets us nowhere. It's easy to write an anti-war play today. The characters in this play are caught up in this game and trying to break out of their roles, but they can't."

Arrick felt he couldn't compare Heller's play with that of any other playwright. "He's really closer to the Jewish sensibility of novelists like Mailer, Roth, Bellow and Malamud who have a kind of self-loathing that is in itself a form of purification — their work comes out of a certain sense of pain and — God!" he said taking a horrified glance at his interviewer's notebook. "What does all that sound like?" He grabbed his jacket. "You can watch the rehearsal if you insist," he said. "But how would you like me to hang over your shoulder while you write your article?" I took the hint.

While Arrick was going through the torments of a mother in labor and Heller was agonizedly pacing the floor like an expectant father and students buzzed around like nurses and interns in various stage of training, Robert Brustein, now in his second year as dean of the drama school, presided over all with the professionally expansive air of an obstetrician who is satisified that everything is going normally. He was ready to discuss such side issues as the difficulties he has encountered in trying to build a more or less permanent acting company, which would include professionals and students. "Actors don't want to miss out on TV and Broadway opportunities," he said sadly. "The problem is to get together actors dedicated to their own development as artists and to certain actor-teacher ethical ideals that would enable them to bypass some personal advantages." As for "We Bombed in New Haven," he felt that there was an extraordinary meeting of minds between actors and playwright. "Heller's script offers a perfect skeleton for using the improvisational and *commedia dell' arte* techniques we are interested in."

Dean Brustein smiled benignly. No reason for him to tense up. The patient would be in labor for another two and a half weeks. In the meantime the students would be learning — and that was what counted.

A week later, playwright Heller, who had stayed away from rehearsals during the interim, was delighted with the play. He said, "At first I was afraid the actors weren't good enough and the director wasn't good enough, but now I am just afraid the script isn't good enough. And I do think I'll write another play."

Première of *We Bombed in New Haven*
Roderick Nordell[*]

Among the obscenities of war, Joseph Heller's first play finds a blend of satire, comedy, and tragedy that cuts to the quick.

It received a remarkably attuned première performance at the Yale University Theater this week before an audience with as many celebrities as a Broadway first night. It was just as if they knew the trip from New York would be worth it. And they could offer the theater-wise responses called for by the play even as it was making deeper demands.

For, from the title on up, "We Bombed in New Haven" is full of comtemporary double-edges. The setting is nominally the Yale theater, but it is probably the role-playing society in general. The characters at first appear to be reluctant bombing crews and officers, but then they emerge as the actors who are playing these parts.

It may sound like Pirandello. But in the hands of Mr. Heller and the Yale School of Drama Repertory Theater, it becomes a fresh amalgam of the Actor's Studio, the Second city, and something all its own.

The unsettling effect may be no surprise to those who felt a reformer's jolt in the bizarre black humor of Mr. Heller's World War II novel, "Catch-22." Though the play deals with a later war—a kind of metaphor for a violent world—it plainly echoes the book.

But the novel ends with an individual defying the system, behaving with that irrepressibility attributed to basic figures of comedy. Now, for all his own brash comic gifts, Mr. Heller seems to think the time for comedy is past. In the play there is no escape for the man who would opt out of the war.

And Mr. Heller is not only cockily putting down the hierarchy of nameless authority that sends men to kill and be killed. He is also trying to break through the callousness he sees in the audience itself.

Here the role-playing of his actors becomes a pointed device for making the spectator examine his own assent or dissent in playing roles he does not believe in. Perhaps the audience can remain comfortably detached when a fictional character is killed. Suppose the actor himself is killed? And what about the people daily killed by war?

If the spectators do care, why don't they do something about it? Why—as a son asks his father in the play—didn't they do something about it when their children were small so they wouldn't have to sacrifice them now to war?

Mr. Heller doesn't argue. He doesn't weigh war against causes worth fighting for. To him war is simply and tragically absurd.

"There's nothing really funny about all this, you know," says another

[*]Reprinted, with permission, from *The Christian Science Monitor*, Dec. 8, 1967, p. 14. © 1967 The Christian Science Publishing Society. All rights reserved.

character, just after one of Mr. Heller's jokes. Hilarious as parts of the play are, it could well make a spectator question his laughter at any war comedy again.

Mr. Heller risks tastelessness in satirizing tastelessness. He can't always resist an irrevelant gag. But for much of the time, his comedy serves the ultimate purpose of his tragedy.

When the tragedy arrives, however, he does not have the restraint to let the audience accuse itself, as O'Casey did with Juno's prayer: "Take away our hearts o' stone, and give us hearts o' flesh!"

Though Mr. Heller says essentially the same thing, he weakens the tragedy by permitting his characters to, in effect, lecture their listeners. But one feels any self-righteousness is unintentional; this is a writer doing his thing to reverse the antihumanity that agonizes him.

And, under Larry Arrick's broad but sensitive direction, the players go from ready-room wisecracks, to fragments of Shakespeare, to a fantastic basketball drill, to more deadly games with an appearance of utter belief.

Ron Leibman, for example, made strikingly acute transitions between mockery and emotion in the pivotal role of the first actor to have doubts about the play he is in. He was part of the production's solid core of profes-. sional actors including Stacy Keach, Anthony Holland, Michael Lombard, John McCurry, and Estelle Parsons.

Robert U. Taylor's effectively nondescript scenery was neatly maneu-vered on a stage that sometimes was bare — or even opened to the backstage work area — while the corrugated reaches of the unadorned walls stretched oppressively overhead.

War Games

Jack Kroll*

Joseph Heller's "Catch-22" is one of the great books of our time, an explosion of cauterizing laughter at the suicidal absurdity of war. Heller's first play, *We Bombed in New Haven*, tries to advance the assault to diffi-cult new terrain. Heller has seen that the issue is no longer war itself, but the deeper, more difficult question of man as role-player, the gap between what men want to do and what they find themselves "forced" to do.

In his play Heller focuses all this through the living metaphor of the actor. His characters are airmen who in some unspecified war are bombing targets from Constantinople to Minnesota. But they take great pains to ex-plain to the audience (and to reassure each other) that they are not "really" soldiers, they are actors — even giving their real names and highlights of their acting careers.

*Reprinted from *Newsweek*, 70 (Dec. 18, 1967), 96. © 1967 by Newsweek, Inc. All Rights Reserved. Reprinted by Permission.

Meanwhile the "war" goes on, guys are getting killed, the absurdities of army life are exploded in gag and slapstick scenes much as in "Catch-22." But the real play is the crescendo of tension between the actors and what they are acting. The actors are saying: "War is so horrible, thank God we're only actors doing a satire on its horror and not real soldiers." But as the play goes on it closes around the actors like a Venus's-flytrap. The sergeant whose "turn" it is to get killed, and who has been the big wisecracker, suddenly says: "I don't want to make believe I'm getting killed." But in the climactic scene he is "killed."

Disturbing: The whole force of the play is to keep the spectator constantly off balance, to disturb him by forcing him to react, not just to the play, but to the reaction of the actors to the play. To put it another way: the audience is instructed in how to react to the play by watching how the actors react to it, how, as a matter of fact, it ceases to be play at all for the actors, and becomes reality — which finally makes it a real play.

Trapping elusive truth with mirrors is fiendishly difficult. The pitfalls are obvious, and Heller falls into plenty of them. And yet the play is very likely the most powerful play about comtemporary irrationality an American has written, with a natural cathartic jolt that comes from the genuinness of Heller as a moral comedian. For all his Chinese-box shenanigans, Heller does not hide the moral concern that gives form and force to his vision. By showing his actors struggling against their play, he challenges the audience to rethink their own "roles" in a tragic absurd reality.

Dynamics: The forces assembled by the Yale School of Drama Repertory Theater must be saluted for their brilliant gallantry, their wit, dedication and theatrical effectiveness. Larry Arrick's direction has remarkable equilibrium in a concept full of booby traps, and he brilliantly modulates dynamics from laughs to shock: the moment in which an MP swings his weapon — a golf club — at the sergeant has a pure, plastic, hilarious terror that is great theater, and there are other such moments. The actors, especially Stacy Keach and Ron Leibman, are from the new young breed who understand in their bones the paradoxes that Heller is evoking, and they perform with masculine gusto and style. Estelle Parsons is strong as the sole female, a Red Cross girl trapped between her "lousy doughnuts" and her misused femininity. Robert U. Taylor's set, which the actors break up and reassemble as they do with the play itself, is perfect. This is one of those rare productions that advance the whole notion of the theater.

Curtains in Connecticut   Tom F. Driver*

When Joseph Heller's *We Bombed in New Haven* bombed in New Haven last winter, one thought that might be the last of it. It's hard to keep a good man down, however, even with the weight of a bomb on his shoulders. Above the sea of criticism Heller now emerges with the play in two new garbs, waiting for the next approaching waves. Knopf publishes the reading version, and Jason Robards, Jr., and Diana Sands are set to appear in the Broadway production come October. So we shall see Robards in the role that requires him to play himself as well as Starkey, the Air Force captain who sends people on missions of death and who marries Ruth, the Red Cross worker, and fathers a child whom he will have to send on missions of death, and all this played out in a spirit of Pirandellan *jeu de thèâtre* and *Grand Guignol*.

I have some advice for Heller. I could just as well call him up and give it to him on the telephone, but as it may have some wider interest, I give it to him here and let him call *me* up on the telephone. "For the love of Mike, get off the radio," I'd say. "For the love of Ivy, you're up against the wall," I'd say. "For the love of God, remember it's dangerous in New Haven, and either write another novel, even if it's only half as good as *Catch-22*, or give us a play of witty prose, but do not under any circumstances imagine that you belong to the theatrical avant garde." And then, if he were still on the line, which is most unlikely, I'd have to explain why there should be such a tirade from someone who thinks Heller is great and *Catch-22* the greatest and *We Bombed in New Haven* a dud of the first magnitude.

I know he would rather not hear anything more about the virtues of that famous novel, the renown of which he bears like a cross. But the fact is that when he wrote it he was himself, and when he wrote *We Bombed* he was somebody else, and it's time for the real Joseph Heller to stand up.

The problem is substance. By which I don't mean moral content or weighty thought or anything like that. *We Bombed* is a very moral sort of a play, and probably no one is going to think that Heller is not serious about it or that a message against killing is out of place in our day. "It's about time," as Heller says twice in the play. The play is about time: the time that we are the servers of until the time we become victims, or until the time when the victims are our own sons. "They are all my sons," as I think a certain playwright said some years ago.

Here indeed is moral substance, but not the substance I'm concerned about first. No author's moral substance is entertaining or convincing without the presence of another kind, which is that of his *métier*. If an artist, craftsman, or doodler of any kind does not make us feel that he has the stuff of his *métier* grasped in hand so that we can hear it, feel it, taste it, see it,

*Reprinted with permission from *Saturday Review*, 51 (Aug. 31, 1968), 22–24.

smell it, then nothing else he does matters. It remains abstract, while we go to art for the concrete feel of emotion and thinking.

Catch-22 was a success because, whatever else one might care to say about it, its language was substantial, in my second meaning of the term. However whimsical was that language, you could hear, feel, taste, see, and smell it. It would run with bases loaded, trip, roll like a ball, and get up to dust itself off at home plate. Change the figure: Heller would pull a sentence like taffy, turn it by magic into a rubber strand, and let it snap in your face. Then for some reason you could see better than ever, perhaps just from the sting of it. The words rang in your ears and swam before your eyes and rattled all around whenever you carried the book (which you did from room to room until you finished reading it once, then twice, maybe more), and whenever you looked at the words, in whatever order, they gave you *déjà vu* and *presque vu* and sometimes *jamais vu*.

All this and much more happened because *Catch-22* is a book that is totally committed, as some books are not, to the notion that the whole world is made up of words, and whatever won't go into words is out of this world. The imagination that created it is totally a verbal imagination, which is what you would also have to say about *Ulysses, Finnegans Wake, Pale Fire*, and a few other very good books of modern times. Heller tied his readers up in his verbal net the same way the Air Force tied up airmen in the system. They couldn't get out, you remember, even by pleading insanity (which anybody knotted up in words the way Yossarian was should have a right to do), because there was catch number 22 in the regulations that said that anybody pleading insanity to get out of the Air Force was, on the very evidence of that attempt, not insane and therefore could not get out by pleading insanity.

More than one husband and veteran who found himself in stitches over *Catch-22* discovered that his enthrallment with it could neither be shared with nor communicated to his wife. I've known a dozen who tried, and all their wives worked like everything to get with it, to no avail. I think these wives saw, pretty quick, that the whole thing was just a verbal construct. "Just words" — there's the whole thing right there. As Shaw made plain in *Man and Superman*, the males of this world do their thing by words, and every Ann Whitefield says to every Jack Tanner, "Yes, dear. Go on talking."

The humor of *Catch-22* depended on taking words with *absolute* seriousness, no bones about it, the same way you'd take the b.m. on the baby's diapers. I mean, there it is. But the women couldn't make out why you had to take mere *words* that seriously. So they smiled indulgently and went back to putting bleach in the diaper wash.

Hell. Their husbands had been in the war and they knew that the whole goddamn Army is run that way. It's not guns and bombs and moral necessity that soldiers take seriously but *words*. A modern army might lose all its ordnance and still remain in the field so long as it had not lost its mimeograph machine. To bring it up to date, the Vietnam War is unaffected by the number of victims, the tons of bombs dropped, the cities won or lost, and such other crap, so long as the Commander-in-Chief can hold onto three words: "International Communist Conspiracy." If you look at the State Department's famous White Paper in February 1965, you will see that it is so locked up in its airtight verbal system that no merely empirical evidence of any kind could ever undo the proposition that the North is the Aggressor. Why? Because (and this is worthy of *Catch-22*) the absence of evidence is said to be the main evidence, since it shows that the Aggressor is so aggressive that he aggressively hides his aggression. To such syntax, falling bombs and flying bodies are no more than commas and semi-colons.

The moral substance of *Catch-22*, then, was an analogy of or corollary to its artistic substance, which was the tactile way in which it treated words and made you sense them with all your senses. And the trouble with *We Bombed in New Haven* is that it does not have any theatrical substance that could be said to be the equivalent of the verbal substance of *Catch-22*. Heller saw the problem I'm describing as it loomed up before him while he dreamed of writing a play. It was like a fast ball coming at him: he swung and missed.

You can tell he saw it because he bent over backwards to write a real sure, bang-up theatrical kind of a play. He figured on hitching up to that most fashionable and important modern phenomenon the theater theatrical. His opening curtain goes up and stops halfway: we're in the theater, and sometimes things go wrong. The audience sees the actors putting scenery in place. Thereafter we are continually reminded by the dialogue that this Captain Starkey is really Jason Robards (or whoever), the very one that played *A Thousand Clowns* and *Long Day's Journey.* In Heller's play, actors, not just characters, really die on the stage, or so we are asked to believe (more or less); and there is a big clock on stage that tells the actual time of the performance. The captain carries this morning's edition of *The New York Times.*

All this sort of thing is meant to be the theatrical material out of which the play is made. In fact, it is immaterial. For it is only an idea in Heller's head, therefore not substance but shadow. You can hear Heller saying to himself: "Let's do something in the theater that you can't do anywhere but in the theater. Let's curtainify the curtain, actorfy the actors, time the time with a clock, write a bomb of a play about bombing and put some real time bombs in it. Let's write a play about playing, which, after Pirandello, Ionesco and Albee, is the only way to do it. And let's have a major who, instead of writing orders, writes the script, and let's make it Relevant by showing that the Air Force, which bombs Constantinople not knowing it's really Istanbul, would just as soon bomb Minnesota next week. Say, that last is pretty good, huh? — because actors (this play will have actors) play now in New Haven or Constantinople or Istanbul or where-the-hell, and next week Minnesota. You have heard of that resident theater in Minnesota, haven't you?"

Well, yes, we have heard of all of this, or could have thought of it ourselves, and it's about time because it's nothing new. There's nothing wrong with it except that it's facetious, and there's nothing wrong with *that* except you need a certain feel to bring it off and not just the notion.

This whole "let's pretend we're not pretending" bit is reminiscent of The Living Theater in its early days on 14th Street. But The Living found out that if you go this road your destination is a theater of improvisation, which is what they came to in their later days on 14th Street before the revenuers got them, and it is what they have made the most of in their influential wanderings in Europe ever since. But the theater theatrical and improvisatory is not, I am sure, Heller's route. He should return to words, mere words. If he wants to put them into the theater instead of a novel that's okay, but then he should turn to the much-neglected art of comic dialogue, should be content to do the old-fashioned thing: let his characters stand around and just talk.

"Just talk"—there's the whole thing right there. Heller should not be intimidated by the anti-verbal bias of the modern theater, should not be afraid of being a *wordy* playwright. Words is where he's at, and if Tom O'Horgan and Richard Schechner and the Becks and lots of other people are now convinced that real theater is pre-verbal or post-verbal, their selling of this perfectly good half-truth should not under any circumstances be allowed to muffle the few real word people we've got.

What we're after in the theater is energy. Not theory, and not fashion. We're after energy sufficiently strong to be shaped by that particular form of intelligence that is useful in the arts and to which we give the name imagination. There are verbal forms of such imaginatively structured energy, and there are nonverbal forms. The form such energy takes matters less than whether it's there or not, and the wrongest thing any talent can do is let itself be hung up on form while the energy gets blocked.

Heller, do your own thing. Don't muck about with what somebody said was real, pure essence of theater. They may be right, but it's got to come through the hair. Your own thing is theater enough.

Yes, dear. Go on talking.

Laughing All the Way to the Truth   Susan Braudy[*]

"At night what do I do? I look at my marquee on 49th and Broadway, and I worry. Because sometimes the bomb on the marquee looks too skinny, sometimes too fat."

"What do I do during the day?" Joseph Heller was staring glumly into Doubleday's window on Fifth Avenue. "I look in bookstore windows. Big

[*]Reprinted, with the permission of the author, from *New York*, 1 (Oct. 14, 1968), 41–45.

deal. Watch me frown when I don't see my play on display." He frowns and sighs and slides a fresh stim-u-dent toothpick in his mouth.

Heller, whose play *We Bombed in New Haven* opens on Broadway October 16 and whose novel *Catch-22* still sells half a million copies a year, is a thick and handsome 45. He looks prosperous. His face is fleshed out and large. His nervous brown eyes seem to stare directly inward as well as outward.

Despite the expensive navy blazer and the nervous eyes, Heller looks tough. Maybe it's the toothpick that hangs out of the side of his mouth. Maybe it's his graying curly hair, long in the sideburns and in back, but slicked back from a widow's peak. It could be his broad shoulders or the slight swagger in his walk.

Twenty years ago, *Esquire* printed a Heller short story along with a picture of Heller, then 24 years old, a junior Phi Bete at NYU, married, and the owner of a good conduct medal from the war.

In *Esquire's* picture, his large nose and eyes sit uneasily on a dark skinny face. He looks scared and underfed. Like almost any picture if you stare at it long enough, the eyes seems to stare directly outward and directly inward at the same time.

Last fall at the Yale Drama School where Heller's play was produced and where he taught playwriting, his students were bewildered by him. Says one student, "I had lunch with Joseph Heller, and you know what he talked about during lunch. Lunch. He talked about lunch. Diet orange drink and hamburgers. Either that guy's wearing a mask or he didn't write *Catch-22.*"

"Joseph Heller, an easy laughing man," was the way *Vogue* magazine saw the writer a year after *Catch-22* was published. *Vogue* held a manicured finger to the fashion winds and called Heller a new trend for the early '60s, along with the high-waisted dress and the overblouse.

But Heller doesn't laugh easily. And he did write *Catch-22*. When Heller, the master of tragi-comic farce, laughs, he sounds only obliging. It's as though he were reading hahahaha from a script of your conversation.

When he writes, Heller uses humor to lure his audience into unexpected confrontations with a tragic truth. But in real life Heller uses his humor to keep people from looking too closely at him.

"Of course he's masked," says a close friend of Heller's. "He'd be an open wound otherwise. There's nothing arty about Joe's mask, either. He's often mysterious because he's so plain."

"Listen, you're crazy," a tired Heller was rubbing the back of his neck in Penn Station. "You've over-researched this article. What do you want to work so hard for. Next time you write an article, take my advice, hand the guy 20 questions and a tape recorder, and that'll be your article."

Heller had agreed to let me interview him on a train ride from New York to Philadelphia. I started to leave him to buy my ticket. "Better take your notes with you," he said, "or I may burn them. Who would be interested in reading all that junk about me anyway?"

Heller has a thing about money. He enjoys talking about it. A few years ago Heller and Edward Albee were both guests at a small dinner party. Albee wanted to talk Art. But he never got the chance. Heller spent all night talking taxes.

"My generation was oriented to the Depression. When I was in school, we all wanted to get out and make a good living. Today most students do not know what they want to do. They only know they *don't* want to do — go to war."

In the dining car of the train, Heller begins. "I'm probably going to fall asleep before I can answer any of your questions. Tell me again why you are writing this article. Somebody must be paying you a lot of money to ride into Philadelphia with me. You're probably crazy."

He leans across the table and whispers, "If you sit here in the dining car, sometimes you can get a free ride."

INTERVIEWER: What did you hope to accomplish by writing *We Bombed in New Haven*, Mr. Heller?

HELLER: (rolls his head to the ceiling and sighs before he puts another toothpick in his mouth. He talks like the guy eating at the deli after Saturday morning golf.) What else, I wanted to make a million dollars.

INTERVIEWER: No really.

HELLER: All right. Right now I want to make every woman cry and every man feel guilty when he has to go home and face his sons. What can fathers do about Vietnam? Up until about a year ago, you could get your son out if you knew a Congressman. My advice to draftees is to keep out. Don't die for something you don't believe in. Anybody who likes war deserves war. Anyone who likes peace deserves freedom. Now people can send their sons to psychiatrists. Or else they can do the kind of massive thing that Spock and Coffin are doing. (Heller pauses and says with emphasis) You ask what did I mean to accomplish. I meant to write a very good play.

Heller believes the play is more relevant now than it was a year ago at Yale. "I have unlimited confidence in the stupidity of our government and all others," he says. "I knew that Congress and the President wouldn't let me down and do something intelligent like ending the war while I was revising my play this year."

"I don't believe in dying for Dean Rusk or Johnson's decisions," Heller has said. "Let them go out and die if they want to fight the war. I loathe the war; I detest it; I hate it. If we really want to protect our fighting men, we should bring them home where they'll be safe."

But World War II, he believes, had to be fought.

Two years ago, *Holiday* sent Heller and his wife and two children back to the air base in Corsica where most of his war took place. From there Heller had flown missions as a wing bombardier. Corsica was no longer the place his war had been; his war was over and gone, and he saw that even his ten-year-old son realized it.

"What the grouchy kid didn't realize though was that his own military service was still ahead; and I could have clasped him in my arms to protect him as he stood there, half hanging out of the car with his sour look of irritation."

In *We Bombed in New Haven*, Captain Starkey (who will be played by Jason Robards) must personally induct his son into the army; Starky always does what he is told. He fits into the system, and the system destroys him.

Heller never read Pirandello, but his spirit is in the play. The characters are both actors and soldiers at the same time. Their parts and their lives are controlled by an existing script which they have read and by a metaphysical script in which only one character, the Major, has access. When a character refuses to die, as the real script dictates, the Major is not surprised. Because he also has the ultimate script, the Major knows how this man must ultimately die.

If all soldiers could know what Heller's characters know about their own deaths, they might take warfare much differently. Says one of Heller's Yale students, "Most guys think they'll go in, play the role of the soldier for two years, and then come back and pick up where they left off. They don't think: go in, play soldier, and be killed. Heller's play metaphor really works."

Heller does not consider the play a comedy — even though, he says, if you call it a comedy, more people will probably buy tickets to see it. Heller's play uses comedy for other ends. There are many jokes in the first act of the play, but in the second act, a soldier says, "There'll be no more laughing tonight," and the play moves swiftly to its tragic conclusion.

Joseph Heller was born in Coney Island in 1923. "Coney Island is beautiful to children and ugly to adults," he once wrote, "and, in this respect, it is often typical of life itself."

After graduating from Abraham Lincoln High School in 1941, Heller went to work as a blacksmith's helper in the Norwalk Navy Yard, though at the time he was too skinny to lift a sledge hammer. He enlisted in the Army Air Corps in 1942, a few months before he would have been drafted. Like Yossarian, Heller figured that the war would be over before he got into it.

"What incredible optimism we had in those days. We believed that any country that tried to take on America would be knocked out in a week."

Yossarian, too, had his moment of truth about the nature of war in a flight over Avignon:

> Yossarian ripped open the snaps of Snowden's flak suit and heard himself
> scream wildly as Snowden's insides slithered down to the floor in a soggy

pile and just kept driping out. . . . "Here was God's plenty, all right," he thought bitterly as he stared — liver, lungs, kidneys, ribs, and bits of stewed tomatoes Snowden had eaten that day for lunch. . . . Man was matter, that was Snowden's secret. Drop him out a window and he'll fall. Set fire to him and he'll burn. Bury him and he'll rot like other kinds of garbage. The spirit gone, man is garbage.
"I'm cold," Snowden said. "I'm cold."

When the war ended, Joseph Heller married, spent one year at USC, got his B.A. from NYU and his M.A. from Columbia, and won a Fulbright to Oxford.

It was while Heller was at NYU that he decided if he couldn't make it as a writer, he would teach. Then from 1950 to 1952, he taught English at Penn State and didn't like it. So, in 1952, Heller moved back to the city to work for 10 years in the advertising departments of *Time, Look,* and finally *McCall's* magazines.

While he was on his way to success in the advertising world, Heller wrote *Catch-22,* the novel about the horrors inflicted on people by both war and peace-time bureaucracies. At night, sitting at his kitchen table, Heller wrote a book attacking the kind of bureaucracy he helped perpetuate during the day.

Friends who summered with the Hellers on Long Beach, Long Island, remember that Joe and Shirley always left parties very early. "The novel, you know," people would say significantly after they'd gone.

During these years, Heller professed to love the advertising game. But he also enjoyed changing jobs. Every time he was offered a raise or a promotion, he began looking for a new job. He also kept working steadily on the novel. He did not want to write just any novel, but a masterpiece.

Heller took a leave of absence from *McCall's* a few months after *Catch-22* was published and he never returned. But when he speaks of his advertising days he still refers to himself as a "born promotion man."

"He's incredible," says a friend. "He comes on like a real Madison Avenue fat cat with that born promotion man business. If I were the author of *Catch-22,* I'd bill myself as a born American author."

When rave reviews started coming in Heller took to carrying them around at work. He signed countless books for *McCall's* people, but he never gave anyone free copies. He chided people who bought their copies discounted at Korvette's.

Heller describes the surprise with which some of his business friends viewed *Catch-22* when it first appeared. "Come on Joe," they would say to me, "a few of the jokes maybe yes, but not that whole book. You don't have that kind of tragic sense."

While Heller was doing reading and speaking tours on *Catch-22,* he conceived of having four actors and actresses do readings from the book plus readings from Shakespeare, the source of a surprising number of *Catch-22* passages.

"Misreading and readings from Shakespeare," was the way Heller described his plan to a Filmways executive who had bought production rights from Columbia.

But as Heller began to look for a device to give his play more form, he decided to drop *Catch-22*, which was becoming a burden, and write an original play. His first draft contained Falstaff's speech on honor, among other Shakespearean passages, most of which have been cut from the final draft. After six months of hard work, Heller sent Robert Brustein, at Yale, the second draft of the whole play. Brustein read it and became so excited by the last act that he read it first to his wife, and was still so excited that he called Philip Roth long distance and read it to him. Brustein then invited Heller to be playwright in residence at Yale, while they produced his play.

The first public reading of the play in October at Yale was a smash hit. At the play's end Heller and Mrs. Brustein were among those moved to tears.

But after one rehearsal Heller was a nervous wreck. He told his playwriting students about a night of fitful sleeping at a local motel, turning and tossing in anguish over what he had seen at rehearsal. All night long, maniacs on either side of his room banged walls and played radios. At 5 A.M. a distraught Heller discovered that, in fact, the radio built into his own night table had been on all night.

After two weeks of rehearsals, Heller was shaken but thoughtful. "I'm learning; I'm learning," he said, "that I wrote a script not a production. In novels the writer defines and limits his characters, but not in plays. If an actor has any talent he will fill out bare words in the script. Anthony Holland and Ron Leibman are adding new comic levels to their parts." (Both actors will play in the Broadway production.)

"Anyway," Heller said, "I'm a veteran of the theatre now. I've learned how to suffer excruciating torture without uttering a sound."

Heller's play had been scheduled for a Broadway production this past April. But a combination of factors including a lukewarm review from *Times* critic Clive Barnes convinced him to delay the opening of the play and re-work parts of it. Other critics were more than lukewarm. *Life* called Heller's play "the best war play of our day," and *Newsweek* said it was "the most powerful play about contemporary irrationality that an American has written."

Heller sold paperback rights for his play for $1,000,000, one of the highest sums ever paid for a play; meanwhile, *We Bombed in New Haven* opened in five major German cities in September. Jason Robards and Diana Sands will headline the Broadway production. Robards was so excited by the play that he ended a self-imposed exile from Broadway and volunteered to play any of several parts.

The Theatre Development Fund, "devoted to the production of plays of artistic merit in commercial theatre," will subsidize ticket sales of Heller's play as its first venture. They have purchased $60,000 worth of tickets for the first six weeks of the play's run. They sell tickets at reduced rates to students, guaranteeing that the play will run six weeks, and that it will be seen by people who might not otherwise be able to afford to see it.

What will you do now after this play, I asked Heller on the train.

"I don't have a work compulsion. I had one when I was younger, but I don't anymore. I don't always have to be doing great art. I just want to write a good novel or play once in a while. I can make enough to live comfortably doing movie polishes."

INTERVIEWER: Isn't it a funny feeling that so many people you don't even know were so moved by your play?

HELLER: Not a funny feeling. It's a good feeling. See that guy over there. (He points to a man across the aisle eating soup and engrossed in a paperback.) When my book first came out in paper, I'd get into the subway or train and look at the books people were reading. If the paperback had blue edges it was Dell. *Catch-22* is in Dell, so then I'd have to try to see the cover. If he was reading my book it was a good feeling.

Heller's *We Bombed in New Haven* Opens

Clive Barnes*

A play is a machine for setting up a dialogue between a playwright and his audience, and a critic's job is to throw on a little oil of interpretation to help it on its way. But what if the dialogue first set up in the critic's mind is too confused to let him interpret as well as he would like to.

You see I am not at all certain what I felt and even less certain what I think, about Joseph Heller's first play, "We Bombed in New Haven," which opened at the Ambassador Theater last night. What do you imagine I should do? Toss a coin to be completely decisive and then lie a little. I am told that many members of the public and those people called producers dislike notices that mugwump on a fence. To Burgundy with them; I intend to vacillate a little.

I have tried to make up my mind. I first read the play before seeing its original production in New Haven, where it was excellently given by the Repertory Company of the Yale Drama School. I reread it, in a slightly revised version, when it was published by Alfred Knopf, and of course I saw it again last night. If I was forced to a judgment I would call it a bad play any good playwright should be proud to have written, and any good audience fascinated to see.

*Reprinted from the *New York Times*, Oct. 17, 1968, p. 51. © 1968 by The New York Times Company. Reprinted by permission.

Mr. Heller's ideas seem to be morally and politically quite unimpeachable, and happily for Broadway quite fashionable. He is against killing people, he is against bombing, he is against the war in Vietnam and, I suspect, against the moral blindness that permits millions of people to treat such a war as a kind of spectator sport to be watched on TV until we are no longer completely sure whether we are seeing our sons and brothers being killed on a newsreel or a few Hollywood actors biting the dust on the Late Late Show.

"We Bombed in New Haven" is a play that has actors pretending to be actors pretending to be airmen. Captain Starkey, a tired regular officer (or perhaps a tired regular actor), is sending out his unit on bombing raids. Today it is Constantinople (it's not Istanbul, it's Constantinople), and tomorrow it will be Minnesota. The aim is to obliterate the target, and the target always is obliterated. But some airmen don't return. Some are killed.

But of course we know, don't we, that the theater is a place of make-believe. We know that they are not genuine airmen and that actors are never killed on active service, not even John Wayne. Equity wouldn't like it, rehearsal time would be impossible, and the blood would mess up the stage.

Mr. Heller's actors know this as well as we do. A Sergeant Henderson about to be killed in the second act — the Major, who is Starkey's superior, carries the script around with him so the cast knows the plot — is not worried about the pretended death, but about the quality of the part he has on stage. Like every actor, he thinks he is worth a better role. Still, it's a job.

But then a corporal is killed on a mission, and Henderson tries unsuccessfully to find him off-stage. Perhaps he has been killed. Perhaps it is not all make-believe. Henderson is scared.

The possibilities of this Pirandellian device of two planes of reality set against each other as in a mirror image are used by Mr. Heller for all they are worth. But although we know that all the world's a stage and all that jazz, the device is neither especially original nor meaningful.

Despite the scattering in the dialogue of actor's camp to mingle with barrack room bull, and the frequent quotations from Shakespeare (when wars were wars and poets would die for them), Mr. Heller does not play fair with his image of an embattled stage.

The air of fantasy was never sufficient to convince me of a phantasmagoric world in which actors might not know where the grease paint ended and the blood began. And the idea itself is a cliché, while the dramatic technique expressing it (and this a first play, remember) is a little rough, a little clumsy. When finally Mr. Heller commits the sentimental coup of showing Starkey sending his own son on a mission, the message of our corporate responsibility becomes almost insupportable in its obviousness.

What then is good? First, the play's ambitiousness; it is a play that tries to extend the theatrical experience of most Broadway playgoers. Second, most of the writing and all of the atmosphere.

Mr. Heller is a writer to the tip of his keyboard. His dialogue flows out, natural, real, amusing, absorbing. Here is the writer of "Catch-22" flying high, high on words of his first theatrical flight.

Then even more there is the "atmosphere" of the play. Mr. Heller has caught the anarchic mood of the present, the callousness, brutality, cynical jokiness, dissent and protest. Every sentence spat out, and many of them are defiantly funny, speaks of today and demonstrates a profound moral concern for what is happening in our own theater of the world.

For this Broadway production Mr. Heller has made a few changes, but perhaps not enough, and it is a pity that the two starring roles are not so well performed as they were in New Haven. Jason Robards, with his disappointed moose face and friendly voice, did not convey the passionate panic of Starkey in the way that Stacy Keach did in New Haven, and Diana Sands was far too beautiful and desirable for Ruth, the coffee girl, originally played by Estelle Parsons with such friendly, battered charm.

But, as perhaps in New Haven, the play is dominated by Ron Leibman and Anthony Holland playing with antic zest and despair their original roles of Henderson and Corporal Bailey. Mr. Leibman goes from the flip to the tragic in a most moving performance, and Mr. Holland conveys a haunted urchin humor and will to survive that is deeply impressive. As the Major, William Roerick was I thought too conventionally authoritarian to convey the Machiavellian menace inherent in the role, but this may have been due to John Hirsch's rather stiff direction.

Finally, all I can say is that this is a play that people should see and make up their own minds. Any way you look at it, this is a pretty remarkable theatrical debut for Mr. Heller. I hope he stays around our theater for a long, long time.

Walter Kerr vs. Joseph Heller   Walter Kerr*

We Bombed in New Haven doesn't work, and I think it's important to know why. What does "work" mean in this case? What *should* happen to us in the theatre as we sit watching war games that turn out to be real and deadly games?

Joseph Heller, novelist and not yet a playwright, has a most specific effect in mind. He has gathered his flight crews in blue fatigues together, given them meaningless orders to bomb Constantinople and then Minnesota, set them to playing with basketballs that may prove to be bombs, had

*Reprinted from the *New York Times*, Oct. 27, 1968, Sec. 2, pp. 1, 5. © 1968 by The New York Times Company. Reprinted by permission.

them turn to the audience to say that they are only actors and not actual men engaged in actual warfare, had them discover that even if they are only actors they can be torn and bloodied by bullets and finally pronounced dead, in order to create in those of us who are watching a sense of direct responsibility.

We watch the play as though it were only play. Mr. Heller wishes to suggest that we watch war, or tolerate war, in much the same way. "J'accuse," say the actors, pointing at us as they take leave of life.

We should shrivel under the accusation, perhaps beat our breasts. We don't. We resist and resent the pointed finger, feeling in some restive way that we've been had. This in spite of what we know about our own failings, inadequacies, weaknesses in the matter under discussion. And this in spite of a swift, polished staging job by John Hirsch and laundry-crisp, sassy performances by Diana Sands, Ron Leibman and Jason Robards.

To say why we respond against the intention of the evening and even against our own private sensations of guilt I'll have to go back to an occasion when we didn't. Several years ago a young playwright named Jack Richardson offered Off Broadway a piece called "The Prodigal." In it, he made use of the ancient narrative of an Orestes called to avenge the murder of his father by responsibly murdering his mother. This was his assigned task, his duty. "They" required it. (In Orestes' case, "they" were the gods; in Mr. Heller's play, the bombings and the deaths are ordered by the men above the men above the men above the men above the major).

Orestes did not wish to do what was being urged — by every social, religious and political force — to do. He shrank from the task, then ran from it. Pursued, badgered, begged to behave as all loyal pawns are expected to behave, he fought off the act of killing with every rational and emotional argument at his disposal. In the end, he gave in. He did not give in to the forces pressing about him onstage. He could hold out against them. He gave in to something else, to someone else. He gave in to us. Turning to the audience for the first time during the evening, he pointed out that he would have to kill his mother, after all, because we expected him to. We *wanted* it. It was what we had come for, and unless our own thirst for blood was satisfied we'd have felt our time and money wasted.

The accusation worked — like a good hard slap in the face — for one simple reason. It was true. We *had* been insisting on murder as the price of our attention, we'd have felt flat and cheated if the play had ended in the rejection of violence, in the refusal to act. The knowledge that this was so stirred in the pits of our stomachs; in some way it hurt. It also caused us to give assent to the play; in some way it *added* to our satisfaction.

That Mr. Heller is after the same awareness, the same savage discovery, is perfectly plain. (I am not, by the way, suggesting that he has in any way borrowed from Mr. Richardson's play; he may not even know it.) Early in the second act of "We Bombed in New Haven," actor Ron Leibman is appalled to discover that he is next in line to be killed on a bombing mission. Who will let such a thing happen? The audience? Won't they *care?* "Why should they?" a buddy snaps back, "it's what they came to see."

Later, after Mr. Leibman has defected, Capt. Jason Robards is arguing his case with Maj. William Roerick. Although Mr. Robards has sent many a man to his arbitrary death, he is gradually developing a conscience, presumably the audience's conscience. The major announces that Mr. Leibman will be shot the instant he is captured. "They won't let you," Mr. Robards exclaims, glancing at the assembled spectators, "They won't just sit there and let you kill him!" (The implication, of course, is that we will, as we do.) Still later, in an obvious and astonishingly mawkish passage, Mr. Robards discovers that his own son is marked for slaughter. Torn between his duty, the commands that "they" give, and his affection, he proclaims his integrity directly. "Do you think I would stand here talking to you," he says, standing alone on the stage and talking to us, "and let my son go off and be killed?" (We are expected, I think, to shout back a loud "yes!", knowing him now for the slave and hypocrite he is because we know that we ourselves have let our own sons go off to be killed. He will be guilty because we already are. Our passion is meant to be turned against ourselves.)

But where we gave assent to "The Prodigal" and felt our knowledge of ourselves increased, here we fight back against the too-plain ironies and feel our knowledge of ourselves inaccurately represented. In an effort to explain our ultimate irration with, both ourselves and the work at hand, we ask all sorts of questions. The evening posits war as a glamorous game in which no one expects really to be killed. It supposes that we regard war in this way; in effect, it accuses us of so regarding it. But who now thinks of war in this way? (Perhaps small children do, like the boy with a rifle in "Summertree." I doubt that a single adult member of the audience attending *We Bombed in New Haven* can flagellate himself for sharing this particular delusion. The accusation, as it is here framed, is off-target.)

Perhaps Mr. Heller, shuttling his players back and forth between their identities as mere actors and as actual sacrifices, means to suggest that in our theatre-going, our public dreaming, we romanticize war (as Joan Littlewood suggested, in "Oh What a Lovely War," that our popular music painted morning glories over the decaying mounds of dead). But when has our theatre last jumped jingoistically, or done retreads of Tennyson? Mr. Heller himself must reach as far back as "Journey's End" to find a reference point, while attacking us as though we were devouring Green Berets on Broadway every night. Again, the apparent target isn't there.

And he surely cannot mean to imply that our constant watching of the nightly news clips from Vietnam on television has deadened our sense of what a bullet through the groin or the head is like, that we have come to regard war as a toy because television can be a toy. Surely it was our watching, our attention to what we knew was real, that stimulated and expanded the large-scale revulsion against the Vietman war and that brought on not only the emergence of McCarthy and the unleashing of Kennedy but the decision of Johnson to bow out of the picture (literally, out of the picture).

If any of these is meant to be the parallel dictating the form of Mr. Heller's conceit, it isn't a parallel. We intuit the fact, and are made uneasy. The charge won't stick because we aren't guilty of *this* particular folly (whatever others we have lodged in our hearts). And if none of them is meant to be the parallel, why has Mr. Heller composed his piece of so many random games, so many references to mere play-acting, so many threats to throw a bomb right into the middle of the audience ("it's only a toy, isn't it?" Mr. Robards sneers as he poises an explosive in our faces, ready to hurl it)?

I think he has tossed all of these gratuitous and sometimes misleading impromptu bits and pieces into the ultimately shapeless hopper because he simply cannot abide the thought of patiently writing a play. He feels too keenly and is in too much of a hurry for that. Why waste time slowly developing characters in whom the audience can believe (when they are only going to be killed), why go to the trouble of having them earn our sympathies as recognizable human beings (when war does not treat them as recognizable human beings), why tease us along a coherent and developing emotional line until we are actively engaged in knowing and perhaps approving its outcome (when war is not coherent and the less engaged we are the better)? Mr. Heller wants not to dramatize war in any way, shape or form, but to talk about it, shout about it, make proclamations about it— *now*.

It is easy to share his feeling (though not his assumption that we are without feeling ourselves) and to understand his hurry. It is not easy to be moved as he wishes us to be moved because the theater—the poor, benighted theater—refuses to function effectively in this way. The whole trick of "The Prodigal" was first to involve us with the characters and the narrative, to make us wish for something, to generate inside us a growing emotion that we may not have bothered, in our absorption, to name. Then Mr. Richardson named it for us and threw us into violent shock. We'd been led into feeling something and were astounded and ashamed to learn what it was we'd been feeling.

Here we cannot be astounded or ashamed because there has been no carefully nourished commitment to begin with; there is no emotion to be reversed, no enlightening shock to be absorbed. The whole content of the evening is on the table from the outset. Within two minutes of starting time, a pilot is asking why a man should bomb Pompeii when it is already in ruins and an officer is answering "it's his job." The next two hours say nothing more than that, do nothing more than that, in spite of a director's canny incidental invention and the fact that Mr. Heller occasionally gives us a line nearly good enough to have gone into "Catch-22."

But what have we come for? Entertainment, in the form of a few lively gymnastics, memories of Pirandello, a spare handful of impertinent lines? Surely not. The issue at hand is obviously too urgent for that, too immediate. It is the first business of our lives (if we are to have any lives). Illumination of the issue, then? But nothing is truly said that we hadn't thought before coming into the theater. The exercise is not only ambiguous, it is superfluous. The theater hasn't done its own possibly powerful work in its own way; and Mr. Heller's way, as things stand, presumes that we will feel guilt gratis, without having committed ourselves to anything at all.

Novels into Film: *Catch-22* as Watershed
Les Standiford*

Prefacing his review of *Catch-22* as film, the *New York Times* critic Vincent Canby charges that a number of filmed novels have failed because of an inability on the director's part to find a cinematic equivalent to the prose of the book.[1] Far better, it would seem, to take a thin novel like Charles Webb's *The Graduate*, where style and scope are austere and the possibilities for serious omission less likely. While the film version was probably the first exposure of an obscure novel for most viewers, *The Graduate* remains one of the few successful examples of novel-to-film adaptation. The bare-boned original gave Director Mike Nichols natural latitude to add the elements he wanted and allowed the filmic elements to superimpose easily on the novel's simple structure.

To be successful in adapting novels to the screen, then, one must actually subordinate the literal reproduction of the story line to more subtle and equally important concerns. In the case of *The Magus*, John Fowles' novel, the filmmaker neglected to find that filmic equivalent to the rich, complex prose of the book and so lost the power of the film. On the other hand, as is successfully demonstrated in Mick Nichols' adaptation of Joseph Heller's *Catch-22*, it may be necessary to find a filmic expression for the pervasive tone of the entire novel. Perhaps a momentary consideration of the failings of *The Magus* as film will underscore the difficulties Nichols had to confront, as well as the distinct film character of the *Catch-22* he created.

*Reprinted, with permission, from *Southern Humanities Review*, 8 (Winter, 1974), 19–25.

While several critics, including Renata Adler, praised *The Magus* on the basis of its imaginative story line without ever acknowledging its novelistic base, at least one noted that the film was taken from John Fowles novel, and that in comparison the film seemed too abrupt. "It needs more interior room in which to let the mysteries sink in, more time in which the audience can catch its breath before being surprised again . . . it needs even more words, more time. . . ."[2]

In this book, Fowles' rich, highly wrought prose style was an integral reflection of the convoluted, mystic nature of the plot. When the film did not substitute a filmic equivalent for that reverberating element within the literary medium, the "feel" of the novel slipped away, and with it the credibility of the highly mystic story line.

These questions of novelistic scope and style stand as the most formidable concerns when adapting a novel to film. Makers of *The Loved One*, while drawn to the manageability of Eveylyn Waugh's short satire and the suitability of its most visible target, Forest Lawn Cemetery, must have recognized after a time the difficulty in conveying the feel of Waugh's light, urbane Briticisms; at any rate, they broadened the gentle satire's scope, hiring Terry Southern as one of the scriptwriters. As might have been expected, what emerged was a heavily drawn, far too broad attack on the whole of American life — with "something to offend everyone" an ironically accurate promotion line.

The process of adaptation is a complicated matter. Traditional picture book production will simply no longer do for an increasingly sophisticated audience looking for something filmic in their films. And the arbitrary omission or adjustment of a novel's verbal style can ruin a filmed version as surely as can the omission, adjustment, or slavish reproduction of story elements.

Imagine the position of Mike Nichols, then, when he approached the making of *Catch-22*, the American counter-culture bible of the 1960's. By 1970 more than five million copies of the novel had been printed, and any professed liberal who had not read the book felt constrained to apologize. A friend of mine tells the story of a boy in his undergraduate dormitory who had once owned and memorized a paper copy of *Catch-22*. The boy had lost the book, but did not need to buy another copy, since he could remember incidents verbatim. He made a list of the forty-two chapter headings and would sit in the bathroom reading titles and laughing to himself.

Not only is *Catch-22* full of incident on each of its four hundred forty-three pages, but also Heller's style works as integrally for comic effect in *Catch-22* as Fowles' reverberates mystery in *The Magus*. How, then, to translate the feel of this narration to the screen:

> The colonel dwelt in a vortex of specialists who were still specializing in trying to determine what was troubling him. They hurled lights in his eyes to see if he could see, rammed needles into nerves to hear if he could

feel. There was a urologist for his urine, a lymphologist for his lymph, an endocrinologist for his endocrines, a psychologist for his psyche, a dermatologist from his derma; there was a pathologist for his pathos, a cystologist for his cysts, and a bald and pedantic cetologist from the zoology department at Harvard who had been shanghaied ruthlessly into the Medical Corps by a faulty anode in an I.B.M. machine and spent his sessions with the dying colonel trying to discuss *Moby-Dick* with him.[3]

Heller himself admitted he did not expect much from any motion-picture adaptation of his work: "I was prepared not to like the movie. . . . My feeling is that complex novels don't make good movies."[4]

But as Vincent Canby notes, *Catch-22's* complexity is that of breadth, not depth. He characterizes Heller's novel as "complex on a horizontal plane," as opposed to the writing of Vladimir Nabokov whom he calls "unfilmable because he is complex on a perpendicular plane."[5] Another critic, Joseph Waldmeir, notes that the book seems an endless repetition of the same joke, "Would you rather walk to work or carry your lunch?"[6] Given the book's nonessential repetition, it could easily be compressed to include only those striking incidents that allow continuity toward the protagonist's bright moment of understanding.

The problem of verbal style, however, is a more complex matter. As G. W. Haslam says in his study, *Forgotten Pages of American Literature,* ". . . language, unlike clay or pigment, is not a neutral medium; it imposes its own unique perceptual pattern and rhythm of expression. As a consequence, many literary forms are simply not transferable. . . ."[7] Nichols, confronted with the formidable difficulty of attempting to transfer Heller's style, has acted wisely; he ignores the novel's exposition, using no voice-over or clumsy mouthing of narrative bridge. What could be kept to suggest the verbal style—the dialogue and the choppy, non-sequitur arrangement of scenes—constitutes enough where there is so much to choose from, all equally evocative.

These changes have made of *Catch-22* a movie that is markedly different from the book. Instead of a rambling, predominantly humorous narrative, the film is a tight progression of scenes which move Yossarian inexorably toward his enlightenment. While the viewer may laugh easily at the early scenes—Nately mugging with his fat whore, Danby fainting away when General Dreedle wants to shoot him, Milo Minderbinder and his all-business attempt at co-opting the U. S. Army—before the film is halfway through, McWatt chops Kid Sampson in half with a plane and then kills himself. Early on in the harshly lit Snowden-Yossarian-gunnery bay sequences, Milo's enterprise goes beyond humor. Looking for a sedative to aid the gravely injured Snowden, Yossarian finds a five-share chit from M&M Enterprises in place of the morphine. In the last shot of the series, when Yossarian discovers the true extent of Snowden's injuries, the viewer keys automatically onto Milo's a-human chicanery even though the "businessman" had nothing to do with the inflicting of the wounds.

And if the unencumbered laughs grow thin after Kid Sampson's death, they cease altogether with the cross-section shot of Snowden's ruptured entrails. Any laughter evoked from that point must carry the weight of the accumulating horror of the film, with scenes originally cloaked in fun suddenly charged in retrospect. Where the scene with the bomber crew ogling Dreedle's WAC once seemed only funny, it becomes in the mind's eye touching and even important. It is a far, far better thing they do there, a more worthy occupation of their time. To test this idea, one should try, during a second viewing, to join in the early raucous laughter of a fresh audience.

With the cutting of humorous but expendable bits like "Huple's Cat" from the original, the serious theme of the film becomes stronger. A book most highly praised and elevated for its rambling comic mode of narration becomes a film most powerful for its sharp juxtaposition of humor against carnage. In the same way, while the bridge of narration is so effective in extending the comic aspect of the novel, maintaining the sense of "a story being told," its omission from the film points up the irony and strengthens the illusion of recreated reality, the strongest aspect of the film medium. As Heller states, "It's really an original creation. . . . I was very glad to see he [Nichols] didn't go for an easy froth of comedy and sex. He went for the somber parts of Catch-22."[8]

The changes are hard to take, of course, if the viewer is a devout believer in the book. Stanley Kauffman holds that there is simply too much material in the book to allow successful translation to the screen,[9] and Vincent Canby guessed that fully half of the preview audience he sat with came prepared to dislike the adaptation; he himself admits there were scenes and characters he missed.[10] But such cutting is necessary, and should be acceptable if the remainder somehow captures the spirit, or even improves upon, the original. Many other unfavorable critiques of the film cite a supposed need to have read the book if one is to make sense of the film's flashbacks within longer flashback. Yet no film critic recalls the fact that the novel itself moves discontinuously, and none considers that the film might gain from the discontinuous mode, that the fragmentation of time and disruption of conventional causal sequence is an organic reflection of the overthrow of conventional values at the heart of both film and book.

War is traditionally viewed as a righteous, quasi-religious enterprise, with heroism a virtue to be rewarded. But central to both book and film is the guiding principle of Catch-22, that nothing follows logically, that injustice interchanges with justice, that merit will certainly be ignored if not actually punished. The concept of a just, ordered universe is directly contradicted; individual survival and self-loyalty become the only standards in the face of absurdity. Yossarian finally realizes his essential aloneness, the necessity of personal choice, when he tells Colonels Korn and Cathcart wonderingly, "What the hell, if they [the other fliers] don't want to fly more missions, let them stand up and do something about it the way I did."

And in moving toward this realization, the normal concept of time is bent across space. Events stay with Yossarian, intrude into his memory un-invited, grow, dovetail progressively, until for Yossarian it all adds up, the Snowden scene completes itself, he understands the a-human indifference that inexorably *will* snuff him out. And if there is no alternative within the system of Catch-22, he must then step outside, create his own frame of ref-erence — in a word, he must escape.

It is not necessary to see the fragmented scenes in a conventional tem-poral order nor to understand them fully at once; certainly Yossarian did not. What is important is a post-understanding of their nature and thematic connection. In this respect, the same is asked of reader and viewer. Thus, because the filmic image is ephemeral and does not allow for easy re-exami-nation, the number of scenes has been reduced, thereby reinforcing as the visual and thematic center, the sequence with Yossarian and Snowden.

All this is not to say that Catch-22 is a film without flaws: the night walk through Rome is overplayed, is out of keeping with the contrapuntal shifting from humor to horror; in the book, with so much surrounding ma-terial diluting the effect of the night-walk sequence, it is hardly noticeable, but in a tight, spare film it glares. Also out of keeping is the Nazi-esque transformation of Milo — far better to have kept him the unaware business-man smilingly oblivious to his vicious influence. The old Italian's moraliz-ing in the whorehouse seems heavy and pointed. And cuts are sometimes made self-consciously, as from the Colonel's advice "kick him in the balls," to Yossarian's howl as the nurse's knee drives into his groin.

Yet these shortcomings are the slips of a director earnestly involved in an adaptation — a distinct, personal artistic endeavor — and are not the gross conceptual errors of a copyist. Actually, the criticism here can be di-rected without reference to the novel, as Susan Lardner shows in her review of *Catch-22* for the *New Yorker*. Recognizing that changes sufficient to make the film a separate work of art have been made, she flatly refuses to compare the novel with the film, then goes on to fault the Nichols work for the specific faults listed above.[11]

Miss Lardner's critical approach seems the most intelligent; she has avoided the tendency to confuse novel with film in a case where the director has avoided that same trap. Because *Catch-22* has become such a revered novel, the distinction is harder to make, but it must be made. Where Nichols falls short of his aims, the shortcomings should be evaluated in terms of his conception, not Heller's. If one thinks that the comic and hor-rific elements seem to split the tone of the film, it does not make sense to say that Heller's book did not have the problem. Responsible criticism should focus on just how the film goes astray.

In the light of these reflections on *Catch-22*, I would be inclined to say that literary works can never be reproduced exactly in film. An identical impulse yields different creations in different media. While one artist may trade on another's concept to create his own work, an attempt to copy the literary work exactly gives only cheap imitation. The viewer who goes to see a filmed version of a novel should be prepared for an *interpretation* and not a reproduction. It is absurd to expect a two-hour film to do the same things that a continually accessible, timeless novel can do. Each medium has its limitations, each its advantages.

Catch-22, the novel, created forty characters and leisurely explored nearly every wartime variation of its cockeyed world. Joseph Heller testifies, "I never though of *Catch-22* as a comic novel. . . . I wanted him [the reader] to be ashamed that he was amused."[12] Mike Nichols as film-maker has held fast to this sense of shame and has created a film that literally turns laughter back on itself. He said once that *Catch-22* struck him as a dream about dying; and he has led viewers into the shocking revelation that they have been laughing at a funeral. Focusing on that irony, Nichols has created a work of his own, a work that stands as an enviable example of film-makers everywhere who would be drawn toward novel-to-film translation.

Notes

1. Vincent Canby, "A Triumphant Catch," *New York Times*, June 28, 1970; II, 1:1.

2. Robert Kotlowitz, "Performing Arts: *The Magus*," *Harper's*, 238 (March 1969), 111.

3. Joseph Heller, *Catch-22* (New York: Simon and Schuster, 1961), p. 15.

4. Joseph Heller, "Pleased with *Catch-22* Film," *New York Times*, June 19, 1970, 24:1.

5. Canby, 1:1.

6. Joseph J. Waldmeir, "Two Novelists of the Absurd: Heller and Kesey," *Wisconsin Studies in Contemporary Literature*, V, No. 3.

7. G. W. Haslam, *Forgotten Pages of American Literature* (Boston: Houghton Mifflin, 1980), p. 84.

8. Heller, "Pleased," 24:1.

9. Stanley Kauffman, "Stanley Kauffman on Films: Catch-22," *New Republic*, 163 (July 4, 1970), 32.

10. Canby, 1:1.

11. Susan Lardner, "No Comparison," *New Yorker*, 46 (June 27, 1970), 62.

12. Heller, "Pleased," 24:1.

In No-Man's Land: The Plays of Joseph Heller

Linda McJ. Micheli*

Students of drama are fond of recalling the difficulties encountered by novelists who turn their hands to the stage. Henry James, Norman Mailer, Ernest Hemingway, and others, they point out, failed to translate their vi-

*This essay was written especially for this volume and is published here by permission of the author.

sions successfully from narrative to dramatic form. Although Joseph Heller's three plays, *We Bombed in New Haven* (1967), *Catch 22: A Dramatization* (1973), and *Clevinger's Trial* (1976), received their share of critical admiration, the consensus at the time seems to have been that the novel remained Heller's metier. Heller may have contributed, half-puckishly, to this judgment. Although he was a longtime student of drama (his graduate and undergraduate work, including his Fulbright to Oxford, was devoted to drama), he asserted, before the opening of *We Bombed*, that he did not much like the theatre and that he considered it a "very limited medium."[1] Nonetheless, by the end of the play's initial run in New Haven, he was interested enough in the theatre to revise *We Bombed* for an eleven-week Broadway engagement in 1968 and to complete three years later his previous attempt to adapt *Catch-22* for the stage.

The plays have received little attention apart from the initial reviews, and they are now out of print. Nonetheless, they merit the attention of Heller scholars and of those for whom the characters and situations of *Catch-22* have become permanent features of the imaginative universe. The plays reaffirm Heller's gift for dialogue and irony, they reveal the darkening of his vision during the Vietnam era, and they testify to his experimental and ingenious approach to dramatic (as well as narrative) structure.

Heller began putting sections of *Catch-22* into dramatic form as early as August, 1962, before the motion picture rights to the novel were sold.[2] When negotiations for the film rights were concluded at the end of that month, Heller set the project aside, since the film contract specified that the theatrical rights could not be exercised until after the film was released. Though completed after the composition of *We Bombed*, the adaptations of *Catch-22* thus have some claim to attention as Heller's first experiments with drama.

Clevinger's Trial was among the first sections of *Catch-22* Heller adapted for the stage, but it was omitted from the final version for reasons of length and published later as a one-act play.[3] It has enjoyed success as a workshop piece and was included in *The Best Short Plays of 1976*. Except for a few lines of narrative transposed as dialogue at the beginning and end, the play follows the central scene of Chapter 8 of the novel almost verbatim. The only significant difference is that the scene is set up as a flashback told to Yossarian by Clevinger as he walks his penalty tours. At the end, as the colonel expresses his hatred for Clevinger and "everybody" (a hatred stated directly in the novel only by the narrator), he orders Yossarian to join Clevinger in the prescribed punishment. Two other details of the play are of interest. First, Billy Petrolle, who remains mysterious in the novel, is identified by the colonel as a professional boxer from Berwick, Pennsylvania, and a veteran of 157 bouts, the number of penalty tours assigned to Clevinger. Second, the colonel is given a closing line that gives the theme of repression and the abuse of authority a more personal note than in the novel:

> Colonel: Do you know why I like to see justice done, Shi —
> Scheisskopf: Scheisskopf.
> Colonel: Scheisskopf? Because I'm the one that does it.[4]

Heller returned to his project of dramatizing *Catch-22* in 1971, while he was completing the final sections of *Something Happened*. Larry Arrick, who had directed *We Bombed* in its premiere run in New Haven, expressed interest in producing *Catch-22* on Long Island in July if Heller could finish the script in time. Heller did, and the play was produced at the John Drew Theatre to favorable reviews that summer (1971) and has since been produced elsewhere in the United States and abroad. Heller credits Arrick with "countless delightful staging and acting surprises" which were later incorporated into the published version of the play.[5]

In dramatic form, *Catch-22: A Dramatization* is straightforward. Influenced perhaps by the movie version directed by Mike Nichols, which appeared in 1970, Heller described the form of the play as "cinematographic": "Characters come in sight when they are ready to speak or be spoken to and leave the stage as soon as they are through, commanding attention to themselves in much the same way that a movie camera directs the gaze of an audience from one person to another."[6] Time and space are handled freely, but Heller took it as axiomatic that the theatre could not accommodate the long, meditative rhythms of his novel or its complex structure. He comments in his foreword that the play of necessity had to be "shorter, swifter, simpler, and more direct" and to display "a distinct, prominent narrative line."[7]

Although Heller said that his dramatization emerged as an independent work "with an identity of its own apart from the novel and the movie,"[8] it is impossible to appreciate the play without establishing its relation to its source. The omissions and conflations which enabled Heller to condense his novel into an acceptable length for a play give the drama its particular effect.

Inevitably, the omissions are many. Of Yossarian's cronies and fellow airmen only Nately, Doc Daneeka, Clevinger, McWatt, the Chaplain, and Milo appear. Gone are Dunbar, Dobbs, Orr, Havermeyer, Hungry Joe, Kid Sampson, Chief White Halfoat, the "roomies," and Captain Flume, although Flume's anxious encounter with the Chaplain is transferred to the "dead" Doc Daneeka. Of the superior officers only Major Major, the Colonels Korn and Cathcart, and Captain Black remain. Major Danby's important role in the denouement is transferred to Major Major; the other colonels and both generals are omitted. Aarfy and the rape and murder of Michaela are included, as are Nately's Whore, the Old Man and Woman of the Roman brothel, and Luciana, but most of the incidents in Rome, including nearly all the "The Eternal City" sequence, are not. Sergeants Towser and Whitcomb, Ex-Pfc Wintergreen, Gus, Wes, and the Hospital staff (Nurse Duckett and the psychiatrist, Dr. Sanderson) fulfill much the same roles as in the novel.

The cumulative effect of these omissions is to limit the scope of the action and the world in which the characters move. Fewer levels of the hierarchy are represented, and fewer forms of defensive madness are exhibited. The important locales are preserved, but none of the combat scenes are dramatized. The absence of those scenes of claustrophobic terror in the cockpit or bomb bay of Yossarian's plane may account in part for Heller's feeling that the play was almost "too funny."[9] The play concentrates on the scenes of authority running amok: the interrogations of Major Major and the Chaplain, and the sinister deal that the colonels offer to Yossarian. Heller associated these scenes with the trials of the Chicago Seven, Bobby Seale, and Angela Davis; all illustrated the "misuses of authority in an atmosphere of war."[10] But without the reminders of death in combat which embrace and to a degree give rise to the paranoia of nearly everyone in the novel, the hilarious illogic of the investigations overshadows their frightening implications.

The structure of the play is streamlined and simplified compared to that of the novel. In his foreword, Heller states that "chronology was put in order."[11] It is true that only one flashback remains; the Snowden scene is re-created fully near the end, as it is in the novel. But the chronology of the play is not the same as the chronology that underlies the structure of the novel. Events that were flashbacks in the novel are part of the dramatic present in the play or are combined with similar events that occurred later. For example, "The Soldier Who Saw Everything Twice" is transferred from Cadet School (which is never mentioned in the play) to Yossarian's stint in the hospital in Pianosa after the Colonel has raised the men to sixty missions. Similarly, Yossarian's theological discussion with Lt. Scheisskopf's wife, his sometime lover at Cadet School, is transferred to a love scene on the beach at Pianosa with Nurse Duckett. And, for a final example, the first two Bologna missions are conflated with the third one. Clevinger, who is already dead when the novel opens, is killed on this mission, and the "chocolate covered cotton" scene between Milo and Yossarian coincides with his funeral, not Snowden's.

None of these conflations severely alters the meaning of any particular incident or the essence of a character, but, as with the omissions, the change in the structure of the whole significantly alters the overall effect. The novel's complex alternation of past and present, its associative shifts from one event to another, stressed the haunting power of the past and the role of memory, guilt, and compassion. It pitted the human consciousness, searching for order, keening its losses, justly anxious about its own survival, against the ambition and cowardice of those in authority, the insanity of war, and the certainty of death. The comedy and the pathos of the novel are fairly represented in the dramatization, but the shadow of death falls more lightly on the stage version.

Although the "cinematographic" form of the play permits something like the fluidity of time and space that characterizes the novel, there are important differences. Scenes that in the novel are conveyed by the third-person omniscient narrator are, in the play, dramatized or reported to the audience by the characters themselves. While this is a natural change for a dramatization, it creates a rhythm and a perspective quite different from that of the novel. The long rhythms of the narrator, who recorded the obsessive musing or complex stream of associations of whichever character happened to be the current center of consciousness, are transformed into the brisker, more cheerful rhythms of dialogue, as in the introduction of the Texan. In the novel the Texan is introduced chiefly through narration; the other characters speak, but his words are merely implied or reported:

> Then there was the educated Texan from Texas who looked like someone in Technicolor and felt, patriotically, that people of means — decent folk — should be given more votes than drifters, whores, criminals, degenerates, atheists and indecent folk — people without means. . . . They put the Texan in a bed in the middle of the ward, and it wasn't long before he donated his views. . . . The Texan turned out to be good-natured, generous, and likeable. In three days no one could stand him.[12]

The parallel passage in the play breaks up the long sentence, distributes the others among several speakers, and weakens the ironic force of the last line by adding a coda:

> Texan: Would you like to know what I think about the republic?
> (Yossarian leaves the bed with a weary groan and hangs up his bathrobe.)
> "I think that people of means . . . decent folk . . . should be given more votes than indecent folk . . . people without means. Don't you? It stands to reason that . . .
> (The Texan exits talking as Yossarian retreats from him toward the Chaplain, who rises to walk with him.)
> Chaplain: The Texan turned out to be good-natured, generous, and likeable.
> Yossarian: In three minutes I couldn't stand him. He drove me out.[13]

Much of the pleasurable irony of the novel's narration is inevitably lost when adapted to relatively "straight" dramatic form.

The dramatic form of *We Bombed in New Haven*, on the other hand, is anything but "straight." First performed by the Yale School of Drama Repertory Theatre in New Haven in 1967, *We Bombed* shares important themes with *Catch-22* (war, freedom and authority, individual responsibility), but it is an independent work and constitutes Heller's most complicated experiment with drama. Like the adaptations, it also illuminates the development of Heller's central themes during the Vietnam era.

The play is self-consciously theatrical. It begins with an apparently premature opening of the curtain, which reveals embarrassed actors still moving props and scenery into position. The actors occasionally refer to themselves by their real names ("Jason Robards" or "Stacy Keach") and al-

lude to other plays in which they have actually appeared. The audience is
frequently mentioned and addressed. There are essentially three layers of
illusion: actors pretending to be actors pretending to be airmen are sent out
on irrational bombing raids—Constantinople, which "doesn't exist," and
Minnesota, which seems an odd target for American airmen. (The significance of the choice of Minnesota is suggested by Heller's remark that Vice
President Hubert "Humphrey wasn't born in Texas.")[14]

Heller's use of multiple levels of illusion and the play-within-the-play
caused *We Bombed* to be linked to the plays of Bertolt Brecht, Thornton
Wilder, and, especially, Luigí Pirandello. Heller responded that he had not
read *Six Characters in Search of an Author* or any of Pirandello's plays
when he wrote *We Bombed*, and that when he did he was not impressed.[15]
The real models for his play were Greek tragedy and comedy, he said, and
his motive had been "to create a new form of literature or at least a new
combination of traditional forms."[16]

Multiple levels of illusion and the use of the play-within are not new
with Pirandello, of course. Shakespeare uses the device in *The Taming of
the Shrew*, *A Midsummer Night's Dream*, and *Hamlet*. A supposed stage
death turns out to be real—as it does in a climactic moment in *We
Bombed*—in an earlier play, Thomas Kyd's *Spanish Tragedy*. Thus Heller
certainly need not have known Pirandello to experiment as he did with multiple levels of dramatic illusion. Nonetheless, a brief comparison with
Pirandello can clarify the nature and significance (if not the originality) of
the form of Heller's play.

In *Six Characters*, a family of "characters," whose author has abandoned them, interrupts the rehearsal of another Pirandello play. The "characters" are clearly distinguished in dress and demeanor from the "actors"
whose rehearsal they disrupt. The two groups are never confused; indeed, it
is part of Pirandello's point that they are hopelessly incapable of even com-
municating with each other. The characters are frustrated by the actors'
obtuseness, and the actors are mystified by the irritability and passion of
their visitors. When the actors attempt to play a scene previously described
and enacted by the characters themselves, they seem wholly unequal to the
task, partly owing to their limited professional skill and talent, and partly
owing to the impossibility of adequately capturing the unique reality perceived by another individual. As the Stepdaughter says to the Leading Lady
attempting to portray her, "Well, to tell the truth, I don't recognize the
scene."[17]

Ultimately, Pirandello's *jeu de theatre* suggests that the characters are
more "real" than the actors. Their roles are clearly defined and imaginatively heightened; their lives are fixed in an "eternal moment" of passion
and suffering. Ordinary mortals, by contrast, live in shallow, fleeting
worlds; their ever-changing, ever-fading present realities prove "mere illusion tomorrow":

> Manager: Then you'll be saying next that you, with this comedy of yours that you brought here to act, are truer and more real than I am?
> Father: But of course; without a doubt![18]

The multiple illusion in *We Bombed* is different in several respects. First, Heller's characters and actors are superimposed, not clearly distinguished. Each figure on the stage has a double role, though some are more fully explored and developed than others. Second, as a result the action does not take place in clearly defined worlds of the "play" and the "real world"; rather the characters often seem to inhabit an ambiguous middle ground. Finally, the issue of the relative potency of the two realities seems to be similar to but is ultimately the opposite of that in Pirandello's play. Heller's characters also discover the potency of imagined realities: actions they supposed to be part of the play turn out to be real. A character is killed, and the actor disappears or dies bloodily on stage. But whereas Pirandello emphasizes the transcendent truth and enduring power of art, in *We Bombed* the play succumbs to rather than transcends the world beyond the theatre. In Pirandello, reality pales beside the deeper, immutable truths of art; in Heller, art is overwhelmed by brutal realities. Make-believe is itself a sham, an attempt to deny reality, but reality will not be denied.

In keeping with this theme, nearly every aspect of Heller's play contributes to the sense of an ambiguous middle ground, a dramatic no-man's land between illusion and reality. The title of the play takes advantage of terms common to the world of the stage and the world of war. Both the professional soldier and the professional actor are familiar with "bombs" and "companies," and both refer to the sphere of their activities as a "stage" or "theatre." Actors also often characterize a poor performance or a bad audience by saying "I died" or "They killed me." Consequently, much of the language of the play conveniently does double duty as both military and theatrical jargon. It refers simultaneously to the actors' real world (the professional stage) and the make-believe world of their play about airmen and bombing raids.

Time is also ambiguous in the play. On the one hand, the stage directions call for a large clock to keep real time throughout the performance. Captain Starkey refers on occasion to the elapsed time between scenes ("You're all due back in exactly eighteen minutes for calisthenics"[19]) and he announces the intermission ("OK, men. You can take a break now. Ten minutes. [To the audience] You, too." [p. 85]). On the other hand, real time and stage time are not always compatible. The men could not possibly execute a bombing raid and return in eighteen minutes, and though the clock shows the passage of some two hours or so, Starkey and Ruth, the Red Cross girl, court, marry, and produce a son who is nineteen years old at the play's end.

The location of the action and the identity of the characters are also often ambiguous. Some of the action takes place "on stage" as part of the play within the play, and one scene is explicitly set "off-stage" in Ruth's dressing room and contains action that clearly departs from the "script."

The bulk of the play, however, consists of the conversation of actors waiting for the action proper to resume. They discuss the play and their roles, but this "backstage" action takes place on stage, in full view of, and often with explicit reference to, the audience. One reviewer sought to resolve these ambiguities by describing the play as a rehearsal, but, as the reviewer acknowledged, rehearsals do not usually involve audiences.[20] Conversely, though the characters discuss their roles in the play-within more often than perform them, they refer to each other by their characters' names. Even in her dressing room, Ruth remains "Ruth" to the others. When the actor playing Sinclair disappears mysteriously after his character is killed, the hue and cry is for "Sinclair" not the actor who is playing him.

While these ambiguities seemed confusing or merely willful to some of the play's early reviewers, their effect can be intriguing and dramatically significant. They enable Heller to develop the action on two levels at once, as in the following exchange between Captain Starkey and Ruth, his lover.

> Ruth: Are you married?
> Starkey: Jesus Christ, Ruthie! Where's your manners? That's a helluva goddam personal question to ask a gentleman you are sleeping with!
> Ruth: Then let's try another. Do you love me?
> Starkey: That's even worse!
> Ruth: Well, I've got to know, dammit. I don't know who I am here or what I mean to anybody. I don't know how I'm supposed to act with you or anybody else. Am I just a goddam Red Cross girl? Is that all I mean to you?
> . . . . . .
> Starkey: OK, I'll tell you. Do you want the truth, or do you want a lie?
> Ruth: Which is better?
> Starkey: I'd go with the lie if I were you.
> Ruth: No, I want the truth. Do you love me?
> Starkey: No.
> Ruth: Let's have the lie.
> Starkey: Yes, I do love you, Ruth, more than I could ever say.
> Ruth: Darling!
> (Ruth flings herself dramatically into Starkey's arms, and the two embrace passionately with an ardor that is definitely histrionic) [pp. 43–45].

The beginning of this scene appears to be spontaneous and not part of the play-within. Ruth has entered uncertainly and addressed the audience as if trying to pass the time until the action begins again. As the scene progresses, she refers to herself as an actress. Her coffee stinks, but, she counters, "So what? I'm an actress not a cook." On the other hand, it is clear that her concern about who she is and what she means to Starkey is equally appropriate to her as Ruth, the Red Cross girl and Starkey's lover; as the actress playing Ruth, who wants to know her character's status and motivation; and as a leading lady who (perhaps) is having an off-stage affair with her leading man. On all three levels, she wants to know if she and Starkey are casual, uncommitted lovers or something more. Here and elsewhere in the play, the dialogue is equally appropriate to the actor as actor and to the character. The different levels of reality are perfectly superimposed.

Whereas the critics assumed the influence of Pirandello and other modern playwrights on *We Bombed*, Heller himself acknowledged only the influence of Greek drama and its quality of inevitability. According to Heller, the catastrophe in Greek drama was inevitable not because of any theory on the part of the dramatists, but "because the audience knew the story. . . . Oedipus had to find out he was married to his mother or the audience would have torn the theatre apart."[21] However, the inevitability of the outcome in Oedipus also arises from the fateful junction of ineluctable forces — divine imperatives and the inner logic of human character. At first glance, the inevitability in Heller's play seems more arbitrary and purely theatrical. As Heller put it, since the audience realizes that the script which the Major carries around dictates the fate of the characters, "the questions are: Do the characters have free will? Can they break away from the script."[22] But, in a sense, the question about Oedipus is also whether he can break away from the script the gods have prepared for him. The answer seems to be that the more Oedipus and the other characters attempt to assert their freedom, the more tightly they bind themselves to their preordained fates. Heller's play does not explore this central irony; his rebels fail not because their rebellion seals their fates but because too few of them have the courage to rebel, and when they do, it is too late.

The central concern of the play is not war *per se* but the individual's capitulation to nameless, bureaucratic authority. In keeping with the ambiguity of *We Bombed*, the metaphors for evil authority are both military (as in *Catch-22*) and theatrical. The Major is both the highest ranking officer in the play and the keeper — perhaps the author — of the script, the ultimate authority for what is supposed to go in the play-within. But the Major is a more sinister and less comic figure than the groveling Colonel Cathcart or the obsessive General Peckem. Unlike these officers, who carry out their destructive, self-serving machinations because (as Colonel Korn explains to Yossarian) they have been taught "to aspire to higher things" (p. 415), the Major's ruthlessness arises from no recognizable human motive other than sheer personal hostility. Talking with the two Sportsmen, financial backers of the play-within who are ultimately cast as MPs, the Major complains that Henderson (or the actor who plays him) is always late. "Why don't you get rid of him?" asks the Hunter. "I'm going to, very soon," replies the Major (p. 65). Earlier, speaking of Starkey, he makes it clear that his ultimate values are authoritarian not theatrical:

> Golfer: That captain's pretty good, isn't he?
> Major: He's all right.
> Hunter: (Surprised) Don't you like him?
> Major: (Without emotion) No.
> Hunter: Why don't you get rid of him?

Major: I won't have to. He does everything I want him to do, and he does
it very well (p. 63).

A mediocre actor can be tolerated if he follows orders and sticks to the
script. In his implacability, his lack of human emotion or motivation, the
Major seems like the embodiment of catch-22 itself rather than the counter-
part of the comically villainous officers of the novel.

By contrast, the other characters in the play have greater professional
ambition than their counterparts in the novel. In *Catch-22*, the noncom-
missioned officers and the enlisted men are consumed by their private
manias and phobias, taking refuge from an intolerable situation in various
forms of insanity, but few of them have any interest in rising in the hierarchy. Survival not status is their goal. The characters of *We Bombed* are
nominally saner and more ambitious. Sometimes their ambition is expressed in purely theatrical terms, as when Ruth complains about the limitations of her role as a Red Cross girl:

> I don't want to carry a stinking coffeepot. (Resumes her trancelike state as
> she moves to the Major and sets the mug of coffee on his desk.) I want to
> carry messages from the life ahead to generations of the life to come. I
> want to deliver poetic tidings of love and tenderness . . . (p. 21).

Frequently, however, the characters' desire for improved status is expressed
in language equally appropriate to their roles as actors and soldiers. Sergeant Henderson eagerly assures the Major that he could stand in for Captain Starkey: "I can handle it all. I could do everything the captain does. I
could take over for him right now if you wanted me to" (p. 101). Corporal
Bailey is ready to step into Henderson's shoes: "Look — I could be a better
sergeant than he is, if you guys would only pitch in next time and cooper-
ate" (p. 69). The irony of this conflation of roles will entrap them in the end,
however, when they must face the truth that their allegiance to both the
script and the authority vested in the Major has implicated them in real
violence and death.

As in *Catch-22*, fear, ambition, and denial of responsibility paralyze
those who are subject to evil and irrational authority. To the extent that
otherwise good people accept and obey such authority, "Every victim [is] a
culprit, every culprit a victim" (p. 396). But this theme is darker in *We
Bombed* than in *Catch-22*. Yossarian finally realizes that "someone had to
do something sometime. . . . Somebody had to stand up sometime to try to
break the lousy chain of inherited habit that was imperiling them all" (pp.
396–97). The wily Orr seems to have done so, and Yossarian takes off at the
end in an attempt to do likewise. The characters in *We Bombed* lack Yossarian's moral vision and, ultimately, his courage.

Perhaps the chief indication of the darkening of Heller's themes in *We
Bombed* is the character of the protagonist. Starkey is clearly one of the
culprits, not merely one of the victims. When Henderson, the rebel, appeals

to him for help, as Yossarian appeals to Major Danby, Starkey promises to support the Sergeant in his attempt to quit the play. (Henderson's relation to Yossarian is suggested by his determination to escape from the life-threatening situation in which he finds himself, and also by his appearance in an earlier scene, when he enters "covered with [the] matted blood" of a comrade killed in action [p. 50]). However, unlike Danby, Starkey loses courage at the crucial moment, abandons Henderson to the Major's power, and thus shares in responsibility for Henderson's death.

Though Starkey later affirms his ignorance of the Major's intentions, he admits his indifference:

> Starkey: I didn't know you were going to kill him.
> Major: Why should you care?
> Starkey: I just didn't know, that's all.
> Major: But what difference does it make, really? Were you so fond of him? Was he anything more to you than just a name? You didn't even care for him, did you? So what difference does it make to you really if he lives or if he dies?
> Starkey: No difference (pp. 179–80).

Indeed, the complicity of all the characters is suggested when Fisher's Kid Brother angrily confronts Fisher: "Hey! I thought you told me nobody got killed here." Fisher responds coldly with no hint of an apology, "I was lying to you" (p. 179).

Starkey's own son, who has been called up as a replacement for Henderson, delivers what seems to be the play's judgment on those who would try to deny or evade their responsibility for the endless cycle of war and oppression:

> Starkey's Son: What were you doing when all this was happening?
> Starkey: My job, I guess.
> Starkey's Son: Pop, you had nineteen years to save me from this. Why didn't you do something?
> Starkey: It didn't seem possible (pp. 184–85).

Unlike Yossarian or even the far less courageous Colonel Danby, Starkey gives up, promising to weep, but unable to perform even the symbolic act of resistance that his son begs from him.

In the closing lines of the play Starkey tries to explain himself by distinguishing between his real and his stage identity:

> Now, none of this, of course, is really happening. It's a show, a play in a theatre, and I'm not really a captain. I'm an actor. (. . . The noise of a plane . . . passes very close and recedes steadily. . . .) I'm ——— ——— (He mentions his real name) . . . Do you think that I, ——— ———, would actually let my son go off to a war and just stand here talking to you and do nothing? . . . Of course not! There is no war taking place here ri—— (In the distance, there is the sound of a single, great explosion. . . .) There is no war taking place here now! (p. 195).

But by now he and the audience know that his two roles cannot be separated; he cannot escape responsibility for the roles he accepts and for the actions he fails to take.

Reviewers were divided in their reactions to Heller's first play. Some found its last scene powerful and affecting, others sentimental and obvious. A few felt that the play was too abstract, that Heller lectured his audience rather than embodied his theme concretely. Nonetheless, reading the play today, one is struck by the ingenuity of its structure and by how uncomfortably relevant the issues that the play raises still are. Moreover, from the vantage point of fifteen years, one is inclined to agree with reviewer Tom Prideaux, who suggested that "no other recent play will convey to people of the next century a better idea of how a large number of Americans felt about war in the late 1960s."[23]

On the evidence of his three plays to date, Heller is a playwright of more than historical interest. His gift for lively dialogue and memorable individual scenes is indisputable, both in the plays and in the novels. *Catch-22: A Dramatization* and *Clevinger's Trial* attest to his mastery of straightforward story-telling in drama, but the full flavor of his novels—their impressive and complex rhythms—does not translate easily into dramatic form. Although *We Bombed in New Haven* does sacrifice many traditional dramatic values—such as well developed characters and situations—for the sake of its moral theme, it is an ambitious and interesting play. Its multiple, superimposed illusions are structurally and thematically significant. Taken together, these three plays merit the attention of students of Heller. The adaptations attest to the enduring delight provided by the characters and situations of Heller's masterpiece, and those who seek out *We Bombed* may recognize in Heller's dramatic no-man's land the discomfitting terrain of American political life in the 1960s and beyond.

Notes

1. Eleanor Lester, "Playwright in Anguish," *New York Times*, Dec. 3, 1967, Section 2, p. 19.

2. Joseph Heller, *Catch-22: A Dramatization* (New York: Delacorte Press, 1973), p. xii.

3. *A Dramatization*, p. xiii.

4. Joseph Heller, "Clevinger's Trial," *The Best Short Plays of 1976*, ed. Stanley Richards (Radnor: Chilton Book Co., 1977), p. 18.

5. *A Dramatization*, pp. ix-xi.

6. *A Dramatization*, p. xxiii.

7. *A Dramatization*, p. xx.

8. *A Dramatization*, p. xi.

9. *A Dramatization*, p. xi.

10. *A Dramatization*, p. xiv.

11. *A Dramatization*, p. xxi.

12. Joseph Heller, *Catch-22* (New York: Simon and Schuster, 1961), p. 9.

13. *A Dramatization*, p. 8.

14. Israel Shenker, "Did Heller Bomb on Broadway?" *New York Times*, Dec. 2, 1968, Section 2, p. 3.

15. Lester, p. 19.

16. Shenker, pp. 1-3.

17. Luigi Pirandello, *Six Characters in Search of an Author*, trans. Edward Storer, in Luigi Pirandello, *Six Plays* (New York: E. P. Dutton, 1922), p. 38.

18. Pirandello, p. 60.

19. Joseph Heller, *We Bombed in New Haven* (New York: Delta, 1969), p. 37.

20. Hobe, "Shows on Broadway," *Variety*, Oct. 23, 1968, pp. 57–58.

21. Shenker, p. 3.

22. Shenker, p. 3.

23. Tom Prideaux, "Joe Heller's Peekaboo with Reality," *Life*, 64 (Jan. 12, 1968), 12.

INDEX